Charles Seale-Hayne Library
University of Plymouth
(01752) 588 588
LibraryandITenquiries@plymouth.ac.uk

SOCIALIZING THE HUMAN–COMPUTER ENVIRONMENT

HUMAN/COMPUTER INTERACTION
A Series of Monographs, Edited Volumes, and Texts
SERIES EDITOR
BEN SHNEIDERMAN

Directions in Human/Computer Interaction
Edited by Albert Badre and Ben Shneiderman

Human Factors in Management Information Systems, Vol. 1
Edited by Jane Carey

Expert Systems: The User Interface
Edited by James A. Hendler

Online Communities:
A Case Study of the Office of the Future
Starr Roxanne Hiltz

Human Factors In Computer Systems
Edited by John Thomas and Michael Schneider

Human Factors and Interactive Computer Systems
Edited by Yannis Vassiliou

Advances in Human/Computer Interaction Vol. 1
Edited by H. Rex Hartson

Advances in Human Computer Interaction Vol. 2
Edited by H. Rex Hartson and Deborah Hix

Empirical Studies of Programmers
Edited by Elliot Soloway and Sitharama Iyengar

Empirical Studies of Programmers Vol. 2
Edited by Gary Olson, Elliot Soloway, and Sylvia Sheppard

Ergonomics—Harness the Power of Human Factors in Your Business
Edited by Edmund T. Klemmer

Human-Computer Interface Design Guidelines
C. Marlin Brown

Online Help Systems: Design and Implementation
Greg Kearsley

Socializing the Human–Computer Environment
Jerry J. Vaske and Charles E. Grantham

In preparation:

The Psychology of Menu Selection:
Designing Cognitive Control at the Human/Computer Interface
Kent L. Norman

Human Factors in Management Information Systems, Vol. 2
Jane Carey

Socializing the Human–Computer Environment

Jerry J. Vaske

University of New Hampshire
Durham, New Hampshire

Charles E. Grantham

Interpersonal Systems Inc.
Berkeley, California

ABLEX PUBLISHING CORPORATION
NORWOOD, NEW JERSEY 07648

Library of Congress Cataloging-in-Publication Data

Vaske, Jerry J., 1951–
    Socializing the human-computer environment / Jerry J. Vaske,
Charles E. Grantham.
        p.   cm. — (Human computer interaction)
    "April, 1989."
    Includes bibliographical references.
    ISBN 0-89391-471-1
    1. Human-computer interaction.   I. Grantham, Charles E.
II. Title.   III. Series: Human computer interaction (Norwood, N.J.)
QA76.9.H85V37   1989
004'.01'9—dc20   89-17745
                                                              CIP

Ablex Publishing Corporation
355 Chestnut Street
Norwood, New Jersey 07648

For our wives,
Maureen and Ellen

Contents

Preface   vii

Chapter 1
Introduction   1
  Why This Book is Needed   3
Theories and Theoretical Perspectives   6
  Social Psychology   7
  Social Organizations   11
  Anthropology   14
Integrating the Perspectives   17
Applying Social Science   18
Book Overview   19
Bibliography   20

Chapter 2
The Social Psychology of Human–Computer Interaction   23
The Scope of Social Psychology   25
  Researcher's Agenda   28
  Manager's Agenda   28
Computer Socialization   29
  Researcher's Agenda   31
  Manager's Agenda   32
Attitude Theory   32
Definition of Attitude   33
  An Attitude is Relatively Enduring   33
  An Attitude is an Organization of Beliefs   35
  An Attitude is Organized Around an Object or Situation   40
  An Attitude is a Set of Interrelated Predispositions to Respond   41
  Attitudes Lead to Preferential Responses   41
  Summary   42
  Researcher's Agenda   42
  Manager's Agenda   43
Attitudes and Behavior   43

Attitude–Behavior Models   43
  Fishbein and Ajzen Model   43
  Bentler and Speckart Model   46
Attitude–Behavior: An Empirical Example   49
Behavior–Attitude Models   51
  Researcher's Agenda   54
  Manager's Agenda   55
Individual Differences   55
Personality Traits   56
  Perceived Locus of Control   58
  Extraversion–Introversion   59
  Fear of Failure/Need for Achievement   59
  Anxiety   60
  Defensive Mechanisms   61
Cognitive Style   62
  Field-dependent/Field-independent   62
  Systematic/Heuristic   63
  Verbalizers/Visualizers   63
  Flexible versus Rigidity   64
Demographic/Situational Variables   64
  Sex-typing and Personality Development   65
  Age   65
  Education   66
  Prior Experience   67
  Usage Classification Schemes   68
  Researcher's Agenda   69
  Manager's Agenda   70
Normative Influences   70
  Social Norms   72
  Personal Norms   72
  The Return Potential Model   73
  Researcher's Agenda   76
  Manager's Agenda   77
Group Productivity and Cooperative Work   77
  Defining Group Productivity   77
Factors Affecting Group Productivity   78
  Group Tasks   78
  Group Size   80
  Group Cohesiveness   81
  Communication Network Structure   82
Social Psychological Aspects of
Computer Mediated Communication   82
Current CSCW Research   85

An Empirical Example   86
  Researcher's Agenda   89
  Manager's Agenda   89
Chapter Summary   90
Bibliography   93

Chapter 3
Organizational Influences and Theories   **105**
The Nature of Human Organizations   106
  Researcher's Agenda   107
  Manager's Agenda   108
Organization Analysis Variables   108
  Authority and Power   108
  Size and Complexity   110
  Efficiency and Effectiveness   111
  Information   111
  Technology   113
  Environment   114
  Researcher's Agenda   115
  Manager's Agenda   116
Theories of Social Organizations   116
The Structural Approach   117
  The Bureaucracy of Max Weber   118
  The Scientific Management Perspective   122
  Applying the Structural Perspective   124
  Summary—The Structural Approach   130
  Researcher's Agenda   130
  Manager's Agenda   131
The Human Relations School   131
Human Needs   133
  Maslow's Need Hierarchy Theory   134
  McGregor's Theory X and Theory Y   136
  Personality and Organization   138
  Ouchi's Theory Z   140
  Critique of the Human Relations Perspective   141
  Researcher's Agenda   142
  Manager's Agenda   143
Open Systems Theory   143
Sociotechnical Design   145
Models of Innovation   147
  Parameter Estimation   148
  An Empirical Example   149
  Researcher's Agenda   151

Manager's Agenda   151
Chapter Summary   152
Bibliography   153

Chapter 4
Anthropology: The Symbols of Meaning   **163**
The Scope of Anthropology   166
  The Concept of Culture   167
  Researcher's Agenda   170
  Manager's Agenda   171
Anthropological Variables   171
  Symbols   171
  Rituals   174
  Myths   176
  Researcher's Agenda   179
  Manager's Agenda   179
Theories in Anthropology   179
Linguistics   181
  Structural Anthropology   181
  Pragmatism   184
Cognitive Anthropology   186
Ecological Theory   189
Symbolic Interactionism   193
  Researcher's Agenda   196
  Manager's Agenda   198
Applying Anthropological Theories   199
  An Example from the Software Games Industry   199
Chapter Summary   200
Bibliography   202

Chapter 5
Measurement and Evaluation   **209**
Overview of the Methodologies   210
Observation of Behavior   213
  Participant Observation   213
  Thinking Aloud   214
  Software Monitor Observation   215
  The Development of a Software Monitor Package   217
  Special Problems of Multiuser System Monitoring   217
Empirical Examples   219
  Empirical Example 1: Office Automation Usage   220
  Empirical Example 2: Electronic Mail   221
  Summary—Software Monitor   224

Ethical Issues   226
Summary—Observation of Behavior   227
Design Team Techniques   228
  Advantages of Committees   230
  Disadvantages of Committees   231
The Delphi Procedure   232
  Conducting a Delphi Sequence   233
The Nominal Group   236
Experiments   237
  Common experimental designs   240
Empirical Example   242
  Results   243
  Example Summary   250
Surveys   251
  The Survey Research Process   253
Types of Questionnaires   258
  Mail versus Telephone versus Personal Interviews   258
  Electronic Surveys   260
Empirical Example   262
  Selected Survey Findings   263
Summary—Surveys   265
Chapter Summary   266
Bibliography   267

Author Index   **275**

Subject Index   **285**

List of Tables

2.1   The effect of attitude and prior behavior on VOX usage.   50

5.1   Overall comparison of the four techniques.   210

5.2   Characteristics of the information provided
by each technique.   211

5.3   Percentage of users' total time in Office Automation
spent in particular functions (per user/day).   221

5.4   Percentage of users' total time in Office Automation
spent in particular functions by position level.   222

5.5   Reported frequency of specific problems with
the terrestrial and satellite services.   244

5.6   Satellite problems reported by frequent and infrequent
telephone users.   246

5.7   Comparisons between other phone services
and the terrestrial service.   247

5.8   Expected versus actual problems with the satellite.   248

5.9   Reported reasons for preferring a particular
communication service.   250

5.10   Procedural guidelines for developing surveys.   254

5.11   Sample mail survey questions.   263

5.12   Reported usage of specific EMail options.   264

List of Figures

1.1 The core concerns of social psychology.   8
1.2 Classification of effects of computer systems.   18
2.1 Relationships among three social sciences
     and social psychology.   27
2.2 The cognitive-affective foundations of an attitude.   36
2.3 Schematic relationship between antecedents, beliefs,
     attitude, behavioral intentions, & behavior.   44
2.4 The Bentler-Speckart attitude–behavior model.   47
2.5 An attitude–behavior model of VOX usage.   48
2.6 The hypothesized model of employee attitudes
     toward working with computers.   52
2.7 Return potential curves for three activities.   74
2.8 Communication networks in five-person groups.   83
3.1 Ouchi's comparison of American and Japanese
     Organizations.   141
3.2 Relationship of General Systems Theory
     to Organizational Theory.   144
3.3 A Sociotechnical approach to systems design.   146
3.4 The generalized "S" curve.   148
3.5 The VOX market projections.   150
4.1 The effect of symbols, rituals, and myths
     on attitudes and behavior.   165
4.2 Examples of different types of symbols.   173
4.3 Relationships between symbols, rituals, and myths.   178
4.4 Theories and variables in anthropology.   180
4.5 Gem desktop icon selections.   184
4.6 Principles of cognitive anthropology.   187
4.7 Social relational matrix of distressful emotions.   197
5.1 Initial and revised send mail forms.   223

Preface

When we began working on *Socializing the Human-Computer Environment* in the fall of 1984, many corporations were in an era of transition with respect to interactive systems. Personal computers were becoming more prevalent as the preferred tool for word processing and spreadsheet tasks, replacing similar functions on minicomputers and large mainframes. Voice-store-and-forward systems and electronic mail were common enough to be viewed by some as substitutes for memos, the telephone, or face-to-face communications. Electronic calendaring facilities were being introduced to coordinate the schedules of busy executives. With these changes, it became apparent that many of the problems faced by system designers and administrators involved a social component that transcended the technology. Electronic communications implicitly involve social interactions.

During the five years it took to complete this book, the trend toward socializing human–computer interactions has grown substantially. Word processing is giving way to group authoring packages. Computer Supported Cooperative Work (CSCW) applications are replacing individual productivity tools. Electronic forms of symbolic communication are increasing the bandwidth of human–computer interaction. Images, graphs, charts, and iconic symbols are now routinely used to facilitate communication. Computing power is moving toward provision of enormous graphical power for the end user. Finally, local area networks, distributed databases, and organizational interfaces are likely to exacerbate this trend even further.

As the technology has evolved, its influence has permeated our interpersonal communication patterns, the structure and functioning of American organizations, and the cultural environment in which we work and live. Norms defining acceptable communication behaviors are evolving as people attempt to cope with new electronic forms of interaction. The established industrial order is giving way to more streamlined ways of work. Flatter organizations, insistence on quality and self-managing groups are demand forces requiring a new generation of software that augments these new organizational styles. From a larger perspective, technology is changing our cultural environment. New subcultures of computer users are emerging, each with their own distinct language, symbols, rituals, and myths. Understanding these cultural variants will give future software its competitive edge.

Our goals in writing this book were to call attention to these social consequences of human–computer interaction and to begin the process of developing a theoretical framework that recognizes the interdisciplinary nature of the interactions that occur between people and machines. We have drawn on the theories found in social psychology, sociology, and anthropology to illustrate how these disciplines can facilitate our understanding of the social processes underlying human–computer interactions and how this understanding benefits the design, development and implementation of computer systems. These theoretical perspectives were selected because they offer a range of viewpoints through which human–computer interactions can be examined. Other theories not presented are also relevant. Our intent was not to detail all perspectives, but rather to suggest some areas where theory development and research may focus.

This book represents a blend of theory, research, and application. The theory chapters offer alternative perspectives on issues that should be considered by system designers and managers. A methods chapter outlining alternative approaches to studying the impacts computers have on people was included to make the procedures commonly used in the social sciences accessible to nonsocial scientists. Throughout the book we have used the results of empirical research—surveys, experiments, design team techniques, and observations of behavior—to illuminate the social processes.

Coverage in the book is broad, and a diversity of topics are discussed. Our synopses, however, should not be taken as comprehensive reviews of the disciplines. One of the most frustrating things we faced in writing this book was the constant tension between comprehensive coverage of a specific topic and the need to be concise. We hope we have reached a happy balance between the two ends of the continuum. The theories and methodologies will not make the reader an expert in the social science disciplines. Rather, our intent was to introduce new ideas for expanding the scope of current human–computer interaction research. Because the disciplines are rich and dynamic, we encourage readers to move beyond the material presented here and to examine areas of interest using our suggested researcher's and manager's agendas. The extended bibliographies at the end of each chapter are intended to encourage further exploration.

Socializing the Human-Computer Environment is intended for professionals in engineering, computer science, human factors, marketing, and the applied social sciences. Individuals who are concerned with designing and implementing computer systems, managing a group of computer users, or maintaining computer installations should find the book helpful. Because the book goes beyond traditional human–

computer interaction theories and research, individuals in academia are afforded an alternative framework for conducting their research. Finally, we hope the book stimulates new interdisciplinary courses which will bring together students from psychology, sociology, anthropology, and the computer sciences.

Although this is a new book, the examples we present are based on our experiences working with software designers, product developers, and system managers. These experiences have indicated that individuals are willing to utilize this information when it is made available to them in a language they can understand.

ACKNOWLEDGEMENTS

Many of our colleagues reviewed one or more chapters of the book and provided useful comments and criticism. We extend thanks to: Jim Bair, Hewlett-Packard; James Bueche, Bull Worldwide Information Systems; Robert Carasik, Pacific Bell; Danielle Detora, Bull Worldwide Information Systems; Maureen Donnelly, University of New Hampshire; Kate Ehrlich, Sun Microsystems; J.D. Eveland; Richard Hoyt; Thomas Irby, Bull Worldwide Information Systems; Robert Janes, University of Maryland; Andy Lafleur, Bull Worldwide Information Systems; Carrol Ostroff, Bull Worldwide Information Systems; Darrell Raymond, University of Waterloo—Ontario; Mary Reed, Pacific Bell; Alan Teubner, Bull Worldwide Information Systems; Ellen Weissinger, University of Nebraska; Eleanor Wynn; and Gus Zaso, University of New Hampshire.

A special thanks are due our editor, Ben Shneiderman. His constant support, encouragement, and expert counseling not only improved the quality of the book, but helped it to become reality.

Responsibility for any mistakes that may remain rests wholly with the authors. Readers are invited to send us a note of recommended additions and corrections. Because this book represents an initial step in a continuing dialog between us and our user group—fellow professionals in the systems design and implementation world—these comments will keep the channels of communication open and hopefully result in a truly integrated and interdisciplinary theory of human–computer interaction.

Many other people contributed to this book. Our managers at Bull Worldwide Information Systems (formerly Honeywell Bull) and Pacific Bell where the early drafts of the book were written supported this effort and supplied us with real life laboratories to test our ideas and learn from experience. Georgia Rouse supplied the creative artwork.

Pat Stokowski at Bull Worldwide Information Systems, and Lilo Tulio and Barbara Crump at Pacific Bell worked diligently at proofing the book and correcting our mistakes. The professional editors at Ablex helped us to clarify our ideas. We extend our appreciation to them all.

Lastly, we express our gratitude to our families. They endured our absence when we were working on the book, listened to our complaints, provided helpful advice when asked, and shared our joy as we achieved milestones.

Jerry Vaske

Charlie Grantham

chapter 1
Introduction

With the development of the first computer came speculation about the impacts this new device would have on individuals and their daily lives. As computers proliferated, so too did the predictions of psychological and social consequences associated with computing. And as the forecasts multiplied, so did the topics of concern. Research, for example, has been conducted on the psychology of programming, ergonomic evaluation, and the teaching of computer skills (Brooks, 1977; Shneiderman, 1980; Card, Moran, & Newell, 1983). Work has also been done on the large scale socioeconomic consequences of computer usage, focusing on such topics as unemployment, privacy, and political ramifications (Forester, 1980; Markus, 1983).

Recent discussions of the social impacts of computers have tended to focus on four central questions: To what extent are individuals and their social organizations affected by the use of computers? Are these effects good or bad? Can system developers increase the positive effects and reduce the negative effects by adhering to formal design guidelines and standards? Can managers of information systems achieve similar results by adopting certain policies of computer use? Although such discussions do address *social issues*, most contemporary research emphasizes design and implementation considerations of the technology. Less attention has been given to the study of computing as a phenomenon in social life (Sim & Anderson, 1976; Forester, 1980; Caporael & Thorngate, 1984).

Limited study of the social consequences of technological innovation is not restricted to computers. It is often difficult to foresee how any invention might impact human social affairs. More than 50 years ago, Cantril and Allport (1935) wrote:

> The radio is a recent invention that has introduced profound alterations in the outlook and social behavior of men, thereby creating a significant social problem for the psychologist. Radio is an altogether novel medium of communication, preeminent as a means of social control and epochal in its influence upon the mental horizons of men. Already its ramifications are so numerous and confused that the psychologist hesitates to take the risks of error and misinterpretation besetting a subject so intricate and new. But a beginning must be made some time, and in the

interests of scientific knowledge as well as practical public policy, the sooner the start is made the better. (p. vii)

The points raised by these social psychologists apply to computers as well as radios. The difference is that the radio diffused rapidly through society without ever becoming an issue in its own right or contributing to an understanding of human social behavior (Caporael & Thorngate, 1984). There are pragmatic, attitudinal, and conceptual reasons for this. Although Cantril and Allport recognized the effects the communication medium had on social control and people's "mental horizons," their investigation focused on implementation issues (speed of speech production and program preferences). With any technological innovation, research on implementation is easier to design, produce, measure, fund, communicate, justify, and rationalize than research on social issues. Implementation research points the investigator toward issues specific to that technology, and consequently, it is difficult to generalize to the broader issues of technology and social behavior. The pressure to begin working on the next version once the initial product is released seldom permits systematic inquiry into what people think about the product, how it is used, and how well it fits into the social environment. Social issues are those associated with technologically induced change. The notion of the *technological fix* for social problems seems to obviate social research on the technology (Caporael & Thorngate, 1984).

There is evidence to suggest, however, that a paradigm shift is occurring in human–computer research and, more generally, software engineering (Schwartz & Ogilvy, 1979; Floyd, 1988). The scope of thinking about the way people interact with computers is broadening to include the social consequences of software design decisions and the social consequences of using computers in a sociotechnical world. This book is testimony to that point. A major thrust of this book is to familiarize the reader with the broad scope of social science ideas. Three theoretical perspectives are considered: social psychology, sociology, and anthropology. The goal is to illustrate how these theories facilitate our understanding of social processes underlying human–computer interactions and how this understanding benefits the design and development of computer system products and services. A second objective is to outline alternative methodological approaches for examining the social changes and impacts computers have on people as they interact with others, including computers. The goal here is to make the methodologies and procedures commonly used in the social sciences accessible to the nonsocial scientists.

Why This Book is Needed

We believe that there are three trends in the development of computer-based information systems which mandate the incorporation of more social science in system development:

1. The movement toward use of small group productivity tools as opposed to individual productivity software. Word processing is giving way to group authoring packages. This trend is exacerbated by local area networking and increased use of distributed data-bases.
2. The changing structural nature of the workplace. The established industrial order is giving way to more streamlined ways of work. Flatter organizations, insistence on quality and self-managing groups are demand forces requiring a new generation of software that augments these new organizational styles.
3. The use of electronic forms of symbolic communication is increasing the bandwidth of human–computer interaction. Images, graphs, charts, and iconic symbols are routinely used to facilitate communication. Computing power is moving toward provision of enormous graphical power for the end user. With this trend comes an increasing use of these tools.

Each of these trends in the workplace increase the need for software to be designed in a larger context than previously. When people use products such as word processing or spreadsheets, the interaction occurs between a single user and a single software application. The extent of usage and the degree to which the product is perceived to be useful is dependent upon the tasks and needs of the individual, and the characteristics and response of the system. Applications such as electronic mail implicitly involve a more social level of interaction. As with face-to-face conversations or telephone calls, electronic mail requires at least two individuals and in many situations more than one computer. The same holds for voice-store-and-forward systems, time management facilities, or computer-supported work tools designed to coordinate the schedules and activities of different people.

The problems of getting individuals to begin using, or increase their usage of, an electronic form of communication essentially represents a social, not a technical issue. Individuals need to believe that the electronic form of communication provides some benefit that can not be realized with more traditional modes of interaction such as memos, the telephone, or face-to-face communication. Moreover, such information and beliefs must be shared by more than one user. If Joe is a firm believer in electronic mail, but none of the people with whom Joe communicates share this opinion, the product will not be efficiently and effectively utilized. When the recipients of electronic messages do not check their mail boxes, the problem of "telephone tag" is simply translated into "EMail lag." Failure to recognize and deal with this shift in levels of interaction is a primary limiting factor in the users' acceptance of any electronic form of communication (Culnan & Bair, 1983; Vaske & Teubner, 1985; Grantham & Vaske, 1985; Kiesler, 1986).

Computer Supported Cooperative Work (CSCW) tools designed to enhance group productivity extend the social consequences associated with human–computer interactions. CSCW applications aim to augment work groups through communications enhancement. The focus on group process rather than individual tasks distinguishes CSCW from the more traditional office automation efforts. Current CSCW software tools include the traditional office automation capabilities (word processing, electronic mail, calendaring) within an integrated and structured framework for facilitating communication. One recent market research analysis indicates that there are no fewer than 17 companies developing software within this rubric (Institute for the Future, 1988). This suite of software products runs the risk of doing little to enhance the effectiveness of work groups unless it explicitly recognizes the social processes that influence human communication.

Interactions between humans encompass both task and social goals. Because computer conversations retain sufficient human-like characteristics, they tend to be judged by many of the same criteria as human conversations. Computer-mediated communication channels affect group productivity because factors such as group tasks, size, and cohesiveness are interrelated with group goals and productivity. The social goals of a group introduce attitudinal factors into the conversation and can conflict with task-related goals. In addition, the norms for appropriate social interaction are often absent from computer communications. This makes it difficult to fulfill task goals and severely limits the range of social goals. From a social psychological perspective, computer-mediated communications are less personal and governed by fewer norms of acceptable behavior (Kiesler, Siegel, & McGuire, 1984). These characteristics reduce social feedback, making it more difficult to coordinate communications and equalize status differentials among participants. An effective CSCW tool must incorporate both the task and social goals of human conversations. The rich tradition of analyzing the characteristics of small group activity in social psychology has much to offer the designer of CSCW packages. The information in this book, especially Chapter 2, can serve as a good primer for these designers.

From a social organizational perspective, modern management theory is struggling with the increased pace of interaction between firms and their environments. The uncertainty of business has increased. Adaptations to this new environment include the use of information systems for strategic advantage and integration across industry segments (Ouchi, 1984). These trends are facilitated by the rapid and accurate movement of information across organizational boundaries, which promotes more dynamic, rapidly changing work structures (Kling, 1987). Just as the telephone gave rise to new organizational functions (e.g., sales force being replaced with telemarketing), these new information systems are creating fundamental changes in business structure. The rules by which businesses operate, the scripts which describe their structure, are being embedded in software. We need to understand these organizational issues to build software to assist people in their new roles. Chapter 3 of this book begins to give a perspective and theoretical understanding of these real world dynamics.

Finally, this book is intended to help designers and developers understand social change associated with symbolic forms of computer communication. The computer and telecommunications industries are rapidly increasing the bandwidth of communication channels. Text, numbers, graphics, and video images can be transmitted with almost the ease of a telephone call. As this capability spreads, it gets used in new and different ways. Adaptation of communication systems, mediated by computers, to work group cultures and values is what will give future software its competitive edge (Morgan, 1987). We need to understand what part these symbolic forms of communication play in human social affairs. Some designers have an intuitive feel of humans' use of symbols and culture, but most do not. In Chapter 4 we present an overview of what we, and others, consider to be the next emerging area of software design; users participating in the actual software development to mold it to their own set of symbols, culture-bound work rituals, and patterns of communication.

Throughout this book we allude to another, more overarching, need for the material presented here; the need to adopt a more integrated theory-based understanding of human–computer interaction as the foundation for system design and development work. The application of human factors engineering, cognitive science, and social science is being integrated into the software development life cycle (Norman, 1980). Software designers are in many cases required to look beyond the technical and individual consequences of human–computer interactions. This shift in orientation ranges from requirements definitions to quality assurance testing (Floyd, 1988). Sound theories of human social behavior are needed if there is to be a logical basis for design modification. Random experiment or pure luck is not enough in today's world. Social evaluation strategies are needed to relate new office technologies to the spectrum of real world requirements (Hopwood, 1983; Shneiderman, 1987).

THEORIES AND THEORETICAL PERSPECTIVES

In any applied field, the theory or theories utilized have to confront reality when they are put to applied test. Another issue, however, is equally important. That is, the theory's point of origin. It is exceedingly difficult to say something meaningful about human–computer interactions in the real world without observation of human–computer interactions in real world settings. Observation and description of the real world are essential points of origin for theories in applied areas like human–computer interaction (Chapanis, 1971; Chapanis, Anderson, & Licklider, 1983; Dubin, 1976; Teubner & Vaske, 1988).

"A *theory* is a set of interrelated propositions that organizes and explains a set of observed facts" (Michener, Delamater, & Schwartz, 1986, p. 8). Theories refer to classes of events rather than any specific event, and go beyond mere observation because they hypothesize causal relationships between concepts. If the theory is valid, the phenomena under investigation can be explained, and events not yet observed can be predicted.

The theoretical development of the social sciences is characteristic of any discipline still in its infancy. As yet there is no common language of descriptive or explanatory concepts that all theorists agree upon. Diversity of concepts and theories is the order of the day, a fact that emerges all too clearly from the studies reported here. One reason for this diversity is the scope and complexity of the problems being addressed: changes in individual attitudes toward computers, organizational influences on user acceptability of computers, or the roles that culture, symbols, rituals, and myths play in human–computer interactions. Each of these issues constitute a complex of more specific problems, which, similar to the larger issues, involve a diversity of phenomena and variables which vary across situations. Understanding a group's attitude change toward computers requires consideration of the organizational pressures to change, as well as the cultural influences (symbols, rituals, and myths) which affect group cohesiveness, group goals, and pressures toward conformity. On the other hand, the study of attitude change as a function of mass media draws attention to the context of the message communicated, the credibility of the source, the order of presentation, etc. To the extent that researchers focus on different variables and different problems (and thereby different individuals and social settings), it is likely that they will stress different variables and explanations in their theorizing.

Theory is not simply a function of what problems are studied, but also of who studies them. Different psychologists may examine the same problem and still end up with different descriptions and explanations. Varying concepts and theories emerge, because researchers make different assumptions about the essential processes necessary to understand social behavior. Different human–computer interaction problems are likely to generate different concepts and theories.

Theory is an important dimension of all social sciences. Each discipline (psychology, sociology, and anthropology) includes a large number of theories that can be classified according to their primary emphasis. One group of theories emphasizes the causal ordering of variables and seeks quantifiable explanations of the conditions that influence social behaviors. Other theories are much broader in scope. Theories of this type make broad sweeping assumptions about human nature and offer general explanations of a wide range of diverse social behaviors. Theories of this latter type are termed *theoretical perspectives* (Michener et al., 1986).

Theoretical perspectives have particular value in the study of human–computer interaction. By adopting a set of assumptions regarding humans and computers, a theoretical perspective offers a viewport through which we can examine a wide range of interaction processes. By emphasizing certain points of view and de-emphasizing others, features of the interaction become more apparent. Of the theoretical perspectives examined here, no two examine exactly the same concepts and processes. Each perspective highlights attributes of a given social situation. The fundamental value of theoretical perspectives lies in their generality and their ability to examine a wide range of social situations and behaviors.

Three theoretical perspectives are examined here: (a) social psychology, (b) sociology as viewed from social organizational influences, and (c) anthropology. These theoretical perspectives were selected because they offer a range of viewports through which human–computer interactions can be examined. Other theories not presented are also relevant. Our intent was not to detail all perspectives, but rather to suggest some areas where initial research may focus. Examples were selected to cross areas of interest to professionals working in the area of human–computer interaction.

Social Psychology

Social psychologists study the nature and causes of human behavior in a social context. There are four major concerns within social psychol-

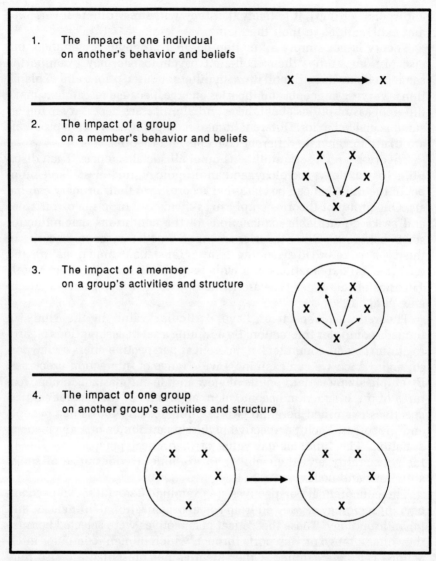

FIGURE 1.1
The Core Concerns of Social Psychology.

ogy (Figure 1.1): (a) the influence of one individual on another person's attitudes and behaviors, (b) the impact of a group on its member's attitudes and behaviors, (c) the impact of a member on a group's activities and structure, and (d) the impact of one group on another group's activities and structure.

The first concern, the impact of one person on another, is perhaps the most researched topic in social psychology. When one person changes the behavior of a second individual, the first is said to have a social influence. The boss who replaces the secretary's typewriter with a computer has a direct influence on the secretary's behavior. Beyond this overt impact on behavior, one person can also affect another's attitudes. Social psychologists define an *attitude* as a learned organization of beliefs and feelings toward a person, an object (e.g., a computer), or a situation predisposing one to respond in some preferential manner. Interpersonal attitudes such as liking, disliking, loving, and hating have received the most attention, but research on people's attitudes toward computers is becoming more common. Because attitudes are learned, they can change. People and technology evolve continuously, and so does our knowledge of their interrelationships. By definition, social change is at the heart of social psychological theory and research, because social influence implies change.

Social psychological theories suggest that, when the cognitive elements of an attitude or behavior are inconsistent, individuals are motivated to change their attitudes, their behavior, or both in order to restore psychological harmony. When individuals freely choose to use a computer because they believe it will improve their job performance, and the machine lives up to their beliefs, there should be considerable cognitive consistency. In situations where a manager dictates the usage of a particular software application, and the employees are generally resistant to computers or dislike the specific application chosen for their use, less consistency will be observed.

Efforts to understand these relationships between individuals' attitudes and behaviors has produced a large and diverse body of literature. Fifty years of research indicates that knowledge of a person's attitudes is a necessary, although not sufficient, condition for predicting behavior. Differences between what people say and what people do are explained in terms of the cognitive structure of the attitude, situation context variables, normative influences, and individual differences.

Although human–computer interaction research has traditionally not emphasized differences in individual users, there is an emerging interest in the topic. Three classes of individual difference variables can be identified: personality, cognitive style, and demographic/situational variables. The psychological study of personality has traditionally been concerned with providing a systematic account of the ways in which individuals differ from one another. Recent personality trait theories have increasingly realized that an adequate approach to the study of traits must examine how qualities of a person and the situation influence each other. This expanded view recognizes that human tendencies are a critical part of personality, but also asserts the need to study the cognitive and affective structures people use to adapt to events, people, and situations encountered in life. Among the personality traits believed to impact human–computer interaction are locus of control, extraversion–introversion, fear of failure/need for achievement, anxiety, and defensiveness.

Theoretical and empirical effort related to individual differences is also concerned with the cognitive processes people employ when dealing with information. Cognitive style refers to an individual's consistent ways of approaching and processing information, especially through perception, memory and thought. At least four cognitive style dimensions have been suggested to have importance to human–computer interactions: field-dependent/field-independent, systematic/heuristic, verbalizers/visualizers, flexibility/rigidity.

Finally, noncognitive variables such as demographic and situation influences (e.g., prior experience) represent another class of moderators affecting attitude–behavior relationships and help to broaden our understanding of individual differences. Prior experience has by far received the most attention in the human–computer interaction literature, but a few studies have examined the impact of demographic indicators.

The second concern of social psychology is the impact of a group on the behavior of its individual members (Figure 1.1). Individuals belong to many social groups which exert influence on their behaviors and attitudes. Groups regulate their members' actions by establishing rules or norms which dictate what people think behavior ought to be in varying situations. Norms are standards that individuals use for evaluating situations, people or computer products as good or bad, better or worse. A distinction is typically made between standards held by an individual (personal norms) and those shared by the members of a social group (social norms). When individuals fail to conform to these social standards, sanctions are sometimes used to maintain the structure and function of the group.

Normative definitions apply to all human–computer interactions, although the amount of shared agreement may vary. While most users would agree that cursor movements should track mouse movements, there is less agreement about what behavior ought to be in electronic messaging systems. Effective cooperative work in these social networks depends on the group's ability to appropriately manage its members and the technology (Eveland & Bikson, 1986). It is also through the group's influence on the individual that members become socialized into the group. Socialization is the process by which individuals selectively acquire skills, knowledge, attitudes, values, and motives current in the groups of which they are or will become members. Through the socialization process, technology is becoming a natural rather than a complex thing. Computer forums influence this socialization process by providing an historical record of the group's thinking and rationale for decisions.

The third concern of social psychology is the impact of individuals on the structure and activities of the group. Similar to the impact groups have on individuals, specific individuals may impact the group itself. An innovative individual who adopts the use of computers for preparing documents and budgets can change the group's norms for these activities. By demonstrating the benefits which accrue from the electronic versions of these activities, the individual serves as the group's leader. Through leadership and innovation, individuals can exert a substantial impact on the group.

The fourth concern of social psychology is the impact of one group on the activities and structure of another group. Relations between two groups may be friendly or hostile, cooperative or competitive. The nature of this relationship can affect not only intergroup interactions, but also larger social organizations to which the groups belong. When marketing, engineering, and human factors cannot agree on an appropriate strategy for the next software release, development and production are delayed and the entire company suffers.

Social Organizations

Social psychology is related to social organizations in the same way that process is related to structure. Social psychology describes the *process* of people interacting with one another. Social organizational literature focuses on the *structure* of this interaction. Study of organizations is intimately linked to social psychological processes because organizations are essentially names we give to patterns of communication. Informal communication networks within an organization are eventually reflected in formal structures, either through acceptance of rituals of behavior or codifying in regulations and rules.

Sociological explanations and descriptions of organizations are concerned with two important properties of *organizing* behavior: structure and function. Structure refers to measurable, observable patterns of communication (Ball, 1978). Computers not only affect organizations, but in some ways *are* organizations. This is especially true in large, complex, formal organizations where computers are applied in everything from the electronic exchange of memos to the heat and lights in the building.

Organizational theories explain the structure and function of corporations in terms of authority and power, size and complexity, efficiency and effectiveness, information, technology, and environment. While different theories emphasize different variables at different times, all theories implicitly or explicitly describe organizations with these constructs. Sociological theories of organizations differ from cognitive and social psychological theories, in that they concentrate more on general observable trends than on the magnitude of variable relationships, a situation dictated partially by the difficulty in obtaining quantitative data. Organizational theories are concerned with identifying consistent patterns of communication between individuals (i.e., structure).

The study of human–computer interaction from an organizational perspective can be classified according to three major theories: (a) the structural approach, (b) the human relations school, and (c) open systems theory. Each theoretical orientation offers an alternative frame of reference for judging particular situations. No single theory will work in every situation.

Structural theories (Weber's bureaucracy and scientific management) emphasize the importance of *formal* roles and relationships, while human relations theories advanced by Maslow, McGregor, Argyris, and Ouchi concentrate on the *informal* relationships that exist between members of an organization. Both the structural and human relations theories represent *closed systems* models—closed in the sense that the organization is studied in isolation from broader influences such as the environment. *Open Systems* theories (sociotechnical design and models of innovation) strive to incorporate these environmental factors and demonstrate the linkages between macro (i.e., formal communication structures) and micro (i.e., informal communication structures) perspectives. Because open systems theories emphasize communication processes, the approaches offer a promising way to analyze the relationship between telecommunications technologies and organizations.

Theories of organizational behavior illustrate important points for human–computer interaction. First, analysis of computer system users within the organizational context is complex and needs to be viewed from theoretical perspectives to be fully understood. A researcher's choice of theory, variables, and method of study should depend upon the question asked. The same is true of the level of analysis (e.g., individual, organization, or culture). Second, organizational theory points to fruitful research pathways by indicating which variables should be correlated with system adoption and use. Computer systems influence organization structure, functional differentiation, and communications patterns. These observations imply that organizational theories should be incorporated into research which aims to discover the patterns which lie behind human–computer interaction, because structure and process variables can account for variation in computer user behavior.

Understanding how technology impacts organizations, the social environment in which the interaction occurs, and the factors related to the occurrence of these impacts requires two separate elements. The first involves a description of the relationships between conditions of use (e.g., types of use, site factors, amount of use) and the impacts associated with these conditions. The second component refers to an evaluative dimension which incorporates value judgments about the acceptability of impacts.

The *descriptive component* is concerned with the observable characteristics of human–computer interactions. Two types of descriptive data are important: management parameters and impact parameters. Anything an organization can directly manipulate is a management parameter. Examples of management parameters include the procedures used for introducing the technology and access privileges for individuals in the organization. Impact parameters describe what happens to users or the environment as a result of computer use patterns and other management parameters. User satisfaction, productivity gains or losses as a function of technology, and the ease with which people can communicate are examples of impact parameters.

In examining how members of an organization use computer technology and the impacts of this usage on the environment and the individual's experience, the descriptive component identifies how the social system works, but it does not determine whether such conditions are appropriate or acceptable. This determination requires input from the second component: evaluation. The *evaluative component* considers the objective states produced by management parameters in an effort to determine their relative merits. It is important that this evaluation result in a set of standards specifying the type of working experience to be provided in terms of appropriate impact parameters as well as the degree of social modification acceptable to management.

The above discussion demonstrates that both scientific and judgmental considerations are necessary to evaluate human–computer interactions. Such evaluations are effective when (a) management objectives specify the social conditions desired in a given situation, and (b) research demonstrates the extent to which existing conditions meet the standards selected. Unfortunately, despite the large volume of literature, little progress has been made on meeting either of these criteria. A major shortcoming in most management plans is the lack of objectives that allow managers to explicitly state the conditions they seek and to measure performance with regard to achieving those objectives. Most research related to the social impacts of organizational computing fails to explicitly state the consequences for different users performing different tasks.

Anthropology

Anthropology studies the human experience through observations of behavior. What differentiates anthropology from the other social science disciplines is the broad, holistic scope of its activities. Anthropologists are concerned with humans in all places of the world, and study all aspects of those people's experiences. They seek to discover the customs and ranges of acceptable behavior that comprise society (or a group in that society) and stress the idea that any society should be viewed within that context. To understand the needs of a group of computer users, the customs and ideals of that group must be examined directly, not interpolated from another group.

Culture is an abstraction employed by anthropologists to clarify the relationships between individuals and the setting in which behavior occurs. The existence of culture is inferred from observed regularities in the behavior of individuals, and from the cultural artifacts that derive from this behavior. Culture in this sense is defined in terms of its external, observable effects. To explain these effects, anthropologists assume the existence of an inner culture, the internalized representation of the person's norms, beliefs, attitudes, and values.

Some beliefs are shared by all of the members of a group, others are specific to one or another subgroup of individuals within the larger group, and still others are held by individuals only. Each of these systems of beliefs refer to different orderings of the world. The system of beliefs held (more or less) by all members of a society is called a *culture*, while the beliefs shared by a limited subgroup is often called a *subculture*. An individual's belief system, the totality of what a person shares with others and what is unique to that person, is an aspect of personality. Anthropologists concentrate on cultural and subcultural variations while cognitive psychologists focus on variations in individuals and their personality.

Anthropological studies of cultural differences typically involve comparisons of dramatically divergent societies. The beliefs and value structures held by modern Western society, for example, might be contrasted against those of the Hopi Indians. Today's anthropologists, however, are broadening their scope of research setting to include the cultures found in corporate organizations. Similar to the social psychologist's theoretical perspective, an anthropologist's study of cultures or subcultures constitutes a basis for understanding the factors that underlie the development of motives, beliefs, and attitudes of corporate cultures. The study of diverse cultural settings provides a basis for determining, not only what is different among groups, but also what is common to the human experience. The concern is not merely with similarities in content, but more importantly, with the determination of the extent to which concepts and theories have validity across human settings.

The influence of culture on any single individual is conditioned by the person's prior experiences. Because people do not share each other's experiences directly, they must convey their ideas and feelings to each other in ways that others will understand. *Symbols* are signs created by humans to convey our ideas, intentions, and actions to others. They are arbitrary stand-ins for what they represent. A commencement ceremony symbolizes the completion of one phase in an individual's life and the beginning of a new one. A gold watch after 25 years of service symbolizes the importance of loyalty and the organization's concern for its people. Meaning is generated from the use of symbols, and there is a constant interchangeability between meaning and symbol in terms of context of use. Through this construction of meaning, *rituals* or rules for structuring meaning evolve. Such structures, built from process, persist over time and become myths or histories of the past. *Myths* are narratives of events having a sacred quality in which at least some of the events neither occurred nor exist in the world outside the myth. The myths associated with software development illustrate that what appears as a reasonable narrative of events can lead to misinformation and confusion. Myths associated with human–computer interaction are also evident in the narratives (stories) told by users. Symbols (computers) are linked to myths (stories) through rituals (behavioral prescriptions). Symbols are embedded in rituals which are in turn embedded in myths. The symbols impart meaning to behavior through the rules prescribed by rituals, but the meaning of behavior only makes sense in the context of the myths that surround that behavior. In terms of the individual, symbols, rituals, and myths influence the person's attitudes and behavior and thus provide a theoretical link to social psychology. From an organizational perspective, symbols, rituals, and myths define corporate culture and thus extend sociological explanations of behavior. The anthropological study of culture, of systems of symbols and meanings, is the science of the basic terms with which we view ourselves as people and as members of society. The way people use these terms determines how they define and experience their world.

Time and space dimensions are important for understanding

human–computer interactions from an anthropological perspective, because the way we think and organize our world is not frozen in time or space. The symbols, rituals, and myths employed by expert computer users are likely to differ significantly from those used by novices. These individual differences partially account for the range of variability among people in the same social setting. Furthermore, no single individual is exposed to all the processes and events that compromise a cultural system. Individuals experience only selected aspects of this social system and much of what is experienced is mediated by other people. Novice computer users do not learn about computing systems in the abstract, but rather are influenced by their own direct experiences and information provided by others. Perceptions of today's computer environment differ from those of the past. Anthropology provides the tools for examining the past to glean a glimpse of the future.

Theories in anthropology focus attention on societal characteristics rather than individual variations. At least four major schools of thought relevant to the analysis of human–computer interaction can be identified: (a) linguistics, (b) cognition, (c) ecology, and (d) symbolic interactionism. *Linguistics* is the study of how people use language. Language is composed of symbols which are linked through speech and transferred from one person to another. Language is bounded by culture and has meaning only in that context.

Cognitive anthropology examines patterns of behavior in terms of culturally variant organizing principles. It assumes that different subcultures employ different cognitive schema. Understanding these cultural-based organizing principles is important for understanding what functionality is needed for different cultures of computer users. *Cultural ecology* examines the influence of environmental factors on culture. Relative to a computer system, ecological theory is concerned with the relationships between the structure of the hardware and software, and how people perceive these relationships in a sociotechnical environment. It assumes that people interact with computing systems in symbolic and ritualistic ways. *Symbolic interactionism* also stresses cognitive processing, but places more emphasis on the interaction process. The theory is based on the premise that human nature and social order are products of a give-and-take process that occurs during interaction. It stresses the central role of symbolic communication in personality development and culture. Human–computer interaction is a symbolic process embedded in larger symbol systems (e.g., a computer is a tool). The theory suggests that an analysis of the relationships between these *symbol systems* is necessary to understand human–computer interactions.

INTEGRATING THE PERSPECTIVES

The three theoretical perspectives differ in the issues they address and those they choose to ignore. They also differ with respect to the variables they consider important and those they treat as irrelevant. Despite these differences, there appears to be five areas where social psychology, sociology, and anthropology overlap with respect to human–computer interactions:

1. **Impact Interrelationships:** Within each discipline (psychology, sociology, anthropology), there is no single, predictable response associated with human–computer interactions. Instead, an interrelated set of impact indicators can be identified (Figure 1.2). Some forms of impact (e.g., employment, a person's functional role in the organization, power aspects in organizations) are more direct or obvious than others (e.g., job satisfaction, alienation, privacy), but any impact indicator or combination of indicators can influence the introduction and use of computer technology. To understand how technology impacts an organization or an individual, it is necessary to consider a range of possible impact variables.
2. **Technology-Impact Relationships:** The relationships between technology and impact variables are neither simple nor uniform. Most impacts do *not* exhibit a direct linear relationship with the technology per se. Computers by themselves do nothing to anybody. Technology-impact relationships are influenced by the implementation procedures, differences in a variety of individual/group variables and situational factors. Technology represents only one of these impact indicators.
3. **Varying Tolerance to Impacts:** One of the most important factors affecting human–computer interactions is the variation in tolerances across individuals. A given scenario may enhance the interaction for some, have no effect on others, and produce dissatisfaction and/or fear for another group.
4. **Task-Specific Influences:** All human–computer interactions do not have the same effects. A given individual may be quite tolerant of a slow system response time when sending a long electronic mail message and very intolerant of a slow response when moving the cursor. Some types of tasks affect one group more than another. Experts may be less tolerant of long or variable response times for a given task than are novices. Impacts can vary within a given task according to the technology used and user characteristics.
5. **Situation-Specific Influences:** The impacts of computer use are in-

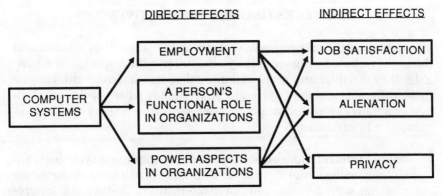

FIGURE 1.2
Classification of effects of computer systems.

fluenced by a variety of situation-specific variables. Given a basic tolerance level to a particular task, the outcome of computer use may still depend on the time and place of the activity.

APPLYING SOCIAL SCIENCE

Two primary factors distinguish *basic* from *applied* research: locus of problem generation (Lazarsfeld & Reitz, 1975) and desired form of results (Suchman, 1967).[1] Locus of problem generation refers to the referent genesis of the research question. With basic research, the research question is generated primarily by the researcher to test the validity of a hypothesis. The goal is to determine the presence or absence of a relationship between two or more variables, independent of social or practical consequences. The following could be a basic research question: "What is the relationship between users' attitudes toward electronic mail and their usage of the software?"

Applied research questions are typically presented to the researcher by someone else to address a practical concern. A similar question could be posed: "What is the relationship between users' attitudes toward electronic mail and usage?" The difference lies in who is asking the question and how the findings will be used. From an applied perspective, the researcher has an additional interest in using the data to help shape policies for introducing the technology and facilitating the acceptance of the software, which goes beyond the validation of theory.

Highlighting these similarities and differences is important, because

---

[1] Quality of research and monetary value are typically not critical distinguishing features between basic and applied research.

it suggests that the same theories and methods used by the *basic researcher* are appropriate for the *applied researcher*. The observation also implies that the same care and attention to detail that is applied to laboratory studies must be carried into field testing. The ability to control extraneous variables may be more constrained in a field setting, but the theory and methods need not be.

Social psychology, sociology, and anthropology rely on observations from empirical studies and utilize explicit methodologies. Methodological differences do exist among the theoretical perspectives, but the differences concern the extent to which the data are quantified and the unit of analysis, not the presence or absence of method. Social psychological studies tend to be highly quantitative analyses of the interactions that occur among individuals or groups. Empirical data found in social organizational studies represent a blend of quantitative and qualitative methods, where the unit of analysis ranges from the organization viewed as an entire system to the linkages that exist among the members of the organization. Empirical work in anthropology tends to utilize qualitative methodologies and in general, focuses on more global societal issues rather than individuals. As these data collection procedures become more comprehensive and the analysis strategies become more sophisticated, relationships between variables are illuminated. Two questions, however, still remain: Can these theoretical perspectives and methodologies facilitate our understanding of the social consequences of human–computer interactions? Can this knowledge be applied to the development and implementation of computer products? This book addresses these questions.

BOOK OVERVIEW

This book represents a blend of theory and application. Each theory chapter isolates a set of variables and examines their interrelationships. A central theme is the relationship between theories and variables. Theories in social psychology are discussed in Chapter 2. Social organizational influences are examined in Chapter 3, and the theoretical perspectives in anthropology are presented in Chapter 4. Each of these chapters follow a similar format. Variables commonly used by a given discipline are examined first, followed by a discussion of the theoretical perspectives relevant to that social science. Each major section in the theory chapters is concluded with a series of questions researchers can consider when designing new projects and managers can use when implementing the technology. Finally, empirical examples are presented to illustrate how the theory can be applied to the practical problems faced by software and system designers. The examples are presented to illustrate practical guidelines for software and system designers. Care is taken to highlight the advantages and disadvantages of placing development projects on a scientific footing. Chapter 5 describes four social science methodologies that can be applied to the study of social human–computer interaction. The methodologies include observation of behaviors, design team techniques, experiments, and surveys. Empirical examples are presented to highlight the application of the methods.

Many of the empirical examples were taken from a series of research projects conducted by the authors. These projects were primarily conducted in two corporations and involved both quantitative and qualitative data collection efforts. We chose to use these data sets as examples for several reasons. First, by focusing on only two organizations, variations in management structures could be controlled. Second, the data sets facilitated the examination of variables relative to each theoretical perspective. Finally, the data permitted real-life illustrations of the concepts being discussed.

BIBLIOGRAPHY

Ball, R. A. (1978). Sociology and general systems theory. *The American Sociologist, 13,* 65–72

Bjorn-Andersen, N., & Rasmussen, L. B. (1980). Sociological implications of computer systems. In H. T. Smith & T. R. G. Green (Eds.), *Human interaction with computers* (pp. 97–123). New York: Academic Press.

Brooks, R. (1977). Towards a theory of the cognitive processes in computer programming. *International Journal of Man-Machine Studies, 9,* 737–751.

Cantril, H., & Allport, G. (1935). *The psychology of radio.* New York: Harper.

Caporael, L. R., & Thorngate, W. (1984). Introduction: Towards the social psychology of computing. *Journal of Social Issues, 40,* 1–13.

Card, S. K., Moran, T. P., & Newell, A. (1983). *The psychology of human–computer interaction.* Hillsdale, NJ: Erlbaum.

Chapanis, A. (1971). The search for relevance in applied research. In W. T. Singleton, J. G. Fox, & D. Whitfield (Eds.), *Measurement of man at work: An appraisal of physiological and psychological criteria in man-machine systems* (pp. 1–14). London: Taylor & Francis Ltd.

Chapanis, A., Anderson, N. S., & Licklider, J. C. R. (1983). *Research Needs for Human Factors.* Washington, DC: National Academy Press.

Culnan, M. J., & Bair, J. H. (1983). Human organization needs and organizational productivity: The potential impact of office automation. *Journal of the American Society for Information Science, 34,* 215–221.

Dubin, R. (1976). Theory building in applied areas. In M. D. Dunnette (Ed.), *Handbook of industrial and organizational psychology* (pp. 17–39). Chicago, IL: Rand McNally.

Eveland, J. D., & Bikson, T. K. (1986). *Evolving electronic communication networks: An empirical assessment.* (Technical report). The Rand Corporation.

Floyd, C. (1988). Outline of a paradigm change in software engineering. ACM SIGSOFT. *Software Engineering Notes, 13,* 25–38.

Forester, T. (Ed.). (1980). *The microelectronics revolution.* Oxford, England: Blackwell.

Grantham, C. E., & Vaske, J. J. (1985). Predicting the usage of an advanced communication technology. *Behavior and Information Technology, 4(4),* 327–336.

Hopwood, A. G. (1983). Evaluating the real benefits. In H. J. Otway & M. Peltu (Eds.), *New office technology: Human and organizational aspects* (pp. 37–50). Norwood, NJ: Ablex Publishing Corp.

Institute For The Future. (1988). *Competitive analysis.* (Special Report SR-315). Menlo Park, CA: Institute For The Future.

Kiesler, S. (1986). The hidden messages in computer networks. *Harvard Business Review, 86,* 46–60.

Kiesler, S., Siegel, J., & McGuire, T. W. (1984). Social psychological aspects of computer mediated communication. *American Psychologist, 39,* 1123–1134.

Kling, R. (1987). Defining the boundaries of computing across complex organizations. In R. Boland & R. Hirscheim (Eds.), *Critical issues in information systems research.* New York: John Wiley and Sons.

Lazarsfeld, P. F., & Reitz, J. G. (1975). *An introduction to applied sociology.* New York: Elsever.

Markus, M. L. (1983). Power, politics, and MIS implementation. *Communications of the ACM,* 68–82.

Michener, H. A., DeLamater, J. D., & Schwartz, S. H. (1986). *Social psychology.* San Diego, CA: Harcourt Brace Jovanovich.

Morgan, G. (1987). *Images of organizations.* Beverly Hills, CA: Sage Publications.

Norman, D. A. (1980). Twelve issues for cognitive science. *Cognitive Science, 4,* 1–32.

Ouchi, W. (1984). *M form society.* Reading, MA: Addison Wesley.

Schwartz, P., & Ogilvy, J. (1979). The emergent paradigm: Changing patterns of thought and belief. *Analytic Report 7 Values and Lifestyles Program.* Menlo Park, CA: SRI International.

Shneiderman, B. (1980). *Software psychology: Human factors in computer and information systems.* Cambridge, MA: Winthrop Publishers, Inc.

Shneiderman, B. (1987). *Designing the user interface: Strategies for effective human–computer interaction.* Reading, MA: Addison-Wesley.

Sim, F., & Anderson, R. E. (1976). Sociology of computing: Conceptual framework and curriculum. *SIGSOC Bulletin, 7.*

Suchman, L. (1967). *Evaluative research.* New York: Russell Sage Foundation.

Teubner, A. L., & Vaske, J. J. (1988). Monitoring computer users' behaviour in office environments. *Behaviour and Information Technology, 7,* 67–78.

Vaske, J. J., & Teubner, A. L. (1985). *A comparative evaluation of Billerica and Phoenix DPS6 Email users.* (Technical Report). Billerica, MA: Honeywell Information Systems, Inc.

chapter 2
The Social Psychology of Human–Computer Interaction

The interactions that occur between people are more than isolated events. People remember and act upon past events and anticipate future interactions; they do not simply react to the present situation (Hollander, 1967). Interactions between humans and computers occur in much the same way. People develop expectations regarding the behavior of a computer system based on their previous interactions and expect future interactions to function the same way. When a software application fails to respond in a manner the user has become accustomed to, the continuity of the interaction is broken. It is this quality of relationships over time, sometimes called *historicity*, that makes the study of human social behavior and human–computer interaction distinct from the study of inanimate matter (Homans, 1961).

Social psychology is the systematic analysis of the nature and causes of human social behavior. It is concerned with the social behaviors of individuals in the context of others, the social interaction processes between two or more individuals, and the relationships between individuals and groups within broader cultural environments (Michener, DeLamater, & Schwartz, 1986). Many social psychologists regard their discipline "as an attempt to understand how the thought, feeling and behavior of individuals are influenced by the actual, imagined or implied presence of other human beings" (Allport, 1969). Human–computer interactions fall within this domain of the imagined or implied presence of others. Weizenbaum (1976), for example, has shown that users sometimes ascribe human-like qualities to interactive computers. In another study, Quintanar, Crowell, Pryor, and Adamopoulos (1982) manipulated the degree that an interactive computer was perceived to be a social stimulus. The computer's responses to the user ranged from human-like to mechanistically nonhuman. The human-like style was seen by the subjects as more human, less honest, and slightly less courteous than the mechanistic style of computer. There was also some evidence that the users perceived the computer as more responsible for their performance under a human-like, as compared with the mechanistic, response style. Under these conditions the computer represents a social influence in the human–computer interaction process.

By describing the nature of social influence processes, social psychology provides a foundation necessary for understanding the causes of social behaviors. In contrast to everyday explanations of the "whys" of social behaviors, it seeks to discover the conditions that produce any social behavior. Everyday or commonsense approaches to understanding social phenomena are insufficient, because they can obscure the actual underlying causal relationships and are themselves often contradictory; for example, "Birds of a feather flock together" versus "Opposites attract." Causal statements in social psychology can be as simple as, "If X occurs, then Y occurs," but in practice the complexities of human social behavior necessitate the specification of conditional relationships. Statements such as "Whenever conditions A, B, C, and D are present and X occurs, then Y occurs," are important building blocks for theories in social psychology.

Understanding these causal relationships is important, because there is currently conflicting advice given to systems designers concerning whether the tendency of users to project human-like characteristics into computer dialogs should be encouraged or discouraged (Murray & Bevan, 1985). Shneiderman (1987) argues that computer systems should be built to behave like tools; human attributes should not be attributed to programs and systems. In his view, "human–human communication is a poor model for human–computer interaction" (p. 434). Others have taken an opposing stance and maintain that a human-like conversational flow enhances computer communications (Cuff, 1980; Spiliotopoulos & Shackel, 1981).

To achieve a systematic understanding of social behavior, social psychologists have developed an explicit methodology that includes experimentation, observation, and surveys.[1] Data collected through this scientific approach helps researchers test the validity of their predictions about social influence. The goal, however, is to go beyond the reward of broadening and deepening of knowledge. It is equally important to use this knowledge to help people organize their interpersonal behaviors more constructively, to facilitate the development of individual potentials, and to reduce the handicaps under which people must work and live.

Given these fundamental characteristics of social psychological inquiry, the social psychology of human–computer interaction may be defined as that branch of scientific study that examines the impacts of

---

[1] Chapter 5 examines these methodologies in detail.

technology on individuals' beliefs (thoughts or cognitions), attitudes, and behaviors as they are influenced by the cognitions, attitudes, and behaviors of others (including computers) in a sociotechnical environment. This chapter explores the benefits obtained from applying the concepts in social psychology to the analysis of human–computer interactions. The goal is to provide a theoretical orientation that complements traditional cognitive psychology models by accounting for the social influences of computers on users' attitudes and performance requirements.

We first examine the scope of social psychological theory and research, highlighting the similarities and differences between social psychology and other social science disciplines—sociology, cultural anthropology, and general psychology.[2] To get a better understanding of social psychology and its approach, we next examine relevant past research on a few selected topics. Among those areas are socialization, attitudes, and the relationship between attitudes and behaviors. Differences between what people say and what people do are explained in terms of attitude structure, definition specificity, situation context variables, individual differences, and norms. Emphasis is placed on quantifying the determinants of users' attitudes toward computers and the influence of these attitudes and experiences on behavior within a social context. In a final section, we explore the concept of group dynamics and identify its relevance to computer supported cooperative work.

THE SCOPE OF SOCIAL PSYCHOLOGY

The central concern of social psychology is the process of social influence. Humans are oriented toward others in their environment and social influence occurs whenever one individual responds to the actual or implied presence of one or more others. People are influenced not only by present interactions, but also by past experiences and the learning that is associated with this interaction. The interactions (human–human and human–computer) of concern to the social psychologist are not static instances, but rather are dynamic and changing relationships in which individuals are both the cause and the consequence of their sociotechnical environment.

---

[2] The term *general psychology* as used here includes the study of perception, thinking, learning, attention, motivation, and other psychological processes. In most instances, these concepts are evaluated in highly controlled laboratory experiments involving the manipulation of physical stimuli in relation to the behavior and experience of the individual.

Any examination of the social psychology of human–computer interaction must thus begin with the premise that human beings (as well as the technology they use) are continuously changing. Just as yesterday's technology is replaced by faster processors with more functionality, computer users evolve overtime. Novice computer users do not stay novices forever, but rather develop new attitudes toward the technology and the social context in which it is used as their experiences increase. This is not to deny the stability of behavior. Individuals seek novelty, complexity, and change to the extent that their social and physical environment is psychologically stable, structured, and secure (McCall, 1974). When people experience contradictions in relation to other individuals, groups, and technologies, the contradictions serve as a basis for change and development (Rappoport, 1977). Just as individual development seems to be stabilizing, new technologies are introduced, with the consequence of never-ending change and development (Riegel, 1976). It is for this reason that the social psychology of human–computer interaction cannot ignore the context of social behavior.

The distinctiveness of social psychology stems from its study of the psychology of the individual in a social context. Although social psychology has close ties with the other social sciences, especially sociology and cultural anthropology, it retains a primary emphasis on the psychological level of analysis (i.e., the individual). Sociologists and anthropologists are concerned with human behavior, but the primary units of analysis are groups of individuals, social organizations, or even larger cultural institutions, not the individual. Social psychology is interdisciplinary in that it attempts to bridge the gaps between sociology, cultural anthropology, and psychology (Figure 2.1).

By focusing on the individual, social psychology bears a close and intimate relationship with *general psychology*. In fact, the task of establishing functional relationships between the properties of the physical world and basic psychological processes (perception, thinking, learning, attention, motivation) has traditionally been the province of general psychology. To distinguish between general and social psychology, it is not enough to observe that the former studies the behavior and experiences of individuals in a physical (laboratory) world, and the latter observes the same phenomena in a social world. If this were the case, it could be argued that, inasmuch as social behaviors and experiences depend on people's capacities to adapt to their physical world, there is no need for a science of social psychology. Whatever the characteristics of basic psychological processes as revealed in a laboratory setting, their influence on the individual's behavior and experience is common. Whether the person is experiencing a point of light in isolation or the behavior of another person in a social situation, the same underlying principles are involved.

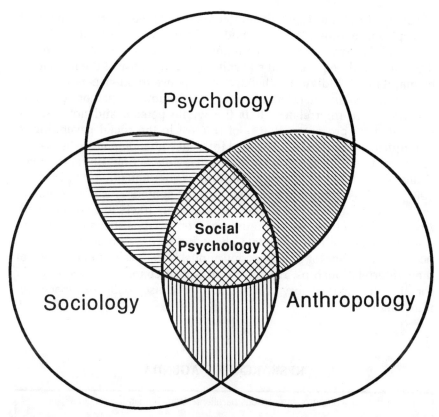

FIGURE 2.1
Relationships among three social sciences and social psychology.

There are three problems with this argument, however, which cast doubt on its validity. First, it ignores the possibility that critical psychological features may occur in complex social situations that are not included or observed in laboratory situations. There is a need to test existing principles in social settings to test their efficacy (Krech, Crutchfield, & Ballachey, 1962). Second, even if we assume the validity of existing psychological principles developed in the laboratory, the question remains of whether they are both necessary and sufficient to explain the complexities of human behavior at increasing levels of social organization. It hardly seems likely that we can acquire "a knowledge of facts and principles of social action by extrapolation from observations of nonsocial conditions" (Asch, 1952, p. 33). Only through the direct observation of social phenomena can we understand fully the nature of social behavior and experience.

Third, the study of basic psychological principles in relation to physical stimuli has typically adopted a segmented approach in which perception, learning, thinking, and other psychological processes are considered independent of each other. The study of social behavior, on the other hand, requires that a *psychological integrity* of the individual be maintained. Individuals behave in response to other persons or social stimuli as an intact organism in which motives, perceptions, and cognitions are interrelated. It is the whole person, and not discrete psychological processes, that is of interest to the social psychologist.

Empirical examples of the social influence phenomena are becoming more common in the human–computer interaction literature (e.g., Kling, 1980; Kiesler, Siegel, & McGuire, 1984; Rafaeli, 1986; Markus, 1987), but it is important to realize that the content area of this emerging field is not fixed. Many social processes are likely to be discovered. At this point in time, we can only report on what has been subjected to scientific inquiry and speculate about future developments. Because people and technology evolve continuously, so does our knowledge of their interrelationships. By definition, social change is at the heart of social psychology theory and research, because social influence implies change.

RESEARCHER'S AGENDA

Should human–computer interactions parallel human–human interactions?

How do social influence processes impact human–computer interactions?

What agents of social change influence computer usage?

In what ways does technology impact users' beliefs and attitudes?

Are there systematic differences in the beliefs and attitudes held by designers and users that interfere with the design of effective systems?

MANAGER'S AGENDA

The social context in which computers are used influences the acceptance and use of technology.

Peoples attitudes toward computers are affected by social influence processes.

Broad based psychological research is required in the current, rapidly changing user environment.

COMPUTER SOCIALIZATION

Socialization is the process by which individuals selectively acquire skills, knowledge, attitudes, values, and motives current in the groups of which they are or will become members (Sewell, 1963). Underlying virtually all contemporary views of the concept is the assumption that socialization is a continuing lifelong process (Bush & Simmons, 1981). Some theories hypothesize distinct sequences in personality and cognitive development. The search for critical or central happenings at different times in life is most characteristic of *stage theories*. Erikson (1963), for example, emphasized key phases in interpersonal development, while other theorists have hypothesized stages in cognitive development (Piaget, 1970) and in moral development (Kohlberg, 1969).

Stage theories suggest that there are distinct qualitative differences in personality and cognitive processes at different ages. The *cognitive development* stage theory hypothesizes that people have cognitive structures or rules for processing information (as in thinking), and that these structures are fundamentally different at different points in development. Kohlberg (1969) believes that these cognitive structures serve to change "stimulus inputs" (information from the environment), and that, in turn, the structures are changed by the inputs. Stage theory hypothesizes that such structures undergo basic transformations during development and thus become qualitatively different. The sequence of transformations, according to stage theory is definite and fixed, but the rate of development may be changed by experience.

Researchers disagree about the validity of stage theories. Some emphasize that certain functions and skills (e.g., walking or talking) develop most rapidly and dramatically at certain critical periods. Others see personality and cognitive development as a continuous process in which learning experiences may accumulate in a variety of sequences, depending on the learning opportunities the person happens to be exposed to. Despite the controversy, it is recognized that socialization is not a haphazard accumulation of bits of behavior, but rather entails some orderly development. This seems especially true to the extent that complex social patterns are sequential. These behaviors require the preexistence of earlier learning and structures. Some things are learned much more readily after other skills have been acquired. Likewise, the absence of certain skills makes the development of behaviors that depend on them less likely and more difficult.

It is also generally recognized that the content and organization of personality may be radically different at different points in development. The ideas, values, skills and interests of a 3-year-old are not those of the same person at age 40. What a person does and is changes with development. Hence, it is interesting to examine people's beliefs and behaviors at different points in time, when different events and crises are salient, and to assess the nature of the stability and of the change found over the years (Block & Block, 1980).

The influence of these stage theory ideas is predominant in Turkle's (1984) book *The Second Self*. She discusses three stages—metaphysical, mastery, and identity—in an individual's relationships with computers. In the "metaphysical stage" very young children are concerned with whether computers can think, feel, and are alive. At this age and stage of development, computer toys and computers serve as a source of reflection; how are the machines like and unlike other objects? Turkle argues that "putting very young children together with computers encourages a rich and continual philosophizing" (1984, p. 137).

Children from age 7 or 8 attach more significance to mastering the computer and place less emphasis on speculations about the nature of the machine. Support for this stage is seen in children playing arcade games and learning how to write computer programs. At this second stage, children want to win the game or test their competence; they want to master the program. Action dominates this developmental phase, not reflection.

By the time the child reaches adolescence, Turkle observed a return to reflection, but at this stage (identity) the source of reflection is about the self. For some adolescents in her investigation, programming became their only major activity. Because of their intense involvement, they began to see themselves and were seen by others as "computer people." Computer clubs or computer centers became the focal point for social interactions, and computers became a way of life for these individuals. Although most adolescents do not adopt this life style, computer experiences during adolescence can serve as a source of self-definition and self-creation. As she describes these individuals:

> They integrate their computer experience into their developing identities in ways that have nothing to do with becoming computer experts. They use programming as a canvas for personal expression and then as a context for working through personal concerns. They use the computer as a constructive as well as a projective medium. (Turkle, 1984, p. 138)

Turkle's book is provocative from at least two perspectives. First, it illustrates the interdisciplinary approach to theory and method that is needed to understand human–computer interactions. The descriptions of the three stages of human–computer interaction development are consistent with the socialization processes discussed by social psychologists. Her enthnographic style of inquiry parallels the methods employed by cultural anthropologists. The individuals in her sample were not average computer users, but rather people for whom computers represented a large part of their lives. These portraits of users who are heavily involved with computing is analogous to the sociological concept of the *ideal type*—examples of present reality in a form larger than life.[3] Through the examination of ideal types it is possible to obtain a clearer picture of how the metaphysical, mastery, and identity stages are manifest in adults' relationships with computers.

Second, Turkle began her study in 1978, when personal computers were first being discovered. Since then, the popularity of home computing and computers in general has grown enormously. We have become a computer-oriented culture in which everything from simple bank transactions, to expanding children's sense of their talents and potentials, to teaching math to adults, to communicating with others is directly influenced by technology. Given this increased exposure, computers cannot help but have an influence on the socialization process. The differences in personality projected by stage theories may still retain a fixed and definite pattern, but the rate of development is likely to be changed by people's experiences with computers.

It is interesting to speculate how such social changes will influence people in the decades to come. Some industry analysts predict that just as almost everyone is telephone-functional today, everyone will be computer-functional in the future. From a system designer perspective, this suggests that the currently nagging problem of accommodating the novice computer user—except those in elementary school—will become a nonissue. Everyone will already have learned, or will easily be able to learn, all he or she needs to know about electronic processing, what it is, and how to do it. Through the socialization process, technology will become a natural rather than a complex thing. The hypothesis is intriguing, but only time and future studies can determine its validity.

RESEARCHER'S AGENDA

How does the socialization process facilitate and/or inhibit user attitudes toward technology?

Do the metaphysical, mastery, and identity stages of human–computer interaction, as identified by Turkle (1984), apply to other populations of users?

---

[3] The ideal type concept is examined in Chapter 3 of this book. We discuss the ethnographic style of inquiry used by anthropology in Chapter 4.

Are there other identifable stages in the computer socialization process?

What ongoing social changes enhance people's acceptance and usage of technology?

What is the nature of the socialization process for new computer technologies?

MANAGER'S AGENDA

The way in which technology is introduced in a social setting is as important as the technology.

Computers are complicated; the socialization process takes time.

Managers can facilitate the introduction of computers by provided support staff to answer questions and calm fears of technology.

ATTITUDE THEORY

The term *attitude* is frequently discussed yet rarely understood in any precise manner. A juvenile delinquent, for example, is said to have a *bad attitude*. In his resignation speech as head of the Department of Agriculture, Earl Butz is quoted as saying: "The use of bad racial commentary in no way reflects my real attitudes." The attitudes of computer users suggest that some see the machine as a "beneficial tool" (Lee, 1970), while others express concern over the possible "dehumanizing effects" (Morrison, 1983) and "threats to society" (Lichtman, 1979). These statements indicate that an attitude, in common parlance, often refers to deeply held opinions that lie close to the heart. When social psychologists discuss attitudes, the concept takes on a more specific meaning, yet even the scientific rhetoric fails to conceal disagreement among scholars as to the components.

Part of the confusion surrounding the definition of *attitude* is that no one has ever actually seen an attitude. Attitudes cannot be weighed, nor can they be counted in any systematic manner. Does the statement "juvenile delinquents have a bad attitude" imply that the youths' are generally unwilling to accept societal norms, or that they hold multiple attitudes which when combined pose a social problem? Do the attitudes of one group of delinquents parallel those of another? Similar problems arise when considering attitudes toward human–computer interactions. To what extent do computer users' attitudes influence their willingness to accept new technologies? Can negative attitudes toward computers be changed? Are the attitudes of users and system designers different, and, if so, how should this influence the design of computer systems?

The concept of attitude only takes on meaning when we attempt to evaluate the actions of others or ourselves against what we believe in or feel is important. This does not mean that attitudes by themselves are not important, or that one should not attempt to define attitudes more precisely. Nuclear physicists do not fully comprehend the atom, yet they continue to study it.

DEFINITION OF ATTITUDE

Most textbook authors review the definitions of *attitude* and then distill the alternatives into their own unique terminology. We have elected to avoid this strategy for two reasons. First, good summaries of the definitions already exist (Shaw & Wright, 1967; Michener et al., 1986). Second, while a discussion of alternative definitions illustrates the range of previously identified ideas, it tends to confuse readers who are unfamiliar with the topic. This section presents one definition that has proven beneficial in our research and discusses the importance of the definitional components. Rokeach (1968, p. 112) defines an *attitude* as follows:

> An attitude is a relatively enduring organization of beliefs around an object or situation predisposing one to respond in some preferential manner.

An Attitude is Relatively Enduring

The first part of this definition implies that an attitude is relatively enduring. The distinction between temporary and enduring is best illustrated by example. When secretaries curse at the department system for having just gone down for the fifth time that day, they are not necessarily displaying a negative attitude toward technology, but rather a frustration with the situation. If later asked to describe their beliefs about word processors, they may still complain about the system going down, but also indicate that the automated approach is faster and easier than retyping an entire document each time a phrase is revised. Moreover, management attempts to revert back to typewriters are likely to be strongly opposed. To do so would imply a loss in the flexibility of editing documents.

Implicit in the previous example is the idea that attitudes are learned. A few short years ago, when typewriters dominated the desks of secretarial pools, the thought of using a computer to type documents represented a foreign concept. Today, the prospect of getting a skilled word processing user to type a letter on a typewriter is akin to asking the individual to etch the document in stone with a hammer and chisel. The positive attitude toward using computers for word processing is a recent acquisition for many people.

The mechanism by which people develop attitudes varies. Direct experience with an object (e.g., a computer) plays an important role in this learning process (Regan & Fazio, 1977; Fazio & Zanna, 1978; Arndt, Feltes, & Hanak, 1983). In one study (Rafaeli, 1986), employees who had more experience working with computers held more positive attitudes toward computers than their peers who were not familiar with computers or for whom the technology was still novel. Individuals with no prior experience are susceptible to viewing what they see during their first computer session as appropriate. The first individuals on a new timesharing system that has relatively few users quickly learn to expect short response times. When more individuals are registered to use the system and the competition for system resources increases, these initial users become dissatisfied as response times lengthen. People who come on later are satisfied because they expect the system to respond more slowly (Shneiderman, 1984). Friends, co-workers, and advertising campaigns also help to shape individuals' beliefs. Even people with no computer experience are probably familiar with IBM's Charlie Chaplin and MASH TV characters and believe that computers should be user friendly. Although such beliefs are not well developed, nonusers have an attitude about computers.

Because attitudes are learned, attitudes can change. The early users' initial positive attitude toward the computer turned negative in the above example, as the system response time increased. As another example, many early personal computer word processors required users to press multiple keys (e.g., Control-Q-Del) to edit text. Individuals who purchased these applications were not enamored with such interfaces but extolled the virtues of the product because it was still faster than the typewriter. Given the adoption of function keys and/or the mouse as replacements for complicated key sequences, the positive attitudes held toward the initial word processing software have undoubtedly changed. When shifts in attitudes occur, dramatic consequences can result. Automobile manufacturers who change their attitude toward robots and replace human labor with machines have a tremendous impact on the displaced employees. Similarly, a company that adopts a favorable attitude toward electronic mail influences the way individuals within the organization interact. Individuals who resist the new attitude may miss information needed to complete assignments and find themselves less effective in their job (Kiesler et al., 1984).

An Attitude is an Organization of Beliefs

An attitude can be dissected into distinct components. Although exist-ing conceptualizations differ in their details, most theorists distinguish between a cognition and an evaluative component. Cognitions, or be-liefs, are information about some aspect of an object or an action. The statement "computers have keyboards for inputting data" represents a belief people hold about computers. The statement is true, but it repre-sents only one interaction method. With a Macintosh or other point device systems, a mouse controls many aspects of data entry without ever touching the keyboard. Alternatively, automobiles use computers for regulating fuel consumption and other vital functions. These exam-ples do not negate the general belief about keyboards and computers, but, rather, highlight the point that any attitude can be differentiated into several beliefs. Efforts to understand computer users' attitudes must recognize this multidimensional nature of individual's beliefs if they are to provide useful feedback to system developers. Such beliefs are usually measured via true-false tests or free association tests (Fish-bein & Raven, 1967).

A second attitude dimension is the evaluative component. Secre-taries who say they enjoy using spreadsheets are expressing an evalua-tive belief about a software package. Evaluative beliefs are typically measured with a series of semantic differential items where the object (e.g., an electronic spreadsheet) of an attitude is rated on bipolar adjec-tives; for example, good–bad, easy–difficult, personal–impersonal, reliable–unreliable, etc. Zoltan's (1981) work on the acceptability of computers to professionals exemplifies this type of questioning. If the evaluative beliefs involve strongly held emotions such as love or hate, the concept is called *affect*. Whatever the terminology, evaluative be-liefs (or affect) refer to a feeling or evaluation which influences the way one behaves toward computer products.

Cognitions and evaluative beliefs are themselves related. If employ-ees believe that a manager uses electronic mail to praise their work (i.e., a cognition), they are also likely to feel that electronic mail is a good way to communicate (i.e., an evaluative belief). This sort of attitude organization is based on the principle of consistency (Festinger, 1957) and constitutes a fundamental building block of cognitive structure. Research efforts in this area have repeatedly demonstrated that people strive for a certain level of balance or consistency in their lives. When inconsistencies arise, individuals expend energy to resolve the conflict and reestablish a steady-state.

Beliefs and evaluative beliefs (affect) can be linked together in syl-logistic form to create new beliefs. The process is analogous to the

Attitude		I love	my computer	
Belief	My computer has a spreadsheet	My business partners use electronic mail to communicate with each other	My personal computer has a package for doing statistical analysis	I paid $10,000 for my computer
Belief		My computer's modem allows me to send electronic messages		
Evaluative Belief	Electronic spreadsheets improve my efficiency	Electronic mail makes me more effective in my job	Statistical analysis capabilities are necessary for any worthwhile computer	Computers should be inexpensive
Evaluative Belief	I enjoy preparing budgets on spreadsheets			I paid too much for my computer

Vertical Structure (left axis)

Horizontal Structure

FIGURE 2.2
The cognitive-affective foundations of an attitude.

syllogisms presented in logic courses: All men are mortal, Socrates is a man, therefore, Socrates is mortal. Such combinations are evident in the attitude, "I love my computer" (Figure 2.2). The belief that "My computer has a spreadsheet package," when combined with the evaluative belief "Electronic spreadsheets make me more efficient," leads to the new evaluative belief "I enjoy preparing budgets on electronic spreadsheets." Similarly, if people believe that electronic mail allows them to communicate with their business partners and that their business associates communicate via this medium, it follows that electronic messaging will be evaluated in a positive manner (Column 2, Figure 2.2). Since the person's computer allows for this networking, the belief string is also consistent with the person's attitude toward the system. Social psychologists refer to this cognitive organization as *vertical structure* (Bem, 1970; Heberlein, 1981; Michener et al., 1986).

The attitude diagramed in Figure 2.2 illustrates a second component of belief structures: *horizontal structure*. With one exception, these stacks of beliefs support the attitude that the person loves his or her computer. The more belief stacks that lead to the same conclusion, the more stable the attitude. Thus, although the last column in Figure 2.2 is inconsistent with the overall attitude, the other vertical belief structures may outweigh the cost limitations such that the attitude does not change.

Cognitive dissonance theory offers another rationale for attitude stability (Festinger, 1957). Similar to balance theory (Heider, 1946, 1958) or personal construct theory (Kelly, 1955), cognitive dissonance predicts that people perceive and evaluate aspects in their environment such that the behavioral implications are not contradictory. Festinger summarizes the basics of his theory as follows:

1. There may exist dissonant or nonfitting relations among cognitive elements.
2. The existence of dissonance gives rise to pressures to reduce the dissonance and to avoid increased dissonance.
3. Manifestations of these pressures include behavioral changes, changes in cognition, and circumspect exposure to new information and new opinions. (1957, p. 31)

The dissonance created by the individual's belief that the computer was too expensive can be reduced. Assume the initial choice was between an expensive workstation and a less expensive clone. Prior to purchase both alternatives may have been judged comparable. If the expensive model was selected, the person may downplay the clone's relative attractiveness by reading all the positive reviews of the higher priced computer and only negative articles about the alternative. Such exposure to more information, albeit selective exposure, reinforces the person's decision. The opinions of others may also help to support the individual's choice. If the person's friends own the same machine, it can be rationalized that, even though the computer costs more, it must be the "right one to own." Such cognitions are more likely in situations where the product is well known and has a good reputation.

The preceding emphasizes that people do not carry around disorganized sets of ideas. Cognitions are systematically interrelated to form organized, abstract, and detailed knowledge structures representing some aspect of social reality (Taylor & Crocker, 1980; Cantor, Mischel, & Schwartz, 1982). The structure and organization of cognitions are as important as their content. Examining any single belief plucked from the structure of a belief system may not provide sufficient information for predicting or understanding behavior. Considering only the cost issue in Figure 2.2, it would be difficult to understand why the person would love his or her computer.

A variety of approaches have been proposed for analyzing belief structures. One method suggests an attitude is equivalent to the summation of beliefs each weighted by the value (i.e., evaluation) ascribed to that belief (Fishbein & Ajzen, 1975). Although this approach results in a single quantitative estimate of an attitude, the process of cognitive integration is inexact and does not necessarily capture the universe of beliefs held toward an object (Bagozzi & Burnkrant, 1979). To understand beliefs, social psychologists have gone beyond simple aggregating measures of a person's beliefs into a single summary index. Recent research stresses the importance of the manner in which beliefs are organized (Schlegel & DiTecco, 1982). Among the aspects of cognitive structure that have been discussed, two of the more important are *differentiation* and *integration* (Zajonc, 1960; Scott, 1969). Differentiation refers to the number of dimensions that underlie a belief system. A greater number of dimensions implies that the person distinguishes objects in several ways, resulting in a more fine-grained and complex structure. One person may perceive computers only in terms of their ability to perform high-speed calculations. Another person, with a more differentiated structure, may view them in terms of word processing, electronic mail, and computational capability. Integration, in contrast, deals with the degree to which the dimensions of belief systems are interrelated. One person may see computers' word processing and quantitative applications as part of larger aspects of information storage and retrieval, while another individual may see these two features as unrelated (Kerber, 1983).

Research suggests that the structure of belief systems varies systematically with the amount of knowledge or experience a person has concerning a particular object (Scott, 1969; Arndt et al., 1983; Rafaeli, 1986). Schlegel and DiTecco (1982, p. 31) reason that, "as one becomes more extensively involved with an object and an elaborated behavioral repertoire is established, an increasingly differentiated and complex [belief] structure is required to represent on a cognitive level this behavioral activity." Their comparison of people with varying levels of involvement with marijuana smoking revealed that belief structures became more differentiated with more experience; increasing knowledge led to reconstruction and reorganization of the belief system. Research on political belief systems suggests that greater involvement in political affairs results in greater integration and coherence of a set of beliefs (Converse, 1964). One of our projects (Vaske, Fleishman, Ehrlich, & Grantham, 1985) compared the belief structures of groups with varying levels of computer experience: nonusers, users with no programming background, users who were formerly programmers, and currently active programmers. Respondents described their beliefs about computers in terms of 16 semantic differential scales. It was hypothesized that the belief structures of people with less experience would be less differentiated and integrated than those of people with more computer expertise. Results indicated that the belief patterns became more organized and interpretable as experience increased. This suggests that the belief structures of more experienced users are more differentiated and more integrated than those of nonusers.

As people's exposure to computers increases, the differentiation concept predicts that individuals' attitudes become more complex. Since the introduction of personal computers (about 1975), the number of people who have used or at least been exposed to computers has increased substantially.[4] Given this social change, the attitudes of the general population should be more differentiated. Although a direct test of this hypothesis would require a longitudinal study that compared people's attitudes at two points in time (e.g., before 1975 and after 1975), some support for the prediction is evident in comparisons of studies. Lee (1970) administered a 20-item questionnaire to 3000 North Americans over 18 years of age. Factor analyses revealed two dimensions. The first factor, which he labeled "beneficial tool of man," was represented by statements such as "They [computers] make it possible to speed up scientific progress and achievements" and "They are very important to the man-in-space program." The second factor, "awesome thinking machines," was represented by agreement with statements like "Electronic brain machines are strange and frightening" and "They sort of make you feel that machines can be smarter than people."[5] Twenty years after Lee collected his data (1963), Morrison (1983) attempted to replicate Lee's findings to see if the same attitude structures persisted. The sample consisted of 412 students at the University of New England in Armidale, Australia. Four dimensions were identified. The beneficial tool and the awesome machine factors identified in Lee's work were each split into two smaller factors. The differences in populations studied (North American versus Australian) and sample sizes (3000 versus 412) make it difficult to directly compare the two

---

[4] A kit for building the Altair personal computer was introduced in 1975 by a small company named MITS.

[5] Further analyses revealed that the factors were virtually independent of each other. The correlation of index scores based on these factors was −.02. This lack of correlation suggests that a person's attitude structure toward computers goes beyond a simple pro–con dimension typically employed in public opinion polls. Pro–con attitude measurement may be acceptable for assessing how individuals might vote for a political candidate, but it is conceptually inadequate for understanding the structure of beliefs in popular perceptions of computers. Lee's study also provides evidence that the conceptual distinction between affect and cognition does not mean the dimensions are empirically distinct. What people believe about computers, what they think this implies for the future, and how they feel about these cognitions are organized into a complex belief structure.

sets of findings. At the same time, the findings do suggest that people's attitudes toward computers have become more differentiated over time.

An Attitude is Organized Around an Object or Situation

Theorists agree that an attitude has an object; that is, one must have an attitude toward something. Users of computer products have attitudes toward keyboards, software packages, and printers. Such objects, however, are comprised of multiple subobjects. Part of the difficulty in determining users' attitudes toward computers is deciphering what subobject(s) the individual is referring to. If a person expresses a negative attitude toward electronic mail, the individual may be reacting to a belief that the application is too difficult to use or that the system is responding too slowly. Alternatively, if the software has a smooth, logical flow and an acceptable response time, the reaction may still be negative if the individual does not feel comfortable with electronic communications or does not believe messages are being delivered. To understand users' attitudes toward a particular object such as electronic mail, it is important to identify the salient subobjects on which users are making their judgments.

Empirical investigations of individuals' attitudes toward a variety of objects are common in the literature. Attitude scales have been developed for describing attitudes about racism (Brigham & Weissbach, 1973), politics (Campbell, Converse, Miller, & Stokes, 1960), natural environments (Dunlap & Van Liere, 1978), and computers (Reece & Gable, 1982; Loyd & Gressard, 1984). Our studies of human–computer interaction have similarly focused on the object of attitudes: electronic mail (Vaske & Teubner, 1985), voice store-and-forward systems (Grantham & Vaske, 1985), and satellite transmissions (Vaske & Grantham, 1985). Less predominant are examinations of attitudes toward varying situations (Rokeach, 1968). If users hold positive attitudes toward electronic mail, do such beliefs persist once individuals have access to voice mail? Under what conditions are users likely to hold positive or negative attitudes toward one form of electronic media as opposed to another? These issues are vital to corporations that develop products that compete for the same market; for example, electronic messaging facilities versus voice store-and-forward systems (Wright, 1986). To account for these situation influences on behavior, researchers have examined the issue from different angles. Personality theorists discuss attitudes toward situations in terms of *trait* concepts, while social psychologists use attitudes and *norms* when examining situation-specific influences on behavior. These concepts are explored in later sections of this chapter.

An Attitude is a Set of Interrelated Predispositions to Respond

The suggestion that attitudes incorporate "a set of interrelated pre-dispositions" is consistent with the idea that attitudes involve a set of organized beliefs. The "to respond" segment of the attitude definition, however, has had different theoretical interpretations, including: "predisposition to respond, predisposition to evaluate; predisposition toward an evaluative response; predisposition to experience, to be motivated and to act" (Rokeach, 1968, p. 119). Rokeach's definition avoids this issue by stating the point from the most general perspective (i.e., predisposition to respond). This more global viewpoint is consistent with personality theorists' concept of trait and with Fishbein and Ajzen's (1975) concept of *behavioral intentions*.

This definition component is important for understanding human-computer interaction, because it suggests that behavior is not determined by a single disposition but rather a set of behavioral intentions. Behavioral intentions are weighed as more or less important in decision-making processes, depending on the object of the attitude (e.g., a word processing application) or the situation in which the object is encountered (e.g., an office setting or the home). If potential buyers indicate an intention to purchase a word processor, they are stating a predisposition to respond. The decision to purchase a particular word processing application, however, is influenced by the characteristics of the product (e.g., quality, functionality, user interface), the demands imposed by the environment in which it will be used (e.g., a single user in his or her home, or multiple users on a office network), and social influences outside the scope of the physical product or intended context of use (e.g., the style and personality of the salesperson). Understanding whether or not predispositions to respond are acted upon requires an evaluation of what components are important to individuals.

Attitudes Lead to Preferential Responses

Attitudes lead to preferential (or discriminatory) responses, but the basis for the preferential response is often not clear. Are preferences driven by an affective liking or disliking of the attitude object/situation, or rather because the attitude is cognitively evaluated as good or bad (Rokeach, 1968)? Conceptual confusion arises because dimensions such as like–dislike and good–bad may be attached to different features of a complex response. People may believe that a computer company makes a good product, but still not buy one because they dislike the user interface. A preferential response (positive or negative) depends on the strength of cognitions relative to the importance attached to the evaluative beliefs in the attitude structure.

Summary

An attitude is "a relatively enduring organization of beliefs around an object or situation predisposing one to respond in some preferential manner" (Rokeach, 1968). Attitudes are embedded in larger cognitive structures and are learned through experience and social interaction. Because attitudes are learned, they can change. The extent to which attitudes can be modified is influenced by the degree of differentiation and integration of the cognitive structure. Highly differentiated and integrated attitudes are more stable. Consistency theories assume that, when cognitive elements are inconsistent, individuals are motivated to change their attitudes, their behavior, or both in order to restore harmony. The next section examines the relationship between computer users' attitudes and their behavior.

RESEARCHER'S AGENDA

What mechanisms facilitate the learning of positive attitudes toward computers?

How are user attitudes toward technology facilitated by the socialization process?

What are the salient beliefs and affect in the structure of computer users' attitudes?

To what extent are attitude structures toward computers consistent across user groups?

To what extent are attitudes about technology consistent across situations?

To what extent are attitudes toward computers differentiated and integrated?

What variables influence the stability of attitudes toward computers?

When inconsistencies in the individual's belief structure arise, what coping mechanisms are employed to reduce the dissonance?

What roles do the characteristics of the technology, the environment in which it is used and social influence processes play in decisions regarding the purchase or use of computers?

What attitudinal characteristics lead to substitution behaviors of one technology for another?

MANAGER'S AGENDA

Similar to computers themselves, attitudes toward computers are complex. To understand human–computer interactions, attitudes toward technology must be examined in their entirety.

Individuals who hold negative attitudes toward computers are not likely to utilize the hardware and software efficiently. Thus, efforts designed to promote more positive beliefs about using technology can result in greater organizational efficiency and effectiveness.

ATTITUDES AND BEHAVIOR

Efforts to understand the relationships between individuals' attitudes and behaviors has been a primary focus of social psychological research since LaPiere's classic 1934 study. Fifty years of research has shown that the relationships between attitudes and behaviors are far from strong (Wicker, 1969; Schuman & Johnson, 1976; Fazio & Zanna, 1978; Hill, 1981; Michener et al., 1986). Nevertheless, knowledge of a person's attitudes is a necessary, although not sufficient, condition for predicting behavior. Numerous explanations have been offered to account for attitude–behavior inconsistencies; however, five lines of reasoning are pertinent here: attitude specificity, attitude structure, situation context factors, individual differences, and normative influences. The impact of these variables is discussed relative to two popular attitude–behavior models.

ATTITUDE–BEHAVIOR MODELS

Fishbein and Ajzen Model

Fishbein and Ajzen (1975) posit that actual behavior depends on one's intentions to perform an action and on one's attitude (*affect*, in their definition). Attitudes are derived from beliefs which are influenced by at least two antecedent variables: (a) social and personal norms, and (b) individual differences. Behavior and attitudes thus ultimately derive from beliefs.

The best predictor of behavior is the individual's intentions to perform that behavior (Figure 2.3). Intentions can be general (I will buy a personal computer) or specific (I will buy a Macintosh). If the decision involves a dichotomous choice (to buy or not to buy the Macintosh),

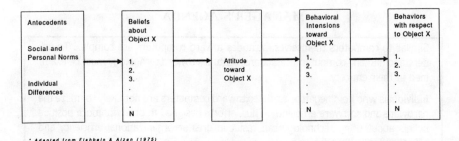

* Adapted from Fishbein & Ajzen (1975)

FIGURE 2.3
Schematic relationship between antecedents, beliefs, attitude, behavioral intentions, & behavior. Adapted from Fishbein & Ajzen, *Beliefs, Attitudes, Intention and Behavior*, © 1975 by Addison-Wesley, Reading, MA. Reprinted with permission.

knowledge of the intention is sufficient for predicting the behavior. When multiple alternatives are available, behavior is determined by the strongest intention. Thus, to understand a decision, it is necessary to evaluate the strength of each behavioral intention available to the person.

Prediction of behavior from knowledge of attitude is accurate only when the attitude influences the intention to perform that behavior (Fishbein & Ajzen, 1975). Attitudes predispose people to perform a *set* of behaviors, not necessarily any *single* behavior. An individual's attitude may be: "My company needs to computerize its operation." This general attitude influences the person's intentions, but does not suggest what specific computer should be purchased. Strong empirical relationships between attitudes, intentions, and behavior are only evident when (a) the variables are measured at the same level of specificity, and (b) the entire attitude structure is examined in context.

Attitude specificity.   Early attitude–behavior investigations tended to correlate general attitudes with specific behaviors and consistently found no significant relationship (Schuman & Johnson, 1976). More recent investigations note that the strength of the attitude–behavior relationship increases when specific attitudes are correlated with specific behaviors or when general attitudes are correlated with general behaviors (Heberlein & Black, 1976; Weigel & Newman, 1976). Ajzen and Fishbein (1977) reviewed 110 studies involving 143 attitude–behavior relations. Only 45 associations were judged to have measured the attitude and the behavior at the same level of specificity or generality. When there was a direct correspondence between the attitude and behavior measures, the correlations were consistently above .40. In studies where the degree of correspondence was questionable, the magnitude of the correlations were lower or nonsignificant. When there was no measurement correspondence, there was no relationship. Attempts to predict usage of a particular software package thus need to focus on individuals' attitudes toward specific applications and not how people feel about computers in general.

Although surveys of attitudes towards computers have been conducted (Ahl, 1976; Lee, 1970; Morrison, 1983; Zoltan & Chapanis, 1982), little is known about attitudes toward specific computer uses. Kerber's (1983) analysis of college students' attitudes toward 32 applications provides an exception. Factor analysis produced three clusters of uses: quantitative applications, decision-making applications, and record-keeping applications. Respondents held favorable attitudes toward quantitative and record-keeping applications but were apprehensive toward decision-making applications. Experience with computers and perceptions of the computer as efficient, humanizing and enjoyable were positively correlated with positive attitudes toward applications.

Attitude structure and situation context.   An individual's attitude is determined by an entire set of beliefs rather than any single belief (Figure 2.3). Changing any one belief about an object (e.g., person, thing, policy, or institution) may not change the attitude toward the object (Fishbein & Ajzen, 1975). To illustrate this concept, consider the following review of Honeywell's Scorpion workstation:

> We all know Honeywell. Respectable. Solid. Stodgy. Boring. Or least we thought until we saw their new Scorpion Unix workstation. Unconventional. Aggressive. Exciting. Sexy. The Scorpion is a workstation with all the right moves: networking, windows, software, mice, ergonomics, bit-mapped graphics. And it has a good price point—under $9,000. (Mackinlay, 1984, p. 80)

The author of this review is expressing two attitudes; one towards the corporation and one towards the Scorpion workstation. Each attitude is based on a number of beliefs. The general attitude about Honeywell is associated with the beliefs that the company is respectable, solid, stodgy, and boring. In essence, Honeywell is perceived to have some positive attributes, but not a company likely to be adventuresome when it comes to developing new computer products. The attitude toward the workstation shows a reversal in thinking. Evaluative beliefs such as unconventional, aggressive, exciting, and sexy are used to describe Scorpion. These affective statements stem from the beliefs that a quality workstation should have features like networking capabilities, windows, mice, etc. Eliminating any one of these features from the product would not have changed the reviewer's positive attitude toward Scorpion: "You can't have all of the above without trade-offs, but then the Scorpion has a lot of bang for the bucks" (Mackinlay, 1984, p. 80). At the same time, the author's overall evaluation of the company remains unchanged, suggesting that historically conservative corporations may find it difficult to change their public image despite efforts to incorporate new technology into the product line.

The preceding example illustrates the importance of situation context on the attitude–behavior relationship. The author of the review had personally experimented with the Scorpion machine before assessing its relative merits. Given that the individual's general attitude about Honeywell was less congruent, it is likely that the workstation would not have been rated as highly, without the direct hands-on experience. From a systems design perspective, this implies that determination of users' perceptions of alternative screen layouts needs to be measured relative to actual experience with the product. Evaluations derived from paper and pencil screen mock-ups are of less value in predicting the actual system's ease-of-use. Given the emergence of relatively inexpensive rapid prototyping programs, developers can more easily incorporate user perceptions early in the design of new products (Cerveny et al., 1987).

In summary, the Fishbein and Ajzen (1975) model indicates that attitude–behavior relationships are mediated by intentions to perform the action. Attitude specificity, attitude structure, and situation context influence the strength of the relationship. Attitudes are themselves determined by an entire set of beliefs, rather than any single belief. Before completing our presentation of the model's variables predicted to influence beliefs, an alternative attitude–behavior model is discussed and contrasted against the Fishbein and Ajzen conceptualization.

Bentler and Speckart Model

In the Fishbein and Ajzen (1975) model, behavioral intention is an immediate determinant of actual behavior. Attitude toward a particular object/situation as well as the antecedent variables have only an indirect influence on overt behaviors.[6] An alternative formulation of the Fishbein-Ajzen model has been proposed by Bentler and Speckart (1979, 1981). In their model, attitude directly affects behavior in addition to indirectly influencing behavior via intentions (Figure 2.4). Prior

---

[6] To support this approach, Ajzen and Fishbein (1977) cite a number of studies demonstrating that behavioral intentions are the single best predictor.

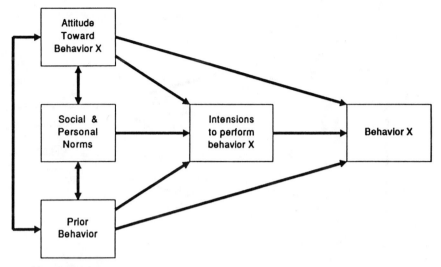

FIGURE 2.4.
The Bentler-Speckart attitude–behavior model.

behavior (e.g., previous computer experience) is also postulated to affect both behavioral intentions and actual behaviors, effects that were not hypothesized by the original Fishbein and Ajzen framework.

Bentler-Speckart's study examined three causal models. The first replicated the Fishbein-Ajzen model. The second added the direct path between attitude and behavior, while a final model included all of the variables and relationships shown in Figure 2.4. Results indicated that the direct paths from attitude to actual behavior, and from prior behavior to both intention and overt behavior, improved the predictive power of the model over that explained with the original Fishbein-Ajzen model. This suggests that behavioral intention does not fully mediate the attitude–behavior relationship.

Although the Bentler-Speckart model was well conceived, several considerations confound the clarity of their findings. The concept of attitude was measured using only the evaluative component (i.e., affect) and did not include beliefs. Behaviors were measured in terms of self-reported behavior rather than by observations of overt behavior. To alleviate these concerns, Fredricks and Dossett (1983) attempted to replicate the Bentler-Speckart study using an attitude measure that more closely approximated the original Fishbein-Ajzen concept and that incorporated observations of actual as opposed to self-reported behavior. Findings provided partial support for the Bentler-Speckart model. Prior behavior directly influenced behavioral intentions and subsequent behavior. Consistent with the original Fishbein-Ajzen

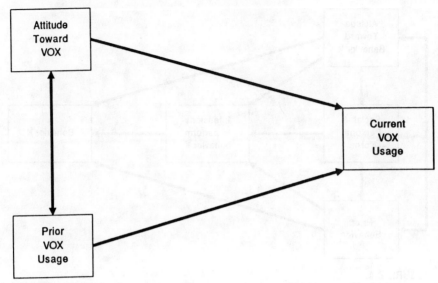

FIGURE 2.5
An attitude–behavior model of VOX usage.

model, however, the direct path between attitude and behavior was not found. Similar findings have been reported by others (Bagozzi, 1981; Burnkrant & Page, 1982; Warshaw, Calantone, & Joyce, 1986).

In summary, this section reviewed two currently popular models of the attitude–behavior relationship. Fishbein and Ajzen (1975) suggest that the influence of attitudes on behavior is mediated by behavioral intentions. Bentler and Speckart (1979, 1981) postulate a direct effect of attitudes on behavior in addition to the indirect impact through intentions. Both models suggest that antecedent variables play a significant role. Fishbein and Ajzen hypothesize that individual differences and normative influences are key antecedent indicators; Bentler and Speckart also include prior behavior. Partial support for both models was shown by others (Bagozzi, 1981; Burnkrant & Page, 1982; Fredricks & Dossett, 1983; Warshaw et al., 1986). To our knowledge, no computer related study has directly examined either the Fishbein-Ajzen model or the Bentler-Speckart model. One of our investigations (Grantham & Vaske, 1985), however, included three of the relevant variables. The model (Figure 2.5) attempted to predict the extent to which individuals used the company's voice store-and-forward system (VOX) from their attitude toward VOX and their prior behavior. Because the study did not include any information on the individuals' intentions to use VOX or their normative expectations about the system, it cannot be considered a complete test of either the Fishbein-Ajzen or the Bentler-Speckart models. The findings are presented here to illustrate the importance of attitudes in influencing human–computer interaction.

ATTITUDE–BEHAVIOR: AN EMPIRICAL EXAMPLE

Variables and hypotheses.   Data were collected during a market survey of 306 Honeywell employees who were subscribers to the voice mail system (Voice Output Exchange—VOX).[7] The dependent variable was the extent of current VOX usage. Similarly to Bentler and Speckart (1979, 1981), a self-reported measure of behavior was utilized. Respondents indicated how frequently they used VOX to plan, coordinate, assign responsibilities and report on the status of projects, and an index was constructed from the four questions. There were three independent variables. The first was an attitude index that evaluated the extent to which respondents believed VOX improved their communication capabilities. Of the two theoretical models, our attitude scale parallels the Bentler-Speckart conceptualization. It was hypothesized that individuals who held a more positive attitude toward VOX would use the product more frequently. Prior behavior was measured by two variables: the length of time respondents had been using VOX and their frequency of daily phone usage. It was predicted that higher current VOX usage rates would be associated with a longer history of use and a greater frequency of phone use.

Results.   Consistent with the hypothesized relationships, attitude toward VOX was positively correlated with behavior patterns (Table 2.1). Individuals who believed that the system enhanced their communications used the system more frequently. Similar findings resulted for the time individuals had spent on the system, with the more frequent users having more prior experience. The relative importance of these independent variables in explaining the variance in VOX usage was examined through a regression analysis. Attitude towards the system was two and a half times more important than prior behavior in accounting for the variance in behavior. Taken together, these predictors explained 30% of the variance in VOX usage.

---

[7] The 12-page questionnaire was distributed through company channels. After one follow-up reminder, 279 completed questionnaires were returned (response rate = 78%). Examination of the respondents' functional activities, span of control, position and length of time with the organization indicated that the sample was representative of the firm's white-collar work force. For a complete description of the study, see Grantham and Vaske (1985).

TABLE 2.1
The effect of attitude and prior behavior on VOX usage.

Independent Variables	Dependent Variable: VOX Usage	
	Zero-order Correlations	Standardized Regression Coefficients
Attitude Toward VOX	.54[*]	.50[*]
Prior Behavior		
Months using VOX	.27[*]	.19[*]
Amount of daily phone usage	.04[*]	n. s.
Explained Variance (R^2)		.30[*]

[*] $p < .001$

Implications.   These data suggest considerations for the design and implementation of computer mediated communication technologies. First, similarly to other studies (Culnan, 1984; Markus, 1987), our findings show that physical access to the technology is not, by itself, sufficient for promoting usage of the system. All of the study participants had a telephone and access to VOX, yet amount of daily phone usage was not correlated with the extent of VOX usage.

Second, the strongest predictor of VOX usage was the respondent's attitude toward the system. This suggests that individuals who have been predisposed to hold positive beliefs about technology will be more willing to experiment with new communication channels. When the voice store-and-forward system in this study was first introduced, relatively little time was devoted to developing a positive attitude about the system among the initial subscribers. As might be expected, some of these early participants terminated the service. More recent marketing efforts have shifted their focus and concentrated more heavily on informing new participants about the range of benefits associated with voice mail. The number of current subscribers is approximately 275% greater than the initial membership.

Third, the findings reveal considerations for the study of attitudes in human–computer interaction. Similarly to both the Fishbein-Ajzen and Bentler-Speckart models, our scale shows that beliefs about technology are linked together to form an overall attitude.[8] Whether or not an individual's actions are influenced by a given belief depends on the number of belief combinations that lead to the same conclusion. Managers may believe that voice mail reduces the amount of time required to communicate with others, yet fail to use the system because they believe none of their peers use it and feel that such technologies are too expensive to install. The important point is that before trying to predict how users might behave it is necessary to determine what people believe and how these beliefs are related. Examining beliefs isolated from the overall attitude structure may not provide sufficient information for predicting behavior.

Fourth, our findings demonstrate that the strength of the attitude–behavior relationship is increased when specific attitudes are correlated with specific behaviors. The correlations and standardized regression coefficients were based on beliefs and usage patterns associated with a single technology, and were larger than .50. Finally, attitude is only one of many factors determining behavior. Prior behavior, for example, was also shown to have a significant effect. Even with both of these variables, however, 70% of the variance in the behavioral scale was not explained. Future investigations need to consider a range of alternative predictors that might influence computer users behavior patterns.

BEHAVIOR–ATTITUDE MODELS

The social psychological literature indicates that attitudes are related to behavior, but the word *cause* is used sparingly. Nevertheless, there has been an implicit assumption that attitudes can sometimes cause behavioral intentions and then, at some later point, cause behavior. At the same time it can be argued that commitment to a course of action is likely to determine future attitudes (Salancik, 1977). The recent racial history in the United States indicates that prointegration attitudes followed forced prointegration behavior (Bem, 1970). Similarly, attitudes toward the purchase of lead-free gasoline became more positive once the nozzle on the regular pump would not fit in the restricted opening of lead-free-only cars (Heberlein & Black, 1981). Because gasoline in

---

[8] The attitude index was constructed from six Likert statements coded on four-point scales (i.e., strongly disagree [1] to strongly agree [4]). A reliability analysis of the belief statements indicated that the six variables resulted in the highest Cronbach alpha. Deleting any item from the scale would lower the remaining scale's reliability.

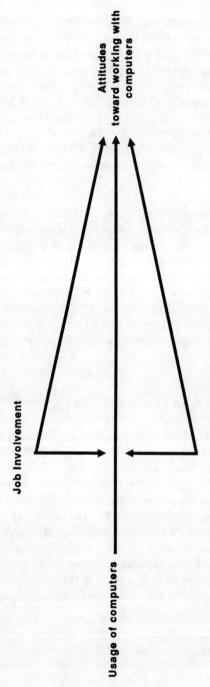

Source: Rafael (1986)

FIGURE 2.6

The hypothesized model of employee attitudes toward working with computers.

purchased on a routine basis, the activity served to increase the consistency between attitudes and behavior. Thus, it is likely that positive attitudes toward computers are likely to follow in situations where individuals use computers as part of their daily work.

Empirical support for the behavior–attitude relationship can be seen in a study by Rafaeli (1986). Rafaeli examined the impact of job involvement, organizational commitment, and current usage of computers on employees' attitudes toward using computers for administrative work. Job involvement and organizational commitment were also predicted to moderate the relationship between usage and attitudes toward computers (Figure 2.6). The results provided at least partial support for all five hypotheses.

Employees who used computers to support their work reported more positive attitudes than those who reported limited usage. For information systems managers this suggests that anxiety about computers can be reduced by having individuals use them in their jobs. Based on Rafaeli's data, however, it appears that actual usage is more likely to enhance positive attitudes than to change negative attitudes. Attempts to modify negative attitudes might more effectively be addressed through employee training, social support, and participation in the computerization process. Employees who were oriented toward their work and were committed to organizational excellence were less concerned about computers than their peers who reported low job involvement and commitment. Finally, job involvement and organizational commitment moderated the relationship between computer usage and attitudes toward working with computers. These findings suggest that the active promotion of an organization's goal to computerize its operations can increase employee's willingness to accept new technologies.

Rafaeli rightly points out that the direction of "causality cannot be inferred from the present cross-sectional data and can only be verified in longitudinal or experimental designs" (1986, p. 102). The relationship between attitudes and behavior is probably reciprocal, and it remains for further work to specify the conditions under which one of the causal orderings is likely to occur. We suspect, however, that the repetitious nature of computerized work serves to enhance attitude–behavior (or behavior–attitude) consistency, much as the consistency (Festinger, 1957; Heider, 1958; Kelly, 1955), attribution (Kelly, 1971), and self-perception theories (Bem, 1970) have implied. Employees may first use a word processor because their co-workers are using one. In reflecting on their usage, they begin to see that the software increases their control over their work (Buchanan & Boddy, 1982; Rafaeli & Sutton, 1985), develop a positive attitude toward word processing (Rafaeli, 1986), and in turn increase their motivation to work (Lawler & Hall,

1970). As their computer usage increases, the consistency between their beliefs, attitudes and behavior is also likely to increase.

This sequences of events, however, assumes a constraint free environment. When individuals freely choose to use a computer because they believe it will improve their job performance, and the machine lives up to their expectations, there should be considerable cognitive consistency. In situations where a manager dictates the usage of a particular software application, and the employees are resistant to computers in general or dislike the particular application chosen for their use, less consistency will be observed.

From the perspective of this chapter, Rafaeli's (1986) study not only supports the existence of a relationship between attitudes and behavior, but also highlights the importance of examining variables that mediate the relationship. Job involvement and commitment mediated the behavior and attitudes of the employees in his study. Both of these organizational variables are considered in greater detail in Chapter 3. The section to follow examines other social psychological variables that influence attitude–behavior relationships.

RESEARCHER'S AGENDA

Under what conditions do attitudes toward technology influence computer users' behavior?

Under what conditions does behavior influence attitudes toward the technology?

To what extent can anxiety about computer usage be reduced by having individuals use them in their work?

Which computer education/training programs are most effective in changing negative attitudes about technology?

To what extent are attitudes, behavioral intentions, and computer usage interrelated?

What variables influence attitude/behavior relationships relative to computer systems? For example:

Behavioral intentions
Prior experience
Personal and social norms
Individual differences
Situation context indicators
Job involvement
Organizational commitment

What attitudes influence specific uses of computer technology?

What sets of beliefs are associated with customers buying behavior in an advanced technology market?

MANAGER'S AGENDA

The belief systems individuals bring to the workplace influences their willingness to accept and use new technologies. Increasing the workers level of job involvement and commitment to organizational excellence promotes positive attitudes toward computer usage.

Negative attitudes toward computer usage can be changed through employee training, social support, and worker participation in the selection of computer equipment.

INDIVIDUAL DIFFERENCES

Although human–computer interaction research has traditionally not emphasized differences in individual users, there is an emerging interest in the topic. Panels on individual differences are now regularly included on the agenda of major computer conferences (e.g., SIGCHI), and researchers are beginning to explore the system design implications for users with differing backgrounds, capabilities, and characteristics (Potosnak, 1986). It has been recognized that individual difference indicators vary in the degree to which they are susceptible to change (van Muylwijk, van der Veer, & Waern, 1983). When user traits cannot or are difficult to modify, the computer system must be adapted to the individual.

In reviewing individual difference variables relative to the success of Management Information Systems, Zmud (1979) identifies three classes of indicators: personality, cognitive style, and demographic/situational variables. Everyday usage of the term personality equates the concept with a person's ability to interact with others. An individual may be said to have a shy personality or a popular personality. More formal conceptualizations presented by psychologists define *personality* as " the dynamic organization within the individual of those psycho-physical systems that determine his characteristic behavior and thought" (Allport, 1961, p. 28), or, more simply, as "a person's unique pattern of traits" (Guilford, 1959, p. 5). Traditionally, the psychological study of personality has been concerned with "providing a systematic account of the ways in which individuals differ from one another" (Wiggins, 1979, p. 395). Individual differences are central definitional components to this branch of psychology, but the term *personality* does not need to be limited to the study of differences between individuals in their consistent attributes. Personality psychology ultimately must encompass the study of how people's thoughts and actions interact with and shape the conditions of their lives (Mischel, 1980). This expanded view recognizes that human tendencies are a critical part of personality, but also asserts the need to study the cognitive and affective structures people use to adapt to events, people, and situations encountered in life (Gough, 1976). In examining personality relative to human computer interactions, researchers have considered a range of variables such as perceived locus of control, extraversion–introversion, fear of failure, need for achievement, anxiety, and defensiveness.

A second area of theoretical and empirical effort related to individual differences concerns the cognitive processes people employ when dealing with information. *Cognitive style* refers to an individual's consistent ways of approaching and processing information, especially through perception, memory, and thought. Researchers working in this area have looked for consistent cognitive and emotional styles that people might habitually use in coping with problems. For example, sex differences have been reported in a cognitive style described as analytic or field-independent as opposed to global or field-dependent (Witkin, Dijk, Faterson, Goodenough, & Kapp, 1962). Boys and men performed better on tasks where subjects were directed to find an embedded figure than girls and women. Similar findings were reported by Maccoby (1966). Drawing inferences from these results, however, must be done cautiously. Maccoby and Jacklin (1974) reviewed the literature on cognitive style tests and concluded that "boys are superior only on problems that require visual discrimination or manipulation of objects set in a larger context; this superior seems to be accounted for by spatial ability . . . and does not imply a general analytic superiority" (p. 110). Boys tend to excel in visual-spatial ability but not in more general analytic skills. Thus, although it is recognized that cognitive style is a multidimensional construct, the number of dimensions and the relationship between dimensions is not clear (Zmud, 1979). At least four cognitive style dimensions have been suggested to have importance to human–computer interactions: field-dependent / field-independent, systematic / heuristic, verbalizers / visualizers, and flexibility / rigidity (Benbasat & Taylor, 1978).

A final class of individual difference indicators are *demographic/situational* variables. Demographic variables include age, sex, and education. Situation variables may include a person's position in an organization or the context in which computers are used, but most existing research has focused on individuals' prior experiences with technology. In the following sections we record and organize a representative sampling of these individual difference variables. The objective is not to formulate a new theory of individual difference dimensions but to highlight critical classes of variables and their influence on attitude–behavior relationships.

PERSONALITY TRAITS

Social psychologists and personality researchers alike believe that, although there is great behavioral variation across people within a particular situation, there is also great consistency within a particular person across situations. To account for this assumed pattern of behavior in their own domains of inquiry, each group of psychologists turned to an individual difference construct. For social psychologists, the concept of attitude was invented to capture the notion of differences among and consistencies within people. For personality researchers, the *trait construct* was invented to perform essentially the same function.

Theorists disagree about the content and structure of the basic traits needed to describe personality, but their general ideas are similar. They all conceptualize traits as underlying properties, qualities, or processes that exist in persons. Traits are viewed as continuous dimensions on which individual differences may be arranged in accord with the amount of an attribute that a person has. Traits are used to account for consistencies in an individual's behavior and to explain why persons respond differently to similar situations. The trait approach has traditionally recognized that behavior varies with changes in social context, but has focused on individual differences in response to the same situation.

Recent trait theories have increasingly realized that an adequate approach to the study of traits must examine how qualities of a person and the situation influence each other. To investigate such interactions, researchers examine how the trait dimensions vary by the psychological situation of the moment. Weinberg (1971) discusses the importance of the trusting–suspicious trait dimension relative to which attribute is best for a programmer. If the task involves debugging a program, it is appropriate for the programmer to be suspicious of each line of code. Without such scrutiny, flaws in the program's design logic are easily overlooked. On the other hand, when the same programmer is placed in a team meeting, the person must to some extent trust his or her fellow colleagues' statements regarding their coding progress.

Trait research has focused on developing quantitative ways of describing important individual differences and their patterning. Participants in the study are typically asked to rate themselves on several bipolar scales (e.g., talkative–silent, adventuresome–cautious, calm–anxious) and may be questioned about their beliefs and attitudes. The results are examined statistically to identify the associations or correlations among the obtained indications of behavior. If multiple dimensions are included, further data reduction techniques (e.g., factor or cluster analysis) are used to clarify the statistical associations among the trait dimensions. The findings from trait research help to illuminate the organization and structure of personality and indicate what kinds of behavior are most likely to occur together.

Evidence of the importance of traits in everyday interactions continues to mount, but much remains unknown. Among the personality traits believed to impact human–computer interaction are locus of control, extraversion–introversion, fear of failure/need for achievement, anxiety, and defensiveness (Zmud, 1979; Shneiderman, 1987). Although this list is far from exhaustive, these dimensions have been subjected to empirical test by human–computer interaction researchers.

Perceived Locus of Control

People differ in the degree to which they believe that they have self-control and feel personally responsible for what happens to them. According to Rotter (1966) such perceptions involve a dimension of perceived *locus of control* (also called *internal–external control*). *Internal control* refers to "the perception of positive and/or negative events as being a consequence of one's own actions and thereby under personal control" (Lefcourt, 1966, p. 207). Conversely, *external control* refers to the "perception of positive and/or negative events as being unrelated to one's own behaviors" (Lefcourt, 1966, p. 207) and hence beyond personal control. Individual differences on this internal–external control dimension have been measured by a questionnaire that has yielded many correlates (Phares, 1978; Rotter, 1966). For example, more intelligent people tend to perceive more outcomes as under their own control, presumably because they can control their fate better than less competent individuals. In situations where the outcome involves luck or chance as opposed to those that are perceived to depend on personal skill, people attribute causality to internal sources more for successful outcomes than for failure outcomes. They tend to credit success to themselves but blame failure on external conditions (Fitch, 1970).

Perceived locus of control may be of special theoretical importance to the social psychology of human–computer interaction because it seems to influence how people react across situations. Efforts to apply the concept, however, have produced mixed results. Arndt et al. (1983) examined secretaries' perceptions of word processing as a function of locus of control. They hypothesized that externally controlled secretaries would view word processing less positively than would internally controlled people. Their findings supported the predicted relationship. Individuals with an internal locus of control were less anxious and more eager to use the software. Similarly, Coovert and Goldstein (1980) show that internals had more favorable attitudes toward computers than externals. Other researchers (e.g., Kerber, 1983), however, have not found a relationship between locus of control and attitudes. Differences in the populations studied (secretaries versus undergraduates) may partially account for the discrepancies, but this explanation is not totally satisfactory given that both Coovert and Goldstein and Kerber studied undergraduates.

Extraversion–Introversion

Extraversion–introversion is a dimension of personality along which individuals can be placed (Eysenck & Rachman, 1965). The typical extravert is sociable, has many friends, needs to have people to talk to, and does not like reading. Extraverts crave excitement, take chances, often stick their necks out, act on the spur of the moment, and are impulsive. The typical introvert is a quiet, retiring sort of person, introspective, fond of books rather than people, and reserved. Such individuals tend to plan ahead, mistrust the impulse of the moment, and like a well-ordered mode of life (Eysenck, 1977).

For human–computer interactions an important difference between extraverts and introverts is their willingness to explore. Extraverts are more willing to explore the capabilities of a computer system than introverts. This suggests that introverts need more careful documentation than extraverts. The more outgoing nature of extraverts may also imply a greater willingness to use computers as a communication medium. Systems designed to facilitate cooperative work may be well suited to the extravert's personality. Such a hypothesis must await empirical verification, however, for three reasons. First, extraverts enjoy tete-a-tete interactions, but whether they derive similar satisfaction from electronic communications where the participants are physically separated remains unknown. Second, although extraverts are more sociable than introverts, they also tend to react on impulse rather than plan ahead. Current computer supported cooperative work systems assume that users are willing to spend the time needed to plan out their activities and adhere to the schedule once developed. Third, electronic communication systems that focus on the task and ignore the social, affective dimension of the interaction may not be acceptable to the extravert personality. Some support for this latter speculation can be found in a case study reported by Hiltz (1984). Her data show that the more successful user groups of a computerized conferencing system had more members who were more emotionally (affectively) committed to their ideas.

Fear of Failure/Need for Achievement

In our achievement oriented society, pressure is exerted on people to compete and excel. Competition is actively encouraged, and children soon learn to make comparisons between their accomplishments and those of others. Some individuals underachieve in situations where their performance is compared to that of others (van Muylwijk et al., 1983). If the competitive component of their work is reduced or eliminated, they perform better. For these individuals, help facilities become a critical element in learning about technology. Algorithmic tutorial sessions are better than heuristic methods for this personality type (De Leeuw & Welmers, 1978). Other researchers have shown that modest levels of need for achievement facilitates performance, while higher levels leads to debilitating anxiety (Wynne & Dickson, 1976).

Anxiety

Just as some people have a fear of heights (acrophobia), open spaces (agoraphobia) or water (hydrophobia), others have a fear of computers (cyberphobia). *Cyberphobia* refers to an intense anxiety about computers which produces physical symptoms such as shaking hands, sweating palms, and conversational difficulties (Kennedy, 1975); high blood pressure, and feelings of inadequacy (Inman, 1983); and queasy stomachs and blank stares (Knight, 1979). A less intense form of this anxiety, *technostress*, can occur in situations where individuals are forced to learn and use new technologies (Brod, 1982). People who suffer from technostress may not exhibit the physical symptoms found in the true phobics, but they do avoid using computers and feel uncomfortable when required to use them. According to Brod, the variables that influence when people will experience technostress include age of the user, previous experiences with technology, perceived control in task selection, and organizational context.

The reasons for either cyberphobia or technostress are varied. Anxiety can arise when computers threaten established procedures for organizational interaction or when employees perceive a loss of personal responsibility associated with the introduction and use of the system. Anxiety levels also increase when people feel that the system is difficult to learn, that it is difficult to use, that the system documentation is poorly organized and inadequate, or that the computer does not perform as advertised. For some users the keyboard is intimidating, and others simply lack the typing skills necessary to effectively communicate. Among novice users, the fear of breaking the system, or the mystique that still surrounds computer technology, can be sufficient to produce a negative reaction. Finally, the computer is one of the few machines people assign anthropomorphic qualities (Curley, 1983). When a computer is perceived to have a brain capable of logical reasoning and analysis, the user may feel powerless against an intellectual superior.

Two related social psychological theories—social facilitation theory and attribution theory—may help to unravel the causes of this latter source of cyberphobia (Quintanar et al. 1982). According to *social facilitation theory* (Geen & Gange, 1977), if users assign anthropomorphic

qualities to computers, the machine becomes a source of personal evaluation. When the interface is easy to learn and use, the interaction is
"socially facilitated." When the converse is true (i.e., the computer is
difficult to learn and use), users' experience a sense of apprehension
and anxiety. A similar logic follows from the application of *attribution
theory* (Heider, 1944; Meyer, 1980). Heider proposed that persons are
more likely to be perceived as causal agents than nonpersons are. When
users' attribute human-like qualities to human–computer interactions,
the machine assumes more responsibility for events during an interactive sequence. The power and intelligence attributed to the computer
can invoke a sense of helplessness in the user.

Computer systems need not always lead to increases in stress and a
deterioration of the working environment. Such negative effects can be
overcome if consideration is given to the users' psychological and social needs in the planning and implementation process. Anxiety can be
reduced through training and education, user support, system design
and psychological-social support. *Training* may involve on-site instruction or sending users back to school. *User support* may range from
improved manuals and online tutorials to administrative personnel
assigned the responsibility of addressing user questions. The former
strategy may be more acceptable to introverts, while the latter fits the
extravert mentality. *System design* considerations include the myriad
of design choices presented here and elsewhere. *Psychological-social*
support includes assuring users that their jobs are secure, involving
users in the planning and introduction of the system, and responding to
users' questions in a timely manner.

Defensive Mechanisms

Humans can create great anxiety in themselves even when they are not
in any immediate external danger. These same individuals can also
cognitively eliminate such internally cued anxiety without altering
their external environment, simply by avoiding or changing their
thoughts or memories. *Defensive mechanisms* are attempts to cope cognitively with internal anxiety-arousing cues. Theorists assume that
these cognitive efforts are at least partly unconscious (i.e., they occur
without the individual's awareness) and have hypothesized many defense mechanisms: repression, denial, sublimation, and reaction formation. Each of these terms refers to a different way of reducing or eliminating anxiety.

The concept of *repression* has been the focus of most research, probably because of the theoretical importance of the concept to Freudian
psychology. According to psychoanalytic theory, repression is an un

conscious defense mechanism through which unacceptable (ego-threatening) material is kept from awareness. Examples include trying not to think about the unknown implications computerization will bring or avoiding tasks that require the use of the computer. The existence of such cognitive avoidance tactics is widely recognized, but the mechanisms underlying the concept are controversial. At issue is whether cognitive avoidance is the unconscious repression of per-ceived threats, or whether the mind consciously inhibits events by suppression. The theoretical distinction is important for human–computer interaction, because the latter (suppression) can be dealt with through improved training and support, while the former (repression) is less susceptible to manipulation. Empirical studies (e.g., Zeller, 1950) have been interpreted as supporting the repression concept, but alternative interpretations are possible (e.g., poorer learning under conditions of anxiety or response interference due to stress).

COGNITIVE STYLE

Cognitive style refers to characteristic modes of functioning in individuals' perceptions and problem solving strategies (Zmud, 1979; van Muylwijk et al., 1983). Ackermann (1983) suggests that difficulties with human–computer interaction in problem solving are caused by the discrepancy between (a) individual mental representations and cognitive styles and (b) the given operations of the scope of action prescribed by the software. Although such behaviors depend on task and situation constraints, individuals display persistent cognitive behaviors, and consistent individual differences have been observed. The range of cognitive style variables examined by psychologists is broad. Our review concentrates on those dimensions that have received the most attention by human–computer interaction researchers and those that seem to offer fruitful avenues for further exploration.

Field-dependent/Field-independent

This construct refers to an individual's ability to distinguish contextual clues or the varying ability to differentiate foreground characteristics from background information. Field-dependent individuals are more influenced by context than field-independent. Although empirical support for this difference is limited, Witkin and associates (Witkin et al., 1962) suggest that the dimension is relevant to both cognitive and social impacts. One area of potentially useful research concerns the use of tiled versus overlapping windows. In a tiled window system, any open window is always visible. The system manages the windows' sizes and locations such that the windows do not overlap. In an overlapping window system, the user manages the location and size of open windows in any way desired. Windows may appear next to each other or on top of each other. Although it is widely believed that overlapping windows are preferable, there is little research that supports this contention. Moreover, one study shows that there are situations where overlapping windows are inferior to tiled (Bly & Rosenberg, 1986). This investigation did not address the issue of individual differences, but performance and preference variations along the field-(in)dependent dimension seem likely. With multiple overlapping windows visible on the screen, the questions become what is foreground versus background, and what difficulties do field-(in)dependent individuals encounter when trying to differentiate foreground from background?

Systematic/Heuristic

People approach problem solving tasks from different angles. Systematic individuals use abstract logical models and processes, while heuristic persons use past experience and intuition (Bariff & Lusk, 1977). When a task is highly structured, a systematic approach is most suitable. When a task is unstructured, experience with related tasks is most helpful. The structured nature of programming readily lends itself to systematic methods, while learning some new applications may be facilitated by knowledge of other software. In situations where the syntactic and semantic structures of a company's word processor are consistent with those of their spreadsheet and graphics software, knowledge of one application reduces the time required to learn a second application. Such transfer effects, however, must be interpreted cautiously in light of recent empirical evidence. Karat, Boyes, Weisgerber, and Schafer (1986) examined the performance of naive subjects as they learned to use a word processing system, as well as the performance of individuals with word processing skills as they learned to use a new system. Results indicated that while general word processing concepts were transferred and contributed to the learning of the two systems, differences in syntax had a negative impact on learning and performance. Other researchers show that performance is reduced when users make analogies between typewriters and word processors (Douglas & Moran, 1983; Allwood & Eliasson, 1987).

Verbalizers/Visualizers

This dimension suggests that people cope with problem solving tasks better when the information is presented in visual images as opposed to verbal structures. The commercial success of programs that support rather simple visual techniques (e.g., spreadsheet applications) points to the utility of building more visually based software. In many cases, however, it is not sufficient to make the invisible visible (Boecker & Nieper, 1985). What is needed are procedures such as intelligent summarizers or filtering techniques that help the user make relevant information and relations visible (Bocker, Fischer, & Nieper, 1986). Second, existing techniques typically only allow the user to generate visual representations of programs. Methods that allow the user to visualize the problem from different perspectives (e.g., programming by example—Gould & Finzer, 1984) may facilitate a user's insight into special cases. Finally, tools are needed to determine what constitutes a "good" visual representation. At present, the empirical relationship between these "make it visual" and computer users' behavior and attitudes remains untested.

Flexible versus Rigidity

Human–computer interaction research on this personality dimension is almost nonexistent (van Muylwijk et al., 1983). It has been recognized, however, that a certain amount of flexibility is essential for the career of any professional programmer (Weinberg, 1971). The nature of software development is such that personnel are frequently switched from project to project, depending on the organization's needs. Those who cannot adjust to new and unrelated programming assignments are likely to find corporate life unappealing. Intuitively this same logic applies to end-users. When changes in software configurations occur frequently, individuals must continually devote some attention to learning the new system. From the perspective of the system (as opposed to a personality characteristic of users), the same scenario applies. The computer must be sufficiently flexible to adapt to changes in the environment, job tasks, and the needs of the user. Inflexible systems occur when system designers emphasize economic and technical aspects rather than user needs. If the computer requires rigid formats and routines, user resentment arises when considerable effort must be expended to add new functions, change screen formats, or alter transaction methods.

DEMOGRAPHIC/SITUATIONAL VARIABLES

The mosaic of findings examining the influence of cognitive styles and related personality traits on human–computer interaction is sketchy at best. Noncognitive variables such as demographic and situation influences (e.g., prior experience) represent another class of moderators affecting attitude–behavior relationships and help to broaden our understanding of individual differences. Prior experience has by far received the most attention, but a few studies have examined the impact of demographic indicators.

Sex-typing and Personality Development

Ideas about people's traits arise from an interaction between the beliefs of the observer and the characteristics of the observed (Cantor & Mischel, 1979). An individual's gender is an immediate and powerful determinant of how people view others and influences the views the individual develops about himself or herself. Sex-typing is the development of patterns of behavior considered appropriate for one sex but not the other (Mischel, 1970). The development of sex roles and sex typing involves biological determinants as well as cognitive processes. Psychological sex differences and sex typing processes through which they develop are critical aspects of personality. Research has consistently found aggressive behavior is one of the main dimensions of sex differences (Sears, 1963, 1965). Males show more physical aggression than females as early as age 3.

In comparing human–computer interaction with human–human research, females have been shown to play against the computer as though they were playing against a male, and males played even more competitively against the computer than in the human male-male condition (Mack, Auburn, & Knight, 1971; Mack & Knight, 1974). In another study, Mack, Williams, and Kremer (1979) observed that virtually all males (98%) and a high percentage of females (85%) attributed male characteristics to the computer.

Age

A study of professional and executive workers' attitudes toward computers suggests that older "knowledge workers" tend to be less receptive to computers than younger managers (Booz, Allen, & Hamilton, 1981). In addition, managers who had spent more years with a firm were more resistant to the introduction of computers than individuals the same age who had just changed jobs. Presumably, those in the former category had developed a preferred mode of operation and perceived computerization as a threat to the established procedures. The mere fact that the executives in the latter category had changed jobs indicates a willingness to experiment with new ideas and methods. Computers simply represented another approach that should be tried and evaluated. Increasing age then is not always associated with negative attitudes toward computers.

Other studies show that older individuals are capable and enthusiastic about using computers. Kearsley and Furlong (1984) conducted computer programming workshops with senior citizens and found them to possess the ability and desire to learn to program. Some elders enjoy using computers to educate themselves, to make writing tasks easier, and to help manage their checkbooks (Krauss & Hoyer, 1984). In a recent experiment comparing older individuals (average age = 70.5) with younger people (average age = 24) in their use of a keyboard editor, the elders were more enthusiastic about using the system than the younger people (Ogozalek & van Praag, 1986). The older users wrote and talked about computers as a hobby, whereas the younger users associated computers with work-related tasks. In this study, no major differences in performance between the two groups were observed in carrying out a composition task.

There are, however, some social and physical differences between older and younger computer users. Younger people are more likely to assume that computers are a natural and integral aspect of living (Krauss & Hoyer, 1984). For them, everything from getting report cards to getting money out of the bank is done by computer. Elderly people are more likely to see computers as a new influence on their lifes—not necessarily a negative influence, but a different influence nonetheless. Physical differences due to the natural aging process are also apparent between the generations. Some older individuals have slower reaction times, decreased sensory acuity, and may be limited by degenerative diseases such as arthritis or rheumatism (Kornbluh, 1984). Hicks (1976) notes that typing difficulties are one of the major problems facing elderly computer users. A solution to this problem is to provide those users who have some physical limitation or who simply lack typing skills, an alternative method of interacting with system. Ogozalek and van Praag (1986) examined this relationship between age and text entry method (voice input versus typing at a keyboard) and found that, although voice input did not improve performance on a composition task, it was the preferred method of data entry for young and old alike. Similar attitudinal results are likely to occur for direct manipulation or pointing device systems (Shneiderman, 1983; Foley, Wallace, & Chan, 1984).

Education

It has been suggested that any person can be trained to be a competent programmer (Weinberg, 1971). Although there is some truth to this

statement, some scholars believe that our educational system is providing the wrong kind of training. Children are becoming increasingly
familiar with computers, but their primary interactions involve running existing software applications such as computer assisted instruction, word processing, or computer games. It is not clear that children
are becoming any more knowledgeable about the principles of computer science. This difference between end-user versus programmer skills
has been shown to influence children's behavior and attitudes toward
computers, and may affect noncomputer related activities such as peer
relationships (Ringle, 1982). Others (e.g., Papert, 1980, p. 5) have gone
so far as to suggest that nonprogramming interactions are potentially
harmful in that the child is programmed by the computer rather than
vice versa.

Not everyone, however, has the desire or needs to be a programmer.
The Macintosh was originally advertised as "the computer for the rest
of us." What the Macintosh offered was a new way of thinking about
computers. Up until the Mac, computers had been developed for institutions, not the individual. The Macintosh was promoted as a personal appliance that increased personal productivity and provided the
opportunity for personal creative expression. But to sell their product,
Apple had to "alter the culture, reshape the public consciousness" and
"lay claim to share of mind" (Sculley, 1987, p. 217). This overt attempt
to change public attitudes, coupled with the notion that Mac users
could accomplish in minutes what used to take hours to master (behavioral change), increased the desire of many individuals to learn about
and use computers. A lesson to be learned from the Macintosh, then, is
that computer education does not have to be painful. The full societal
impact of this educational and cultural revolution, however, remains to
be seen.

Prior Experience   I hate Macs!

Individuals vary in their previous experiences with computers. Experts
may have vast amounts of experience with several systems, programming languages, and software applications. The experience of other
users may be limited to a single operating system and word processor,
while a third group may have no exposure whatsoever to computers.
These differences in prior experience influence individuals' attitudes
toward human–computer interactions. Experts might believe that typing commands at the prompt level is the most appropriate method of
interaction, while those with less experience may feel more comfortable selecting items from a menu (Gilfoil, 1981). Even experts, however, sometimes prefer menus on software packages they use infrequently, and novices do not stay novices forever but rather continue to

learn and change their attitudes about preferred interaction styles. Recognizing this diversity, some software packages provide users with a choice of interaction methods. Some applications provide users with the option of picking an item from a menu or keying the command directly. This design logic is based on the assumption that it is impossible to satisfy all users with a single interface. Attempting to do so would only satisfy the "average or typical" user (Rich, 1983).

Examination of a person's prior computer experiences is useful for at least two reasons. First, prior experiences represent a frame of reference through which people evaluate particular situations. Second, varying amounts and types of participation suggest differing motives for using a computer. Understanding a person's history of computer usage may provide a link between internal beliefs (e.g., expectations and preferences) and computing behavior. Prior experience, then, can be thought of as an indicator of the cognitive processes that influence behavior and perception. Persons with differing amounts of experience are drawing on different amounts and types of information concerning participation.

Usage Classification Schemes

To compensate for the diversity that is masked by average user profiles, researchers have also developed typologies to characterize users into more homogeneous groups. Despite attempts to classify computer users, no generally agreed upon methodology has emerged in the literature (Ramsey & Atwood 1979; Zmud, 1979; Potosnak, 1986; Shneiderman, 1987). Chapanis, Anderson, and Licklider (1983) discuss several approaches to classifying computer users. One method categorizes individuals on the *amount* of prior computer experience. Typologies based on this strategy vary widely in subgroup definitions and have an extensive range of categories; for example: casual users (Cuff, 1980), experienced users (Shackel, 1981), first-time users (Al-Awar, Chapanis, & Ford, 1981), inexperienced users (Dzida, Herda, & Itzfeldt, 1978), naive users (Thompson, 1969), and occasional users (Hammond, Long, Clark, Barnard, & Morton, 1980). A second approach to classifying users has focused on the *type* of usage. Categories resulting from this approach include: analysts (Smith, 1981), clerical workers (Stewert, 1974), technical users (Ramsey & Atwood, 1979), and programmers and nonprogrammers (Martin, 1973). Finally, other researchers have considered both amount and type of computer usage when classifying individuals. Vaske et al. (1985) examined the belief structures of four distinct groups of individuals: nonusers, users with no programming backgrounds, users who were formerly programmers, and currently active programmers. The findings from this investigation and other similar studies (Zoltan, 1981) suggest that *diversity* of use is an important consideration when classifying computer users.

These classification strategies revolve around criteria the researcher judges to have a priori relevance. Other investigators demonstrate that classifications based on user perceptions of themselves are better predictors of behavior than those based on the experimenters decisions (Iso-Ahola, 1980; Vaske, Donnelly, & Tweed, 1983). Categorizing individuals via user-defined measures has received little attention in the human–computer literature.

RESEARCHER'S AGENDA

What computer tasks are most susceptible to individual differences?

To what extent are personality traits situation specific?

In what situations does perceived locus of control influence attitudes toward and usage of computers?

Are systems designed to facilitate cooperative work activities better suited for individuals with particular personality traits (e.g., extraversion versus introversion)?

Under what conditions are algorithmic tutorial sessions better than heuristic methods?

Do computer systems that project human-like characteristics increase or reduce technostress?

Does the cognitive avoidance associated with computer usage represent an unconscious repression or a conscious suppress of fear?

To what extent are cognitive-style variables related to one's ability to learn and use alternative interface designs (e.g., tiled versus overlapping windows)?

In what ways does a person's knowledge of software enhance and/or inhibit the learning of a new application?

When does a visual representation of a task facilitate problem solving?

To what extent are demographic indicators related to attitudes about and usage of computers?

Among the alternative methods of interacting with a computer (keyboard, voice, point device, direct manipulation), which are best suited for overcoming the physical limitations of the user?

MANAGER'S AGENDA

Anxiety brought on by the use of computers can be reduced through training and education, user support, system design, and psychological-social support.

Training may involve on-site instruction or sending users back to school.

User support may range from improved manuals and online tutorials to administrative personnel assigned the responsibility of addressing user questions.

System design considerations include the myriad of design choices presented here and elsewhere.

Psychological-social support includes assuring users that their jobs are secure, involving users in the planning and introduction of the system, and responding to users' questions in a timely manner.

The average computer user does not exist. Individual differences in computer users' attitudes and behavior are important and should be examined empirically.

NORMATIVE INFLUENCES

Computer manufacturing organizations explicitly recognize the importance of standards (norms) for developing and maintaining computer products. There are ANSI (American National Standards Institute) standards, ISO (International Standards Organization) standards, etc. Standards come into existence in two ways. First, a single dominant manufacturer can define a standard for its own products, and the rest of the industry may follow. The second and more common method of creating a standard is through a committee which serves as a forum for examination of needs, discussion between interested parties, and compromise. The notion of a group standard or a social norm is also implicit in human–computer interaction research (Hannemyr & Innocent, 1985). Shneiderman's (1984) review of studies examining response time and display rate in human performance with computers suggests that people employ different standards when evaluating the acceptability of system responses.

At least three issues influence user standards for system response times (Shneiderman, 1984). First, standards are shaped by the individuals' prior experiences. People who perform repetitive tasks on a computer system quickly learn how long it takes the system to react to specific commands. When the computer responds more quickly than usual, user satisfaction increases, provided the response is not too quick. In this latter situation, the individual is left wondering whether the system actually carried out the desired command. Second, people develop tolerances for delays. Novices who lack prior experience with a given application may be willing to wait a considerable period of time before becoming annoyed. Experts, on the other hand, who are cognizant of how long it should take to execute a particular command, may be less tolerant of long delays.[9] Third, people adapt to changes in response times. With a multiuser system, individuals who realize that the system responds more slowly at certain times of the day may adjust their work schedule to avoid the system during these periods. They may not prefer this situation, but still adjust their behavior because they know what to expect. These explanations for variations in users' expectations are consistent with the idea that there is some kind of normative standard that is used to evaluate a particular system response time as "too fast, just right, or too slow."

Although normative explanations of behavior have been posited by many social psychologists (Homans, 1950; Blake & Davis, 1964; Cancian, 1975; Schwartz, 1977), there has not always been perfect agreement about the components to be included in the concept. Many definitions are broad enough to include behavioral expectations derived from habit or convention (Black & Heberlein, 1979). Scott (1971) suggests that norms are socially determined behavior. The problem with this approach is that, "if norms are taken to be regularities of behavior, they have no analytical significance at all; they are merely another name for behavior itself, and cannot contribute to an understanding of behavior" (Blake & Davis, 1964, p. 464). To avoid this tautology, Blake and Davis use the term to "designate any standard or rule that states what human beings should or should not think, say or do under given circumstances" (p. 456). This is similar to Homans' (1950, p. 124) definition, "norms are not behavior itself, but rather what people think behavior ought to be." Our use of the concept parallels the definition offered by Blake and Davis (1964).

Despite the significance that has been attached to normative influences on behavior, few theorists or researchers have suggested systematic methods for differentiating and measuring the properties of norms. This section applies an analytical approach for identifying and examining the structure of norms called the *return potential model* (Jackson, 1965). In doing so we hope to demonstrate the role norms play in users' evaluations of computer products. The distinction between social and personal norms is discussed first.

---

[9] Other variables in addition to the novice–expert continuum, such as differences in the task to be completed or personality variations, may also influence the tolerance limits of specific users. The important point here, however, is that people's tolerance for varying response times is variable.

Social Norms

The central theme in most discussions is that norms are standards that individuals use for evaluating situations, people or computer products as good or bad, better or worse. Standards shared by the members of a social group are labeled *social norms* (Black & Heberlein, 1979). For example, many people believe that the programming language "C" should be used when developing new applications. This is a prescription of what people think behavior ought to be (a social norm), not actual behavior.

Individuals belong to many social groups which influence their evaluations of varying situations. Some groups have a definite membership and interact on a daily basis (e.g., a person's work group). Other groups consist of members with whom the individual may have limited direct contact (e.g., a professional society like ACM or IEEE). These latter groups might be termed a *collective* of individuals, who by virtue of their affiliation in the same organization share a sense of solidarity and common values (Merton, 1968).

Many activities involving humans and computers fit into this latter social group. Software developers may share a similar set of social norms regarding acceptable approaches to screen design, because they view other developers as their reference group. Similarly, new secretaries in a typing pool soon learn the social norms regarding what format is to be used when preparing memos and how much work is expected of them. Failure to adhere to such norms leads to sanctions by their peers or management. Individuals who produce too much are viewed as "rate breakers" among the other secretaries. Not typing enough material leads others to believe the individual does not carry his or her own share of the load.

When people are highly attracted to a group, they are more likely to conform to the group's norms, because they wish to be personally accepted by the other members or because achieving a desired goal dictates adherence to the norm (Jackson & Saltzstein, 1958; Michener et al., 1986). The success of a software development team depends on the group members conforming to the norms regarding acceptable design strategies.

Personal Norms

While individuals often share the values and norms with a large collective of people, not all social norms become internalized by every member of the group. The individual is an active participant in creating his or her own personal norms (Kluckholn, 1951). *Personal norms* refer to the individuals' own expectations, learned from shared expectations and modified through interaction. They represent ideals against which events are evaluated (Schwartz, 1977).

This definition implies that there is not a perfect symmetry between the personal norms held by a given individual and the social norms posited by the members of a collective. Fishbein (1967) points out that, while the individual's personal norm is usually close to the social norm, it may in some cases be different. Programmers may believe that the company expects them to write a certain number of lines of code each month. Motivated by a desire to excel in the corporation's management structure, some programmers may set higher personal norms for their production of lines of code. Such differences in personal standards may exist among individuals working on the same task as well as among people engaged in different tasks. Identification of these differences requires an analytical tool to show the relationship between personal and social norms.

The Return Potential Model

Jackson (1965) proposed a model which describes the structural characteristics of norms by means of a graphic device called a *return potential curve*. Because this terminology is rather unwieldy, we will simply refer to *norm curves* when applying Jackson's work to human–computer interaction. To illustrate how norms can be described with Jackson's model, three norm curves are presented (Figure 2.7). The horizontal axis is called the behavioral dimension. In this example, the behavior is system response times, but, obviously, in other cases it may be acts such as error rates, productivity estimates, or software usage rates. The vertical axis is an evaluation of the behavior as favorable or unfavorable. Evaluations of behavior can range from strong approval to strong disapproval, through some point of indifference. A personal norm can be described by a line connecting the individual's ratings at each point along the horizontal axis, while the social norm can be described by a line connecting the mean ratings for all members of a group.

For sending short electronic messages, Figure 2.7 shows that the tolerable system response time is from 0 to 3 seconds. For longer E-mail documents, response rates under 3 seconds can be evaluated as negatively as longer delays. With a small response time, the individual may think the mail item was not processed, while longer delays prohibit moving on to other tasks. For the person sending mail through the U.S. Postal Service, response time is not an issue until days have passed. Although theoretical, the plots in Figure 2.7 demonstrate that the distinction between user evaluations and system response times is essentially a normative concept that defines acceptable rates of interaction in a particular situation.

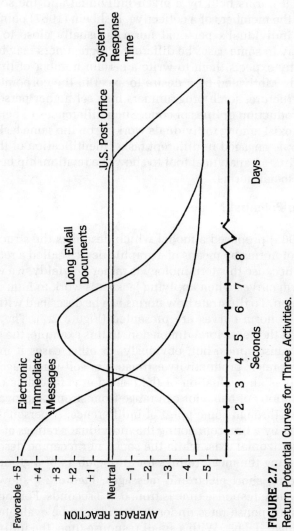

FIGURE 2.7.
Return Potential Curves for Three Activities.

Normative definitions apply to all human–computer interactions, although the amount of shared agreement may vary. Shneiderman's (1984) review article of system response times points out differences in terms of users' prior experiences, tolerances for delays, and the time of day when the interaction occurs. These variables influence the user's evaluations of the situation.

The model described by Jackson suggests that an analysis of the shape of the curve reveals a number of structural characteristics of norms—the range of tolerable actions, the intensity of the norm, and the crystallization of the norm.

Range of tolerable actions.   In one sense, the entire curve defines the norm, since it describes how actions are evaluated over the entire range. A range of tolerable actions is that portion of the behavioral dimension which members of a group or an individual approve and evaluate positively (Michener et al., 1986). In Figure 2.7, the range of acceptable response rates for short messages is 0 to 3 seconds; for longer E-mail documents the range is 3 to 7 seconds, and for U.S. mail the range is measured in days. Behaviors outside these ranges are not approved or tolerated.

In each situation, personal and social norms define the boundaries of acceptable response times for that task. This range is dictated by the consequences delays have on the individual's or group's ability to achieve desired goals. The greater the consequences the behavior has for the individual/group, the narrower the range of tolerable behavior (Sherif & Sherif, 1956). For some activities (e.g., moving a cursor), the range of acceptable response rates is extremely small. For other activities (e.g., compiling a program), the tolerable response period is much wider. Response times that exceed users' normative expectations in either situation are likely to result in negative evaluations.

Norm intensity.   "The intensity of a norm is indicated by the height of the return potential curve, both above and below the point of indifference" (Jackson, 1965, p. 305). Defined in this manner, *intensity* is the distance from the neutral line at each point on the norm curve, independent of the direction of the evaluation (i.e., favorable or unfavorable). Since the entire curve represents the norm, an individual's intensity index can be operationalized as the sum of the absolute values at each system response time. The larger the value, the stronger the group's feelings about system response.

When the range of tolerable response times for a task is narrow, the intensity of the norm may be increased. This seems particularly likely when violation of the norm is linked symbolically with violations of other norms (Black & Heberlein, 1979). An individual's negative evaluation of an 8-second response time may be a reaction, not to the response time per se, but rather a general dislike of electronic mail. Secretaries who have always typed their managers' memos may view electronic communications as detracting from their usefulness, because the executives now handle their own correspondence (Kiesler et al., 1984).

Norm crystallization. *Crystallization* is the amount of shared agreement about the norm. A measure of crystallization can be derived by computing the standard deviation for each point on the behavioral dimension, and then calculating $100 - D^2$ (Cronbach & Gleser, 1953). A small standard deviation implies that the norm is crystallized. When the dispersion is great, the collective's members have not crystallized a norm for that behavior. If the curve describing the norm is flat (indicating low intensity), it might be argued that there is no norm for that activity (e.g., sending mail through the U.S. Postal Service). Similarly, novice electronic mail users lack the experience necessary for judging the acceptability of different response times. Norm crystallization increases with experience.

These examples illustrate that changing the definitional characteristics of the situation (i.e, sending a short electronic message, sending longer E-mail documents, or using the U.S. Postal Service) alters users' expectations of acceptable system response times. Conceptually, Jackson's return potential model offers the potential for quantitatively identifying and measuring three structural properties of normative expectations—range of tolerable behavior, norm intensity, and norm crystallization.

RESEARCHER'S AGENDA

What standards (norms) do individuals use when evaluating computer technology?

How much agreement is there between an individual's personal norms regarding computer usage and a group's social norm?

Which social groups influence an individual's normative evaluations?

Under what circumstances do computer related norms vary?

Does a current product offering conform with the users' ease of learning and ease of use norms?

To what extent do the norms held by expert users differ from those of novices?

How much variation in norms exists across organizational boundaries?

What is the range of acceptable system response time norms for different hardware and software products?

How intensely are these system performance norms held?

To what extent do users agree on acceptable system response time norms?

MANAGER'S AGENDA

Similar to the existing ANSI and ISO standards for developing and maintaining computer technology, users have norms of acceptable computer behavior.

People are willing and able to express their norms regarding specific technologies.

Understanding user norms facilitates the design and implementation of computer technology.

GROUP PRODUCTIVITY AND COOPERATIVE WORK

The use of computers to enhance work group productivity has increased at a dramatic rate since the introduction of data processing systems in the work place. The latest of these efforts has been labeled *Computer Supported Cooperative Work* (CSCW), which aims to augment work groups through communications enhancement.[10] The focus on group process rather than individual tasks distinguishes CSCW from the more traditional office automation efforts. However, because CSCW has become a buzz concept in the computer industry, it is difficult to define precisely (Johansen, 1987; Karon, 1988). Applications ranging from electronic mail packages to multiuser database programs and calendaring facilities now claim to support group work activities. Despite this confusion, the basic idea of developing software to facilitate intra- and intergroup communications is a logic extension of current product offerings. Many professionals work in groups, and their productivity depends on their ability to work together and boost each other's skill and knowledge. In this section we examine the concept of CSCW from a social psychological perspective. We begin by defining the idea of group productivity and then examine some of the factors that influence the success or failure of group productivity. The section closes with a discussion of recent efforts in the field of CSCW and an empirical example illustrating the use of a CSCW software program in an office environment. Because the concept of CSCW is still evolving, this section raises more questions than it answers.

Defining Group Productivity

Group productivity refers to the output or end state resulting from group activity. A group's productivity is judged relative to what is

---

[10] The first technical conference on the topic was held in late 1986 in Austin, Texas (Grief, 1987).

produced rather than group activities themselves. The unit of measurement depends on the goals of the group. A software development group might be evaluated on the speed of producing applications, the number of problems or bugs detected in the released product, or the software's performance. Human Factors groups may base productivity on the percentage of software modifications successfully negotiated with management or development groups, the clarity of the documents they produce, or the speed of responding to developers' questions.

Differences in group productivity can be noted even when the members are working on similar tasks and have comparable talent. Some development groups produce more lines of code than others and commit fewer errors, while some problem-solving groups achieve better solutions. This observation suggests a number of questions about group productivity:

1. In what ways is productivity governed by the task(s) confronting a group?
2. To what extent is productivity affected by group size? Is there some optimal size for efficient and effective group interaction?
3. Does a group's cohesiveness affect the quality of its productivity? Under what conditions do pressures for conformity enhance and/or reduce productivity?
4. In what ways does a group's communication structure influence its members style of interaction? Can the communication structure foster a high level of performance in a group?

FACTORS AFFECTING GROUP PRODUCTIVITY

Group Tasks

Understanding group productivity requires an analysis of the task to be completed. The nature of the task affects performance because it interacts with other group attributes such as group size or method of communication. To understand how computer mediated communication channels affect group performance, it is necessary to first evaluate what the group is trying to accomplish.

Tasks can be classified according to the difficulty of completion, the procedures employed to accomplish them, and the criteria used to determine when they are complete. Researchers note that divisibility is another defining characteristic of a task (Steiner, 1972, 1974; Shiflett, 1979). With some tasks, all group members perform identical activities. Secretaries in a typing pool at a state's motor vehicle department, for example, might all process new vehicle registration requests, modify the existing database of registered vehicles to reflect address changes, and issue forms for renewals. Such tasks are unitary, because the secretaries have similar typing skills and perform all activities.

When members perform different, but complementary activities, the task is called *divisible*. A divisible task can be divided into smaller subtasks and involves a division of labor among the members. Software development activities are often divisible tasks. Some members of the organization specify the interface design, others write the application code, and still others test the performance of the resulting product. If the application is part of an integrated software offering, individual developers typically depend on code produced by others. The person charged with developing the interface to a graphics application may use code needed to display help messages that was built by other software developers.

Group productivity for a unitary task requires three conditions for successful performance. First, all group members must possess the skills needed to do the task. If some of the secretaries in a typing pool are only marginal typists, productivity will be below acceptable standards. Second, the group members must be sufficiently motivated to perform the activity. Extrinsic rewards such as pay can enhance motivation, but, unless the members feel their contribution is important and valued (intrinsic motivations), productivity suffers. When group morale is low, productivity declines. Third, the group must understand what is expected of them and have feedback regarding their performance. The secretaries in the motor pool example may be happy with processing 200 vehicle registration requests per day until they are told that other typing pools handle 400 requests each day. It is management's responsibility to establish and convey to the group reasonable expectations.

Successful performance is more difficult to achieve for divisible tasks than unitary tasks. In addition to the skill, motivation, and feedback requirements, individual group members must be assigned to subtasks commensurate with their abilities and goals. Rules for coordinating the group's activities must be carefully established and conveyed to the members. Failure to follow the prescribed course of action will negatively impact the objective of completing the task in a timely manner. Unless the interface design specialists, application developers, and testers coordinate their activities, the released product is likely to be difficult to use, lacking in desired functionality, contain errors, and be behind schedule. Although these issues apply to all divisible tasks (e.g., multiple co-authors on a manuscript), the important point here is that existing CSCW software is most appropriate for divisible tasks. In situations where all group members perform the same (unitary) task, the utility of CSCW remains to be determined.

Group Size

Group size can influence group productivity, but the nature and magnitude of this relationship is complex. A large software development team has a greater information and skill pool to draw on when attempting to resolve problems and consequently, may be more productive than a smaller group of developers. On the other hand, large groups need extensive organization and coordination among members, which may inhibit productivity.

Determining the effects of group size on productivity requires an analysis of the type of task to be performed (Thomas & Fink, 1963). For some classes of tasks (called additive tasks), the addition of extra personnel facilitates completion of the job. Assuming a software product has been thoroughly planned and the developers understand the overall design goal, 10 people can write software code faster than two. Even here, however, there is some maximum point beyond which the addition of extra personnel no longer improves productivity. If 50 people tried to produce the software, difficulties in coordination might increase to the point where the group is actually less productive than the group of 10.

Tasks can also be classified as *disjunctive* or *conjunctive* (Steiner, 1972). A disjuntive task is one in which group performance depends entirely on that of the strongest or fastest member, while a conjunctive task is one in which group performance is constrained by the efficiency and effectiveness of the weakest or slowest member. Tasks performed by a software development group may be either disjunctive or conjunctive. If the problem entails resolving a particularly sticky but basic design issue, the task is disjunctive, because a solution by any member is equivalent to a solution by the entire group. If the problem is one of typing application code, the task is conjunctive, because the group's performance (as measured by the speed of completing the project and number of errors encountered) will be constrained by its slowest member.

Steiner hypothesizes that performance will (a) increase directly with group size when the task is disjunctive and (b) decrease with group size when the task is conjunctive. When the task is disjunctive, larger groups are more likely to contain members of high ability. Since a solution offered by any member solves the problem, performances increases with group size. When the task is conjunctive, an opposite outcome is possible. Larger groups are more likely to have some members who are weak in some area. Because these weak members can reduce the overall productivity of the group, large groups should perform less well than small ones on conjunctive tasks.

Accurately defining how many individuals should comprise a large versus small group for any type of task (additive, conjunctive, disjunctive) is not well understood. In situations involving the electronic exchange of information, the number of people who actively read and respond to messages appears to be more important than the physical size of the group (Hiltz, 1984). Determining this effective size varies as function of critical mass (Markus, 1987) and type of task. Palme (1981a, p. 17) comes to a similar conclusion:

> The real value . . . will of course depend on whether the person can through COM communicate with a sufficiently large number of other persons, with which the person has a need to communicate. How large this group is depends on how large the need to communicate is in the group. If this need is large, and if alternative satisfactory communications means are not available, then COM may work even for a person who communicates in a small group of e.g., 5–10 people. But for persons who use COM mainly for the exchange of experience, communication with at least 30 other people seems to be necessary before this person feels that the value of using COM is larger than the trouble.

The final version of Palme's (1981b) report backs away from specifying a precise number (e.g., 30) and merely suggests that the optimal size of an electronic conference ranges between 10 and 80 participants.

Group Cohesiveness

Highly cohesive groups are not always more productive. Cohesiveness does impact productivity, but only when combined with other variables such as group norms and task structure. If a group is highly cohesive and has norms of high productivity, it will exert more influence on the members and will be highly productive. On the other hand, if the group is highly cohesive but has norms of low productivity, it will spend more time socializing than working (Berkowitz, 1954). In general, cohesiveness enhances whatever productivity norms exist within the group rather than directly affecting the amount produced.

Group cohesiveness also interacts with task structure to affect performance (Nixon, 1977). In organizations where there is a division of labor (a divisible task structure), successful performance depends on a harmonious coordination among the respective groups. If the goals of the marketing department are not effectively communicated to the engineering departments, the products may not meet the customers needs. When product development teams working on complementary projects do not function as a cohesive unit, schedules slip and the ultimate product may lack desired functionality.

In situations where team members work on essentially independent and identical projects (a unitary task structure), a negative relationship between cohesiveness and successful group performance has been noted (Landers & Luschen, 1974). Unitary tasks do not require much coordination among the team members. If the group contains a number of star performers, rivalry among the members can motivate higher levels of individual excellence. Thus, in organizations based on a unitary task structure, low levels of group cohesiveness may actually improve productivity.

Communication Network Structure

A *communication network* is the pattern of communication opportunities within a group. Communication patterns among the members of a group are affected by the relative status of its members, the nature of the group's task, the physical distance between members, and the size of the group. For example, communication patterns for a group of five individuals can result in a variety of networks (Figure 2.8). A completely connected network (*comcon*) allows each member to talk freely with all other members. Other networks impose restrictions on communication. In the wheel network, one individual (or computer) is at the hub and all communication must pass through that person (machine). With a chain network, information transmitted from the person at either end must pass through other individuals (nodes) to reach the other end. Different network configurations thus affect opportunities for interaction among a group's members and can influence productivity. Examination of these opportunities for interaction is central to understanding the nature and function of cooperative work (Jefferson, 1972; Suchman & Trigg, 1986).

Because messages flowing from the wheel, the chain and the Y networks must pass through a central hub, these networks are centralized. The circle and the comcon networks are decentralized, because messages need not pass through a central hub. The impact of computers on centralization versus decentralization of an organization's structure is considered in Chapter 3. The next section reviews the social psychological aspects of computer mediated communication networks.

SOCIAL PSYCHOLOGICAL ASPECTS OF
COMPUTER MEDIATED COMMUNICATION

Conversations between humans go beyond the task of giving and receiving information; they also involve the social goals of making a good impression, increasing one's status and influencing others (Murray & Bevan, 1985). The nature of a conversation is influenced by the person's initial attitudes toward the recipient of the information and the

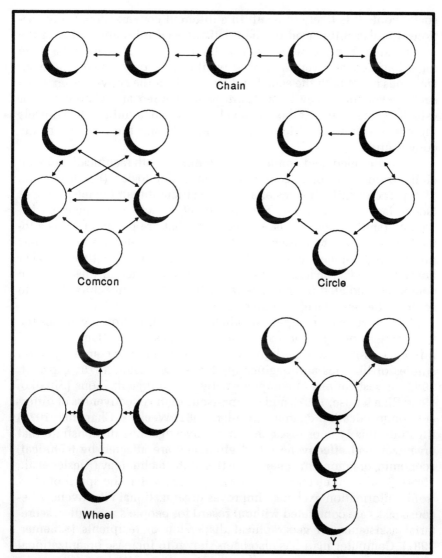

Source: Adapted from Leavitt (1951)

FIGURE 2.8
Communication networks in five-person groups.

individual's attitude toward the subject of the conversation. Each social situation contains nonverbal cues that influence the initial attitudes, even before the participants are present. A casual conversation, over lunch, on the nature of a person's work establishes a different atmosphere than would be found if the person were interviewing for a new job. Although the topic of the conversation is the same, the different social context is likely to result in a different conversation. Conversations are also influenced by the relative social roles and status of the participants. The interaction during the interview is likely to be more formal and constrained than what would occur over lunch. These social roles affect both the social and task goals of the conversation. On a social level there may be a desire to strengthen an existing role or establish a new one. At the task level, the roles determine who controls the conversation, what topics are acceptable and the duration of the conversation.

Computer mediated communication differs both technically and socially from traditional communication technologies (Kiesler et al., 1984). Technically, it is faster and more efficient than the telephone or face-to-face conversations. Socially, it often lacks the nonverbal behaviors (smiles, head nods, eye contact) that are common in face-to-face encounters. The presence of these cues in face-to-face interactions provide the listener with an efficient vehicle for letting the speaker know the subject matter is understood. The absence of these cues in computer-mediated interactions restricts the communicators ability to achieve the same level of understanding.

Most research on computer-mediated communications evaluates the technologies on task and technical capabilities, rather than the social influence processes underlying their usage. Computer communication studies of libraries and engineering firms (Lancaster, 1978; Tapscott, 1982), investigations of computer networks in organizations (Sinaiko, 1963; Rice & Case, 1982), and comparisons of the effectiveness of different communication channels (Geller, 1981; Weeks & Chapanis, 1976) illustrate this type of research. These investigations demonstrate that organizational effectiveness and efficiency are affected by technical, economic, or ergonomic characteristics of the technology (Kiesler et al., 1984). Studies of electronic mail systems show that the speed of electronic information exchange improves organizational effectiveness because tasks are completed without regard for people's schedules, secretarial assistance, or geographical dispersion of recipients (Kraemer, 1981). Computer mail has also been shown to increase organizational efficiency by discouraging off-task interaction (Weeks & Chapanis, 1976) and because individuals read more efficiently than they listen (Hiltz & Turoff, 1978).

Such investigations provide a necessary component to understanding human–computer interactions, but real life technological functions do not exist in isolation. Technological components are embodied in larger social contexts which trigger social psychological processes (Williams, 1977). Computer mail not only increases the amount of communication but also increases communication up and down the organization's hierarchy. This change in channels of information flow raises social psychological issues (Kiesler et al., 1984). The nature of such organizational impacts, however, remains controversial. Online computer conferences that increase the rate of information flow can result in premature decisions (Dutton & Kraemer, 1980). Conversely, because computer-mediated communication channels reduce status and power differentials, and lessen the impact of other social cues, the quality of the decision can be enhanced. The influence of charismatic and high status people is reduced, and group members may participate more equally in computer communication (Edinger & Patterson, 1983).

Computer mediated communications have at least two interesting characteristics from a social psychological perspective: (a) depersonalizing technical qualities and (b) few rules governing their use (Kiesler et al., 1984). These authors suggest three areas that affect communication via a computer:

1. Reductions in social feedback and unpredictable message style complicate efforts to coordinate communications.
2. Social influence among communicators tends to equalize because hierarchical dominance and power information is hidden.
3. Social standards are less important and communication is more impersonal because the rapid exchange of text alone, the lack of social feed back, and the absence of norms governing social interaction redirect attention to others as compared to the message itself (Kiesler et al., 1984).

Because human–computer interactions comprise a subset of the behavior of a human communicator, the user applies to the situation the habits, skills, and reactions appropriate to conversations with another human. With most existing software, however, only certain types of human conversations can be emulated. Murray and Bevan (1985) identify four underlying dimensions of people's perceptions of interpersonal relations: cooperative/competitive, equal/unequal, intense/superficial, and formal-task/informal. Most computer conversations are tended to be cooperative, equal, intense, and task oriented. This predetermined social style and role impacts the effectiveness of computer mediated communications.

CURRENT CSCW RESEARCH

At least 17 different approaches to computer supported cooperative work have been identified (Johansen, 1987). These approaches can be classified according to software that supports (a) face-to-face meetings [e.g., group decision support systems], (b) electronic meetings [e.g., computer conferencing], or (c) between-meeting interactions [e.g., project management software]. Most existing CSCW applications fall into the latter two classifications. DeCindo, DeMichelis, Simone, Vassallo, and Sanaboni (1986) discuss one such tool (called CHAOS) and note that "organization rules" of interaction accompany work mediated by computers. They suggest that the sociolinguistic rules of communication impart a dynamic organizational meaning, a concept that bridges the gap between individual and organization. Such symbolic interactions also imply a relationship between the variables considered by social psychologists and those examined by anthropologists (Chapter 4).

The Coordinator is another example of a current CSCW tool. Based on the theory that language is a primary dimension of human cooperative activity (Flores, 1982; Winograd, 1987), the Coordinator assumes that language itself is action in the context of human social behavior. Language is seen as a symbolic interaction which gives meaning to people through pragmatic, semantic and syntax uses. By combining electronic mail, calendaring, and word processing within a framework for conversations, the Coordinator claims to improve group productivity by making communications within a group more productive and focussed. The intent is to provide an environment that fits the structure of everyday communication such that the user need no longer be aware of the software or its interface.

An essential feature of the Coordinator is the use of *conversational templates*, also known as *speech acts*. Speech acts are judged relative to their appropriateness to a context rather than their semantics or meaning (Austin, 1962). The basic unit of work in the Coordinator is a conversation, not a message. Two types of conversations are supported. *Conversations for Action* have a structure which lead toward closure by fulfilling a request, declining to fulfill a request, accepting or declining an offer, or explicitly cancelling a commitment. *Conversations for Possibility* do not necessarily lead toward closure and, as such, do not have a formal structure. Messages and responses are linked in the software so that one can always retrieve the context of any given message. The dates of commitments and promises in one's conversations are automatically included in the calendaring function. The software does not attempt to understand the content of the messages, only to maintain the conversation structure.

AN EMPIRICAL EXAMPLE

A research project was initiated in Pacific Bell to evaluate the potential value of the Coordinator and to help knit together a diverse group of professionals scattered across a number of mail systems and office locations (See Carasik & Grantham, 1988, for a complete discussion). The test group consisted of 15 professionals who provide consulting services to information systems activities within the organization. Some group members are located in San Francisco, while others have their offices in an administrative center, about 35 miles away. Members of the group are frequently traveling, attending meetings, or working at home, so phone tag is an endemic problem.

A simple pre/post within group comparison methodology was used to evaluate the subject's usage and reactions toward the Coordinator. Changes in participants intragroup communication patterns were measured using a network analysis questionnaire (Schmeideck, 1978). Changes in subjects cognition were assessed using a series of semantic differential scales.

Results.   The level of system use was neither uniform nor intense. At the completion of 6 weeks, the users voted to discontinue use of the Coordinator as a work group tool and return to using the electronic mail system that had been in use prior to the study. Lack of language clarity, difficulty in learning the tool, and lack of cross-system compatibility were cited as reasons for discontinuance. Other anecdotal evidence indicated a negative reaction to the Coordinator by most study participants. Comments ranged from "worse than a lobotimized file clerk" to "this doesn't fit the way we work" and "I learned it in spite of the interface."

Implications.   These findings suggest that the affective nature of work tasks mediate the relationship between system acceptance and use. Recent theoretical work in linguistics support this observation (Scheff, 1986). Language provides an interpretive understanding and introduces affective states in individuals. Individual affect in human interaction is related to the extraction of meaning from the situation. A person's interpretation of the situation can vary greatly, suggesting that CSCW tools should pay attention to the affective nature of human–computer interactions. The Coordinator severely constrained the affective states in the present investigation and focused on the task component of the interaction.

These constraints move beyond specifying a priori status and power differentials. They delineate rules of exchange such as rationality, reciprocity, consistency and competition. Such norms of exchange develop during interaction and violation of these norms generate emotional states which must be acknowledged in order to effectively manage group interaction. The Coordinator may in certain circumstances, force violation of established norms of interaction. In some groups, the norm of reciprocity suggests that only certain statements require a response. Nonresponse might signal acceptance of the situation and by implication, acknowledgment of the group norm. Communication devices explicitly requiring a response violate this norm. One way to augment group interactions is to negotiate these norms of interaction among group members and to incorporate these norms into the software itself. The Coordinator does not permit such negotiation of interaction norms. Failure to recognize and facilitate the renegotiation of these norms can lead to a breakdown of communication.

Cooperative work systems require a substantial investment in training and support. By their very nature, they imply a change in the way an organization functions. Successful implementation will be affected by the existing corporate culture. The results of this study reflect the characteristics of the tool and the degree to which it fit the group. Since other electronic mail and word processing systems were already in place at Pacific Bell, the anticipated benefits of the language/action paradigm had to be communicated to the test group. Group training was limited to one 4-hour block of familiarization. During this period little effort was devoted to explaining the underlying theory embodied in the product. While the vendor claimed that understanding of the language/action paradigm was not needed to use their product, we found that interest in, and use of, the tool correlated with interest in understanding the language/action paradigm. The lack of intensive training may partially account for the lack of group level affect. More focus on system implementation methods is needed if CSCW software is to demonstrate significant positive changes in cognition and associated attitudes or behavior.

The specialized terminology in the Coordinator was also considered confusing to most participants in this study. Considerable work was needed to use the conversation templates in even a rudimentary way. The function-key driven interface of the Coordinator was difficult to learn, although, once mastered, it was fairly easy to use. A novice mode with a visual interface might enhance the learning curve. For technically sophisticated users, the interface requires more flexibility in interaction style. The interface should give the user a sense of control while allowing for fast response. Further work with the Coordinator's "conversation manager" subsystem may enable the use of tailored conversational scripts better suited to actual work situations.

The conversational templates constrained the communications medium. This perceived rigidity reduced the motivation of participants to learn the tool. Moreover, the templates did not conform to the existing actual work situation. For instance, an FYI notice had to be sent as either a *Conversation for Possibilities* or a *Conversation for Action*. The Conversation for Action template is better suited to environments characterized by negotiations and frequent status reporting among members of the same group. Since only a small proportion of communication done by members of the trial group took place within the group, a threshold level of involvement with the tool was never reached.

For a CSCW tool to be useful to a variety of organizations, it must have a structure for communications that can be tailored to the organization's needs. The Coordinator, while promising in concept, has proven somewhat inadequate in execution. Future research should explicitly incorporate the affective dimensions of human–computer interaction.

RESEARCHER'S AGENDA

In what ways is productivity governed by the task(s) confronting a group?

To what extent is productivity affected by group size?

Is there some optimal size for efficient and effective group interaction?

Does a group's cohesiveness affect the quality of its productivity?

Under what conditions do pressures for conformity enhance and/or reduce productivity?

In what ways does a group's communication structure influence its members style of interaction?

How do communication structures enhance and impede group performance?

In what ways can Computer Supported Cooperative Work (CSCW) software facilitate group productivity?

Does communication through text alone reduce coordination of communication?

What quantitative dimensions of existing communication will be altered with the use of CSCW tools?

What type of work processes are most amiable to use of CSCW techniques?

MANAGER'S AGENDA

Understanding group productivity requires an analysis of the task to be completed. The nature of the task affects performance because it interacts with other group attributes such as group size or method of communication.

CSCW software is most appropriate when group members are required to perform different, but complementary tasks (i.e., divisible tasks). In situations where all group members perform the same (unitary) task, the utility of CSCW software remains to be determined.

Group performance will increase directly with group size when the task is disjunctive (i.e., tasks where group performance depends on the capabilities of the strongest member).

Group performance will decrease directly with group size when the task is conjunctive (i.e., tasks where group performance depends on the limitations of the weakest member).

The definition of what constitutes a large versus small group depends on the type of task (additive, disjunctive, conjuntive) to be completed.

Highly cohesive groups are not always more productive. If the group is highly cohesive but has norms of low productivity, it will spend more time socializing than working. On the other hand, if a group is highly cohesive and has norms of high productivity, it will exert more influence on the members and will be highly productive.

Computer mediated communication differs both technically and socially from traditional communication technologies.

To be effective, computer-supported cooperative software needs to consider both the affective and task-oriented structure of the situation.

Strategic planning, user training, and support are needed to facilitate the use of CSCW tools.

CHAPTER SUMMARY

- Social psychology is the systematic analysis of the nature and causes of human social behavior. Its central concern is the process of social influence. The distinctiveness of social psychology stems from the study of the psychology of the individual in a social context.
- The social psychology of human–computer interaction may be defined as that branch of scientific study that examines the impacts of technology on individuals' beliefs (thoughts or cognitions), attitudes, and behaviors as they are influenced by the cognitions, attitudes, and behaviors of others (including computers) in a sociotechnical environment.
- Empirical examples of the social influence phenomena are becoming more common in the human–computer interaction literature, but the content area of this emerging field is not fixed. Because people and technology evolve continuously, so does our knowledge of their interrelationships. By definition, social change is at the heart of social psychology theory and research because social influence implies change.
- Socialization is the process by which individuals selectively acquire skills, knowledge, attitudes, values, and motives current in the groups of which they are or will become members. Through the socialization process, technology is becoming a natural rather than a complex thing.

- An attitude is a relatively enduring organization of beliefs around an object or situation predisposing one to respond in some preferential manner. Attitudes are embedded in larger cognitive structures and are learned through experience and social interaction. Because attitudes are learned, they can change. The extent to which attitudes can be modified is influenced by the degree of differentiation and integration of the cognitive structure. Highly differentiated and integrated attitudes are more stable.

- Consistency theories assume that, when cognitive elements are inconsistent, individuals are motivated to change their attitudes, their behavior, or both in order to restore harmony. When individuals' freely choose to use a computer because they believe it will improve their job performance, and the machine lives up to their expectations, there should be considerable cognitive consistency. In situations where a manager dictates the usage of a particular software application and the employees are resistant to computers in general or dislike the particular application chosen for their use, less consistency will be observed.

- Efforts to understand the relationships between individuals' attitudes and behaviors has been a primary focus of social psychological research. Knowledge of a person's attitudes is a necessary, although not sufficient, condition for predicting behavior. Differences between what people say and what people do can be explained in terms of attitude specificity, attitude structure, situation context variables, individual differences, and normative influences. Strong empirical relationships between attitudes and behavior are only evident when (a) the variables are measured at the same level of specificity, and (b) the entire attitude structure is examined in context.

- Although human–computer interaction research has traditionally not emphasized differences in individual users, there is an emerging interest in the topic. Three classes of individual difference variables can be identified: personality, cognitive style, and demographic/situational variables.

- The psychological study of personality has traditionally been concerned with providing a systematic account of the ways in which individuals differ from one another. Recent personality trait theories have increasingly realized that an adequate approach to the study of traits must examine how qualities of a person and the situation influence each other. This expanded view recognizes that human tendencies are a critical part of personality, but also asserts the need to study the cognitive and affective structures people use to adapt to events, people and situations encountered in life. Among the personality traits believed to impact human–computer interaction are locus of control, extraversion-introversion, fear of failure/need for achievement, anxiety, and defensiveness.

- A second area of theoretical and empirical effort related to individual differences concerns the cognitive processes people employ when dealing with information. Cognitive style refers to an individual's consistent ways of approaching and processing information, especially through perception, memory and thought. At least four cognitive style dimensions have been suggested to have importance to human–computer interactions: field-dependent/field-independent, systematic/heuristic, verbalizers/visualizers, flexibility/rigidity.

- Noncognitive variables such as demographic and situation influences (e.g., prior experience) represent another class of moderators affecting attitude–behavior relationships and help to broaden our understanding of individual differences. Prior experience has by far received the most attention, but a few studies have examined the impact of demographic indicators.

- Norms are standards that individuals use for evaluating situations, people or computer products as good or bad, better or worse. Standards shared by the members of a social group are labeled social norms. Personal norms refer to the individuals' own expectations, learned from shared expectations and modified through interaction. They represent ideals against which events are evaluated.

- Normative definitions apply to all human–computer interactions, although the amount of shared agreement may vary. The return potential model suggests that norms can be systematically evaluated in terms of three structural properties—the range of tolerable actions, the intensity of the norm, and the crystallization of the norm. An example was presented to illustrate that changing the definitional characteristics of the situation (i.e, sending a short electronic message, sending longer E-mail documents, or using the U.S. Postal Service) alters users' expectations of acceptable system response times.

- Computer supported cooperative work aims to augment work group activities through communication enhancements. Group performance can be examined in terms of the tasks confronting the group, group size, cohesiveness and communication structure. To understand how computer-mediated communication channels affect group productivity, it is necessary to first evaluate how these factors affecting performance interact.

- Interactions between humans encompass both task and social goals. Social goals introduce attitudinal factors into the conversation and can conflict with task-related goals. Computer conversations retain sufficient human-like characteristics to be judged by many of the same criteria as human conversations. Although computer conversations involve the exchange of information, the norms for appropriate social interaction are often absent. This makes it difficult to fulfill task goals and severely limits the range of social goals.

- From a social psychological perspective, computer mediated communications are less personal and governed by fewer norms of acceptable behavior. These characteristics reduce social feedback making it more difficult to coordinate communications and equalize status differentials among participants. An effective CSCW tool must incorporate both the task and social goals of human conversations.

BIBLIOGRAPHY

Ackermann, D. (1983). Robi Otter oder die Suche nach dem operativen Abbildsystem. Interner Bericht der Studienarbeiten SS.

Ahl, D. H. (1976). *Survey of public attitudes toward computers in society.* Morristown, NJ: Creative Computing Press.

Ajzen, I., & Fishbein, M. (1977). Attitude–behavior relations: A theoretical analysis and review of the empirical research literature. *Psychological Bulletin, 84,* 888–918.

Al-Awar, J., Chapanis, A., & Ford, W. R. (1981). Tutorial for the first-time computer user. *IEEE Transactions on Professional Communication, PC-24,* 30–37.

Allport, G. W. (1961). *Pattern and growth in personality.* New York: Holt, Rinehart and Winston.

Allport, G. W. (1969). The historical background of modern social psychology. In G. Lindzey & E. Aronson (Eds.), *The handbook of social psychology* (Vol. 1, 2nd ed., pp. 1–80). Reading, MA: Addison-Wesley.

Allwood, C. M., & Eliasson, M. (1987). Analogy and other sources of difficulty in novices' very first text-editing. *International Journal of Man-Machine Studies, 27,* 1–22.

Arndt, S., Feltes, J., & Hanak, J. (1983). Secretarial attitudes toward word processors as a function of familiarity and locus of control. *Behavior and Information Technology, 2,* 17–22.

Asch, S. (1952). *Social psychology.* Englewood Cliffs, NJ: Prentice-Hall.

Austin, J. (1962). *How to do things with words.* Cambridge, MA: Harvard University Press.

Bagozzi, R. P. (1981). Attitudes, intentions, and behavior: A test of some key hypotheses. *Journal of Personality and Social Psychology, 41,* 607–627.

Bagozzi, R. P., & Burnkrant, R. E. (1979). Attitude organization and the attitude–behavior relationship. *Journal of Personality and Social Psychology, 37,* 913–929.

Bariff, M. L., & Lusk, E. J. (1977). Cognitive and personality tests for the design of management information systems. *Management Science, 23,* 820–829.

Bem, D. J. (1970). *Beliefs, attitudes and human affairs.* Belmont, CA: Brooks/Cole.

Benbasat, I., & Taylor, R. N. (1978). The impact of cognitive styles on information system designs. *Management Information System Quarterly, 2,* 43–54.

Bentler, P. M., & Speckart, G. (1979). Models of attitude–behavior relations. *Psychological Review, 86,* 452–464.

Bentler, P. M., & Speckart, G. (1981). Attitudes "cause" behaviors: A structural equation analysis. *Journal of Personality and Social Psychology, 40,* 226–238.

Berkowitz, L. (1954). Group standards, cohesiveness and productivity. *Human Relations, 7,* 509–519.

Black, J. S., & Heberlein, T. A. (1979). *Emergent norms and environmental action: Reciprocal causation of personal and perceived social norms in the purchase of lead-free gasoline.* Paper presented at the annual meeting of the Rural Sociology Association. August.

Blake, J., & Davis, K. (1964). Norms, values and sanctions. In R. E. L. Faris (Ed.), *Handbook of modern sociology.* Chicago, IL: Rand McNally.

Block, J., & Block, J. (1980). The role of ego-control and ego resiliency in the organization of behavior. In W. A. Collins (Ed.), *The Minnesota symposium on child psychology* (Vol. 13). Hillsdale, NJ: Erlbaum (Wiley).

Bly, S. A., & Rosenberg, J. K. (1986). A comparison of tiled and overlapping windows. In *Proceedings: CHI'86 Human Factors in Computing Systems* (pp. 101–106). New York: ACM.

Bocker, H-D., Fischer, G., & Nieper, H. (1986). The enhancement of understanding through visual representations. In *Proceedings: CHI'86 Human Factors in Computing Systems* (pp. 44–50). New York: ACM.

Boecker, H-D., & Nieper, H. (1985, September). Making the invisible visible: Tools for exploratory programming. In *Proceedings of the First Pan Pacific Computer Conference.* Melbourne, Australia: The Australian Computer Society.

Booz, Allen, & Hamilton. (1981, March 29). How to conquer fear of computers: Executive guide. *Business Week,* pp. 176–178.

Brigham, J. C., & Weissbach, T. A. (Eds.). (1973). *Racial Attitudes in America: Analyses and Findings of Social Psychology, 90,* 285–289.

Brod, C. (1982). Managing technostress: Optimizing the use of computer technology. *Personnel Journal, 61,* 753–757.

Buchanan, D. A., & Boddy, D. (1982). Advanced technology and the quality of working life: The effects of word processing on video typists. *Journal of Occupational Psychology, 55,* 1–11.

Burnkrant, R. E., & Page, T. J., Jr. (1982). An examination of the convergent, discriminant, and predictive validity of Fishbein's behavioral intention model. *Journal of Marketing Research, 19,* 550–561.

Bush, D. M., & Simmons, R. G. (1981) Socialization processes over the life course. In M. Rosenberg & R. H. Turner (Eds.), *Social psychology: Sociological perspectives* (pp. 133–164). New York: Basic Books.

Campbell, A., Converse, P. E., Miller, W. E., & Stokes, D. E. (1960). *The American voter.* New York: Wiley.

Cancian, F. M. (1975). *What are norms.* New York: Cambridge University Press.

Cantor, N., & Mischel, W. (1979). Prototypes in person perception. In L.

Berkowitz (Ed.), *Advances in experimental social psychology* (Vol. 12). New York: Academic Press.

Cantor, N., Mischel, W., & Schwartz, J. (1982). Social knowledge: Structure, content, use, and abuse. In A. Isen & A. Hastorf (Eds.), *Cognitive social psychology*. New York: Elsevier North-Holland.

Carasik, R., & Grantham, C. (1988). A case study of computer-Supported cooperative work in a dispersed organization. In *Proceedings of SIGCHI 88* (pp. 61–65). Association of Computing Machinery.

Cartwright, D., & Zander, A. (Eds.). (1968). *Group dynamics: Research and theory*. New York: Harper and Row.

Cerveny, R. P., Garrity, E. J., Hunt, R. G., Kirs, P. J., Sanders, G. L., & Sipior, J. C. (1987, August). Why software prototyping works. *Datamation*, pp. 97–103.

Chapanis, A., Anderson, N. S., & Licklider, J. C. R. (1983). *Research needs for human factors*. Washington, DC: National Academy Press.

Converse, P. E. (1964). The nature of believe systems in mass publics. In D. E. Apter (Ed.), *Ideology and discontent*. Glencoe, IL: Free Press.

Coovert, M. D., & Goldstein, M. (1980). Locus of control as a predictor of users' attitude toward computers. *Psychological Reports, 47*, 1167–1173

Cronbach, L., & Gleser, G. C. (1953). Assessing similarity between profiles. *Psychological Bulletin, 50*, 456–473.

Cuff, R. (1980). On casual users. *International Journal of Man-Machine Studies, 12*, 163–187.

Culnan, M. J. (1984). The dimensions of accessibility to online information: Implications for implementing office information systems. *ACM Transactions on Office Information Systems, 2*, 141–150.

Curley, P. (1983, April). Confessions of a cyberphobe. *Best's Review*, p. 80.

DeCindo, F., DeMichelis, G., Simone, C., Vassallo, R., & Sanaboni, A. (1986). Chaos as coordination technology. In *Proceedings of the CSCW '86 Conference* (pp. 325–342). Austin, TX: ACM.

De Leeuw, L., & Welmers, H. (1978). The need for help during problem solving instruction in relation to task complexity and personality variables. In *Proceedings of XIXth International Congress on Applied Psychology*. Munich.

Douglas, S. A., & Moran, T. P. (1983). Learning text-editor semantics by analogy. In *Proceedings CHI'83: Human Factors in Computing Systems* (pp. 207–211). New York: ACM.

Dunlap, R. E., & Van Liere, K. D. (1978). Environmental concern: A bibliography of empirical studies and a brief appraisal of the literature. *Public administration series bibliography*. Montecello, IL: Vance Bibliographies.

Dutton, W. H., & Kraemer, K. L. (1980). Automating bias. *Society, 17*, 36–41.

Dzida, W., Herda. S., & Itzfeldt, W. D. (1978). User-perceived quality of interactive systems. *IEEE Transactions on Software Engineering, SE-4*, 270–276.

Edinger, J. A., & Patterson, M. L. (1983). Nonverbal involvement and social control. *Psychological Bulletin, 93*, 30–56.

Erikson, E. (1963). *Childhood and society*. New York: Norton.

Eysenck, H. J., & Rachman, S. (1965). *The causes and cures of neurosis: An introduction to modern behavior therapy based on learning theory and the principles of conditioning.* San Diego, CA: Knapp.

Eysenck, M. W. (1977). *Human memory: Theory, research and individual differences.* Oxford: Pergamon Press.

Fazio, R. H., & Zanna, M. P. (1978). Attitudinal qualities relating to the strength of the attitude–behavior relationship. *Journal of Experimental Social Psychology, 14,* 398–408.

Festinger, L. (1957). *A theory of cognitive dissonance.* Evanston, IL: Row, Peterson.

Fishbein, M. (1978). Attitudes and behavior prediction: An overview. In J. M. Yinger & S. J. Cutler (Eds.), *Major social issues: A multidisciplinary view* (pp. 377–389). New York: The Free Press.

Fishbein, M., & Ajzen, I. (1975). *Beliefs, attitude, intention, and behavior: An introduction to theory and research.* Reading, MA: Addison-Wesley.

Fishbein, M., & Raven, B. H. (1967). The A-B scales: An operational definition of belief and attitude. In M. Fishbein (Ed.), *Readings in attitude theory and measurement.* New York: John Wiley and Sons.

Fitch, G. (1970). Effects of self-esteem, perceived performance, and choice on causal attribution. *Journal of Personality and Social Psychology, 16,* 311–315.

Flores, F. (1982). *Management and communication in the office of the future.* Berkeley, CA: Logonet.

Foley, J. D., Wallace, V. L., & Chan, P. (1984, November). The human factors of computer graphics interaction techniques. *IEEE Computer Graphics and Applications,* pp. 13–48.

Fredricks, A. J., & Dossett, D. L. (1983). Attitude-behavior relations: A comparison of the Fishbein-Ajzen and the Bentler-Speckart models. *Journal of Personality and Social Psychology, 45,* 501–512.

Geen, R. G., & Gange, J. J. (1977). Drive theory of social facilitation: Twelve years of theory and research. *Psychological Bulletin, 84,* 1267–1288.

Geller, V. J. (1981). *Mediation of social presence: Communication modality effects on arousal and task performance.* Murray Hill, NJ: Bell Laboratories.

Gilfoil, D. M. (1981). Warming up to computers: A study of cognitive and affective interaction overtime. In *Proceedings: Human Factors in Computer Systems* (pp. 245–250). Gaithersburg, MD: ACM.

Gough, H. (1976). Personality and personality assessment. In M. D. Dunnette (Ed.), *Handbook of industrial and organizational psychology.* Chicago, IL: Rand McNally.

Gould, L., & Finzer, W. (1984). *Programming by rehearsal* (Tech. Rep. No. SCL-84–1). Palo Alto, CA: Xerox Palo Alto Research Center.

Grantham, C. E., & Vaske, J. J. (1985). Predicting the usage of an advanced communication technology. *Behaviour and Information Technology, 4,* 327–335.

Grief, I. (1987, December). *Proceeding of the CSCW '86 Conference.* Austin, TX: ACM.

Guilford, J. P. (1959). *Personality.* New York: McGraw-Hill.

Hammond, N. V., Long, J. B., Clark, I. A., Barnard, P. J., & Morton, J. (1980,

September). Documenting human–computer mismatch in the interactive system. In *Proceedings of the Ninth International Symposium on Human Factors in Telecommunications* (pp. 17–24). Holmdel, NJ.

Hannemyr, G., & Innocent, P. R. (1985). A network user interface: Incorporating human factors guidelines into the ISO standard for open systems interconnection. *Behaviour and Information Technology, 4*(4): 309–326.

Heberlein, T. A. (1981). Environmental attitudes. *Zeitschrift fur Umweltpolitik, 2,* 241–270.

Heberlein, T. A., & Black, J. S. (1976). Attitudinal specificity and the prediction of behavior in a field setting. *Journal of Personality and Social Psychology, 33,* 474–479.

Heberlein, T. A., & Black, J. S. (1981). Cognitive consistency and environmental action. *Environment and Behavior, 13,* 717–734.

Heider, F. (1944). Social perception and phenomenal causality. *Psychological Review, 51,* 358–374.

Heider, F. (1946). Attitudes and cognitive organization. *Journal of Psychology, 21,* 107–112.

Heider, F. (1958). *The psychology of interpersonal relations.* New York: John Wiley and Sons.

Hicks, B. (1976). *Computer outreach.* Washington, DC: National Institute of Education.

Hill, R. J. (1981). Attitudes and behavior. In M. Rosenberg & R. H. Turner (Eds.), *Social psychology: Sociological perspectives.* New York: Basic Books.

Hiltz, S. R. (1984). *Online Communities: A case study of the office of the future.* Norwood, NJ: Ablex Publishing Corp.

Hiltz, S. R., & Turoff, M. (1978). *The network nation: Human communication via computer.* Reading, MA: Addison Wesley.

Hollander, E. P. (1967). *Principles and methods of social psychology.* New York: Oxford University Press

Homans, G. C. (1950). *The human group.* New York: Harcourt Press.

Homans, G. C. (1961). *Social behavior: Its elementary forms.* New York: Harcourt, Brace.

Inman, V. (1983). Learning how to use computers is a frightening experience for many. *The Wall Street Journal,* April 12.

Iso-Ahola, S. E. (1980). *The social psychology of leisure and recreation.* Dubuque, IA: William C. Brown.

Jackson, J. (1965). Structural characteristics of norms. In I. D. Steiner & M. F. Fishbein (Eds.), *Current studies in social psychology* (pp. 301–309). New York: Holt, Rinehart, & Winston.

Jackson, J., & Saltzstein, H. D. (1958). The effect of person-group relationships on conformity processes. *Journal of Abnormal and Social Psychology, 57,* 17–24.

Jefferson, G. (1972). Side sequences. In D. Sudnow (Ed.), *Studies in social interaction.* New York: Free Press.

Johansen, R. (1987, May). *User approaches to computer-supported teams.* Paper presented at the Symposium on Technological Support for Work Group Collaboration, New York.

Karat, J., Boyes, L., Weisgerber, S., & Schafer, C. (1986) Transfer between word processing systems. In *Proceedings: CHI'86 Human Factors in Computing Systems* (pp. 67–71). New York: ACM.

Karon, P. (1988). The on-line team: Computing in a group. *PC Week, 5,* 59, 64.

Kearsley, G., & Furlong, M. (1984). *Computers for kids over 60.* Reading, MA: Addison-Wesley.

Kelly, G. A. (1955). *The psychology of personal constructs* (Vol. 2). New York: W. W. Norton.

Kelly, H. H. (1971). *Attribution in social interaction.* New York: General Learning Press.

Kennedy, T. C. S. (1975). Some behavioral factors affecting the training of naive users of an interactive computer system. *International Journal of Man-Machine Studies, 7,* 817–834.

Kerber, K. W. (1983). Attitudes towards specific uses of the computer: Quantitative, decision making and record keeping applications. *Behavior and Information Technology, 2,* 197–209.

Kiesler, S., Siegel, J., & McGuire, T. W. (1984). Social psychological aspects of computer mediated communication. *American Psychologist, 39,* 1123–1134.

Kling R. (1980). Social analysis of computing: Theoretical perspectives in recent empirical research. *Computing Surveys, 12,* 61–110.

Kluckholn, C. (1951). Values and value—Orientations in the theory of action. In T. Parsons & E. A. Shils (Eds.), *Toward a general theory of action* (pp. 388–433). New York: Harper and Row.

Knight (1979). A hands-on workshop for reducing computer anxiety. *Journal of College Student Personnel, 26,* 167–168.

Kohlberg, L. (1969). Stage and sequence: The cognitive-developmental approach to socialization. In D. A. Goslin (Ed.), *Handbook of socialization theory and research* (pp. 347–480). Chicago, IL: Rand McNally.

Kornbluh, M. (1984). *Computer and telecommunications applications to enhance the quality of life of our elderly citizens.* Washington, DC: Congressional Research Service, Library of Congress.

Kraemer, K. L. (1981). *Telecommunications-transportation substitution and energy productivity: A re-examination.* Prepared for the Directorate of Science, Technology and Industry Organization for Economic cooperation and Development, Paris.

Krauss, I., & Hoyer, W. (1984). *High technology and the older person: Age and experience as moderators of attitudes towards computers.* Unpublished study. Syracuse University.

Krech, D., Crutchfield, R. S., & Ballachey, E. L. (1962). *Individual in society.* New York: McGraw-Hill.

Lancaster, F. W. (1978). *Toward paperless information systems.* New York: Academic Press.

Landers, D. M., & Luschen, G. (1974). Team performance outcome and the cohesiveness of competitive coacting groups. *International Review of Sport Sociology, 2,* 57–69.

LaPiere, R. T. (1934). Attitudes versus action. *Social Forces, 13,* 230–237.

Lawler, E. E., & Hall, D. T. (1970). Relationship of job characteristics to job involvement, satisfaction and intrinsic motivation. *Journal of Applied Psychology, 54,* 305–312.

Leavitt, H. J. (1951). Some effects of certain communication patterns on group performance. *Journal of Abnormal and Social Psychology, 46,* 38–50.

Lee, R. (1970). Social attitudes and the computer revolution. *Public Opinion Quarterly, 34,* 53–59.

Lefcourt, H. M. (1966). Internal versus external control of reinforcement: A review. *Psychological Bulletin, 65,* 206–220.

Lichtman, D. (1979, January). Survey of educator's attitudes toward computers. *Creative Computing,* pp. 48–50.

Loyd, B. H., & Gressard, C. (1984). Reliability and factorial validity of computer attitude scales. *Educational and Psychological Measurement, 44,* 501–505.

Maccoby, E. E. (1966). Sex differences in intellectual functioning. In E. E. Maccoby (Ed.), *The development of sex differences* (pp. 25–55). Palo Alto, CA: Standard University Press.

Maccoby, E. E., & Jacklin, C. N. (1974, December). What we know and what we don't know about sex differences. *Psychology Today,* pp. 109–112.

Mack, D., Auburn, P. N., & Knight, G. O. (1971). Sex role identification and behavior in a reiterated prisoner's dilemma game. *Psychometric Science, 24,* 280–282.

Mack, D., & Knight, G. P. (1974). Identification of other players characteristics in the reiterated prisoner's dilemma. *The Psychological Review, 24,* 93–100.

Mack, D., Williams, J. G., & Kremer, J. M. D. (1979). Perception of a simulated other player and behavior in the reiterated prisoner's dilemma game. *The Psychological Review, 29,* 43–48.

Mackinlay, B. (1984). Honeywell's Scorpion. *Unix/World, 1*(3) 80–92.

Markus, M. L. (1987). Toward a critical mass theory of interactive media communication research. *Communication Research, 14*(5), 491–511.

Martin, J. (1973). *Design of man-computer dialogues.* Englewood Cliffs, NJ: Prentice Hall.

McCall, R. B. (1974). Exploratory manipulation and play in the human infant. *Monograph Social Research Child Development, 39,* 150.

Merton, R. (1968). *Social theory and social structure.* New York: Free Press.

Meyer, J. P. (1980). Causal attribution for success and failure: A multi-variate investigation of dimensionality, formation, and consequences. *Journal of Personality and Social Psychology, 38,* 704–718.

Michener, H. A., DeLamater, J. D., & Schwartz, S. H. (1986). *Social Psychology.* San Diego, CA: Harcourt Brace Jovanovich.

Mischel, W. (1970). Sex typing and socialization. In P. H. Mussen (Ed.), *Carmichael's manual of child psychology* (Rev. ed.). New York: Wiley.

Mischel, W. (1980). Personality and cognition: Something borrowed, something new. In N. Cantor & J. Kihlstrom (Eds.), *Personality, cognition, and social interaction.* Hillsdale, NJ: Erlbaum.

Morrison, P. R. (1983). A survey of attitudes toward computers. *Communications of the ACM, 26,* 1051–1057.

Murray, D., & Bevan, N. (1985). The social psychology of computer conversations. In *Proceedings of the IFIP Conference on Human-Computer Interaction* (pp. 268–273). London: Elsevier Science.

Nixon, H. L. II (1977). "Cohesiveness" and team success: A theoretical reformulation. *Review of Sport and Leisure, 2*, 36–57.

Ogozalek, V. Z., & van Praag, J. (1986). Comparison of elderly and younger users on keyboard and voice input computer-based composition tasks. In *Proceedings: CHI'86 Human Factors in Computing Systems* (pp. 205–211). New York: ACM.

Palme, J. (1981a). *Experience with the use of the COM computerized conferencing system* (Draft Report). Stockholm, Sweden: Swedish National Defense Research Institute.

Palme, J. (1981b). *Experience with the use of the COM computerized conferencing system*. (FOA) Report C 10166E-M6(H9). Stockholm, Sweden: Swedish National Defense Research Institute.

Papert, S. (1980). *Mindstorms*. New York: Basic Books.

Phares, E. J. (1978). Locus of control. In H. London & J. E. Exner, Jr. (Eds.), *Dimensions of personality*. New York: Wiley.

Piaget, J. (1970). *Structuralism*. New York: Basic Books.

Potosnak, K. M. (1986). Classifying users: A hard look at some controversial issues. In *Proceedings: CHI'86 Human Factors in Computing Systems* (pp. 84–89). New York: ACM.

Quintanar, L. R., Crowell, C. R., Pryor, J. B., & Adamopoulos, J. (1982). Human computer interaction: A preliminary social psychological analysis. *Behavior, Research, Methods and Instrumentation, 14*, 210–220.

Rafaeli, A. (1986). Employee attitudes toward working with computers. *Journal of Occupational Behaviour, 7*, 89–106.

Rafaeli, A., & Sutton, R. I. (1985). Word processing technology and perceptions of control among clerical employees. *Behaviour and Information Technology*.

Ramsey, H. R., & Atwood, M. E. (1979). *Human Factors in Computer Systems: A Review of the Literature*. (Tech. Rep. No. SAI-79–111–DEN). Englewood, CO: Science Applications, Inc.

Rappoport, L. (1977). Symposium: Towards a dialectical social psychology. *Psychological Bulletin, 3*, 678–680.

Reece, M. J., & Gable, R. K. (1982). The development and validation of a measure of general attitudes toward computers. *Educational and Psychological Measurement, 42*, 913–917.

Regan, D. T., & Fazio, R. H. (1977). On the consistency between attitudes and behavior: Look to the method of attitude formation. *Journal of Experimental Social Psychology, 13*, 28–45.

Rice. R. E., & Case, D. (1982). Electronic messaging in the university organization. *Psychological Bulletin, 94*, 239–264.

Rich, E. (1983). Users are individuals: Individualizing user models. *International Journal of Man-Machine Studies, 18*, 199–214.

Riegel, K. F. (1976). The dialectics of human development. *American Psychologist, 31*, 689–700.

Ringle, M. (1982). *The impact of turnkey systems on naive users.* Unpublished report.

Rokeach, M. (1968). *Beliefs, attitudes, and values: A theory of organization and change.* San Francisco, CA: Jossey-Bass.

Rotter, J. B. (1966). Generalized expectancies for internal versus external control of reinforcement. *Psychological Monographs, 80* (Whole No. 609).

Salancik, G. R. (1977). Commitment and the control of organizational behavior and belief. In B. Shaw & G. R. Salancik (Eds.), *New directions in organizational behavior.* Chicago, IL: St. Clair.

Scheff, T. (1986). Micro-linguistics and social structure: A theory of social action. *Sociological Theory, 4,* 71–83.

Schlegel, R. P., & DiTecco, D. (1982). Attitudinal structures and the attitude–behavior relation. In M. P. Zanna, E. T. Higgins, & E. P. Herman (Eds.), *Consistency in social behavior.* Hillsdale, NJ: Erlbaum.

Schmeideck, R. A. (1978). *The personal sphere model.* New York: Grune and Stratton.

Schuman, H., & Johnson, M. P. (1976). Attitudes and behavior. *Annual Review of Sociology, 2,* 161–207.

Schwartz, S. H. (1977). Normative influences on altruism. *Advances in experimental social psychology, 10,* 221–279.

Scott, W. A. (1969). Structure of natural cognitions. *Journal of Personality and Social Psychology, 12,* 261–278.

Scott, J. F. (1971). *Internalization of norms.* Englewood Cliffs, NJ: Prentice-Hall.

Sculley, J. (1987). *Odyssey: Pepsi to Apple . . . A Journey of adventure, ideas and the future.* New York: Harper and Row.

Sears, R. R. (1963). Dependency motivation. In M. R. Jones (Ed.), *Nebraska Symposium on Motivation* (pp. 25–64). Lincoln, NE: University of Nebraska Press.

Sears, R. R. (1965). Development of gender role. In F. A. Beach (Ed.), *Sex and behavior* (pp. 133–163). New York: Wiley.

Sewell, W. H. (1963). Some recent developments in socialization theory and research. *The Annals of the American Academy of Political and Social Science, 349,* 163–181.

Shackel, B. (1981 September). *The concept of usability.* Paper presented at the Software and Information Usability Symposium, IBM, Poughkeepsie, NY. (Also presented at the ITT Symposium on Human Factors and the Usability of Software, Shelton, CT, October, 1981).

Shaw, M. E., & Wright, J. M. (1967). *Scales for the measurement of attitudes.* New York: McGraw Hill.

Sherif, M., & Sherif, C. W. (1956). *An outline of social psychology.* New York: Harper and Row.

Shiflett, S. (1979). Toward a general model of small group productivity. *Psychological Bulletin, 86,* 67–79.

Shneiderman, B. (1983). Direct manipulation: A step beyond programming languages. *IEEE Computer, 16,* 57–69.

Shneiderman, B. (1984). Response time and display rate in human performance with computers. *Computing Surveys, 16,* 265, 285.

Shneiderman, B. (1987). *Designing the user interface: Strategies for effective human–computer interaction.* Reading, MA: Addison-Wesley.

Sinaiko, H. W. (1963). *Teleconferencing: Preliminary experiments* (Research Paper P-108). Arlington, VA: Institute for Defense Analysis.

Smith, S. L. (1981, October). *The usability of software: Design guidelines for the user-system interface.* Paper presented at the ITT Symposium on Human Factors and the Usability of Software, ITT Advanced Technology Center, Shelton, CT.

Spiliotopoulos, V., & Shackel, B. (1981). Towards a computer interview acceptable to the naive user. *International Journal of Man-Machine Studies, 14,* 77–90.

Steiner, I. D. (1972). *Group process and productivity.* New York: Academic Press.

Steiner, I. D. (1974). *Task-performing groups.* Morristown, NJ: General Learning Press.

Stewart, T. F. M. (1974). Ergonomic aspects of man-computer problem solving. *Applied Ergonomics, 5,* 209–212.

Suchman, L., & Trigg, R. (1986). A framework for studying research collaboration. In *Proceedings of the CSCW '86 Conference* (pp. 221–228). Austin, TX: ACM.

Tapscott, D. (1982, March). Investigating the electronic office. *Datamation,* pp. 130–138.

Taylor, S. E., & Crocker, J. C. (1980). Schematic bases of social information processing. In E. T. Higgins, E. P. Herman, & M. P. Zanna (Eds.), *Social cognition: The Ontario Symposium, Vol. 1.* Hillsdale, NJ: Erlbaum.

Thomas, E. J., & Fink, C. F. (1963). Effects of group size. *Psychological Bulletin, 60,* 371–384.

Thompson, D. A. (1969). Man-computer system: Toward balanced cooperation in intellectual activities. In *Proceedings, International Symposium on Man-Machine Systems* (IEEE Conference Record Number 69C58–MMS, Vol. 1). New York: Institute of Electrical and Electronics Engineers.

Turkle, S. (1984). *The second self: Computers and the human spirit.* New York: Simon and Schuster.

Van Muylwijk, B, Van Der Veer, G., & Waern, Y. (1983). On the implications of user variability in open systems: An overview of the little we know and of the lot we have to find out. *Behaviour and Information Technology, 2*(4), 313–326

Vaske, J. J., Donnelly, M. P., & Tweed, D. L. (1983). Recreationist-defined versus researcher-defined similarity judgments in substitutability research. *Journal of Leisure Research, 15*(3), 251–262.

Vaske, J. J., Fleishman, J. A., Ehrlich, K., & Grantham, C. E. (1985). Variations in belief structures about computers as a function of prior experience. In *Proceedings: 9th Annual Honeywell International Computer Sciences Conference* (pp. AA1–AA12). Minneapolis, MN: Honeywell.

Vaske, J. J., & Grantham, C. E. (1985). *HVN versus satellite communications: A comparison of users evaluations.* (Tech. Rep.). Billerica, MA: Honeywell Information Systems.

Vaske, J. J., & Teubner, A. L. (1985). *A comparative evaluation of Billerica and Phoenix DPS6 Email users.* (Tech. Rep.). Billerica, MA: Honeywell Information Systems, Inc.

Warshaw, P. R., Calantone, R., & Joyce, M. (1986). A field application of the Fishbein and Ajzen intention model. *Journal of Social Psychology, 126,* 137–139.

Weeks, G. D., & Chapanis, A. (1976). Cooperative versus conflictive problem-solving in three telecommunication modes. *Perceptual and Motor Skills, 42,* 8779–917.

Weigel, R. H., & Newman, L. S. (1976). Increasing attitude–behavior correspondence by broadening the scope of the behavioral measure. *Journal of Personality and Social Psychology, 33,* 793–802.

Weinberg, G. M. (1971). *The psychology of computer programming.* New York: Van Nostrand Reinhold.

Weizenbaum, J. (1976). *Computer power and human reason.* San Francisco, CA: Freeman.

Wicker, A. W. (1969). Attitudes versus actions: The relationship of verbal and overt behavioral responses to attitude objects. *Journal of Social Issues, 25,* 41–78.

Wiggins, J. S. (1979). A psychological taxonomy of trait-descriptive terms: The interpersonal domain. *Journal of Personality and Social Psychology, 37,* 395–412.

Williams, E. (1977). Experimental comparisons of face-to-face and mediated communication: A review. *Psychological Bulletin, 84,* 963–976.

Winograd, T. A. (1987). *A language/action perspective on the design of cooperative work* (Report No. STAN-CS-87–1158). Palo Alto, CA: Department of Computer Science, Stanford University.

Witkin, H. A., Dijk, R. B., Faterson, H. F., Goodenough, D. R., & Kapp, S. A. (1962). *Psychological differentiation: Studies of development.* New York: Wiley.

Wright, J. (1986). E-Mail and voice-mail systems: Conspirators or competitors? *Infosystems, 6,* 74–76.

Wynne, B. E., & Dickson, G. W. (1976). Experienced managers' performance in experimental man-machine decision system simulations. *Academy of Management Journal, 18,* 25–40.

Zajonc, R. B. (1960). The process of cognitive tuning in communication. *Journal of Abnormal and Social Psychology, 61,* 159–167.

Zeller, A. (1950). An experimental analogue of repression II. The effect of individual failure and success on memory measured by relearning. *Journal of Experimental Psychology, 40,* 411–412.

Zmud, R. W. (1979). Individual differences and MIS success: A review of the empirical literature. *Management Science, 25,* 966–979.

Zoltan, E. (1981). How acceptable are computers to professional persons. *Proceedings of conference on Human Factors in Computer Systems* (pp. 74–77). Gaithersburg, MD.

Zoltan, E., & Chapanis, A. (1982). What do professional persons think about computers? *Behavior and Information Technology, 1,* 55–68.

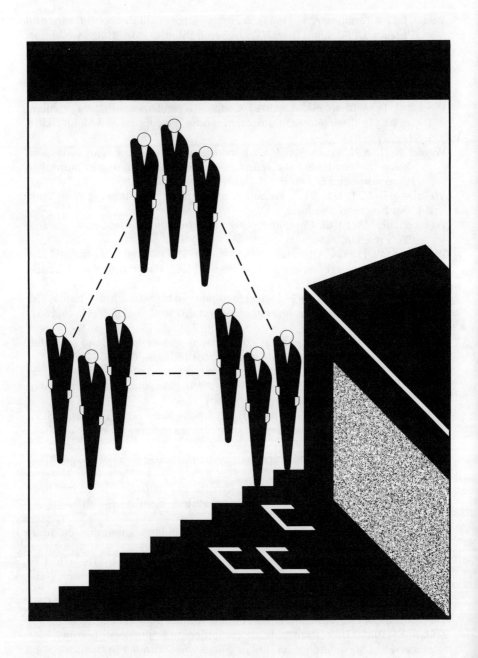

chapter 3
Organizational Influences and Theories

Efforts to improve organizational efficiency and effectiveness have become increasingly popular in American corporations. Such interests are fueled by increased competition from multiple vendors, the threat of foreign companies usurping traditionally U.S. dominated markets, and the public's declining confidence in corporate management. Numerous books and articles have discussed strategies for enhancing organizational excellence, changing the corporate culture and comprehending the mysteries of Japanese management. Although readers of this popular literature have welcomed any suggestions that will improve their corporate image and make them more productive, it is often difficult to determine which strategy is most appropriate. Moreover, because different authors emphasize different issues, it is difficult to place recommended changes into a usable framework.

This chapter provides an *organizational* perspective to the study of human–computer interaction.[1] We review approaches to understanding organizations that are based on theory and supported by empirical evidence. By focusing on established social science theories, the intent is to differentiate the fundamental from the fashionable popular literature. To that end, it is important to note that there is no single theory that will work in every situation. Rather, the theoretical orientations offer alternative frames of reference for judging particular situations. In the context of this book, this chapter bridges the theoretical gap between the individual level variables found in social psychology (Chapter 2) and the situation-context variables employed by anthropology (Chapter 4).

A relationship between organizational structure and human–computer interaction has been suggested by several authors. Some draw a parallel between the structure of computer programs and formal organizations to develop design rules for computer programs (e.g., Malone, 1982). Malone (1985) has also argued that organizational theories can be applied to the design of interfaces, suggesting that organizations

---

[1] For those interested in a more in-depth coverage of organizational theory, Hall (1977), Grusky and Miller (1970), or Silverman (1971) provide particularly good sources of information.

themselves can be seen as end-users. Fox (1981) examined the similarities between organizational theory concepts and a system designed to understand connected speech (Hearsay II). Other researchers (e.g., Lincoln, 1985) have pointed to shifts in organizational theories since the introduction of computers into the workplace. Our own work (Grantham & Vaske, 1985) has found that organizational position is correlated with usage rates of advanced computer technologies. Finally, in a review of current empirical literature, Kling (1980) found distinct organizational perspectives being increasingly used in the analysis of computers.

Organizational context does not explain all of the variance in computer usage patterns, however, it accounts for a significant portion of the variation. Data reported by Bikson and Gutek (1983), for example, show that organizational environment is one of the best predictors of overall satisfaction with new technology. Before examining organization theories and their relationship to human–computer interaction, the nature of all human organizations and the variables used to describe them are reviewed.

THE NATURE OF HUMAN ORGANIZATIONS

Although organizations vary in size and complexity, a number of characteristics are common to all organizations. All "organizations have goals, boundaries, levels of authority, communication systems, coordinating mechanisms and distinctive cultures" (Bolman & Deal, 1984, p. 29). These characteristics are evident in small start-up software firms as well as large multinational conglomerates. For instance, both IBM and a start-up company have a goal of selling computer products. Where they differ is in terms of the number of goals that are pursued. Because of its resources, a corporation the size of IBM may also decide to engage in community service activities and provide scholarships to universities. Financial constraints prevent smaller organizations from such actions even though the members may believe in their worth. All organizations have goals, although the number and type of goals may vary. As a second example, both IBM and start-up firms have levels of authority. In small organizations this chain of command may be short, with a single individual wearing many hats, but the concept is still pertinent.

Two important constructs emerge from these properties of human organizing behavior: *structure* and *function*. Deciding on an appropriate structure is a central concern for any organization. A company's structure may be depicted in terms of lines and boxes on an organizational chart, but structure goes beyond these simple diagrams. Structure influences a corporation's activities and establishes patterns of communications among subdivisions. It also shapes employees' expectations for certain interactions and, in general, influences their attitude toward policies.

All organizations have a structure and perform certain functions. Parsons (1960) and Merton (1957) divide this structural–functional relationship into four categories. In their framework, organizations provide people with mechanisms to:

1. adapt to change in environmental conditions
2. produce things
3. integrate people through networks
4. maintain patterns of interaction over time, through norms of behavior and rituals.

Computers are evident in each of these structural–functional categories. For example, Hebenstreit (1983) discusses the need for coupling the introduction of computer technology into the workplace with training programs to facilitate the process. Word processing, graphics, and database software have been shown to provide individuals with the tools needed for increasing organizational productivity (Buchanan & Boody, 1983; O'Malley, 1986). Electronic mail packages facilitate the growth and integration of both formal and informal social networks (Vaske & Teubner, 1985). Norms defining the appropriate use of this technology function to maintain and encourage such interactions over time (Kiesler, 1986).

In general, these organizational functions parallel the psychological hierarchy of human needs outlined by Maslow (1954) and applied by others (Kaplan, 1976; Fried, 1986). Fried (1986) used Maslow's theory to suggest ways of enhancing user acceptance of integrated office support systems, an approach which reinforces the connection between psychology (the study of the person) and sociology (the study of organizations).

RESEARCHER'S AGENDA

Are the existing computer capabilities meeting the structural and functional needs of the organization?

To what extent can organizational productivity be attributed to the use of computer technology?

What new organizational forms are emerging today as the result of computer technology?

MANAGER'S AGENDA

Social organizational theories provide a frame of reference for evaluating situations. It is important to remember, however, that no single theory will work in every situation.

The introduction and use of computer technology can influence an organization's goals, boundaries, levels of authority, communication systems, coordinating mechanisms, and culture. Understanding the reciprocal relationships between technology and these organizational characteristics can lead to improved decision making.

ORGANIZATION ANALYSIS VARIABLES

Distinct variables have been used to describe organizations. Most organization theories employ these same variables, but vary as to the nature, direction and strength of the predicted variable relationships. The major variables used in organizational analysis are:

Authority and Power
Size and Complexity
Efficiency and Effectiveness
Information
Technology
Environment

The pairing of variables like authority and power stems from previous research (e.g., Perrow, 1968; Blau, 1974) that has consistently found associations among the variables. Individuals who have more authority in an organization are likely to have more power. As organizations increase in size, complexity also tends to increase. Efficient organizations are often effective organizations, although the strength of this relationship varies from one organization to the next. Alternative naming conventions have been employed to identify these variables, such as combining efficiency—effectiveness and labeling the new construct *productivity*.

Authority and Power

Authority is a quality vested in a position which gives the right to obtain, control, and use resources (Etzioni, 1964; French & Raven, 1959; Levine, Carter, & Gorman, 1976). When data processing activities are centralized, the authority to make changes in applications software is vested in the data processing department, not with specific people. Power, on the other hand, is the ability of a person to influence, obtain control, and use resources. While powerful individuals often have authority, power tends to be more subjective and informal than authority (Blau, 1964). Power is evident in organizations where individuals use their personalities to obtain and use resources which would not normally be available to any one individual by sole virtue of rank or position. The concept of power also has a dimension of interdependence. The power a person exerts over another is to some degree a function of the other person's willingness to accept the legitimacy of the relationship (Kling, 1980).

Human factors departments exemplify this interdependence and the general distinction between authority and power. Such departments assist both engineering and marketing groups by recommending design modifications and clarifying the characteristics of users. Conversely, both engineering and marketing rely on human factors personnel to provide answers to user interface questions as they arise. The human factors department may not have the authority to change design, but individuals may effect desired changes if developers and marketing trust the person's judgment.

In computer-using, as opposed to computer-producing, organizations, automated information systems enhance the power of already powerful groups. Danziger (1977) found that computer-based systems increased the power of those who had access to the technology, since they could organize the data to their advantage. Bjorn-Anderson and Pederson (1977) examined the role of production scheduling systems in altering the power among production planners, plant managers, and production managers. Results indicated that production managers, individuals with up-to-date knowledge of the scheduling system, increased their power over the other two groups. This shift in influence occurred despite the fact that no such consequences were intended.

Kraemer and Dutton (1979) investigated the role of automated information systems in altering power relations among key participants in American municipal governments. In each of 42 cities, researchers coded the extent to which actors (e.g., mayor and staff, council members, planners) gained or lost power because of computer-based reports. Results indicated that, in most cities, some participants discernibly gained or lost power as a result of computer use. However, in different cities, different types of actors were gainers and losers. City councilmen were most likely to lose (20%) and rarely gained power (5%). Top-level administrators often gained (27%) and rarely lost power (3%). Planners (direct data custodians), on average, gained the most power, but their position remained relatively weak. Similar observations have been reported by others (Downs, 1967; Kraemer & Dutton, 1979; Kling, 1978a).

Kling (1980) has argued that computer-based information systems reinforce the structure of power in an organization, simply because such systems are expensive to develop and use. Top officials who can authorize such expenditures will ensure that the analyses serve their interests. When there are major conflicts over the control of critical organizational resources, computers serve as political instruments. Albrecht (1979) discusses a tracking system that was introduced by judges on the legal staff in a Southern court to manage the work of the probation staff. The legal staff was concerned about processing cases in an efficient and orderly manner. The probation staff emphasized rehabilitating individuals. When the information system was being designed, each group proposed a reporting structure that minimized its accountability and maximized its authority over the other group. The system that was ultimately installed represented a compromise between the two alternatives. Albrecht interprets these findings as a power struggle between the legal staff and the probation staff, a struggle in which neither group could exert enough influence over the other to force it to submit to their form of measurement and management. Since the data that was produced by the system served no ones needs, it became a sterile tool and was removed.

Size and Complexity

Size represents the number of subdivisions in the organization. Subdivisions may be defined as groups of people, regiments, divisions, or any other appropriate unit (Hall, 1967; Hage, 1965). Counts of the number of people employed in a particular unit (e.g., marketing, engineering, human factors, etc.), or the number of operating units, are measures of organizational size. Complexity refers to the pattern of interconnections among subdivisions of an organization (Hall, 1967; Hage & Aiken, 1967). Complexity can also be viewed as the web of communication among organizational subunits. A complex organization is likely to have formal communication channels between marketing, software development, testing, and human factors. In a less complex organization, these channels of communication are commonly informal or unstructured. Danziger and Dutton (1977) examined the role of institutional needs and the social features within and outside of American local governments to predict the rates at which they would adopt computing applications. Results indicated that governmental size and complexity accounted for about half of the explained variance in computing adoption.

Efficiency and Effectiveness

Efficiency refers to the rate at which goods are produced *inside* the organization (Etzioni, 1964; Hall, 1967). One measure of the efficiency of a software engineering group is the ratio of person-hours worked to lines of code produced. Effectiveness is the ratio of goods produced within the organization and those sold in the *external* environment (Georgopoulos & Tannebaum, 1957). Effectiveness can be measured by the ratio of market size to the number of application packages sold. Human factors specialists influence efficiency when their recommendations help engineers and marketing focus on the most desirable alternatives. Effectiveness is facilitated by human factors when studies of user groups identify new market niches.

The impact of computers on organizational efficiency and effectiveness is difficult to address, because the relationship is dependent on the criteria used to measure success. Systems that perform well according to a narrow efficiency criteria may be problematic when viewed more broadly. Conversely, computerized systems that seem ineffective when evaluated with respect to a narrow criteria of internal efficiency may be of substantial value to their users in the larger context of social relations. Kling's (1978b) study of a welfare agency showed that computers did little to improve the internal efficiency of the organization, but greatly improved the agency's image as an efficient administration, a perception that increased the organization's ability to attract new funding. In other words, because others perceived the agency as efficient, it could be effective. Whatever the relationship, researchers (Lucas, 1975; Kraemer, Dutton, & Northrup, 1980) note that efficiency and effectiveness gains attributed to the use of computers should be empirical findings rather than a priori assumptions.

Information

The evaluation of computer based information systems is a complex problem because information plays a key role in any organization (Hopwood, 1983). *Information* has been defined as a measure of reduction in uncertainty (Buckley, 1967; Maruyama, 1963; Weiner, 1948), but the concept is broader than this definition. Information delineates organizational structures, the responsibilities of particular units, the nature of managerial authority, and associated positions of power. Flows of information disseminate organizational goals and missions, define linkages between organizational units, and assist the coordination and integration of the complicated interactions between specialized tasks. The major operational indicators of information flow are:

Input/output.   Input/Output variables define what goes into a system and what comes out (Boulding, 1968). Marketing, for example, may receive input from customers regarding desired features in a given electronic mail facility. This input is translated by developers into enhanced functionality in the next release (i.e., the output). Information flow when viewed from this perspective is similar to the engineering concepts of *signal* and *noise*. Signal variables are those software enhancements which serve to differentiate the product from the competition in some positive manner. Noise indicators are those modifications which result in changes to the existing release, but do not necessarily improve the quality of the product or the number of subsequent sales. Sorting through these signal and noise variables is primarily a marketing function, but one that may be facilitated by input from development or by systematic data collection efforts.

Feedback/feedthrough/feedforward.   These terms, borrowed from information theory, refer to the path information flow takes in an organization. Their directional nature suggests that the analysis is relative to the perspective of the observer (Bogart, 1980). Expanding on the software development example, *feedback* may be represented by information from customers about what they like or dislike about the software. *Feedthrough* is the cycle of information coming in, moving to developers, and resulting in changes in the next release of the software. *Feedforward* is illustrated by the changes visible to customers such as a streamlined menu structure, additional functionality, or improved documentation.

Social network analysis.   A social network is a structural description of who talks to whom, about what, when, and how (Grantham, 1982). Computerized communication channels are suggested to influence both social network structures and information flow. In a case study of a voice store-and-forward system, Ehrlich and Akiba (1986) show that the technology enhanced communication networks by eliminating the time dependency problems and increasing the quality of the message. Trauth, Kwan, and Barber (1984) found the use of electronic messaging resulted in improved information flow. Some individuals are more willing to discuss issues through electronic mediums than they are in person-to-person conversations (Aronson, 1971; Beattie, 1971), thus facilitating the flow of information.

Although these investigations are beginning to shed light on the impact of electronic communications on social networks, much remains unknown (Eveland & Bikson, 1986). Their study of electronic mail usage in the Rand Corporation raises a number of practical issues. For example, the results did not support the anticipated growth pattern in system usage (i.e., initial surge attributed to novelty effects, followed by a decline and then steady growth). Rather, the aggregate findings from the Rand users show a slow and irregular pattern of usage. Also contrary to common belief, the electronic messaging system did·not stimulate significant changes in the social communication norms and patterns of interaction. Research professionals used the system to inter- act with individuals in their own departments, but not necessarily with those in other research programs or administrative functions. Taken together, these findings demonstrate that providing access to technolo- gy is, by itself, not a sufficient condition for promoting cross corporate system usage.

Technology

There appears to be little doubt that office technology impacts informa- tion flow and organizational change (Hopwood, 1983; Gabel, 1986). Word processors influence the ease with which memos can be created and edited. Spreadsheet programs allow for the systematic exploration of "what if" alternatives in planning budgets, while business graphics applications facilitate the presentation of data. The relationship be- tween technology and organizational structure, however, is not yet well understood (Robey, 1977; Buchanan & Boody, 1983). When personal computers are introduced into an office, professional workers often assume many of the clericals' duties (Bjorn-Anderson, 1983; Wynne, 1983). If the manager or executive is at least a marginally competent typist, composing a memo on the screen is faster than dictating the letter to the secretary, having it typed, proofing the copy, and waiting for the final version.

This shift in what people do and what they delegate raises practical questions for any organization. For example, are such activities a wise use of the professional's time and the company's resources? Both pro and con arguments have been suggested (Gabel, 1986). Including the clerical in the writing–rewriting loop might result in a 2-day turn- around for the final memo. If the professional can produce the same memo in a couple of hours, the information flow is faster and the company benefits. Moreover, in corporations concerned with produc- ing office technology, managers who use the company's own products quickly see both the benefits and limitations of the software, observa- tions which can directly influence future enhancements because of their direct link to the development process. On the negative side, a professional's productivity may decline if the person becomes enam- ored with tinkering with alternative fonts or page layouts and never gets the memo produced. It is because of these practical issues that an analysis of technology as a distinct characteristic of organizations is necessary.

Environment

Bolman and Deal (1984) define *environment* as "everything outside the boundaries of the organization" (p. 44). The environment provides the raw materials and information that the organization needs to stay in existence. Depending on the organization, raw materials may range from components provided by original equipment manufacturers (OEMs) to requests from customers for a particular product. It is also the environment that receives the organization's output and the arena in which the organization must compete for a market share with other organizations.

Other theorists and researchers focus upon the relationships between conditions in the organization's task environment and its structure (Lawrence & Lorsch, 1967; Thompson, 1967; Robey, 1977). The term *task environment* is defined in terms of environmental components which influence the organizations ability to achieve desired goals (Dill, 1958). Factors such as customers, competitors, and supplies are included in the analysis.

An organization's environment has been shown to vary along several dimensions. Thompson (1967) examines the importance of stability and degree of homogeneity. Scott (1981) discusses the dimensions of uncertainty and dependence. As environments move from homogeneous to heterogeneous and from stable to dynamic, uncertainty increases and the organization becomes more dependent on influences outside of its direct control. Organizations in high technology industries continually deal with uncertain environments where success or failure depends on the attitudes of customers and the competition's product line. State-of-the-art products quickly become out of date because the environment is unstable and diverse.

Robey (1977) reviews the impact of computers on the centralization versus decentralization of the organization's structure. Four positions are offered: (a) computers increase centralization, (b) computers increase decentralization, (c) computers have no effect, and (d) computer impact on an organization's structure is moderated by other influences. When the organization exists in relatively stable, homogeneous, and predictable environments, computer usage is associated with centralization. Studies of life insurance companies (Delehanty, 1967; Whisler, 1970), the American Airlines SABRE system (Gallagher, 1961), and gas utility companies (Rief, 1968) all support this observation. In these situations, however, computers did not lead to increased centralization because the organizations were already highly centralized. Rather, computers facilitated the existing organizational structure.

Other studies show that computers are associated with decentralization. In contrast to Rief's (1968) investigation of a gas utility company which showed a correlation between centralization and computers, Wagner's (1966) study of a natural gas utility in Nebraska found that the introduction of computers did not change the organization's decentralization philosophy. Schultz and Whisler (1960) and Stewart (1971) report similar findings in studies of large international oil companies. Computers in these organizations were used for specific applications (e.g., a personnel system and linear programming models), where a decentralized structure was appropriate for the environmental constraints. Based on this evidence, it seems that computers can facilitate either centralized or decentralized structures depending on the environment in which the organization operates (Robey, 1977).

The relationship between computerization and an organization's environment is difficult to predict, because computers perform different functions (Kling, 1978c; Butera & Bartezzaghi, 1983) and because different parts of the same organization face different environments (Bolman & Deal, 1984). The customer–supplier relationship, for example, differs for marketing, accounting, software engineering, and human factors. Each of these organizational units may use computers, but the influence of technology varies because of environmental requirements.

Summary. Organizational theories use the variables authority and power, size and complexity, efficiency and effectiveness, information, technology, and environment to explain the processes and structure within corporations and to identify the effect of organizations on people. While theories emphasize different variables at different times, all theories implicitly or explicitly describe organizations with these constructs.

RESEARCHER'S AGENDA

To what extent and in what ways does computer technology alter power relationships among organizational members?

What types of computer applications are most appropriate for organizations of different size and complexity?

Researchers have argued that efficiency and effectiveness gains attributed to the use of computers should be empirical findings rather than a priori assumptions. At issue is what operational criteria should be used to measure the constructs for a given situation.

To what extent do computerized communication channels influence social network structures and information flow?

Under what circumstances do electronic messaging systems stimulate changes in an organization's social communication norms and patterns of interaction?

Given the proliferation of personal computers, professional workers often assume more clerical duties (e.g., typing their own memos). Has this change in work patterns increased or decreased the flow of information through the organization?

What is the relationship between technology and organizational structure?

Under what conditions do computers increase the centralization of an organization's structure? Under what conditions do computers increase the decentralization of an organization's structure?

What is the relationship between computerization and an organization's environment?

MANAGER'S AGENDA

Organizational theories are pathways for research; not answers to questions.

An organization's goals, structure, technology, and environment are mutually interdependent variables.

Organizational structures should not be altered without first examining the underlying social processes that will be affected.

THEORIES OF SOCIAL ORGANIZATIONS

Sociological theories of organizations differ somewhat from other approaches in the social sciences. In contrast to cognitive or social psychology where empirical data are routinely generated to test theories, examination of variable relationships in organizational theories is more difficult to explore quantitatively (Cook & Campbell, 1976). This does not imply that systematic study is unfeasible, nor does it suggest that empirical support is impossible. Rather, the point is that the control of variables extraneous to any given theory poses a larger methodological problem. Laboratory experiments cannot be set up to determine which companies will succeed and which will fail under different management structures. Even field studies are difficult, because successful corporations are sometimes reluctant to share information that will weaken their competitive edge. Less successful organizations may react negatively to participation in scientific studies for fear of bad publicity.

For these reasons, organizational theories and research concentrate more on general, observable trends than on the magnitude of correlations among variables.

Organization theories are concerned with structure (Inkeles, 1964; Ball, 1978). *Structure* here means a measurable, consistent pattern of communication between individuals. Organizational studies have traditionally focused on how these patterns of interactions affect the organization, however, organizations are also powerful influences on peoples' attitudes and behaviors. An organization can provide employees with access to computers, and thereby enhance their communication opportunities. The employees' attitude toward and usage of the technology, however, influences the organization's effectiveness and efficiency. Such relationships vary considerably because there are systemic limits to how effective people and technologies are in creating change. Discussions of organizational theories constantly return to this frame of reference, because the mutually interactive association between people and organizations is the keystone of sociology.

Social organizational theory development is embedded in a long history. We discuss three major theories roughly in order of their historical development: (a) the structuralist approach, (b) the human relations school, and (c) open systems theory. The present state of organizational theory is the result of years of research, incorporating a broad spectrum of ways of evaluating organizations. These theories provide a basic understanding of the organization as it influences the study of human–computer interaction.

THE STRUCTURAL APPROACH

The structural approach emphasizes the importance of formal roles and relationships (Bolman & Deal, 1984). Structures are created through policies designed to coordinate organizational activities and assign responsibilities to particular management hierarchies. The ordering of authority structures permits role differentiation and increases specialization. Relationships between roles are created by structures which perpetuate existing rules of action and restrict access to information. Because organizations are complex and evolve over time, an organization's structure needs to be flexible enough to accommodate changes in the ways members interact with each other and their environment. As computer technologies alter the way organizations function, the importance of this latter point increases. In situations where the structure does not fit the needs of the organization, some form of action is necessary to correct the mismatch.

The structuralist's view of organizations is represented by two schools of thought. The first can be labeled *scientific management* and stems from the work of industrial psychologists concerned with maximizing efficiency. Frederick Taylor's (1911) time-and-motion studies, for example, were based on the premise that organizational efficiency can be improved by first understanding the tasks workers perform and then changing those behaviors that do not result in maximum payoff. The second branch of structuralist thought began with the work of Max Weber (1947), who was primarily interested in analyzing large, complex social organizations. This work and subsequent research (e.g., Parsons, 1960; Blau & Scott, 1962) sought to conceptualize an ideal form of organization that maximized rationality.

Through the construction of an ideal organization model, the most rational management structure could be identified. Comparing the ideal type against reality highlights discrepancies for corrective action.

The Bureaucracy of Max Weber

Weber wrote at a time when patriarchal organizations dominated by a single father figure were being replaced by formal organizations. The metaphor he coined, *bureaucracy*, to describe organizations identified seven characteristics of formal organizations:

1. Decisions are made on a rational means-ends basis.
2. Authority is arrayed in hierarchical fashion.
3. Status and power are ascribed to positions, not persons.
4. Fixed rules govern the decision making process.
5. Organizational power comes from knowledge of the rules.
6. Definitive career patterns of promotion exist.
7. Written materials are maintained in files and exist as permanent records.

Bureaucracies of the past were built on the premise that the most rational and efficient form of decision making occurs when policies are formulated at the top level and implemented at lower levels of the organization (Crozier, 1983). Studies of innovative organizations have found that this top-down approach is not always the most rational, because individuals at all organizational levels can effect change (Kanter, 1972). Today's scholars build upon Weber's work by distinguishing between *calculative* (traditional Weberian) and *generative* rationality (Westrum, 1984).

Calculative rationality is found in production environments where the rules for acceptable behavior and the methods for accomplishing tasks are based on the efficiency goals. Such environments tend to be relatively stable, promote standardized operating techniques, and have established procedures for implementing change. This rationality is the driving force behind the desire for automated software production (Shneiderman, 1980) and is evident in the growing popularity of robots. Apple Computer, for example, used robots to replace about 80% of its manufacturing workforce in the production of the Macintosh computer.

Generative rationality is characteristic of a product development group where the goal is to create or invent technologies. Rapid prototyping is an example of generative rationality (Wasserman & Shewmake, 1985). There is a rational, systematic process operating, but the results are often unpredictable. The interface that is ultimately implemented may differ dramatically from the initial design.

It is also apparent that interface designers and users sometimes employ different types of rationality in their approach to computers. Hammond, Jorgensen, MacLean, Barnard, and Long (1983) interviewed five software designers on aspects of user interface design. Results indicated that the designers tended to be focused on the logical structure (calculative rationality) of the task interface, whereas the users were focused on the psychological components of the task (generative rationality). The software developers were primarily concerned with correctly programming the computer to perform tasks, while the end-users were mainly interested in getting the task completed with a minimal amount of effort.

Another defining characteristic of Weber's bureaucracy argues for a hierarchical ordering of authority. Two distinct types of authority structures can be identified: traditional and charismatic. Traditional authority is best seen in terms of long established, "we have always done it this way" companies such as IBM. Charismatic authority stems from the power of the individual and is common in entrepreneurial companies such as Apple Computer.

The study of authority structures is difficult because organizations rarely have a single pure authority structure. This is evident from two perspectives. First, authority structures evolve over time. During 1985, for example, a charismatic authority type directed Apple in the person of Steven Jobs. A traditional authority structure was also emerging at this time in new management figures who had been brought in to move the company from a high growth to a stable market environment. This traditional structure became more powerful, and the charismatic leader who started the process was deposed in late 1985. Second, different authority structures can coexist at the same time in a single organization. A structure found in the computer science department may differ dramatically from that found in the president's office of the same university.

Computers can influence each of the defining characteristics of bureaucracies. Access to computer technology may bypass traditional organizational structures through the use of shared data files and the blurring of jurisdictional boundaries. Since information is stored on mass storage devices, executives who have traditionally controlled access to vital information can be replaced by people who understand how to manipulate information processing technology. If organizational power and promotion opportunities come from knowledge of the rules for using information, and access to this information is gained through a position and not a person, knowledge of computer systems can circumvent traditional power structures.

Bureaucracy becomes the most rational and efficient form of mass administration when social relationships are characterized by an administrative staff which perpetuates the organization by creating formal rules of action. Because of this emphasis on formal roles and relationships, bureaucracies are often viewed as rigid monoliths. The structural perspective, however, is not intended to be totally inflexible. Rather, Weber and his followers saw bureaucracy as a mediator between the individual and larger political-economic structures. A social welfare bureaucracy, for example, mediates between the political system and the individual. This mediation of exchange between person and society is based on a belief in rationality and assumes that the right structure can minimize organizational problems.

Bolman and Deal (1984, pp. 31–32) summarize these assumptions of the structural perspective as follows:

1. Organizations exist primarily to accomplish established goals.
2. For any organization, there is a structure appropriate to the goals, the environment, the technology, and the participants.
3. Organizations work most effectively when environmental turbulence and the personal preferences of participants are constrained by norms of rationality.
4. Specialization permits higher levels of individual expertise and performance.
5. Coordination and control are accomplished best through the exercise of authority and impersonal rules.
6. Structures can be systematically designed and implemented.
7. Organizational problems usually reflect an inappropriate structure and can be resolved through redesign and reorganization.

An organization's goals, structure, technology, and environment can be considered mutually interdependent variables. Changes in one variable influence the status of others. For example, universities (Brown, Carnegie-Mellon, Drexel, Dartmouth College, and the University of Wisconsin) have shifted from centralized computer resources to distributed workstation environments. This change in technology affects the goals, structure, and environment in which the university functions.

Pallatto (1986) describes the situation at the University of Wisconsin. Before microcomputers arrived on campus, computer resources were concentrated in the Wisconsin Instructional Time-Sharing System (WITS). There were approximately 6400 PCs in use at that time on the Madison campus with the number expected to increase dramatically. With the development of PC networks, the demand for time-sharing services dropped considerably. An advisory committee established to study the status of instructional computing facilities recommended a plan to further supplant much of the existing time-sharing system with an even broader PC-based computer network that provided communication links between the departments. At the core of this plan was a proposal to provide a ratio of one computer for every 10 of the full time Madison students.

Orchestrating such an effort poses organizational problems (Pallatto, 1986). First, the university's mandate to provide high quality education to all qualified residents makes it difficult to require students to purchase their own computer hardware. To expedite their plans, the university established a microcomputer outlet which sells PCs to faculty, staff, and students at low markup. Although such an arrangement provides a valuable service, it places the university in direct competition with local retail establishments and changes the function of the school. Changes in the technology thus added a new goal (i.e., to provide low cost PCs) which influenced the university's environment.

Second, because of the decentralized structure of the university's management, no single committee or department has the authority to dictate a university wide computerization plan. Moreover, because deans and department chairs retain the authority for budgeting money to buy software and hardware, volume discounts and license agreements are difficult to negotiate. The results are that efforts are duplicated and the bureaucracy is less efficient. By introducing a new technology, the decentralized structure needed to be modified to accommodate changes in the goals and environment. The advisory committee's recommendation that the Madison Academic Computing Center (MACC) assume a leadership role in the transition from a time-sharing system to PCs implicitly recognizes the importance of these relationships. The success of the reorganization plan, however, depends on the extent to which individual departments accept MACC's authority.

In general, the introduction and use of PC technology in organizational settings can be characterized as a swinging pendulum. During phase one, microcomputers represent an alternative source of productivity, with little influence on the overall structure of the organization. As their popularity spreads, PCs begin to threaten the viability of existing centralized data processing structures. The next phase is the co-opting of the new technology through the exercise of traditional authority over fiscal and personal resources. The final outcome of this shifting balance of power between formal and informal structures has yet to be determined. It appears, however, that the balance between existing centralized structures and decentralized computer networks will shift back and forth as newer technologies continue to be introduced in organizations.

The Scientific Management Perspective

By describing organizations in terms of their formal roles and relationships, Weber set the stage for the scientific management approach to administration. Proponents of this perspective hold that certain principles can be discovered by quantifying an organization's structure and function (Perrow, 1972; Mouzelis, 1968). Similar to engineering and economics, emphasis is placed on the reduction of complex behaviors to mathematical equations. Frederick Taylor's (1911) time/motion studies, for example, attempted to understand the diversity of activities an individual performs by dissecting behaviors into discrete identifiable units of analysis. From this perspective, scientific management compliments Weber's thinking by providing a quantitative analysis of the ideal-type concept.

A variety of schools of thought can be included in this perspective: scientific management (Taylor, 1911), management by objective (MBO), cooperative management (Barnard, 1938), and the transactions cost approach (Ouchi, 1980). Each of these frameworks stress efficiency in the work place through increased production and maximum use of employees. IBM's Charlie Chaplin and MASH TV characters exemplify the approach.

To achieve this maximum efficiency, workers must accept the organization's goals and comply with management's directives (Barnard, 1938; Etzioni, 1961). Employee compliance with the formal regulations is suggested to increase the organization's profit and to result in more pay for the worker. Individuals who receive more pay are predicted to increase their performance and be more satisfied (Taylor, 1911; Tausky, 1977). It follows from this logic that workers should embrace computer technologies that help them become more productive and the company

more profitable. The weakness in this argument occurs when computers displace workers and anxiety about job security rises (Flaherty,
1986).

Organizational studies based on the scientific management perspective frequently employ econometric models as a primary analytical tool
(March & Simon, 1958) Greenberger, Crenson, and Crissey (1976) studied the role of econometric models in such diverse tasks as developing
U.S. fiscal policy for simulating the "limits to growth" and an operations research model for locating fire stations in New York. Results
indicated that policy makers were rarely directly influenced by model
based analyses. Rather, the models were used to generate support for
policies selected in advance. The failure of these models to influence
policy can be traced to the simplifying assumptions underlying any
econometric approach.

The scientific management approach assumes that differences in
social settings are inconsequential in the use or utility of analytical
models (Licklider & Vezza, 1978). Studies have shown, however, that
the conditions under which computers are adopted are strongly influenced by social setting (Danziger & Dutton, 1977; Greenberger et al.,
1976; Kling, 1974, 1978a, 1978c; Rule, 1974). Computer usage is influenced by both technical benefits and bureaucratic politics (Keen, 1975;
Kling, 1974, 1978c; Laudon, 1974). When computer systems serve as
political instruments, the management scientists emphases on rationality and efficiency become less important.

Other assumptions inherent to the scientific management perspective include:

1. Behavioral choices stem from a desire to obtain the maximum
    award possible.
2. Participants are cognizant of and understand all of their options.
3. Individuals have the ability to prioritize actions.
4. All costs and benefits can be accurately measured.
5. If the relevant variables can be identified and described in mathe-
    matical terms, the social system can be manipulated by changing
    equation parameters and varying system inputs.

Violation of these assumptions introduces uncertainty in the model.
For example, the managerial perspective predicts a direct correlation
between a software developer's paycheck and the number of lines of
code produced. When individuals do not believe this relationship is
valid (i.e., an uncertainty in the model), their behavior is more difficult
to predict given a certain level of pay. The prediction also assumes that
the best award possible is increased pay. Studies by Perrow (1972) have

cast doubt on this direct correlation between pay and satisfaction, especially in innovative companies where the emphasis is on creativity rather than routine tasks. In these situations, Deci (1975) shows that intrinsic motivations (e.g., the desire to develop a quality user interface) often outweigh extrinsic motivations (e.g., pay).

The assumptions regarding participant awareness of all options and their ability to prioritize actions are also questionable. Computers increase the amount of information that is available to decision makers, but unless the data are organized and presented simply, the impact is minimal. This suggests that, although individuals can prioritize their actions, decisions are based on suboptimal certainty. Simon (1977) has argued that for most important decisions, comprehensive knowledge about the costs and benefits of alternative lines of action are too costly and time consuming to obtain, and that decision makers must select satisfactory but suboptimal choices. Each of these considerations, coupled with the difficulty of accurately measuring all relevant variables, weakens the application of mathematical models inherent to the scientific management approach.

Scientific management theories tend to be more successful in a closed system where the relationships among resource inputs and finished products follow predictable patterns of development. For example, studies of systems running routine operations such as traffic ticket processing show that computers do improve efficiency (Colton, 1978; Kraemer et al., 1980). In work groups where cooperation among individuals is necessary for task completion or where innovation is key, scientific management techniques have more limited applications. Corporations concerned with producing advanced computer technologies stretch the limits of scientific management applications. As the pace of innovation increases, the need for coordination among marketing, engineering, and human factors increases. When research and development cycles become longer than the normal half-life of the product, determining which designs should become products is not a perfectly rational process and hence not subject to scientific management.

Applying the Structural Perspective

Despite the limitations, a structural perspective to the study of organizations does offer advantages. First, because organizations are complex, diverse, and specialized, it is difficult to identify the most appropriate structure for the organization. Weber's approach to bureaucracy facilitates such efforts by making explicit those properties (e.g., goals, technology, environment) of an organization which influence its structure and function. The complexities of reality are reduced to a more manageable subset for analysis by practitioners or researchers. The mathematical models employed by scientific management carry this thinking further by quantifying the relationships between structural elements.

Second, because almost all organizations reorganize, recognition of why the restructuring was needed helps decision makers plan a rational course of action. Bolman and Deal (1984) identify five reasons organizations modify their structure:

1. Organizations grow
2. Changes in political climate
3. Changes in environment
4. Changes in technology
5. Changes in leadership

Growth affects an organization's structure. Apple Computer shifted from a charismatic authority structure to a traditional authority structure in an effort to move from a high growth to a stable market environment. At Digital Equipment Corporation (DEC), Kenneth Olsen has been the guiding force for the last 30 years, yet the impact of growth is clearly evident on the organization's structure (Petre, 1986). Olsen's strategy has been to develop a series of minicomputers that use the same operating system coupled with a communication system to speed the flow of information. Corporations that had purchased Digital computers for their factories also bought DEC equipment for their office, because the smaller models could communicate across the product line. This approach allowed Digital to carve out a sizable portion of the overall computer market. As DEC grew into a multibillion-dollar organization, the flexible and informal structure which had characterized the corporation's early years developed into formal rules and hierarchies of authority. This company-wide reorganization affected all levels of the corporation as is evidenced by the departure of some of the company's best-known and promising executives (Petre, 1986). Similar structural changes occurred at Wang Laboratories. What started as a sole proprietorship evolved into a formal structure as the organization became a leader in office automation.

Apple, DEC, and Wang grew because they had successfully followed a strategy which opened new market niches. Other companies grow by consolidating resources. Computer industry participants, for example, have reacted to increased competition in the marketplace by cooperating on joint projects. The Department of Defense's VHSIC (Very High Speed Integrated Circuit) program was one of the first cooperative R&D efforts to bring together industry sponsors (Allison, 1986). DARPA (Defense Advanced Research Project Agency) is another long standing DOD funded program that sponsors research into artificial intelligence.

In addition, two private corporations have been established in the U.S. to encourage collaboration. The first was the Semiconductor Research Corporation (SRC), established to extend knowledge in semiconductor-related areas by funding university research. The second was the Microelectronics and Computer Corporation (MCC), which was created to consolidate the research dollars of the participating organizations. The member companies recognized that, individually, their limited resources did not permit the funding of basic research which is necessary to maintain a competitive edge.

Slumps in the computer industry have also facilitated organizational growth through merger, the marriage of Burroughs and Sperry into Unisys being one example. Growth through merger, however, occurs in good times as well as bad. In 1970, Honeywell Inc. recognized the influence computers would have on its control-system capabilities. To enhance its computing potential and marketing opportunities, Honeywell purchased General Electric's Information Systems group. The two companies complemented each other's strengths. Honeywell provided a successful marketing organization, while GE provided technological and production expertise. The merger also created a comprehensive product line. Through this single acquisition, Honeywell added GE's large mainframes, the Italian Olivetti small computer, and the French Bull GE mid-size computer to its own mid-range computer line. Finally, the two companies complemented each other in terms of geographic concentration. Honeywell marketed in North America, while GE was active in Europe.

In summary, three distinct channels for organizational growth have been identified: (a) identification of new market niches, (b) consolidation of resources, and (c) merger. Regardless of the technique employed, increasing the size of a corporation alters the structure of the organization. Sometimes this change is manifested by shifts in the authority structure (e.g., charismatic to traditional management hierarchies). Other times, the existing management structure remains in place, but the rules for conducting business become more formalized. In the case of consolidation of resources, organizational growth necessitates changes in the philosophical structure of the corporation. When cooperation with competitors makes survival essential, traditional beliefs about proprietary information must be realigned. If growth occurs through merger, domestic markets can be expanded to international environments, and the structure for coordinating activities becomes more complex. Consistent with the structuralists emphasis on rationality, these examples illustrate that organizations modify their structure to compensate for changes in the goals, technology, and environment.

Changes in the political climate are another major reason organizations restructure. The agreement that allowed Honeywell to acquire Bull GE changed when a new French government nationalized the computer industry. Controlling interest over 66% of the organization's shares was reduced to 19%. More recently, the threat of Japanese domination has invoked national and international responses. The Common Market has established two major projects—ESPRIT and Eureka—to encourage members to cooperate on high technology projects. Although worthwhile in spirit, each project is "susceptible to political squabbling, uncertain funding and diffuse objectives" (Allison, 1986). Similarly, the U.S.–Japanese semiconductor agreement to prevent the dumping of electronic chips in the United States sounds rational on the surface. As witnessed by the steel, auto, and textile industries, however, protectionist policies do not always result in the intended outcome.

Environmental changes also effect an organization's structure, as is evident in the case of AT&T (American Telephone and Telegraph). Shifting the environment from regulation to competition resulted in a total revamping of the Bell System. Finally, examples provided throughout this section illustrate that changing the technology or the leadership results in a restructuring of the organization.

The structural perspective recognizes that there is no one best way to organize. Rather, the structure must be tailored to meet the existing situation. Hard working, talented people will not be effective if the structure imposes roadblocks to their productivity. By changing the structure, the overall effectiveness of an organization's members can be increased. For this reason, structural consultants typically explain organizational problems in terms of structural characteristics:

1. overload
2. excessive interdependence or excessive autonomy
3. too many meetings
4. too few or too many rules
5. diffuse authority
6. structure/technology mismatch
7. structure/environment mismatch

Overload.   When the organization's structure imposes unrealistic deadlines, creative and innovative activities are at best difficult. Computer manufacturing firms continually confront this problem because of the pace of technological change. Software developers faced with the pressures of meeting the next release date have tended to concentrate on getting the functionality to work and de-emphasize how the interface appears to the ultimate user. If human factors specialists are requested to address several interface design problems simultaneously, the probability of overlooking critical flaws increases exponentially.

Excessive interdependence or excessive autonomy. When an organization dictates that all activities must be approved at each level in the authority hierarchy, coordinating activities becomes difficult. As computer technologies increase the pace of organizational change, the time span between an issue arising and action being taken is shortened. To be effective, some slippage in the organization's formal operating procedures is necessary. Conversely, when the linkages between units are too loose, integrating efforts is equally difficult.

There are too many meetings. A typical response to the problems associated with excessive autonomy is to hold a meeting to inform those who are affected. Carried to an extreme, an organization's members may find that their entire day is spent in one long continuous meeting. Productivity declines, because the structure does not facilitate work.

There are too few or too many rules. If the guidelines for accomplishing tasks are only loosely defined, it is difficult for individuals to know which approach should be followed. Specifying that an interface should be consistent and easy to use are common guidelines given to software developers. Many software engineers recognize the importance of conforming to these rules but are unsure of when the objectives have been met. A solution is to explicitly state the rules for interface design for all to follow, but even here problems can arise. In corporations where products have been evolving over time, developers must address the issue of compatibility with previous releases. Compatibility may mean that radical interface design changes are sometimes not possible. In other situations where the goal is to integrate the software (e.g., word processing, graphics, and images), a design that is appropriate for one application may be inconsistent with another. If the developers' management structure recognizes this diversity, arguments over consistency for consistency sake are avoided.

Diffuse authority. As organizations increase in size and complexity, the responsibility for performing tasks can be lost. A human factors department may be theoretically responsible for the design of user interfaces. If this authority has not been structurally mandated through sign-off responsibility or some other formal mechanism, the department's ability to fulfill the function is limited. This seems especially likely in organizations where interface issues have traditionally received minor attention or where the human factors department represents a relatively new unit in the company. In recent years, market pressures for easy to use and consistent/integrated interfaces have increased the number of human factors departments (Grimes, Ehrlich, & Vaske, 1986). Establishing such organizational units without the structural linkages to other divisions is unlikely to result in the desired software improvements.

Structure/technology mismatch. Mismatches between structure and technology occur at all levels of an organization. Because of their position, executives are typically the first to receive the latest technological innovations. Yet a 1986 survey of 100 top level executives revealed that more than half never used the technology (Call, 1986). The reasons range from a lack of time to learn the hardware and software, to a general perception that the technology is for support personnel. This situation may change as the next generation of computer literate professionals are promoted, but for the moment, a mismatch between structure and technology exists for many managers.

Similar mismatches occur in the clerical ranks. Today's word processing software offers a broad spectrum of functionality, ranging from simple editors to sophisticated desktop publishing packages. The former tend to be easy to learn but limited in their ultimate capabilities. The latter provide a full range of functionality but have a steeper learning curve, and, more importantly, may contain features that inhibit productivity because of the number of options available. Frustration sets in when the user changes one parameter and the system modifies other variables which the user did not want changed.

As a final example, software development groups often suffer from the "shoemaker's children" syndrome. Just as the shoemaker's children are the last to receive new shoes, software developers are in some companies the last group to get new hardware and software. Computer organizations reason that it is better to sell products than to give employees the latest technology where there is no direct profit margin. While this rationale appears logical, problems arise when developers make design decisions based on dated technology. Working from structural theory, a consultant might argue that it is more rational for the organization to provide its developers with the latest hardware/software to avoid inconsistencies in the logic of human–computer interaction.

Structure/environment mismatch. Honeywell Inc., best known for its dominance in the thermostat and control systems industry, has traditionally had little trouble with competitors. When Honeywell's Information Systems (HIS) Division was created through the acquisition of General Electric's Information Systems group, the organization's environment changed dramatically. Rather than dominating the competition, the company struggled to find an identity alongside corporations such as IBM, DEC, and Wang which had had a strong presence in office automation for years. The organization's structure was not equipped to cope with the new environment. To correct this mismatch, a new company—Honeywell Bull—was created, consisting of HIS, Groupe Bull in France, and NEC in Japan. A goal of this action was to make product sourcing as efficient as possible and to allow all three companies to compete more effectively in the world market.

Summary—The Structural Approach

By focusing on organizational context and making explicit those variables which influence a corporation's structure and function, the structuralist perspective facilitates an understanding of organizations. Placed in historical context, Weber's overriding emphasis on rationality was a necessary transition away from the idiosyncratic tendencies of the then dominant patriarchal organizations. Through the construction of an ideal form of organization, problems stemming from structural constraints could be identified. The scientific management school, which can be characterized as neo-Weberian, sought to lend rigor to organizational analysis by incorporating explicit measurement tools (e.g., econometric models).

Although these structural approaches are appropriate when analyzing routine tasks, both have been found wanting in certain respects. First, explanations offered by structural consultants tend to be descriptive of what has happened in the past rather than predictive of the future. In situations where the technology and environment change rapidly, predictive models are less effective. Second, not all organizational problems stem from structural issues. Structuralists forget that restructuring will not be effective if the rank and file do not support the new alignments. Meyer, Scott, and Deal (1981), for example, show that structure has little effect on the activities engaged in by the members of an organization. Third, because of the exclusive emphasis on rationality, the structural framework fails to account for noneconomic rewards, extraorganizational influences, and the subjective side of behavior. These variables are central to the human relations school, which is examined next.

RESEARCHER'S AGENDA

How is the structure of an organization influenced by the introduction and use of computers?

Structural theorists identify two types of rationality—calculative and generative. There is some evidence to suggest that interface designers and end-users employee these forms of rationality differently. To what extent can these findings be generalized?

Weber's bureaucracy argues for a hierarchical ordering of authority. Studies of innovative organizations have found that this top-down approach is not always the most rational, because individuals at all organizational levels can effect change. In what ways are computers influencing hierarchical authority structures?

Are computers introducing new forms of organizational structure?

To what extent should the formal and informal role relationships within an organization be embedded in computer systems?

What process and structure implications are associated with the adoption of integrated telecommunication and computer systems?

To what extent do telecommunication systems enhance the effectiveness of the organization?

MANAGER'S AGENDA

An organization's goals, structure, technology, and environment are mutually interdependent. Changes in one variable influence the status of others.

Long term organizational goals are just as important as short run costs.

Because authority structures in an organization evolve over time, the roles computers play in the organization must evolve to compensate for these changes.

Changing technology can modify authority and power relationships within organizations.

Changing technology can influence the efficiency and effectiveness of an organization's structure.

Scientific management theories tend to be more successful in a closed system where the relationships among resource inputs and finished products follow predictable patterns of development.

THE HUMAN RELATIONS SCHOOL

Approximately 10 years after the scientific managers began publishing their recommendations for organizing workers, Elton Mayo initiated a series of studies at the Western Electric Company designed to examine the relationship between worker productivity and working conditions. Although no relationship was found, an interesting finding emerged. During a light-intensity experiment, the researchers noticed that even when the lights were practically turned off, worker productivity increased. This effect (called the Hawthorne effect, after the name of the Western Electric plant) was attributed to the fact that the workers were receiving more attention. These studies marked the beginning of the human relations movement in industry. For the first time, evidence of such variables as worker attitudes, needs, and motivation were shown to influence productivity. No longer was it possible to claim that production was totally a function of organizational structure.

As the name suggests, the human relations model conceived of organizations as social systems in which the attitudes and relationships of workers toward each other and toward the total organization influenced their job output. In contrast to the structuralists' focus on formalized patterns of interaction, the human relations proponents emphasized the importance of informal patterns of communication within an organization (Roethlisberger & Dickson, 1939; Whyte, 1959; Argyris, 1964; Etzioni, 1964). The approach recognizes that people rarely relate to the organization per se; rather, they relate to individuals in the organization in terms of committee members, project members, task teams, etc. Through these interactions, employees develop attitudes toward their fellow workers and the organization as an entity. Such attitudes stimulate either a positive or negative motivation toward job productivity.

Human relations theory stresses improved productivity through better designed reward systems and internalized job satisfaction, as opposed to merely providing better tools (e.g., computers). The goal is to restructure jobs to fulfill basic human needs, provide opportunity for growth and satisfy communication requirements of workers. Computers influence these variables when their usage increases employees' sense of control and mastery of their environment and promotes higher performance standards. When employees fear that the introduction of computers will result in a loss of jobs, computers have a negative impact (Evans, 1983; Flaherty, 1986).

Empirical studies of computing in the work place have been dominated by the human relations perspective (Argyris, 1971; Kling, 1974, 1977, 1978c; Mann & Williams, 1960; Lucas, 1975; Mumford & Banks, 1967; Robey, 1979; Swanson, 1974). Many of the early human factors engineering studies grew out of concerns similar to those of human relations. Ergonomically designed keyboards, monitors and office furniture implicitly focus on the needs of the user. Sociotechnical analyses (to be discussed later) attempt to optimize both human and technical factors in organizational design (Trist, 1981). Others (Swanson, 1974; Kling, 1980) argue that, in addition to being technically correct, the computer systems must meet the needs of the user.

At the heart of these investigations and human relations theory are assumptions regarding the relationship between individuals and organizations:

1. Organizations exist to serve human needs (and humans do not exist to serve organizational needs).
2. Organizations and people need each other. Organizations need the ideas, energy, and talent that people provide, while people need the careers, salaries, and work opportunities that organizations provide.
3. When the fit between the individual and the organization is poor, one or both will suffer: The individual will be exploited or will seek to exploit the organization, or both.
4. When the fit is good between the individual and the organization, both benefit: Humans are able to do meaningful and satisfying work while providing the resources the organization needs to accomplish its mission (Bolman & Deal, 1984, p. 65).

Determination of this goodness of fit between the individual and the organization requires an initial evaluation of the concept of need.

HUMAN NEEDS

It is recognized that individuals have different needs (Maslow, 1954; McGregor, 1960; Argyris, 1964). Some needs are as basic as food, sleep, and air. Other needs relate to psychological constructs such as stress release, self-respect, or acceptance by peers. An organization's ability to satisfy either the basic or higher-order needs of its employees depends, at least partially, on what the individual expects from the organization and the employee's motivations for engaging in the activity.

At a general level, people engage in behaviors with the expectation that their participation will lead to certain rewards (Vroom, 1964). The expectations that people have for a given experience are influenced by individual and environmental factors such as the amount and type of previous experience, the degree of communication with others, situational variables, and personality characteristics (Lawler, 1973). Research related to expectancy theory yields important conclusions for the examination of needs in organizations. First, most people participate in activities to satisfy multiple needs. The range of needs considered has extended from the basic dichotomy of intrinsic versus extrinsic motivations (Deci, 1975) to extensive lists of psychological outcomes or satisfactions (Ives, Olson, & Baroudi, 1983; Jensen, 1983; Baroudi, Olson, & Ives, 1986; Rushinek & Rushinek, 1986). Second, the motivations for engaging in a particular behavior may vary considerably. Certain expectations tend to be associated with particular behaviors, but considerable variation in expectations may be found among individuals engaged in the same behavior, or even within a given individual at different times.

Recognition that individuals have multiple needs is an important but common-sense realization. The more difficult questions concern the identification of needs and the roles that computers play in either helping or hindering individuals to satisfy them. Theories have been proposed to address these questions, although none have been universally accepted. The sections to follow examine four theoretical models common to the organizational literature: (a) Maslow's Hierarchy of Needs, (b) McGregor's Theory X and Theory Y, (c) Argyris' views on personality and organization, and (d) Ouchi's Theory Z.

Maslow's Need Hierarchy Theory

Of the theories describing human needs, Maslow's (1954) theory of motivation has been one of the most influential. The theory starts with the premise that all individuals have multiple needs but recognizes that some needs are more fundamental than others. Maslow categorized needs into a five level pyramid. From "lowest" to "highest," the order is as follows:

1. Physiological Needs (e.g., food, clothing, shelter)
2. Safety Needs (e.g., assurances that the use of VDTs is not associated with cancer)
3. Affiliation and Belonging (e.g., the need to feel associated with a particular community of users)
4. Esteem (e.g., the desire for stable, high evaluations of one's work)
5. Self-actualization (e.g., the desire to become everything that one is capable of becoming).

Each subsequent level is engaged when needs of the previous level are satisfied. For many individuals in the western world, the physiological needs (level 1) of food, clothing, and shelter are no longer major issues. As one moves up the hierarchy, the potential for achieving a particular need decreases. To illustrate this point, Maslow suggested that people on average satisfy 85% of their physiological needs, 70% of the safety needs, 50% in affiliation and belonging needs, 40% in self-esteem, and 10% in self-actualization.

Except for those situations where the loss of a job due to computers threatens a person's ability to provide food, clothing, and shelter, it is difficult to draw a parallel between human–computer interaction and level 1 needs. Instances of the impact of computers on the other needs discussed by Maslow, however, are common in the literature. Matula (1981) compiled a bibliography of 174 references pertaining to job and health safety issues associated with the use of visual display terminals (VDT). Some of these investigations show a positive relationship between VDT usage and the safety concerns (Dainoff, Happ, & Crane, 1981; Laubli, Hunting, & Grandjean, 1981; Mourant, Lakshamanan, & Chantadisai, 1981), while others find no or few effects (Starr, Thompson, & Shute, 1982; Sauter, Gottleib, Jones, Dodson, & Rohrer, 1983). Although the weight of the objective empirical evidence suggests only a minor association at best, as long as people believe there is a negative relationship, computers will have an impact on safety needs.

The effects of technology on Maslow's affiliation and belonging needs are also prevalent. People want to be part of the process of introducing computers. Resistance to new technology is minimized when employees participate in the decision to purchase new hardware and software (Kanter, 1985; Leonard-Barton & Kraus, 1985; Mainiero & De-Michiell, 1986). To be effective, however, employee participation must involve more than simply giving them the opportunity to voice their opinion. The individuals must have an affiliation with the team that is making the decision and believe that their recommendations are being heard. In organizations which have a strong union presence, failure to create this sense of belonging may delay implementation until the concerns of the members are satisfied, or result in a total rejection of the technology.

The need for affiliation and belonging is also evident in computer producing corporations. Keen and Gerson (1977) emphasize the importance of ensuring that the responsibility and ownership of new product lines is shared by designers, managers, and human factors people alike. Our own experiences with implementing standards for software development reinforce their argument. When developers and human factors personnel share the same concerns, the chances of success increase.

The need for self-esteem, level 3 in Maslow's hierarchy, is strongly coupled with the implementation and use of computers. Most managers and professionals are now expected to be computer literate and capable of using a computer. In such an environment, executives who resist using the company's electronic mail facility, or secretaries who refuse to use the word processor, run the risk of losing the esteem of their colleagues. This resistance to using technology has been referred to in a variety of ways: computer phobia (Weinberg & Fuerst, 1984), cyberphobia (Curley, 1983), and technostress (Brod, 1982). Whatever the label, the reason for the anxiety has been attributed to a fear of embarrassment, loss of responsibility, or a general loss of self-esteem (McElhone, 1982; Gardner, Render, Ruth, & Ross, 1985).

Maslow's highest order need—self-actualization—suggests that, having satisfied the lower order needs, people strive to be the best they can be. Unfortunately, since self-actualization is specific to each individual, it is difficult to determine the meaning of this term. How does one know when he or she is self-actualized? Although such a question raises an interesting academic debate, managers need not be excessively concerned about this need level. First, if employees are striving for self-actualization, the organization has, by implication, satisfied all of the lower-order needs (Fried, 1986). Such individuals have sufficient self-motivation to accept and utilize new technology as it is introduced. Second, as noted by Maslow and others (Zaleznick, Christensen, & Rothlisberger, 1958), few individuals fit into this category of self-actualized.

In general, Maslow's ideas on motivation have had an enormous impact on both managers and researchers, primarily because of the theory's intuitive appeal. Describing instances where a need level is either satisfied or inhibited by human–computer interaction, however, does not demonstrate that the theory is right or wrong. Research efforts designed to test the validity of the theory have produced only limited support (Alderfer, 1972). A review by Wahba and Bridwell (1976) shows that none of the past studies verified all of the five levels as independent factors. More typically, the results show that the need categories overlap, with no consistent rank ordering. Despite these limitations, the theory is important because of its impact on the thinking of other theorists (e.g., McGregor, 1960; Argyris, 1964; Ouchi, 1981).

McGregor's Theory X and Theory Y

Among the theories of motivation in organizations, McGregor's (1960) ideas stand out predominantly. Building on Maslow's hierarchy of needs framework, McGregor added the notion that a manager's perception of subordinates influences their responses. From McGregor's perspective, traditional management approaches assume that most people do not like to work, that motivating subordinates can only be achieved by tight controls over their activities, and that employees would rather be told what to do than think for themselves. He labeled this authoritarian view Theory X and suggested that management options ranged from a "hard" to a "soft" version of the theory. The hard version involves coercion, tight controls, threats, and punishment. Worker response to this style of management is typically opposition to directives, reductions in productivity, and obstruction of organizational goals. The soft version of Theory X uses an opposite tact. Managers attempt to satisfy every need and avoid conflict by creating a permissive atmosphere. Although soft management practices may lead to a shallow harmony, it more often results in apathy and indifference.

Some evidence of McGregor's Theory X can be found in the computer literature. Braverman (1974) argues that managers perceive workers as general purpose machines which they operate. Computers represent a managerial strategy to replace unreliable and finicky human machines with more reliable, more productive, and less self-interested electronic machines. He suggests that computerized information systems are organized to routinize white-collar work and weaken the power of lower-level participants in an organization. Consistent with Theory X, these observations exemplify management frameworks designed to control employee activities by restructuring their jobs or reducing their power.

Similarly to our discussion of Maslow, however, citing examples does not validate theory. Most individuals can recall instances where management has entertained the assumptions of Theory X, and, similarly, most of us have witnessed workers whose behavior seemed to validate the assumptions. At this point a cycle emerges which makes the assumptions of Theory X self-fulfilling. People shape their environments, but the environment also shapes their behavior. Argyris (1957) indicates that, if workers are subjected to work environments which are designed to account for Theory X behavior, they will come to behave accordingly.

In opposition to this traditional view of man, McGregor postulated a second set of ideas about motivation in organizations, which he called Theory Y. The assumptions underlying Theory Y are as follows:

1. People do not inherently like or dislike work, but rather develop an attitude toward employment based on past experience.
2. While authoritarian methods do sometimes get things done, they are not the only method available. In addition, there is nothing inevitable about them and their undesirable side effects do not have to be tolerated.
3. People select goals for themselves if they see the possibility of some kind of reward. Having selected a set of goals, employees will pursue them in the same manner as if their superiors were attempting to pressure the same activity.
4. In certain situations, people seek rather than shun responsibility.

In essence, Theory Y says that Theory X is not necessary. It is a plea for flexibility and innovation, but since most management approaches historically favor a singular philosophy of tight control over employees, a move toward flexibility imposes considerable stress on traditional modes of operation. Theory Y aims for an integration of individual goals and organizational goals, rather than the subjugation of one by the other. "The task of management is to arrange organizational conditions so that people can achieve their goals by directing their efforts toward organizational rewards" (McGregor, 1960, p. 61). Examples of strategies for achieving this integration of individual and organizational goals are discussed in the sections to follow.

As was the case with Theory X and Maslow's hierarchy of needs, however, the existence of organizations which appear to have adopted the assumptions of Theory Y, and the presence of individuals who bear out the assumptions, does not validate the theory. Again, the implication is that the assumption of Theory Y by management encourages worker behavior which proves the theory. To this extent Theory Y is self-fulfilling.

What then can be said of McGregor's ideas? First, Theory X and Y represent the extremes of managerial perceptions of the workforce. They are the ends of a vaguely defined continuum of worker behavior. Second, depending on an employee's past experiences, it is as natural to behave according to Theory X assumptions as it is to behave according to Theory Y. Third, either Theory X or Theory Y may be appropriate, depending on the existing environmental conditions. One study by Sadler (1966) found that 21% of the workers actually preferred an authoritarian leadership style to alternative forms of management. However, within the context of high technology organizations, characterized by rapid environmental changes and the constant influx of new ideas, the premises of Theory Y are likely to be viewed more favorably. Many individuals in such firms are accustomed to, within limits, defining for themselves what activities are necessary to accomplish the task at hand.

Personality and Organization

Another classic statement of human resource ideas is found in the work of Argyris (1957, 1964). Similarly to McGregor, Argyris saw a basic conflict between human personality and the ways organizations are traditionally structured and managed. Both believed that organizations create an environment that forces workers to be dependent on their superiors and gives employees little control over daily activities. In essence, the logic of industrial organizations is to treat adults as much like infants as is technologically possible. Under such conditions people feel and experience psychological failure.

When conflict exists between individuals and organizations, people adopt one or more strategies to cope with the situation; for example:

1. withdraw from the organization by quitting or frequent absenteeism
2. psychological withdrawal by passivity, indifference, or apathy
3. resisting the organization by restricting output, deception, featherbedding, or sabotage
4. attempts to move up in the hierarchy and thus avoid the frustrations associated with mechanized work
5. creating groups such as labor unions which seek to correct the imbalance of power.

Thus, McGregor and Argyris believed that management practices are inconsistent with people's needs and that the conflict produces resistance and withdrawal. To reduce this conflict, Argyris encouraged both job enrichment and participative management.

Job enrichment.   Job enrichment involves redefining narrow, fragmented worker positions into opportunities that encourage thinking and promote personal growth opportunities. Support for this approach can be seen in Herzberg's (1966) Two-Factor theory of motivation.

Herzberg interviewed 203 American engineers and accountants. Subjects were asked to describe situations when they felt "extremely good" or "extremely bad" about their jobs. From these replies, Herzberg identified two categories of job factors—*motivators* and *hygiene factors*. Included among the motivators were achievement, advancement, recognition, responsibility, and the possibility of growth. These motivators were the dominant themes in the respondents' descriptions of their good work experiences. The bad experience stories (the hygiene factor) included themes such as company policy and administration, supervision, security, and salary. In essence, Herzberg's Two-Factor theory is a need hierarchy similar to Maslow's, except that there are only two levels to the pyramid. Items in the hygiene factor are consistent with the first three levels advanced by Maslow, while the motivator factor parallels Maslow's self-esteem and self-actualization levels. Herzberg suggested that the motivators describe intrinsic aspects of work, while hygiene factors refer to extrinsic components of the work environment. He concluded that the motivator events lead to job enrichment and satisfaction because of the need for growth and self-actualization.

Although the Two-Factor theory has been criticized in terms of the research methodology (Vroom, 1964) and the inconclusiveness of the results (Ullrich, 1968), Herzberz's ideas are consistent with other human relations theorists—(e.g., Maslow, 1954; McGregor, 1960; Argyris, 1957). Views expressed by each of these individuals suggests that job enrichment produces a better fit between employees and organizations.

Participative management. A second approach to reducing conflict between workers and management is participation; giving employees the opportunity to influence policies that affect their work. Over the past decade, participative management has become extremely popular. The introduction of *quality circles* in many large organizations is an example. Although such activities are positive in spirit, research efforts to determine the influence of participation on employee—manager relationships have produced mixed results. Some studies have found participation to be positively correlated with both morale and productivity (Blumberg, 1969; Katzell & Yankelovich, 1975). Others suggest that participative management is more myth than reality (Argyris & Schon, 1974; Bolman, 1975). Managers believe in participation for themselves more than they believe in it for their subordinates (Bolman & Deal, 1984). Moreover, because participation creates a need for change, it is resisted by other parts of the organization. The preceding is not intended to discourage participative management, but simply to recognize that merely establishing quality circles does not solve organizational problems. Unless management is willing to actively integrate employee ideas into the decision-making process, human relations becomes a pseudo-participation destined to failure.

Ouchi's Theory Z

Cognizant of McGregor's Theory Y, Ouchi (1980) advanced Theory Z in an attempt to blend Japanese and American approaches to management (Ouchi, 1980). Ouchi observed major differences between organizations in the two countries (Figure 3.1). Although these differences in culture suggest that management styles in American and Japanese organizations may never parallel each other perfectly, valuable lessons can be learned from a comparative evaluation of the two countries. Such lessons are evident in the prescription Ouchi offers for moving an organization toward Theory Z.

1. Create strong emphasis on corporate philosophy—a statement of the organization's basic goal and its commitment to its workers.
2. With philosophy in place, begin working on improving interpersonal skills, including skills of understanding group processes.
3. Collect evidence to see how well your organization is meeting its objectives.

AMERICAN	JAPANESE
Short term employement	Lifetime employment
Rapid evaluation and promotion	Slow evaluation and promotion
Specialized career paths	Non-specialized career paths
Explicit control mechanisms	Implicit control mechanisms
Individual decsion-making	Collective decision-making
Individual responsiblity	Collective responsiblity
Segmented concern	Holistic concern

FIGURE 3.1.
Ouchi's Comparison of American and Japanese Organizations.

Consistent with human relations ideas, these steps emphasize that humanizing work conditions, not only increases worker productivity, but also worker self-esteem. Theory Z differs from traditional human relations in that it emphasizes corporate culture, the symbols, rituals, and myths that pervade organizational life (topics to be discussed in the following chapter).

Critique of the Human Relations Perspective

The theoretical strength of human relations is that it emphasizes a less formal study of organizations and begins to show the linkages between macro level value structures and micro level behaviors. Human relations emphasizes the person and small groups in the organization, particularly the relation of power and communication patterns (Cartwright & Zander, 1968). For these reasons, the human relations school is closely linked to theories in social psychology.

There are, however, some limitations to the human relations perspective. Because the individual is the primary focus, the formal structures and routine processes of large, complex organizations are not considered. In today's organizational environment, the impact of these larger events can overshadow individual level factors. Downturns in the computer industry illustrate the point. Low cost Japanese imports, and the emergence of a world wide computer market, have had a more powerful influence on manager/employee relations than localized attempts to increase productivity.

Finally, and most importantly, human relations approaches neglect the conflicts resulting from differential power distributions in organizations (Ritzer, 1972). Egalitarian ideas of industrial democracy based on old established orders are difficult to overcome, especially in the context of increased competition and rapidly advancing technology. Such bureaucracies are capable of stopping change through inaction. A human relations perspective, on the other hand, seeks increased communication as a means of resolving differences and promoting change. Although admirable, the goal fails to appreciate fully the pervasive influence of other organizational features, such as differing authority structures or subcultural norms of conflict resolution.

RESEARCHER'S AGENDA

Most human relations research has described instances where the needs of employees are either satisfied or inhibited by human–computer interactions. Research is needed to test the reliability and validity of human relation theories.

Of the human relations theories discussed in this chapter, which ones offer the most promise for explaining human–computer interactions under differing circumstances?

What role(s) should computers play in satisfying the needs of individuals in organizations?

Efforts to improve employee–manager relationships typically incorporate participative management techniques such as quality circles. Research efforts designed to evaluate the effectiveness of these techniques have produced mixed results. Some studies have found participation to be positively correlated with both morale and productivity, while others suggest that participative management is more myth than reality. Under what circumstances will participative management enhance employee–manager relations?

Training programs are often established to help people learn new computer systems. To what extent are these programs meeting their objective? In what ways can training programs be improved?

MANAGER'S AGENDA

Organizations and computers exist to serve human needs. Humans do not exist to serve organizational or computer needs.

When the fit between the individual and the organization is poor, one or both will suffer. When the fit between the individual and the computer is poor, the individual suffers.

When the fit is good between the individual and the organization, both benefit: Humans are able to do meaningful and satisfying work while providing the resources the organization needs to accomplish its mission. When the fit is good between the individual and the computer, both the individual and the organization benefit.

Employee participation in decisions to purchase new hardware and software means more than simply giving individuals the opportunity to voice their opinion. The individuals must have an affiliation with the team that is making the decision and believe that their recommendations are being heard.

When technology becomes a normal part of worklife, people need assurances that their privacy will be protected and their jobs are secure.

OPEN SYSTEMS THEORY

Organizational theory development has increasingly emphasized communication as the defining characteristic of human organizations (Maruyama, 1963; Shibutani, 1968). The structural and human relations theories suggest that communication by its nature, function, and pattern gives definition to what we call organizations. Weber's bureaucracy and the scientific management approaches examine the formal structure of these communication patterns, while the theories of Maslow, McGregor, Argyris, and Ouchi highlight informal communication roles. Both the structuralist and human relations theories represent *closed systems* models, closed in the sense that the organization is studied in isolation from broader influences such as the environment. *Open systems* theories, the focus of this section, strive to incorporate these environmental factors and demonstrate the linkages between macro (i.e., formal communication structures) and micro (i.e., informal communication structures) perspectives. Because open systems theories emphasize communication processes, the approaches offer a promising way to analyze the relationship between telecommunications technologies and organizations (Malone, 1982; Eason, 1983; Crozier, 1983).

Understanding open systems theory relative to the other theories we have been discussing requires some comprehension of *general systems theory* (see Figure 3.2). Boulding (1968) describes general systems theory (GST) as a level of theoretical model building which lies somewhere between the highly generalized constructions of pure mathematics and the theories of the specialized disciplines (e.g., psychology or sociology). GST does not posit a series of variable relationships, but rather, a perspective for highlighting key features. A parallel argument can be advanced for the relationship between computer science and social

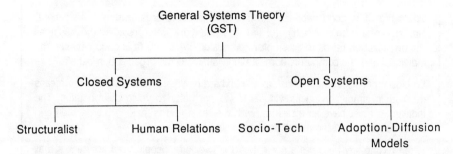

FIGURE 3.2.
Relationship of General Systems Theory to Organizational Theory.

science explanations of human–computer interaction. Human–computer interactions extend beyond the higher order cognitive aspects of the interaction and include social, organizational, environmental, and symbolic factors (Crozier, 1983; Hewitt, 1986; Mumford, 1983).

Open systems theory contends that human organizations have some similarity in their behavior to physical systems found in biology and physics (Boulding, 1968). The theory posits an association between an organization, its internal processes, and the external environment within which it exists. For example, a goal of many established computer vendors is to grow at a steady rate, while newer, evolving, organizations strive for rapid growth and domination of specialized markets. Both types of firms exist in an open environment, but have different goals and strategies for collecting, translating, and expending information resources. Each organization sets its priorities based on its own assessment of the environment. As environmental factors change, priorities for action may also change. Modifying one priority often impacts other parts of the organization, which in turn influences the organization's overall goals.

This natural cycle is evident when organizations attempt to anticipate external market demands to maximize their internal benefits from environmental changes. Environmental factors such as market demand are intrinsically tied to internal production and developmental processes. Just as systems designers strive to build equipment that can connect to a variety of systems in the "open world" of communications, organizations need to connect to the larger world. Failure to recognize and cope with such linkages leads to reductions in profit and layoffs in personnel, and brings into question the survival of the company. Use of the open systems perspective points to a specification of internal tasks, factors external to the company, and technology within a unified framework of organizational analysis.

When computers influence the environment in which we work, it becomes important to examine how these technologies change organizational communication patterns. More specifically, how does the introduction of computers and advanced communications technologies impact the way in which people interact with one another and the way people interact with computers themselves? Study of advanced communication processes are of special interest, because computer technology is fundamentally communications technology which controls, translates, and speeds the transfer of information from place to place and person to person. The open systems approach comes closest to translating the concepts presented up to this point into a measurable framework for analyzing communication network structures.

To illustrate how computers influence organizations and their environment, two approaches to open systems theory—*socio-technical* and *models of innovation*—are examined. An empirical example focusing on the adoption-diffusion process of a voice mail product is presented.

SOCIOTECHNICAL DESIGN

Sociotechnical design represents an integration of jobs, organizations, and technology to provide the best business results (Assunto, 1986). Trist (1981) summarized the main principles of sociotechnical design:

1. The basic design unit is the overall work system comprising a number of logically integrated tasks or unit operations rather than single tasks or operations which form the system.
2. The work group becomes the primary social unit, not the individual job holder.
3. Internal regulation of the system is by the work group itself.
4. Jobs are multiskilled because the work group, rather than the individual, is the primary social unit.
5. Greater emphasis is placed on the discretionary as opposed to the prescribed part of worker roles.
6. People are treated as complementary to machines, not as extensions of, or subservient to, machines.
7. Work organization is aimed at increasing rather than decreasing job variety.

These principles have evolved into a variety of design methods and tools for introducing computer technologies. Mumford (1983) describes one approach, labeled ETHICS (Effective Technical and Human Imple-

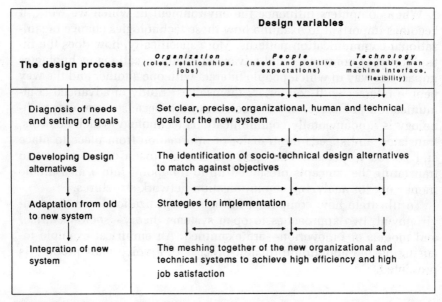

	Design variables		
The design process	*Organization* (roles, relationships, jobs)	*People* (needs and positive expectations)	*Technology* (acceptable man machine interface, flexibility)
Diagnosis of needs and setting of goals	Set clear, precise, organizational, human and technical goals for the new system		
Developing Design alternatives	The identification of socio-technical design alternatives to match against objectives		
Adaptation from old to new system	Strategies for implementation		
Integration of new system	The meshing together of the new organizational and technical systems to achieve high efficiency and high job satisfaction		

Source: Mumford (1983)

FIGURE 3.3
A Sociotechnical approach to systems design.

mentation of Computer-based Systems), which has been successful in both the U.K. and the U.S. (e.g., DEC). There are four discrete stages included in Mumford's design process (Figure 3.3). Information collected at each stage provides input for the next stage. By making explicit the goals for each of the design variables (i.e., organization, people, and technology) at each design stage, the implementer is afforded some assurance that the needs and concerns of all affected are being heard. Mumford's contribution is valuable, not simply for the process she sets up, but for her realization that the people in jobs, the jobs themselves, and the technologies supporting these jobs all combine to influence the organization.

Although the sociotechnical perspective has an intuitive appeal, there are a number of practical barriers associated with its actual implementation. First, in most companies, business managers, systems custodians, and human resources personnel have each had a narrow view of their responsibilities and the responsibilities of the other two. To change this view, individuals in each operational unit must broaden the scope of their focus and appreciate their interconnections with the organization, its employees, and technology. Second, although the introduction and use of new office technologies is believed to stimulate changes in job design and work flow, specifying the exact nature of such changes is often difficult to predict (Drucker, 1986). Even if accurate predictions were available, most personnel departments lack the experience to tackle the required integration process. Finally, the training of most systems professionals reinforces the idea that the human is less important than the machine (Assunto, 1986).

Although these barriers inhibit the application of sociotechnical design efforts, the problems represent limitations of traditional management structures and not the basic thrust of the theory. Given a sufficient amount of time and experience with overcoming the existing problems, the sociotechnical perspective offers the potential of integrating organizations, people, and technology.

MODELS OF INNOVATION

Innovation research is the study of the relationship of "acceptance over time of some item—an idea or practice, by individuals, groups, or other adopting units, linked to channels of communication, to a social structure and to a given system of values, or culture" (Katz, Levin, & Hamilton, 1963, p. 237). Adoption-diffusion theories assume that the acceptance of new ideas, products, and technologies within organizations occurs gradually, and that the rate of adoption is linked to patterns of communication (Bass, 1980; Meade, 1984; Randles, 1983; Robertson, 1971).

Two types of individuals—innovators and imitators—are commonly identified in the innovation literature. Innovators are individuals who find, adopt and use new products, ideas, and technologies independent of outside influence. Most of us are familiar with individuals who are consistently the "first to try something." Imitators are those individuals who follow the behavior patterns of innovators. Computers, for example, come to be used in organizations partly because people see others using them and are influenced by their evaluations of the systems. Innovation research suggests that there is a combination of *innovators* and *imitators* in any market segment. The empirical questions center around the relative size and impact of each group (e.g., innovators and imitators) on the resultant overall diffusion pattern.

Tarde (1903) proposed that the empirical pattern found in the diffusion process took the shape of an "S" (logistic) curve (Figure 3.4). The curve suggests that the adoption of products is slow at first introduction because of the small number of innovators. Once a critical mass is reached, the behavior of imitators begins to appear and the slope of the curve increases rapidly. As the market approaches saturation, the process slows down and the curve declines or remains flat. Such a pattern was evident with the sales of personal computers. The slow sales in the late 1970s was followed by a dramatic increase between 1982 and 1985.

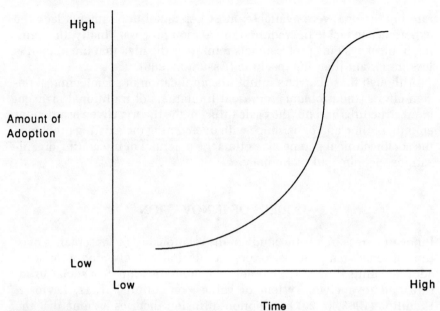

FIGURE 3.4
The Generalized "S" Curve.

By the late '80s, the pace of computer sales slowed considerably as the diffusion process for this cycle of products reached a peak.

The mathematics describing the "S" curve can be expressed in the general form given by Bass (1969):

$$S(T)^2 = pm + (q - p)Y(T) - (q/m)[Y(T)]$$

where:
    $S(T)$ = initial adopters at time T
    p = coefficient of innovation
    q = coefficient of imitation
    m = market potential
    $Y(T)$ = number of previous adopters at time T

Parameter Estimation

The parameters found in the general diffusion model refer to the relative effect of innovator and imitator behavior. The coefficient of innovation (p) and the coefficient of imitation (q) are the two respective group's behavior. Estimation of the coefficients p and q constitutes a major empirical problem of innovation-diffusion research. Small changes in these parameters yield large changes in predicted behavior. In general, the faster the rate of information transfer between innovators and imitators, the more rapidly diffusion occurs. Slower diffusion rates result when there are few innovators in the communication system and when imitators do not rapidly substitute new products for ones currently in use. Several approaches have been used to obtain estimates for these parameters.

Past sales records are the most predominant means of estimating the number of people who adopt a technology at any one time. Histories of past consumer behavior with similar products have been used to arrive at beginning estimates (Thomas, 1985). If regression models are applied to a record of product sales performance, q and p refer to the estimated market size of each group; m (market potential) is usually estimated from primary market studies. Use of past sales records is a fairly reliable method of estimating parameters, if the product or innovation in question is similar to past products.

There are, however, limitations of this historical record approach (Tigert & Farivar, 1981). New computer and communications technologies are often not directly comparable to existing products. Thomas (1985) presents an alternative method of parameter estimation based on the idea of analogous product attribute ranking. In the absence of directly comparable product sales data, Thomas argues that the equation parameters may be estimated by comparing multivariate attributes of new and candidate products. Weights are assigned to customer preferences, beliefs and perceptions. Combination of these subjective judgments yield estimates for p and q. Following a method presented by Mahajan and Peterson (1978), m is estimated and the values inserted in the Bass (1969) equation. Thomas reports that this method yields results reflective of the rate of product diffusion.

An Empirical Example

This part of the chapter reports the results of an investigation which applied the Bass model to the adoption of an advanced communication technology in an office environment. The empirical questions involved determining how to increase the use of the product among existing users, and how to increase the rate of innovative behavior among non-users. Although the example is limited to the introduction of voice mail, the same concepts and procedures apply to any product.

Open systems theory predicts that functional units of organizations concerned with collecting and processing information from external sources have different communication patterns than those which are more concerned with internal processes, such as administration. Applying this perspective to the process of technology diffusion, we would expect differences in the equation parameters across functional groups in the organization.

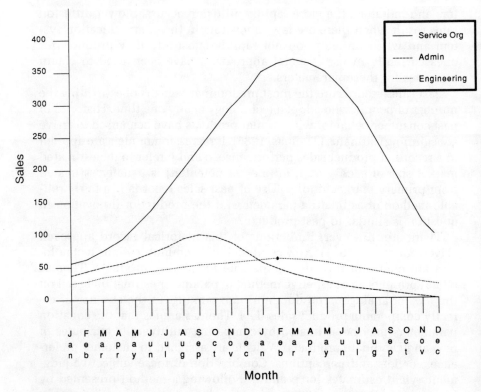

FIGURE 3.5
The VOX Market Projections.

The voice mail system examined in this study was used by 260 people at Honeywell. If we disaggregate the data by functional group (i.e., marketing/sales, engineering, administration, and customer service) and fit the usage pattern for each group to the diffusion equation, organizational theory would predict different estimates for each of the groups. Figure 3.5 displays the results obtained by fitting the Bass model to each of the functional groups. The curves describing the diffusion behavior for the voice mail product clearly differ between groups. These findings indicate that the diffusion parameters do, in fact, vary according to organization function. Further, the process of diffusion occurs at a higher rate in marketing and sales groups than it does in administrative groups, data which support the hypotheses predicted from organizational theory.

There are at least two implications of these findings for computer system designers and marketing personnel. First, the data suggest that organizational structure (i.e., functional group in the organization) does bear some relationship to how people adopt advanced technologies in organizations. Organizational theory has also given us some insight into which groups can be predicted to adopt these technologies more rapidly than others. Organizational units concerned with external communication and coordination are more apt to use telecommunication technologies than production oriented (e.g., engineering) units. The second implication is that groups, because of their communication requirements, may find different types of system interfaces more effective than others.

RESEARCHER'S AGENDA

In what ways does the introduction of advanced communication technologies change organizational communication patterns?

In what ways should the organization be modified structurally to accommodate the potential of the new technologies?

Do new office technologies stimulate changes in job design? In what ways are such modifications evident?

How can communications technologies create faster response to changing customer demands?

How can these new technologies decrease the organizational impedance of information flow among all corporate units?

How can feedback/feedforward systems be facilitated by communications systems?

Can these technologies help the organization to adapt more quickly to globalization of the economy in general and our market in particular?

What is the adoption diffusion rate of different technologies?

MANAGER'S AGENDA

Business managers, systems custodians, and human resources personnel have traditionally each had a narrow view of their responsibilities and the responsibilities of the other two. Open systems theory calls for individuals in each operational unit to broaden the scope of their focus and appreciate their interconnections with the organization, its employees, and technology.

Sociotechnical design represents an integration of jobs, organizations, and technology to provide the best business results.

Innovation research is the study of the relationship of acceptance over time of some item-an idea or practice, by individuals, groups, or other adopting units, linked to channels of communication, to a social structure, and to a given system of values, or culture. Understanding the models of innovation facilitates efforts to integrate communication technologies into an organization.

CHAPTER SUMMARY

- This chapter examined the study of human–computer interaction from an organizational perspective. Three major organizational theories were discussed: (a) the Structuralist approach, (b) the human relations school, and (c) open systems theory. Each theoretical orientation offers an alternative frame of reference for judging particular situations. It was emphasized that no single theory will work in every situation.

- Organizational theories explain the structure and function of corporations in terms of authority and power, size and complexity, efficiency and effectiveness, information, technology, and environment. While different theories emphasize different variables at different times, all theories implicitly or explicitly describe organizations with these constructs.

- Sociological theories of organizations differ from cognitive and social psychological theories in that they concentrate more on general observable trends than on the magnitude of variable relationships, a situation dictated partially by the difficulty in obtaining quantitative data. Organizational theories are concerned with identifying consistent patterns of communication between individuals (i.e., structure).

- Structural theories (Weber's bureaucracy and scientific management) emphasize the importance of *formal* roles and relationships, while human relations theories (Maslow, McGregor, Argyris, and Ouchi) concentrate on the *informal* relationships that exist among members of an organization. Both the structuralist and human relations theories represent closed systems models, closed in the sense that the organization is studied in isolation from broader influences such as the environment.

- Open systems theories (sociotechnical design and models of innovation) strive to incorporate these environmental factors and demonstrate the linkages between macro (i.e., formal communication structures) and micro (i.e., informal communication structures) perspectives. Because open systems theories emphasize communication processes, the approaches offer a promising way to analyze the relationship between telecommunications technologies and organizations.

- This application of theories of organizational behavior has illustrated important points for human–computer interaction. First, analysis of computer system users within the organizational context is complex, and needs to be viewed from theoretical perspectives to be fully understood. A researcher's choice of theory, variables, and method of study should depend upon the question asked. The same is true of the level of analysis (e.g. individual, organization, or culture). Second, we have shown that organizational theory can point to fruitful research pathways by indicating which variables should be correlated with system adoption and use.

- The empirical example used to illustrate the applicability of organizational theory centered on the diffusion of computer based technology within a complex, formal organization. The data indicated that use of computer systems is influenced by organization structure, functional differentiation, and communications patterns. These findings imply that organizational theories should be incorporated into research which aims to discover the patterns which lie behind human–computer interaction, because structural and process variables can account for variation in computer user behavior.

- Chapter 2 discussed the range, scope, and application of social psychology as it relates to problems of human–computer interaction. This chapter was concerned with human–computer interactions from the context of social organizations. This progression of theoretical approaches leads to an appreciation of the social interaction processes operating within and between people and organizations.

- Social psychology is related to social organizations in the same way that process is related to structure. Social psychology describes the process of people interacting with one another. Social organizational literature focuses on the structure of this interaction. Study of organizations is intimately linked to social psychological processes, because organizations are essentially names we give to patterns of communication. Informal communication networks within an organization are eventually reflected in formal structures, either through acceptance of rituals of behavior or codifying in regulations and rules. The next chapter extends the evaluation of human–computer interactions by examining the role of anthropological theories in the analysis of culture, symbols, rituals, and myth.

BIBLIOGRAPHY

Albrecht, G. (1979). Defusing technical change in juvenile courts: The probation officer's struggle for professional autonomy. *Sociology of Work and Occupation, 6*, 259–282.

Alderfer, C. P. (1972). *Existence, relatedness, and growth.* New York: Free Press.

Allison, A. (1986, June). Computer vendors consolidate resources. *Mini-Micro Systems*, pp. 54–63.

Argyris, C. (1957). *Personality and organization.* New York: Harper & Row.

Argyris, C. (1964). *Integrating the individual and the organization.* New York: John Wiley.

Argyris, C. (1971). *Management and organizational development.* New York: McGraw-Hill.

Argyris, C., & Schon, D. A. (1974). *Theory in practice: Increasing professional effectiveness.* San Francisco, CA: Jossey-Bass.

Aronson, S. A. (1971). The sociology of the telephone. *International Journal of Comparative Sociology, 12,* 153–167.

Assunto, K. (1986, July). *How jobs, organizations and technology interact: The case for planned interaction.* Aetna Life & Casualty.

Ball, R. A. (1978). Sociology and general systems theory. *The American Sociologist, 13,* 65–72

Baroudi, J. J., Olson, M. H., & Ives, B. (1986). An empirical study of the impact of user involvement on system usage and information satisfaction. *Communications of the ACM, 29,* 232–238.

Bass, F. M. (1969). A new product growth model for consumer durables. *Management Science, 15,* 215–227.

Bass, F. M. (1980). The relationship between diffusion rates, experience curves, and demand elasticities for consumer durable technological innovations. *Journal of Business, 53,* S51–S67.

Beattie, G. W. (1971). They ring and I obey. *New Society, 10,* 448–449.

Bernard, C., (1938). *The functions of the executive.* Cambridge, MA: Harvard University Press.

Bikson, T. K., & Gutek, B. A. (1983). *Advanced office systems: An empirical look at utilization and satisfaction.* Santa Monica, CA: The Rand Corporation.

Bjorn-Andersen, N., & Pedersen, P. (1977). *Computer systems as a vehicle for changes in the management structure.* (Working paper 77–3). Copenhagen, Denmark: Information Systems Research Group, University of Copenhagen.

Bjorn-Anderson, N. (1983). The changing roles of secretaries and clerks. In H. J. Otway & M. Peltu (Eds.), *New office technology: Human and organizational aspects* (pp. 120–137). Norwood, NJ: Ablex Publishing Corp.

Blau, P. (1964). *Exchange and power in social life.* New York: John Wiley and Sons.

Blau, P. (1974). *On the nature of organizations.* New York: John Wiley.

Blau, P., & Scott, W. R. (1962). *Formal organizations: A comparative approach.* San Francisco, CA: Chandler.

Blumberg, P. (1969). *Industrial democracy: The sociology of participation.* New York: Schocken Books.

Bogart, D. H. (1980). Feedback, feedforward and feedwithin: Strategic information in systems. *Behavioral Science, 25,* 237–248.

Bolman, L. (1975). The client as theorist. In J. Adams (Ed.), *New technologies in organization development.* La Jolla, CA: University Associates.

Bolman, L. G., & Deal, T. E. (1984). *Modern approaches to understanding and managing organizations.* San Francisco, CA: Jossey-Bass Publishers.

Boulding, K. E. (1965). Towards a general theory of growth. *General Systems Yearbook, 1,* 65–75.

Boulding, K. E. (1968). General systems theory: The skeleton of science. In W. Buckley (Ed.), *Modern systems research for the behavioral scientist.* Chicago, IL: Aldine.

Braverman, H. (1974). *Labor and monopoly capital: The degradation of work in the twentieth century.* New York: Monthly Review Press.

Brod, C. (1982). Managing technostress: Optimizing the use of computer technology. *Personnel Journal, 61,* 753–757.

Buchanan, D. A., & Boody, D. (1983). *Organizations in the computer age: Technological imperatives and strategic choices.* Aldershot: Grower Publishing Company, Ltd.

Buckley, W. (1967). *Sociology and modern systems theory.* Englewood Cliffs, NJ: Prentice-Hall

Butera, F., & Bartezzaghi, E. (1983). Creating the right organizational environment. In H. J. Otway & M. Peltu (Eds.), *New office technology: Human and organizational aspects* (pp. 102–119). Norwood, NJ: Ablex Publishing Corp.

Call, B. (1986, June 17). Chief executives adjust slowly to using PCs. *PC Week,* p. 52.

Cartwright, D. & Zander, A. (1968). *Group dynamics: Research and theory* (3rd ed). New York: Harper and Row.

Colton, K. (Ed.). (1978). *Police computer technology.* Lexington, MA: Lexington Books.

Cook, T. D., & Campbell, D. T. (1976). The design and conduct of quasi-experiments and true experiments in field settings. In M. D. Dunnette (Ed.), *Handbook of industrial and organizational psychology* (pp. 223–253). Chicago, IL: Rand McNally.

Crozier, M. (1983). Implications for the organization. In H. S. Otway & M. Peltu (Eds.), *New office technology: Human and organizational aspects* (pp. 86–101). Norwood, NJ: Ablex Publishing Corp.

Curley, P. (1983, April). Confessions of a cyberphobe. *Best's Review,* p. 80.

Dainoff, M. J., Happ, A., & Crane, P. (1981). Visual fatigue and occupational stress in VDT operators. *Human Factors, 23,* 421–437.

Danzinger, J. (1977). Computers and the litany to EDP. *Public Administration Review, 37,* 28–37.

Danzinger, J., & Dutton, W. (1977). Computers as an innovation in American local governments. *Communications of the ACM, 20,* 945–956.

Deci, E. L. (1975). *Intrinsic motivation.* New York: Plenum.

Delehanty, G. E. (1967). Computers and organization structure in life insurance firms: The external and internal economic environment. In C. A. Meyers (Ed.), *The impact of computers on organizations.* Cambridge, MA: M.I.T. Press.

Dill, W. R. (1958). Environment as an influence on managerial autonomy. *Administrative Science Quarterly, 2,* 409–443.

Downs, A. (1967). A realistic look at the final payoffs from urban data systems. *Public Administration Review, 27,* 204–209.

Drucker, P. (1986, May 22). Goodbye to the old personnel department. *Wall Street Journal.*

Eason, K. (1983). Methodological issues in the study of human factors in teleinformatic systems. *Behavior and Information Technology, 2*(4), 357–364.

Ehrlich, S. F., & Akiba, E. A. (1986). Successful implementation of voice store and forward technology: A case study. *SIGOA Bulletin, 6*, 19–26.

Etzioni, A. (1961). *A comparative analysis of complex organizations.* New York: Free Press.

Etzioni, A. (1964). *Modern organizations.* Englewood Cliffs, NJ: Prentice-Hall.

Evans, J. (1983). Negotiating technological change. In H. J. Otway & M. Peltu (Eds.), *New office technology: Human and organizational aspects* (pp. 152–168). Norwood, NJ: Ablex Publishing Corp.

Eveland, J. D., & Bikson, T. K. (1986). *Evolving electronic communication networks: An empirical assessment.* (Technical report). Santa Monica, CA: The Rand Corporation.

Flaherty, D. (1986). *Humanizing the computer: A cure for the deadly embrace.* Belmont, CA: Wadsworth Publishing.

Fox, M. S. (1981). An organizational view of distributed systems SMC-11. *IEEE Transactions of System, Man, and Cybernetics, 11*, 70–80.

French, J. & Raven B. (1959). The bases of social power. In D. Cartwright (Ed.), *Studies in social power.* Ann Arbor, MI: Institute for Social Research.

Fried, L. (1986, Summer). Motivating user acceptance for integrated office support systems. *Journal of Information Systems Management*, pp. 50–55.

Gabel, D. (1986, June 24). The changes PCs bring. *PC Week*, pp. 85–87.

Gallagher, J. D. (1961). *Management information systems and the computer.* New York: American Management Association.

Gardner, E., Render, B., Ruth, S., & Ross, J. (1985, November). Human-oriented implementation cures 'cyberphobia'. *Data Management*, pp. 29–46.

Georgopoulos, B. S., & Tannebaum, A. S. (1957). A study of organizational effectiveness. *American Sociological Review, 22*, 534–540.

Grantham, C. (1982). *Social networks and marital interaction.* Palo Alto, CA: R & E Research Associates, Inc.

Grantham C. E., & Vaske, J. J. (1985). Predicting the usage of an advanced communications technology. *Behavior and Information Technology, 4*, 327–336.

Greenburger, M., Crenson, M. A., & Crissey, B. L. (1976). *Models in the policy process: Public decision-making in the computer era.* New York: Russell Sage Foundation.

Grimes, J., Ehrlich, K., & Vaske, J. J. (1986). User interface design: Are human factors principles used. *SIGCHI Bulletin, 17*, 22–26.

Grusky, O., & Miller G. A. (1970). *The sociology of organizations: Basic studies.* New York: Free Press.

Hage, J. (1965). An axiomatic theory of organizations. *Administrative Science Quarterly, 10*, 300.

Hage, J., & Aiken, M. (1967). Relationship of centralization to other structural properties. *Administrative Science Quarterly, 12*, 79–80.

Hall, R. H. (1967). Organizational size, complexity and formalization. *American Sociological Review, 32*, 906.

Hall, R. H. (1977). *Organizations: structure and process* (2nd ed.). Englewood Cliffs, NJ: Prentice-Hall.

Hammond, N., Jorgenson, A., Maclean, A., Barnard, P., & Long, J. (1983, December). Design practice and interface usability: Evidence from interviews with designers. In *Proceedings of conference on Human Factors in Computer Systems* (pp. 40–44). New York: ACM.

Hebenstreit, J. (1983). Training for future office skills. In H. J. Otway & M. Peltu (Eds.), *New office technology: Human and organizational aspects* (pp. 205–220). Norwood, NJ: Ablex Publishing Corp.

Helmer, O. (1966). *Social technology.* New York: Basic Books.

Herzberg, F. (1966). *Work and the nature of man.* Cleveland, OH: World.

Hewitt, C. (1986). Offices are open systems. *ACM Transaction of Office Information Systems, 4,* 271–287.

Hopwood, A. G. (1983). Evaluating the real benefits. In H. J. Otway & M. Peltu (Eds.), *New office technology: Human and organizational aspects* (pp. 37–50). Norwood, NJ: Ablex Publishing Corp.

Inkeles, A. (1964). *What is sociology.* Englewood Cliffs, NJ: Prentice-Hall.

Ives, B., Olson, M. H., & Baroudi, J. J. (1983). The measurement of user information satisfaction. *Communications of the ACM, 26,* 785–793.

Jensen, S. (1983). Software and user satisfaction. In H. J. Otway & M. Peltu (Eds.), *New office technology: Human and organizational aspects* (pp. 190–205). Norwood, NJ: Ablex Publishing Corp.

Kanter, J. (1972). *Management-oriented information-systems.* Englewood Cliffs, NJ: Prentice-Hall.

Kanter, R. M. (1985, April). Managing the human side of change. *Management Review,* pp. 52–56.

Kaplan, A. (1976). Maslow interpreted for the work environment. *Man-Environment Systems, 6,* 246–248.

Katz, E., Levin, M. L., & Hamilton, H. (1963). Traditions of research on the diffusion of innovation. *American Sociological Review, 28,* 237–252.

Katzell, R. A., & Yankelovich, D. (1975). *Work, productivity, and job satisfaction.* New York: Psychological Corporation.

Keen, P. (1975, Spring). Computer-based decision aids: The evaluation problem. *Sloan Management Review,* pp. 13–21.

Keen, P. G. (1981). Information systems and organizational change. *Communications of the ACM, 24,* 24–33.

Keen, P. G. W., & Gerson, E. M. (1977). *The politics of software systems design, or: What do you do when the systems analysis doesn't work?* San Francisco, CA: Pragmatica Systems, Inc.

Kiesler, S. (1986, January–February). Thinking ahead: The hidden messages in computer networks. *Harvard Business Review,* pp. 46–60.

Kling, R. (1974). Computers and social power. *Computer Society, 5,* 6–11.

Kling, R. (1977). The organizational context of user-centered software design. *MIS Quarterly, 1,* 41–52.

Kling, R. (1978a). Information systems in public policy making: Computer technology and organizational arrangements. *Telecommunications Policy, 2,* 22–32.

Kling, R. (1978b). Automated welfare client-tracking and service integration: The political economy of computing. *Communications of the ACM, 21*(6), 484–493.

Kling, R. (1978c). *The impacts of computing on the work of managers, data analysts and clerks* (Working Paper). Irvine, CA: Public Policy Research Organization, University of California–Irvine.

Kling R. (1980). Social analysis of computing: Theoretical perspectives in recent empirical research. *Computing Surveys, 12*, 61–110.

Kraemer, K., & Dutton, W. H. (1979). The interests served by technological reform: The case of computing. *Administration and Society, 11*, 80–106.

Kraemer, K., Dutton, W. H., & Northrup, A. (1980). *The management of information systems*. New York: Columbia University Press.

Laubli, Th., Hunting, W., & Grandjean, E. (1981). Postural and visual loads at VDT workplaces: Lighting conditions and visual impairments. *Ergonomics, 24*, 933–944.

Laudon, K. (1974). *Computers and bureaucratic reform*. New York: Wiley Interscience.

Lawler, E. E. (1973). *Motivation in work organizations*. Monterey, CA: Brooks/Cole.

Lawrence, P. R., & Lorsch, J. W. (1967). *Organization and environment*. Cambridge, MA: Harvard University Press.

Leonard-Barton, D., & Kraus, W. A. (1985). Implementing new technology. *Harvard Business Review, 63*, 102–110.

Levine, D. N., Carter, E. B., & Gorman, E. M. (1976). Simmel's Influence on American Sociology: 2. *American Journal of Sociology, 81*, 1113–1133.

Licklider, J. C. R., & Vezza, A. (1978). Applications of information networks. In *Proceedings IEEE, 66*, 1330–1346.

Lincoln, Y. S. (1985). *Organizational theory and inquiry: The paradigm revolution*. Beverly Hills, CA: Sage Publications.

Lucas, H. (1975). Performance and use of an information system. *Management Science, 21*, 908–919.

Mahajan, V., & Peterson, R. A. (1978). Innovation diffusion in a dynamic potential adopter population. *Management Science, 15*, 1589–1597.

Mainiero, L. A., & DeMichiell, R. L. (1986, July). Minimizing employee resistance to technological change. *Personnel*, pp. 32–37.

Malone, T. W. (1982). *Organizing information processing systems: Parallels between human organizations and computer systems*. (Working Paper). Palo Alto, CA: Xerox Palo Alto Research Center.

Malone, T. W. (1985, April). Designing organizational interfaces. In *Proceedings of CHI' 85* (pp. 66–71). New York: ACM.

Mann, F. C., & Williams, L. K. (1960). Observations on the dynamics of change to electronic data processing equipment. *Administrative Science Quarterly, 5*, 217–256.

March, J. G., & Simon, H. (1958). *Organizations*. New York: John Wiley and Sons.

Maruyama, M. (1963). The second cybernetics: Deviation-amplifying mutual causal processes. *American Scientist, 51*, 164–179.

Maslow, A. H. (1954). *Motivation and personality*. New York: Harper and Row.

Matula, R. A. (1981). Effects of visual display units on the eyes: A bibliography (1972–1980). *Human Factors, 23*, 581.

McElhone, A. (1982, July). Training perspective: Take the awe out of automation. *The Office*, p. 86.

McGregor, D. (1960). *The human side of enterprise*. New York: McGraw-Hill.

Meade, N. (1984). The use of growth curves in forecasting market development—A review and appraisal. *Journal of Forecasting, 3*, 429–451.

Merton, R. (1957). *Social theory and social structure*. New York: The Free Press.

Meyer, J., Scott, W. R., & Deal, T. E. (1981). Institutional and technological sources of organizational structure: Explaining the structure of educational organizations. In H. Steen (Ed.), *Organization and human services: Cross-disciplinary perspectives*. Philadelphia, PA: Temple University Press.

Mourant, R., Lakshamanan, R., & Chantadisai, R. (1981). Visual fatigue and CRT display terminals. *Human Factors, 23*, 529.

Mouzelis, N. (1968). *Organization and bureaucracy*. Chicago, IL: Aldine.

Mumford, E. (1983). Successful systems design. In H. J. Otway & M. Peltu (Eds.), *New office technology: Human and organizational aspects* (pp. 68–85). Norwood, NJ: Ablex Publishing Corp.

Mumford, E., & Banks, O. (1967). *The computer and the clerk*. London: Routledge and Keegan-Paul.

O'Malley, C. (1986, August). Driving your point home. *Personal Computing*, pp. 86–105.

Otway, H. J., & Peltu, M. (Eds.). (1983). *New office technology: Human and organizational aspects*. Norwood, NJ: Ablex Publishing Corp.

Ouchi, W. G. (1980). Markets, bureaucracies and clans. *Administrative Science Quarterly, 25*, 129–141.

Ouchi, W. G. (1981). *Theory Z*. Reading, MA: Addison-Wesley.

Pallato, J. (1986, April 29). The University of Wisconsin at Madison. *PC Week*, pp. 69–74.

Parsons, T. (1960). *Structure and process in modern society*. New York: The Free Press.

Perrow, C. (1968). The effect of technological change on the structure of business firms. In B. C. Roberts (Ed.), *Industrial relations: Contemporary issues* (pp. 205–219). London: MacMillan.

Perrow, C. (1972). *Complex organizations: A critical essay*. Glenview, IL: Scott, Foreseman and Company.

Petre, P. (1986, October). America's most successful entrepreneur. *Fortune*, pp. 24–32.

Proshansky, H. M., Ittelson, W. H., & Rivlin, L. G. (1976). *Environmental psychology* (2nd ed.). New York: Holt, Rinehart and Winston.

Randles, F. (1983). On the diffusion of computer terminals in an established engineering environment. *Management Science, 29*, 465–476.

Rief, W. E. (1968). *Computer technology and management organization*. Iowa City, IO: University of Iowa, Bureau of Business and Economic Research.

Ritzer, G. (1972). *Man and his work: Conflict and change*. New York: Basic Books.

Robertson, T. S. (1971). *Innovative behavior and communication.* New York: Holt, Rinehart and Winston.

Robey, D. (1977). Computers and management structure: Some empirical findings reexamined. *Human Relations, 30,* 963–976.

Robey, D. (1979). MIS effects on managers task scope and satisfaction. In *Proceedings: 1979 AFIPS National Computer Conference* (pp. 391–395). Arlington, VA: AFIPS Press.

Roethlisberger, F., & Dickson, W. (1939). Human relations. In *Management and the Worker.* Cambridge: Harvard University Press.

Rule, J. (1974). *Private lives and public surveillance: Social control in the computer age.* New York: Schocken Books.

Rushinek, A., & Rushinek, S. F. (1986). What makes users happy? *Communications of the ACM, 29,* 594–598.

Sadler, P. F. (1966). *Leadership style, confidence in management and job satisfaction.* Berkhamsted, England: Ashridge Management College.

Sauter, S. L., Gottlieb, M. S., Jones, K. C., Dodson, V. N., & Rohrer, K. M. (1983). Job and health implications of VDT use: Initial results of the Wisconsin-NIOSH study. *Communications of the ACM, 26,* 284–294.

Schultz, G. P., & Whisler, T. L. (Eds). (1960). *Management organization and the computer.* New York: Free Press.

Schwartz, P., & Oglivy, J. (1979). *The emergent paradigm: Changing patterns of thought and belief.* Menlo Park, CA: SRI International.

Scott, W. R. (1981). *Organizations: Rational, natural, and open systems.* Englewood Cliffs, NJ: Prentice-Hall.

Shibutani, T. (1968). A cybernetic approach to human motivation. In W. Buckley (Ed.), *Modern systems research for the behavioral scientist* (pp. 330–336). Chicago, IL: Aldine.

Shneiderman, B. (1980). *Software psychology.* Norwood, NJ: Ablex Publishing Corp.

Shneiderman, B. (1983). The psychology of serving the user community: Management strategies for interactive systems. *Journal of Capacity Management, 1,* 328–343.

Silverman, D. (1971). *The theories of organizations.* New York: Basic Books.

Simon, H. A. (1977). *The new science of management decision-making.* Englewood Cliffs, NJ: Prentice-Hall.

Starr, S. J., Thompson, C. R., & Shute, S. J. (1982, April 14). *Effects of video display terminals on telephone operators.* Bell Laboratories Internal Report.

Stewart, R. (1971). *How computers affect management.* London: Macmillan.

Swanson, B. (1974). Systems heroes. *General Systems, 19,* 91–95.

Tausky, C. (1977). *Work organizations: Major theoretical perspectives* (2nd ed.). Itasca, IL: F. E. Peacock Publishers.

Tarde, G. (1903). *The laws of imitation.* New York: Holt, Rinehart and Winston.

Taylor, F. (1911). *Principles of scientific management.* New York: Harper and Row.

Thomas, R. J. (1985). Estimating market growth for new products: An analogical diffusion model approach. *Journal of Productivity Innovation and Management, 2,* 45–55.

Thompson, J. D. (1967). *Organizations in action.* New York: McGraw-Hill.

Tigert, D., & Farivar, B. (1981). The Bass new product growth model: A sensitivity analysis for a high technology product. *Journal of Marketing, 45,* 81–90.

Trauth, E. M., Kwan, S. K., & Barber, S. (1984). Channel selection and effective managerial decision making. *ACM Transactions on Office Information Systems, 2,* 123–140.

Trist, E. (1981). The evolution of sociotechnical systems as a conceptual framework and as an action research program. In A. H. Van de Ven & W. F. Joyce (Eds.), *Perspectives on organization design and behavior.* New York: John Wiley.

Ullrich, R. A. (1968). *A study of the motivating and dissatisfying forces in an isolated work situation* (No. PB 178 324 1968). Springfield, MA: Clearinghouse for Federal Scientific and Technical Information.

Vaske, J. J., & Teubner, A. L. (1985). *A comparative evaluation of Billerica and Phoenix DPS6 EMail users.* (Tech. Report). Billerica, MA: Honeywell Information Systems, Inc.

Vroom, V. H. (1964). *Work and motivation.* New York: John Wiley and Sons.

Wagner, L. G. (1966). Computers, decentralization, and corporate control. *California Management Review, 9.*

Wahba, M. A., & Bridwell, L. G. (1976). Maslow reconsidered: a review of research on the need hierarchy theory. *Organizational Behavior and Human Performance, 15,* 212–240.

Wasserman, A. I., & Shewmake, D. T. (1985). The role of prototypes in the User Software Engineering (USE) methodology. In R. Hartson (Ed.), *Advances in human–computer interaction 1* (pp. 191–210). Norwood, NJ: Ablex Publishing Corp.

Weber, M. (1947). *The theory of social and economic organizations.* (Trans. by A. M. Henderson and Talcott Parsons). New York: Oxford University Press,.

Weick, K. E. (1969). *The social psychology of organizing.* Reading, MA: Addison-Wesley.

Weinburg, S., & Fuerst, M. (1984). *Computer phobia: How to slay the dragon of computer fear.* Wayne, PA: Banbury Books.

Weiner, N. (1948). *Cybernetics of control and communication in the animal and machine.* Cambridge, MA: MIT Press.

Westrum, R. (1984). *The effect of electronic communications technologies on the large corporation: Basic theoretical framework.* Minneapolis, MN: Honeywell Corporate Information Management.

Whisler, T. L. (1970). *The impact of computers on organizations.* New York: Praeger.

Whyte, W. F. (1959). *Man and organizations: Three problems in human relations training.* Homewood, IL: Richard D. Irwin.

Wynne, B. (1983). The changing roles of managers. In H. J. Otway & M. Peltu (Eds.), *New office technology: Human and organizational aspects* (pp. 138–151). Norwood, NJ: Ablex Publishing Corp.

Zaleznick, A., Christensen, C. R., & Rothlisberger, F. J. (1958). *The motivation, productivity and satisfaction of workers.* Norwood, NJ: The Plimpton Press.

chapter 4
Anthropology: The Symbols of Meaning

This chapter focuses on how people construct meaning from their experiences. To a large extent this process is symbolic in nature. A stop sign on a highway, for example, conveys a certain meaning to motorists. Similarly, computers convey a symbolic meaning to both users and nonusers. In situations where individuals perceive computers as tools for increasing productivity, computers impart a positive symbolic meaning. When computer technology replaces jobs, or when it is difficult to understand, computers promote a negative connotation. These symbolic definitions of computers have taken on new meaning as personal computers have become more common. Computers no longer symbolize large machines in glass cages of corporate offices, but rather tools for performing tasks in the home and at work. In many corporations, computers also serve as symbolic objects which function to convince others that decisions were made carefully. Kling (1978) found engineers shifted from paper-and-pencil calculations to computers to give the appearance of improved accuracy. Managers sometimes adopt computers to gain more credibility for their plans (Keen & Scott-Morton, 1978). These variations in the meanings users attach to computers determine, to a large extent, whether or not the introduction of computer technology will be successful. Individuals who are initially reluctant to use electronic forms of communication may change their evaluations once the system is perceived to enhance decision-making processes (Kiesler, 1986).

Changes in meaning over space and time are a major concern of anthropology. The interfaces which predominated 20 years ago were batch mode environments where input was through punch cards and output came in the form of printouts. Data structures were organized around the "80 column" metaphor and magnetic tapes were a primary mode of data storage. Although some might consider these interfaces relics in today's technology, could system designers of 20 years ago have anticipated the changes which occurred? Would those anticipated changes have made a difference in the designs? Although such questions are academic, the point is that designers are concerned about product acceptance over time. Today's designers strive for compatibility with previous software releases, while attempting to incorporate desirable new features. Systems developed today need to be sensitive

163

to existing users, yet flexible enough to accommodate the users of tomorrow. Nowhere is this more evident than in the development of graphical interface designs.

Scientists and designers interested in graphical interfaces have suggested that, "In the same way that books support man's linear and verbal thinking, machines will support his graphic and intuitive processes" (SRI, 1984, p. 2). Given the emerging use of symbolic processing in computer technology, the importance of understanding the meanings people attach to symbols becomes critical for systems designers and programmers. Questions like "When are symbols more appropriate than words?" need to be addressed as systems are put together and tested. For at least one task (making a withdrawal from an automated teller machine), symbols are inferior to text, or text and graphics combined (Stern, 1984).

The construction of meaning over time results in rituals or rules for structuring meaning. Just as structures arise in the interaction between people (Chapters 2 and 3), people also develop structures of symbols (i.e., rituals) which allow them to continuously construct meaning (TenHouten & Kaplan, 1973). Such structures, built from experiences, persist over time and become myths or histories of the past. By examining these variables (symbols, rituals, and myths) in different cultural contexts, anthropology has contributed greatly to what we know about man's history. An analysis of human–computer interaction maps readily into these anthropological variables. Computers symbolize packages of tools for performing a variety of tasks (Kling, 1980) and may symbolize the task itself, such as image processing. The meanings users attach to these symbols evolve into rituals or rules for interacting with the system. As their usage and experience increases, myths are associated with the software and hardware.

Symbols, rituals, and myths define a business's corporate culture and extend the human relations and sociotechnical organization analysis approaches to an anthropological perspective. Theories of organizations indicate that corporations change as the introduction and use of computers changes communication patterns. Computer-based communications cut across previously established organizational boundaries and result in new informal social networks. These changes in corporate culture impact the symbolic meaning of work and create new subcultures bounded by rituals and myths.[1] The social effects of these computer networks represents a conceptual bridge between the organi-

---

[1] When anthropologists talk about *culture*, they are typically referring to the shared customs of a society or population of people. When they talk about the shared customs of a subgroup within a society or population, they are referring to a *subculture*.

zational effects discussed in Chapter 3 and the symbolic meanings users associate with computer technology. This realization is important for systems designers because "one simply cannot change pieces of stable culture without creating potential mass anxiety" (Schein, 1986, p. 33).

Symbols, rituals, and myths also influence a user's attitudes and behavior (Figure 4.1), providing a theoretical link between anthropology and social psychology. Theories in social psychology concentrate on evaluations of users' belief structures, which influence their attitudes toward technology and affect their behavior patterns. As computer usage increases, these belief structures become more differentiated and include the symbols found in the technology, the rituals defining appropriate computer usage for that social environment, and the myths associated with that usage.

Each theoretical orientation—social psychology, sociology, and anthropology—provides a lens through which we view the world (Schwartz & Ogilvy, 1979). To understand the components of this world requires the inclusion of the constructs from all three disciplines. System design principles appear to be moving in this direction. The increasing use of symbols, and their relationship to belief structures and organizational contexts, is facilitating a change in the way new interfaces are being built. The theories of anthropology presented in this chapter contain elements of this change. Moreover, the very use of an anthropological approach to system design is a reflection of the paradigm shift occurring in computer system design.

Through the examination of symbols, rituals, and myths, anthropology seeks to explain cultural differences (Ember & Ember, 1977), cultural change (Bateson, 1972), and cognitive relativism (Geertz, 1983). An objective of this chapter is to provide applied researchers and systems

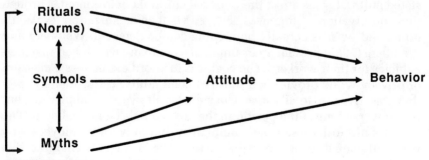

FIGURE 4.1
The effect of symbols, rituals, and myths on attitudes and behavior.

developers with guidelines for incorporating these cultural variants into their analyses and designs. Theories and variables common in anthropology are emphasized, but the linkages to other conceptual frameworks are also noted. Design problems that involve the use of language, cognition, pattern recognition, and the manipulation of symbols are particularly appropriate for the use of the material presented here. Similar to the other theory chapters, we begin by outlining the scope of anthropology and then review the common variables and major theoretical orientations. The application of anthropological theory to human–computer interaction, however, is still an emerging area, and as such there is a paucity of published research. This shortage of empirical evidence makes it difficult to offer numerous examples, as we have done previously. We have included this chapter to provide a theoretical basis for what we feel will become increasingly important areas of investigation in future years. Our discussion reflects traditional approaches and current developments in anthropology.

THE SCOPE OF ANTHROPOLOGY

Anthropologists are often stereotyped as scientists studying exotic peoples in obscure corners of the world, or reconstructing the daily life and customs of prehistoric peoples from fossil remains. Such stereotypes are at least partially accurate, because anthropologists seek answers to a wide variety of questions about human evolution and existence. The questions range from "How and where did humans first appear on earth?" to "In what ways are human societies similar and different?" The stereotypes are inaccurate in the sense that today's anthropologists are moving out of the equatorial jungles and into the corporate ones (Friedland, 1987).

Corporations are hiring anthropologists to observe how a company's stated cultural goals affect the informal cultural environment. Through these observations differences between what an organization thinks it's doing and what is actually happening can be detected. Weinberg and Weinberg (1985) present an example of a company which had installed cubicles for their workers. The goal was to afford employees a measure of privacy while providing a sense of community. Unfortunately, neither objective was totally met. The cubicles allowed visual privacy, but the conversations of the person in the next cubicle could be heard. The cubicles did foster a sense of community, but only for employees who were tall enough to see over the barrier. The Weinbergs analyzed this situation as a case of misplaced boundaries. Because the boundaries were tangible and movable, the solution was easy to solve.

The more difficult problems involve identifying and removing intangible, subjective boundaries that exist between different groups and cultures. People from different cultures see the world differently and consequently apply their own interpretation of what is appropriate behavior in a given situation (Hallowell, 1955; Sahlins, 1976). These studies draw their conclusions from comparative analyses of disparate cultures, but there is no inherent reason to believe that the same variation does not exist across smaller subculture groups. System users and system developers in many ways belong to different subcultures, even when they work for the same company (Weinberg & Weinberg, 1985). Evidence for this statement can be seen in the way members of the two groups dress, the language each group uses, and the hours they keep. These differences define what a group is by providing an unconscious symbol of the group's identity. By studying cultural variations, anthropologists sensitize us to the important but subtle differences that separate cultures and subcultures.

What differentiates anthropology from the other social sciences is the broad scope of its activities. Anthropology is explicitly and directly concerned with all varieties of people throughout the world. In addition, anthropologists include numerous aspects of the human experience when describing a group of people. The history of the area (or organization), the physical environment, the formal and informal organization of operational units, the features of the language (both verbal and nonverbal), and the political and economic climate are all topics of anthropological inquire.

Anthropology seeks to generalize observations of human behavior from overall experiences; thus, the theories employed by anthropologists tend to be global or holistic. While a social psychologist would differentiate between belief and affective components of an attitude, the anthropologist would fuse these dimensions into a single global symbol (D'Andrade, 1981). As a simple example, one might say that a stove is 200 degrees Celsius (a belief or statement of fact) and that it is painful to touch objects at this temperature (an affect or feeling). The anthropologist would say that the stove is hot, fusing together a representation of how things are with how we feel about them into a holistic concept. A society's culture provides the background information needed to simultaneously represent both the external event and the internal reactions. By fusing fact and affective evaluation reaction, cultural schemata come to have powerful impact on implicit values.

The Concept of Culture

Individuals are unique in the sense that each may ascribe to a personal set of beliefs and attitudes, yet most individuals share a surprising number of beliefs and attitudes with other members. A *culture* may be defined as the set of beliefs, values, and behaviors generally shared by the members of a society or population (Ember & Ember, 1977). If only one person believes in or engages in a certain behavior, that belief or action is a personal habit, not a pattern of culture. For something to be considered cultural, it must be generally shared by some population or group of individuals. Examples of shared beliefs, values, and behaviors can be seen among people who have similar regional origins, religious, and/or professional affiliations.

Another defining feature of culture is that it is learned. The way we communicate with each other, the procedures used to perform certain actions, and the behaviors we consider inappropriate are learned rather than being innate qualities of humans. Cultural learning, however, occurs in subtle and complex ways. A great deal of childhood learning occurs through observation, modeling, trial and error, and occasional instruction. Rarely is anyone explicitly taught the precise set of steps to follow to accomplish a task. People more typically learn about culture through a process of guided discovery (D'Andrade, 1981).

However it is defined and learned, culture is what's behind the behavior and the structure that you see in a society or organization (Friedland, 1987). Signs of corporate culture can be seen in the way people interact in meetings: who attends, where they sit, how many voice an opinion. Understanding corporate culture is important because culture influences business strategies. Problems arise when there is a mismatch between an organization's culture and the environment in which it operates.[2] AT&T is a frequently mentioned example in this regard. AT&T's culture was based on the assumption of a universal service with a centralized organizational structure. Today this model is inconsistent with the demands of a decentralized and marketing-oriented information technology environment.

Anthropologists seek to discover the customs and ranges of acceptable behavior that comprise the culture of the society under investigation. Their focus is on general or shared patterns of behavior rather than on individual variations. Anthropologists believe that a society's customs and ideas should be understood in the context of that society's problems and opportunities (sometimes called *cultural relativity*). Rather than comparing a group's behavior against our own, behavior should be judged relative to the appropriateness of the behavior in that group. For software developers, this means that, to understand which functionality and design logic is appropriate for a user community, they must understand the customs and culture of that community.

Every society develops a series of cultural ideal patterns which most

---

[2] A similar point is made in Chapter 3.

members of that society believe to be correct behavior in particular situations. The concept is analogous to Weber's concept of the ideal type (Chapter 3). Similarly to social psychologists, anthropologists refer to such ideal patterns as norms. As we saw in Chapter 2, society's norms do not always agree with actual behavior. Some of our ideal patterns differ from actual behavior, because the ideal is outmoded, based on what that society used to be. Other ideal patterns may never have been actual patterns and may merely represent what people would like to see as the correct behavior. Examination of these differences between the ideal and actual cultural patterns suggests three basic issues about culture:

1. Culture is generally adaptive.
2. Culture is mostly integrated.
3. Culture is always changing.

Culture is generally adaptive.   Culture is generally adaptive to the particular conditions of the physical and social environment. When computers are introduced into an organization, the members of that culture must adapt to new ways of processing information and interacting with other individuals. Some individuals may welcome the new procedures and readily adapt. Others resist the change and cling to the previous mode of operation. What is important for system designers to recognize is that what may be adaptive in one environment may not be adaptive in another. Moreover, a given custom represents one group's (or a society's) adaptation to its environment; it does not represent all possible adaptations. Different groups may choose different means of adjusting to the same situation. Why a group develops a particular response to a problem depends on whether or not a particular response is possible, given existing capabilities. If not all members of a work group are registered to use electronic mail, electronic messaging will not prove to be an effective means of communication.

It is important to remember that a group is not forced to adapt its culture to changing environmental circumstances. First, even in the face of changed circumstances, people may choose not to give up what they have. Second, although people may alter their behavior according to what they perceive will be helpful to them, what they perceive to be helpful may not prove to be adaptive. Third, changing a corporation's culture is difficult, because it embodies the values found in the larger societal culture. Corporations do not simply shape the values of their employees. Rather, they select people from the larger culture who have values that fit its culture and then mold those further (Friedland, 1987). Considering the large number of cultures that have survived, however, we can assume that cultures are generally adaptive.

Culture is mostly integrated.   Culture is mostly integrated in that the elements or traits that make up the culture are mostly adjusted to or consistent with each other. If certain traits are more adaptive in particular settings, then those bundles of traits will generally be found associated under similar conditions. Some aspects of culture may tend to be integrated for another reason. Social psychological research suggests that there is a tendency for people to modify beliefs or behaviors when beliefs or behavior are not cognitively consistent with other information. If we assume cognitive consistency is generally found in humans, we might expect aspects of culture to also be integrated. Cultural integration, then, may be cognitively as well as adaptively induced.

Culture is always changing.   Cultural adaptation is cultural change in response to environmental changes. Cultural integration occurs if one aspect of culture changes in response to other cultural changes. The raw material for cultural change is often the result of individual variation. Something that starts out as unusual or peculiar may be picked up by others as an appropriate response in the face of changing circumstances. When enough people adopt the new behavior, it becomes cultural by definition. The human–computer interaction literature discusses a similar process, using technology transfer as the defining label.

If cultures are more than random collections of behaviors, beliefs, and values (cultures are adaptive, integrated, and changing), then the similarities and differences between cultures should be understandable. In other words, similar circumstances within and outside the culture will give rise to similar cultural responses. Although we may assume that cultural variation is understandable, the task of discovering which particular circumstances favor which particular cultural patterns is a large and difficult one. In the sections to follow we examine some of the variables and theories anthropologists use to explain cultural variations.

RESEARCHER'S AGENDA

In what ways do the members of a culture adapt to new ways of processing information and interacting with other individuals when computers are introduced into an organization?

To what extent and in what way does organizational culture influence system acceptance and use?

How does understanding emerge from the experience of using advanced computer systems?

How many different subcultures exist within the organization or setting of interest?

In what ways are these subcultures similar and different with respect to ideas toward and usage of computers?

MANAGER'S AGENDA

Signs of corporate culture are evident in the way people interact in meetings: who attends, where they sit, and how many voice an opinion. Understanding corporate culture is important because culture influences business strategies.

People, tasks, and culture co-evolve with new technologies. Jobs change as computers are introduced and used.

Anticipate cultural change by incorporating open architectures.

Direct manipulation of a corporation's culture is difficult because it embodies the values found in the larger societal culture.

View the computer as the end-user sees the computer. To understand which functionality and design logic is appropriate for a user community, you must understand the customs and culture of that community.

System users and system developers in many ways belong to different subcultures, even when they work for the same company.

ANTHROPOLOGICAL VARIABLES

Rather than decomposing human–computer interactions into a series of isolated variables such as the mode of interface presentation, number of functions, and the users' prior computing experience, the usability of systems is measured in terms of overall reactions to the computer and the environment in which the activity occurs. As we have been discussing, however, there are three variables common to most studies in anthropology: symbols, rituals, and myths.

Symbols

Because people do not share each other's experiences directly, they must convey their ideas and feelings to each other in ways that others will understand. *Symbols* are signs created by humans to convey our ideas, intentions, and actions to others. They are arbitrary stand-ins for what they represent. The color green in a traffic light could just as easily stand for *stop* as for *go*. The arbitrariness of symbols becomes obvious when travelling in foreign countries. A North American who wishes to express satisfaction with his or her dinner to the waiter by making a circle with thumb and index finger will find the symbol has different meanings in different countries. In Ghana the waiter might interpret the gesture as a sexual invitation, while in Venezuela the sign is likely to be interpreted as a sexual insult. To interpret symbols as they are intended, their meanings must be socially shared. Because individuals associate different meanings to interactions with computers, a major task for systems designers is to identify symbols that minimizes the interpretative variance users attribute to human–computer interactions.

Symbolic representations of actions may (or may not) be effective in conveying meaning to computer users. The trash can icon used in Apple's Macintosh stands for throwing something away and an object to throw it into. Because of our cultural norms, the symbol (trash can) is easily associated with the action (throwing something away). Cultural norms in this example provide a convenient vehicle for communicating between man and machine. Similarly, an icon showing a painter's palette might suggest a drawing program. A picture of a telephone could imply a communication package, and the typewriter is sometimes used to symbolize word processing functionality. The extent to which these meanings are shared by people with different computer backgrounds, however, remains unresolved (Cahill, 1975). New users, for example, have been shown to perform better on command and menu systems than on iconic systems (Whiteside, Jones, Levy, & Wixon, 1985). The performance of individuals who lacked experience with the test system but were experienced computer users was also poorer on the iconic systems than on all the other systems considered together. The care with which an interface is crafted thus appears to be more important than the style of interface (Whiteside et al., 1985, p. 190). The directness of the link between the icon and the command it represents affects both initial comprehension and subsequent retention (Hemenway, 1981).

Symbols can be represented by words as well as pictures (Figure 4.2). Words like DELETE or INSERT denote a set of complex behaviors. The word DELETE implies the behaviors of initiating a subroutine, locating and erasing a file (or some other object), and exiting the subroutine. The choice of which words to use impacts users' reactions to and performance on the system (Booher, 1975; Remington & Williams, 1986). Violent messages such as FATAL ERROR, RUN ABORTED, or obscure code like IEH2191 can be confusing even to experienced computer users (Shneiderman, 1987).

Symbols may also be structural or physical in nature (Figure 4.2). In

Type of Symbol	Example

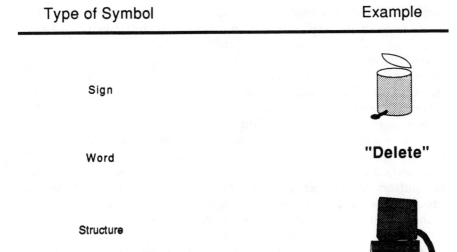

Sign

Word "Delete"

Structure

FIGURE 4.2
Examples of different types of symbols.

this sense, most architecture can be seen as symbolic. Grand cathedrals symbolize the importance people attach to the church. Similarly, the physical structure of a computer has a symbolic meaning that is imparted to the system user. The sheer size of many early computers symbolized the power of electronic data processing. Interestingly, the significance attached to such size attributes has changed as the power of desktop micros approaches and in some cases exceeds the capabilities of minicomputers. Bigger is not always perceived as better.

The physical design of computer furniture has also changed over the years. When relatively few individuals were directly involved in the use of computers, little attention was given to the dimensions of tables and chairs on which terminals were placed. Now that many office workers have their own terminal or PC, companies have emerged that specialize in ergonomically constructed workstations. Entire offices have been redesigned to accommodate these new furnishings, and books have been written to describe the most appropriate placement of computer equipment (Van Cott & Kinkade, 1972; Grandjean & Vigliani, 1980; Woodson & Conover, 1966). Each of these symbolize the role computer technology plays in our everyday lives.

Symbols are constructed by people to denote value states (Schultz, 1964). Computers are often considered valuable because they symbolize tools for improving productivity. Characterizing computers as tools is appropriate for such things as pocket calculators, but may be an oversimplification for larger, more complex computers (Kling, 1980). Kling suggests that computers are more appropriately symbolized as a package which consists, not only of the hardware and software, but also of the diverse sets of skills, support mechanisms, affected organization units, and individual beliefs about computers. Couched in this manner, many of the difficulties that users face in exploiting the value of computer-based systems lie in the way the package is embedded in the complex set of social relationships.

When computing is symbolized as a complex social setting, it becomes a social object and the development and use of computer-based services a social act (Kling & Scacchi, 1979; Scacchi, 1980). As this computing milieu becomes more technically and socially complex, problems can arise, especially if policies are introduced reactively to management problems after the issues have surfaced (King & Kraemer, 1979). The package view of computing suggests that computers symbolize more than simple tools which impact work life. Rather, computers involve a complex array of social interactions, and man–machine interactions represent a symbolic reality that serves multiple purposes.

Rituals

If symbols can be considered "words" which describe reality, rituals represent the rules by which we combine and use these words. This relationship is most easily seen in the language employed by computer users. People familiar with data tapes for storing information sometimes use terms like *at-rewind* (@rewind) in normal conversation with other computer users. The linguistic symbol in this situation denotes the idea the speaker wishes to back up and repeat the last statement.

Any interaction process (human–human, human–computer) is bounded by rules of etiquette and prescription. Such rules are transmitted through time and space by means of ritual. *Rituals* are prescribed behaviors that help form attitudes by providing a meaningful context. Rituals, like social norms (Chapter 2), are prescriptions for what behavior ought to be, not actual behavior. Computer system documentation prescribes appropriate actions for using a system, but the manuals do not physically perform the actions. The procedures required for *booting up* a system illustrate the range of these ritualistic behaviors in a computer environment. Booting up a Macintosh requires a relatively simple set of actions. Start-up procedures for a large mainframe demand a more complex set of events performed in predefined order. The system designers in this latter situation bound the human–computer interaction process by prescribing ritual behaviors.

Rituals are propagated by cultural history that places people and their behavior in context. Ritual prescriptions for computer systems involve issues such as who turns the system on, what instructions are given first, and how the instructions are given. Command languages also serve the ritualistic function of propagating the culture by using sacred knowledge to appropriately interact with the machine. Because rituals are often transparent to people in everyday use, they only become evident when the environment forces change. The use of Latin in the Roman Catholic church has become almost nonexistent in the past few decades. This evolution denotes a change in ritual. The meanings of reverence and respect have not changed, but the means of expressing these symbols have. Changes in the ritualistic use of computers were apparent with the development of timesharing, interactive processing as compared to batch processing. Rather than submitting a program, waiting for the run to be completed, and then returning to examine the output, users could adopt a more conversational approach to computer interactions. The ritual (norm) changed, and so did the symbolic meaning; computing became less mysterious and less sacred.

The increasing use of personal computers raises questions with respect to changes in rituals. Should designers make personal computer interfaces similar to user interfaces on timesharing systems to minimize the effect of changing the ritual of interaction? Or conversely, should the interface be different to reinforce the idea of change? Answers to these questions are related to the individual's expectations and preferences for a particular type of interaction (Chapter 2) and the context in which the work is to be performed (Chapter 3).

Many of today's younger computer users have little, if any, experience with mainframes, and thus have not developed normative expectations for the traditional rituals. For these users, the rituals of human–computer interaction are defined by personal computer interfaces. Predicting the appropriate personal computer interface for individuals with experience on several computers is more difficult, because different groups of users may expect and prefer different modes of interaction. One solution is to allow users to select the style of interaction they feel comfortable with. Some commands on the Macintosh or other window-based systems, for example, can be issued either by keyboard sequences (i.e., similarly to editors on a mainframe) or by menu selections picked via the mouse. Such dual-mode personalities reinforce traditional rituals for those familiar with that interaction style while introducing a different style for new users.

Situational context also plays a role in the impacts associated with the use of PCs. In an office environment where rituals for performing certain tasks are well defined, shifting from a shared logic system to a

PC can be traumatic. Such shifts in technology disrupt traditional work patterns that have been reinforced by co-workers and managers. PC usage in the home is a relatively new phenomenon and thus there is no history of ritualistic behavior to be modified. There are no traditional patterns of using the tool (PC) in the home. The relatively low penetration of PCs into the home market might be explained by a failure to develop the technology to fit the ongoing rituals (patterns of behavior) of home life. Market surveys of people's buying habits continually come to the same conclusion: "OK, so what do I use it for?" Technology that requires a modification of ritual must be closely attuned to everyday behaviors, so that it augments them. When new technologies do not fit the existing situational context, their chances of adoption are decreased.

Myths

Myths are typically used in a pejorative sense (e.g., it is only a myth), the implication being that there is no truth in myths (Bolman & Deal, 1984). Although myths may contain a considerable amount of truth, they differ from theories in that myths are not testable. The chief characteristics of myths are:

1. a myth is a narrative of events
2. the narrative has a sacred quality
3. the sacred communication is made in symbolic form
4. at least some of the events and objects which occur in the myth neither occur nor exist in the world other than in the myth itself
5. the narrative refers in dramatic form to origins or transformations (Cohen, 1969, p. 337).

The myths associated with software development illustrate that what sometimes appears as a reasonable narrative of events can lead to misinformation and confusion. Pressman (1982) argues that software myths have contributed to many of the current problems in software development. The paragraphs below (taken from Pressman, 1982, pp. 25–26) examine some of the more common software myths and present a statement of reality (as perceived by Pressman):

Myth: A general statement of objectives is sufficient to begin writing programs—we can fill in the details later.

Reality: Poor up-front definition is the major cause of failed software efforts. A formal and detailed statement of function, performance, interfaces, design constraints, and validation criteria is essential. These characteristics can be determined only after thorough communication between requestor (customer) and developer.

Myth: Once we write a program and get it to work, our job is done.

Reality: A software life cycle exists. Initial work concentrates on planning (not "writing programs"); subsequent work focuses on development (design, coding, and testing), and finally, on-going work is required to maintain the software once it is "complete."

Myth: Project requirements continually change, but change can be easily accommodated because software is flexible.

Reality: It is true that software requirements change, but the impact of change varies with the time at which it is introduced. . . . If serious attention is given to up-front definition, change can be accommodated easily. . . . When changes are requested during software design, cost impact grows rapidly. . . . Changes, when requested late in a project, can be more than an order of magnitude more expensive than the same change requested early.

Myth: Reviews are superfluous, too time consuming, or impossible to initiate.

Reality: Reviews are the only known mechanism for management and technical control.

Myth: If we get behind schedule, we can add more programmers and catch up (sometimes called the Mongolian horde concept).

Reality: Software development is not a mechanistic process like manufacturing. . . . As new people are added, the need for learning and communication among staff can and does reduce the time spent on productive development effort.[3]

Myth: The only deliverable for a successful project is a working program.

Reality: A working program is only part of a configuration. . . . Documentation forms the foundation for successful development, and more importantly, provides guidance for the software maintenance task.

Myth: Once software is "working," maintenance is minimal and can be handled on a catch-as-catch-can basis.

Reality: . . . Over 50 percent of the budget is actually expended on maintenance. Therefore, software maintenance should be organized, planned, and controlled as if it were the largest project within an organization.

Myth: Give a good technical person a programming book, and you've got yourself a programmer.

Reality: . . . If we are to accept the need for formal training of hardware engineers, we should recognize that software engineering compe-

---

[3] See Chapter 2 (Section—Group Productivity and Cooperative Work) for additional discussion on this topic.

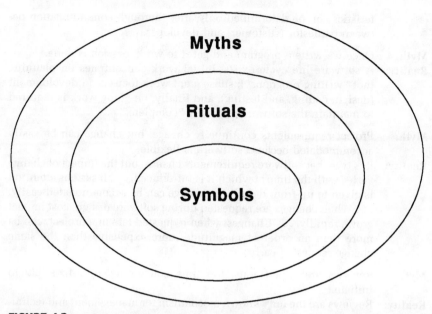

FIGURE 4.3
Relationships between symbols, rituals, and myths.

tence can be achieved only through formal education and worthwhile experience.

Myths associated with human–computer interactions are also evident in the narratives (stories) used by everyday users. Unix users may
believe that Unix machines are powerful, secure, and the only system
to use.[4] As these beliefs are propagated through usage, a myth is born
and the machines almost take on a life of their own. Computer forums
illustrate this propagation of myths and their narrative quality. Forums
act as a natural history of the events which surround discussions of a
particular topic. Initiation rites for new users into the subculture often
take the form of reading this natural history. As the forum evolves over
time, new subcultures define additional rituals which function to establish more myths.

These cycles of symbol, ritual, and myth are intertwined and mutually reinforcing among groups. Symbols (machines) are linked to myths
(stories) through rituals (norms). Symbols are embedded in rituals
which are in turn embedded in myths (Figure 4.3). The symbols impart

---

[4] Consistent with Cohen's defining characteristics of myths, these beliefs illustrate
that some elements in the narrative may be true. Unix machines may be powerful and
secure, but they are not the only system that can be used.

meaning to behavior through the rules prescribed by rituals, but the meaning of behavior only "makes sense" in the context of the myths that surround that behavior. Describing and understanding these relationships between symbols, rituals, and myths in a cultural context is a major focus of anthropology.

RESEARCHER'S AGENDA

What symbolic meaning do people take from the systems they use?

To what extent are the same symbols used by different subcultures?

Should system designers make personal computer interfaces similar to interfaces on timesharing systems to minimize the effect of changing the ritual of interaction? Or conversely, should the interface on the PC be different to reinforce the idea of change?

What icons should be used to symbolize different functionality?

What myths surround the use of computer systems?

MANAGER'S AGENDA

The introduction of computers into a corporate culture impacts the symbolic meaning of work and creates new subcultures.

Allow users room to develop their own subcultures.

Hidden assumptions and dimensions of the culture need to be explicit.

When designing and introducing new systems consider the symbolic cultural significance of the work task the system will fit into.

What are the central myths of the organization that no one questions?

Technology that requires a modification of ritual must be closely attuned to everyday behaviors, so that it augments them.

THEORIES IN ANTHROPOLOGY

Theories in anthropology focus attention on societal characteristics. Some approaches are concerned with the *biological* characteristics and *physical* artifacts of human populations, while others examine *cultural* characteristics, values, and belief systems. Within each of these broad classifications of subject matter, anthropological theories have demonstrated a continual ebb and flow of ideas. One theory may dominate the

| | Variables | | | |
Theory	Symbol	Ritual	Myth	Research Focus
Linguistic	X			Words
Cognition	X	X		Thoughts
Ecology		X	X	Form
Symbolic Interaction	X	X	X	Interaction Patterns

FIGURE 4.4
Theories and variables in anthropology.

intellectual thought for a period of time, only to be displaced by another orientation that attempts to compensate for the shortcomings of the former. In this section we outline three major theoretical orientations in cultural anthropology (*linguistics, cognition,* and *ecology*) and introduce the theory of *symbolic interactionism.* Although symbolic interactionism is typically identified as a subdiscipline of social psychology, we present the theory in this chapter because of the theory's emphasis on symbols in a social/cultural context. Discussion of symbolic interactionism here also reinforces the linkages between anthropology and social psychology.

Anthropological theories influence, not only the types of information the researcher collects, but also the way the anthropologist organizes, interprets, and explains the information. Figure 4.4 relates the four theoretical approaches to the variables commonly used in the anthropology.[5] Theories of linguistics are primarily concerned with the study of symbols, whereas symbolic interactionism incorporates the analysis of symbols, rituals, and myths. From the perspective of research focus, linguistics examines words, cognition is concerned with thoughts, ecology emphasizes form, and symbolic interactionism is primarily interested in patterns of interactions. Although these distinctions are far from mutually exclusive, Figure 4.4 provides an overview of the differences among the theories.

[5] It is assumed that the use of computers has developed to the extent that computers have become symbols in themselves, that rituals for their use have become routine, and that myths regarding their usefulness are commonplace for many individuals.

LINGUISTICS

People have created numerous symbol systems (mathematics, music), but language is the main vehicle of human communication. All peoples possess a spoken language. Although communication is not limited to spoken language, language is of overriding importance, because it is the primary vehicle through which human culture is shared and transmitted. *Spoken language* can be defined as a socially acquired system of sound patterns with meanings that are agreed on by the members of a group. Language is thus composed of symbols which are linked through speech and transferred from one person to another.

Linguistics is the study of how people use language. In order to study the diversity of human languages, linguists have developed ways of describing languages that enables them to compare languages systematically. Spoken languages include sounds, words, meanings, and grammatical rules. To understand a string of sounds and to produce an appropriate response, people must recognize:

1. the distinct sounds of which the language is composed (the phonetic component)
2. the combination of sounds into words (the morphologic component)
3. the common meanings of the words (the semantic component)
4. the convention of putting words together built into the language (the syntactic component or grammar).

Unspoken languages such as computer languages and the sign languages for the deaf lack a phonetic component, although they do possess the remaining components. For a communication system to be considered a language, morphology, semantics, and syntax are all essential. Linguists study these components, seeking to uncover the rules that give structure to language. Similarly, computer scientists examine these components to identify how people use language when communicating with computers. Anthropologists are more interested in how language facilitates the way people perceive their world and organize experience. Two linguistic approaches in anthropology that have relevance to the study of human–computer interaction are: (1) the *structuralist* approach, and (2) the *pragmatic* approach.

Structural Anthropology

Structural anthropology posits a relationship among language, cognition, and social structure. Symbol systems such as language influence how members of a social system think about and resolve issues as they arise. At the individual level, the structure of the symbol system describes how a person's knowledge about the different segments of his or her environment are related to each other. At the cultural level, the structure of symbol systems describes the attribute relations between individual systems that make up the interpersonal symbolic systems.

To some theorists (Levi-Strauss, 1963, 1966), linguistic constructs are universal structures which are invariant across cultures. If languages are molded by the beliefs, values, and ideals all people share, languages should also have certain features in common. *Linguistic universals* are features common to all languages. For example, every language has nouns and verbs, because people must refer to objects and actions. Every language appears to have terms that express height, length, distance, and direction (left–right, up–down), because all humans have the same basic need to orient themselves in relation to the physical world (Clark & Clarke, 1977). The origins of these universals lie in the human capacities for thought about events and relations. Of most interest to anthropologists are universals rooted in the social and cultural conditions of life.

Other theorists (Sapir, 1921; Chomsky, 1965) hypothesize a relationship between cognitive and social structures, but view language as culturally dependent. Rather than discussing the influence of thought and experience on language, this approach suggests that language influences the way we think and experience the world. The Sapir-Whorf *linguistic relativity hypothesis* is the most frequently mentioned theory on this question. This hypothesis holds that language "is not merely a reproducing instrument for voicing ideas, but is itself a shaper of ideas, the program and guide for the individual's mental activity" (Whorf, 1956). Both strong and weak versions of this hypothesis have been proposed.

According to the strong version, language determines our perceptions of reality such that we cannot perceive or comprehend distinctions that do not exist in our own language. The suggestion is that we cannot talk about ideas or objects for which we lack the words. The ways we think about the world are determined by the way our language slices up reality. This strong version of the linguistic relativity hypothesis has found little empirical support. For example, some languages have only two basic words (*dark* and *white*) to cover the spectrum of colors, yet people from these cultures can discriminate and communicate about whatever large numbers of colors are shown to them (Heider & Olivier, 1972).

The weaker form of the hypothesis says each language facilitates particular forms of thinking, because it makes events more easily cod-able and symbolized. Support for this hypothesis is substantial, with two clear effects resulting from the availability of linguistic symbols for objects and events. First, it improves the efficiency of communication about these objects and events, and, second, it enhances success about remembering them. To demonstrate the value of language labels for memory, one study exposed subjects to a large number of nonsense shapes that were either verbally labelled or not (Santa & Ranken, 1972). When later asked to recognize the shapes they had seen, subjects re-called shapes better if they had been originally labelled. The verbal labels helped people to discriminate more completely among the shapes and to store them more distinctly in memory.

Based on the available evidence, we can conclude that language is more a reflection of human capacities and culture than a determinant of thought. Language influences memory and perhaps the efficiency of thought, but even if language constructs are assumed to be universal, the form in which these universals are expressed may vary between groups (Friedrich, 1970). Most people in North America would recog-nize an icon of an upright cabinet as a place to store things. Individuals from other cultures who do not file records in a similar manner may find such a symbol confusing. Similarly, a *rolodex* is generally defined "as a place to keep addresses," but the icon used to illustrate a rolodex may vary dramatically. One rolodex could be round and contain index cards for holding address information. Another may be flat and similar to a ring binder, while a third is simply an address book. From a system design perspective, the empirical questions are: What icon should be used to represent the intended functionality? To what extent are the symbols employed by one subculture (e.g., system designers) shared by another subculture (e.g., office automation users)?

Debate over these issues is not likely to be resolved in the immediate future. One solution, however, is to let the user select, from a range of possible candidates, the icon that will represent the functionality. Digi-tal Research's GEM desktop manager allows for this user specification. When a new application is installed, the user selects an icon from the options shown in Figure 4.5. If the user lives in the United States or Canada, some of these symbols (e.g., the $ icon for accounting pro-grams) are easily associated with the intended functionality. The mean-ing of other icons may not be as readily apparent; for example, the two choices provided for multifunction activities or the options for outlin-ing programs. Another solution is to provide individuals with the capa-bility of creating their own symbolic representations. This approach allows users the greatest amount of flexibility in customizing their interface to suit their preferences and needs.

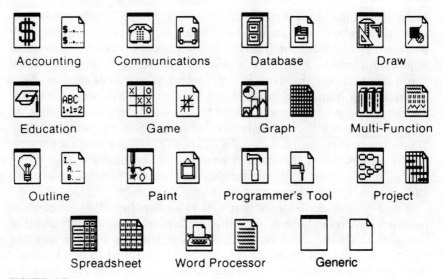

FIGURE 4.5
Gem desktop icon selections.

Pragmatism

A second major linguistic theory in anthropology which has direct application to system design is the *pragmatic* approach. Language develops from our surrounding culture and has meaning only in that context (Ruesch & Bateson, 1951). Problems occur when the rules of contextual behavior are not shared by all users. The *PRINT* command has traditionally implied hardcopy output. In a PC environment, however, the concept of *PRINT* may mean any of several output devices (e.g. printer, hard disk, floppy disk, etc). Confusion arises when a user familiar with the concept of printing hardcopy finds the system writing the document to hard disk. The point is that the meanings of words are derived from usage and may not bear a direct relationship to the same word in a different task or system environment.

The study of pragmatic linguistic structures provides some guidance in understanding why people don't use computers in the way designers intended them (Campbell, 1982). The logic in use during design has been shown to be quite different from that employed by system users. In the study by Whiteside et al. (1985), the function keys on the menu system varied from application to application causing user frustration. Subjects in this experiment perceived inconsistencies which were not detected by the developers. Given that most human–computer communication systems are based on logical structures, paradoxes are created in peoples' minds because of the pragmatic discontinuous nature of language (TenHouten & Kaplan, 1973).

The way in which people use language mediates the relationship between the individual and larger social structures. Underlying all social interaction is a microworld (Scheff, 1986). This microworld connects individuals in shared meanings and feelings and also connects them to the social structure of their society. Linking the individual to society through language implies that language can illustrate how the connections emerge and how individuals attune themselves to larger social institutions.

The process by which people take meaning from symbolic structures is based on their "mastery of the language" (Dolgin, Kemnitzer, & Schneider, 1977). Cultural norms inherent to language provide a basis for extracting meaning. Extracting meaning from symbols, however, goes beyond the capabilities of a language. A great deal of information is communicated nonverbally during human–human interactions. When we wave to departing friends at an airport, we are communicating through a visual channel. Our facial expressions may convey a sense of sadness with their departure. By one estimate, the human face can make some 250,000 different expressions (Birdwhistell, 1970). Combining these with other nonverbal cues, the number of nonverbal communication possibilities is infinite. Like language, these nonverbal cues are learned rather than innate. As a result, the meanings of nonverbal cues may vary from one culture to another. Information exchange in human–human interaction is usually conveyed through both nonverbal and verbal channels. Multiple cues add information to each other, reduce ambiguity, and increase accuracy. But if the cues are inconsistent, people must determine which cues reveal the speaker's true intentions. Computer-mediated communication also allows people to engage in interaction with larger groups, but electronic messaging often truncates the bandwidth of communication (Winograd, 1984).[6] Attenuation of bandwidth and decreasing channels (e.g., the absence of a nonverbal language) lessens the understanding of the extended context of language (Sacks, Schlegoff, & Jefferson, 1974).

In face-to-face interactions, four major types of nonverbal communication are: paralanguage, body language, interpersonal spacing, and choice of personal effects. *Paralanguage* refers to the vocal aspects of speech other than words (Scherer, 1979). These vocal aspects include loudness, pitch, speed, emphasis, inflection, breathiness, clipping of words, pauses, etc. *Body language* conveys meaning through

---

[6] A similar point is made in Chapter 2 in the section on Group Productivity and Cooperative Work.

the participants' movements. Scowls, smiles, nods, gestures, and postural shifts are all examples of body language. *Interpersonal spacing* is positioning ourselves at varying distances and angles from others (e.g., standing close or far away, facing head-on or to one side, adopting various postures). As with the other nonverbal cues, interpersonal spacing rituals are culture bound. American and Northern European tourists often feel uncomfortable at the closeness of interaction if they engage an Arab male in conversation. Different cultures have different norms for interaction distances. A final form of nonverbal communication is a person's *choice of personal effects*. This refers to the selection and display of objects that others associate with an individual. A person's choice of cars, home decoration, clothing, for example, can communicate social status, life style, and occupation, revealing a great deal about the individual.

The very nature of computer-mediated communication in its truncated format calls for an increased understanding of basic human linguistic communication. The development of systems to augment human interaction by connecting and extending their intelligence requires a broad perspective to be successful. Linguistic analysis is a powerful tool in analyzing this augmentation process. To understand any given utterance, the participants must have access to the extended context of the utterance, all events which took place or could have taken place before, during, and after the particular moment (Scheff, 1986). The design of computer systems should inherently recognize the importance of this fact and build into systems a capability to facilitate people having access to the extended context of the conversations (interactions) being transmitted.

COGNITIVE ANTHROPOLOGY

Cognitive anthropology is a relatively new area of inquiry within the social sciences (Tyler, 1969). Emphasis is placed on explaining behavior patterns in terms of culturally variant organizing principles. Two types of questions are typically asked: What phenomena are important to people? and How do people organize these phenomena? (Figure 4.6). It is assumed that different subcultures employ different cognitive schema. In contrast to traditional linguistic theory which suggests that people impose a preexisting order, cognitive anthropologists argue that people attempt to discover the underlying order that exists outside themselves (Douglas, 1970, 1975). Cognitive psychologists investigate similar issues but focus on intrapersonal variation rather than cultural differences. Viewed from this perspective, cogni-

Questions: What phenomena are important to people?

                  How do they organize these phenomenon?

Theory: Order is given to the environment.

                  Organizing principles vary as a function
                  of culture.

Unit of Analysis: Principles, not things.

Method: Linguistics, Symbolic Analysis

FIGURE 4.6
Principles of Cognitive Anthropology.

tive anthropology supplements the work of cognitive psychologists
(e.g., Norman, 1983).

Cultural variations affect the ways people organize physical space
(Hallowell, 1955; Sahlins, 1976). Concern over the way people perceive
and organize information displayed on a computer workstation is evident in the desktop metaphor used on Apple's Macintosh, IBM's Top-
view, Digital Research's GEM desktop, and Microsoft's Windows. In
each of these environments, users are provided with a visual way of
organizing their work. Users can arrange their desktops anyway they
want. Objects on the desktop can be moved around similar to the way
users would manipulate things in any office. At issue is the discovery
of how groups organize the world around them.

One approach is to examine how people arrange or manipulate
things in a noncomputer environment. Arrangements can be characterized along several dimensions. Malone (1983) shows that desktop arrangements not only assist individuals in finding desired information,
but also the function of reminding people of things to do. Electronic
desktops which include both of these functions may enhance the perceived usefulness of the system. Another approach that offers potential
benefits to system designers has been described as *Environmental
Knowing* (Moore & Golledge, 1976). This method concentrates on how
people conceptually organize categories in their physical environment
and how groups' develop mental schemata of that environment. Three
major areas of study are included in the environmental knowing perspective: meaning, cognitive chunking, and mental maps.

Meaning. There is a difference between giving meaning to the
world and having knowledge about it. The process of giving meaning

implies that people actively impose order onto the world. The converse is that people passively take knowledge from the world. Such differences have important implications for the study of man's use of computers. If people actively give meaning to their environments, the process is interactive rather than linear. Human–computer interactions where the person switches from word processing, electronic mail, and spreadsheet applications at irregular intervals do not follow a linear pattern. Similarly, computer users learn new systems by interactively imposing previously learned metaphors. Programmers might learn a new system by applying their knowledge of other systems. Novice users rely on metaphors drawn from other domains. When individuals' first attempt to learn a text editor, they typically use their knowledge about electronic typewriters. To facilitate this paired-associate learning, Carroll and Thomas (1982, pp. 111–115) identify eight recommendations for system designers:

1.   Find and use appropriate metaphors in teaching the naive user a computer system.
2.   Given a choice between two metaphors, choose the one that is most congruent with the way the system really works. The more aspects of the system that can be "covered" by a single metaphor, the better.
3.   Take care to ensure that the emotional tone of the metaphor is conducive to the desired emotional attitude of the user.
4.   When it is necessary to use more than one metaphor for a system, choose metaphors drawn from a single real-world task domain (i.e., similar enough) but do not choose objects or procedures which are exclusive alternatives from within that domain (i.e., not too similar).
5.   Consider the probable consequences to users and system designers of each metaphor used.
6.   When introducing a metaphor, explicitly point out to each user that it is not a perfect representation of the underlying system and point toward the limits of the metaphor.
7.   Keep in mind from the beginning that any metaphors presented to the user are to give an overview of the system and that there may be a time, at least for the continual user, that the metaphor is no longer useful.
8.   Provide the user with exciting metaphors for routine work and eventually present the user with a variety of scenarios which present different views and require different actions but whose underlying structure is identical.

Chunking. The second component of Environmental Knowing suggests that people *chunk* or aggregate information into manageable units (Rapoport, 1976). Similar ideas have been widely used by psychologists to understand memory and recall processes (Miller, 1956). Anthropology extends this traditional psychological view by proposing that chunking effects are culturally variant, maybe not in absolute numbers, but in the "kinds of symbols and metaphors" that are used to aggregate information. Thus, even though all people may use approximately seven units or chunks, your seven units may be quite different from mine. Metaphors used by experienced users typically vary from those employed by novice users. As individuals gain experience, the metaphors that initially facilitated learning the system often break down and are replaced by more elaborate symbols. For instance, a computer terminal does not work exactly like a typewriter; the terminal displays information on a screen rather than on paper, text typed on a terminal is not necessarily saved automatically, footnotes may be positioned by the system rather than the individual, and formatting may be handled by style sheets rather than manually moving tab markers. Understanding which chunks of information are used by groups of individuals will facilitate the design of computer systems and extend their useful life as the metaphors become more differentiated.

Mental maps.   People's *mental maps* of the world also vary in relation to cultural dimensions. One subculture of users (e.g., Unix hackers) are likely to have a different map of a computer system than do those from another subculture (e.g., office automation users). Just how far into subcultural distinctions this phenomenon penetrates is an empirical question that remains to be examined. If the supposition of cultural variance is true, system designers need to be aware of such differences when developing new hardware and software products. Cognitive anthropology facilitates such efforts by providing a set of tools for investigating cultural variations. Agar and Hobbs (1985) describe a methodology for "growing schemata out of interviews." Their system represents a merging of traditional ethnographic concerns with those of artificial intelligence. The system specifies how to look for themes in personal interviews and how to structure the data collection process to achieve manageable results. Colby (1985) also discusses the development of a computerized content analysis system which seeks to describe and model culture through the study of recorded human speech. The system automates the content analysis process to describe the relationship between the use of semantic symbols and affect.

ECOLOGICAL THEORY

Cultural ecology examines the influence of environmental factors on culture. To the cultural ecologist, cultural variations are influenced by the physical and social conditions within which the culture exists. Relative to a computer system, ecological theory is concerned with the relationships between the structure of the hardware and software, and with how people perceive these relationships in a sociotechnical environment. The fundamentals of human–computer interaction can be summarized by ecological theory as follows. People interact with computing systems in symbolic and ritualistic ways. The form of this interaction is qualitatively different from the content of the interactive process. The form of the interaction is represented by patterns; the content gives rise to the meaning people take from the interaction. Changes in human–computer interaction patterns comes from the interaction of form and content dimensions. The context of the interaction (i.e., meta-message or grouping of patterns) is part of the form of the interaction.

The "ecological laws" developed by Bateson (1972) provide a starting point for understanding this phenomenon. These laws are presented here to suggest an alternative way of viewing human–computer interaction. They are:

1. **Science Never Proves Anything:** The scientific model of reality is only valid within a certain historical and cultural context. Data from a survey of hackers' perceptions of which features should be included in a new computer product may not reflect the needs of office automation users. Science doesn't prove things, it only provides explanations of events within a sociocultural context.

2. **The Map is Not the Territory:** Descriptions of reality are only that, descriptions, not reality itself. A description of a series of computer users' behaviors is not the same thing as the interaction itself. It follows that map and territory are always mismatched and not accurate reflections of one another.

3. **There is No Objective Experience:** All experience is perceived, sensed, and recorded through a process of filtering, or reorganization. Experience becomes subjective and therefore is different for each person.

4. **Image Formation Processes are Unconscious:** The images we develop of the world around us can be identified, counted, and measured, but the process we use to form these images is not readily assessable.

5. **Perception of Parts and Wholes is Convenient:** Organizing reality into pieces and putting pieces together helps us understand, but there are different ways of separating and combining these pieces. A computer system can be divided into parts (e.g., CPU, memory storage, input/output devices), but the system can be divided in different ways for different purposes, such as separating it into things that move around and those that don't.

6. **Divergent Sequences are Unpredictable. Convergent Sequences are Predictable:** Things that move apart from one another are oriented to the future, things coming together are seen as emerging from the past. Cognitively, we sense a pattern to convergence based on past events. We only see a pattern, and hence our predictive ability increases from past events. Computer users familiar with one operating system can often predict how a new system might function based on their past experiences. Novices who lack this background have more difficulty in understanding the relationships between the hardware and software.

7. **Number is Different from Quantity:** Numbers are the product of counting, while quantities are the product of measurement. Measuring the amount of CPU usage is different from counting the number of users on a system.

8. **Quantity Does Not Determine Pattern:** Patterns are relationships between two or more quantities. Patterns are not determined by any single quantity, although they bear a relationship to it. Monitoring the number of times individuals send mail to each other is different that determining the pattern of interaction among the users.

9. **Logic is a Poor Model for Cause and Effect:** Logic is a time-constrained way of describing relationships between events. The typical "if. . . . then" model is logical in a closed system of behavior. In an open system, however, where multiple factors relate to the "then" event, the simple "if . . . then" logic breaks down. Cause and effect are by nature more probabilistic than deterministic. The logical physics of Newton has been replaced by the more relativistic model of Einstein. Bateson suggests that the same is true of theories of human behavior.

10. **Causality Does Not Work Backward:** Pressing a key on a keyboard can "cause" a computer to change a bit in an address space. But changing that bit, by some other means, will not "cause" a key to be depressed on the keyboard.

11. **Language Commonly Stresses Only One Side of Any Interaction:** The point of view of the speaker is inherent in our common subject–predicate relationship in language. People talk about interacting with someone, but the overall pattern of the interaction is better understood when considering all the viewpoints of the group. Electronically monitoring computer users' behavior provides a vehicle for capturing the "language of the computer" as well as that of the user. By comparing user linguistic descriptions to computer descriptions of the same interaction, a certain richness emerges from having both languages as source material.

12. **Stability and Change are Necessary for Description:** The concepts

of stability and change are descriptions of parts of a process. To present a complete picture of an event requires an understanding of how elements change over time. Descriptions of measures from a single point in time are incomplete.

Overall, ecological theory represents a paradigmatic shift in anthropological thought. Emphasis is placed on the analysis of *patterns of interaction* between man and computer. Bateson's work seeks to push this shift further into a study of patterns that connect human–computer–environment metaphors. Ecological theory, and Bateson in particular, offers two basic issues to the design of computer systems: (a) a change in the nature of questions asked by researchers, and (b) a focus on interaction pattern recognition. Bateson defined his approach to social science as being a different epistemology. *Epistemology* is a subdiscipline in philosophy concerned with ways of knowing. It assumes that there are different ways to come to know, understand, and experience social phenomena. Central to Bateson's thinking is the idea that there is another way to understand behavior besides linear cause and effect models. The ecological laws are key principles meant to help researchers change their perspective on what to look at in human–computer interaction.

Research in information system design is beginning to echo the importance of developing a different perspective (Lyytinen, 1987). Improvements in information system use are being limited by the way designers come to understand the design problem itself. "The IS [Information System] use process is also affected by the epistemological strategies preferred by the individual. Epistemological strategies are classes of evidence generators or guarantors. Each evidence generator exhibits an archetypical way of generating evidence for decision-making" (Lyytinen, 1987, p. 31). In other words, the model of reality brought to the research/design situation can limit the identification of design alternatives. The principles of ecological theory can be used by system designers to switch perspectives—and begin asking different questions—leading to alternative system designs. This demand for different strategies in system design can only be met with the use of a wider variety of design assumptions—epistemologies. The work of Bateson is seminal within this perspective.

The second way that ecological theory can be used is to emphasize a search for patterns connecting humans and computers. As a different epistemology is used, the way in which we analyze the data produced should also change. Ecological theory points to looking at patterns of mutual causality, systemic connections, and feedback. These ways of looking at data are vastly different than traditional social science. The use of ecological theory implies a search for the patterns which connect people and computers.

Ten Houten and Kaplan (1973) provide an example of this approach in their discussion of Guttman scaling. Data viewed from one perspective may appear to be a straight line, yet the same data could form the pattern of a circle. This ability to look at the same data from a number of perspectives is a sensitivity that ecological theory is intended to inter-ject into the research process. The batch mode method of processing information during the 1960s was a pattern of many people relating to one computer, a many-to-one relationship. The advent of personal computing in the 1970s changed this pattern of relationships from many-to-one to one-to-one. As computer technology advances we are seeing another change in the way people and computers interrelate, for example, a shift from individual productivity tools to software that facilitates work group activities. Such groupware represents a complex hybrid of existing forms of human–computer interaction. Ecological theory stresses the importance of trying to find, describe and explain the dynamics of these changing patterns. Ecological theory is a tool for designers, a different way of looking at human–computer interaction.

SYMBOLIC INTERACTIONISM

Symbolic interactionism provides a conceptual bridge between cognitive anthropology/psychology and social psychology. Like the cognitive perspectives, symbolic interactionism stresses cognitive processes (thinking, reasoning, planning), but places more emphasis on the inter-action process (Mead, 1934, 1938; Blumer, 1962, 1969; Stryker, 1983). The theory is based on the premise that human nature and social order are products of communication among people. An individual's be-havior is constructed through a give-and-take during interaction with others. Behavior is more than a response to stimuli or an expression of biological drives. Rather, human behavior emerges through communi-cation and interaction with others. The bases for such communications are verbal and nonverbal (gestures, voice qualities, etc.) symbol sys-tems.

People are successful in communicating with one another to the extent that they ascribe similar meanings to objects (symbols) in a situa-tion. The meaning associated with an object is influenced more by what the person might do with the object than the physical properties of the object itself. Objects take on meaning only in relation to a person's plans. A secretary might see a computer as only a word processing tool; a manager might see it as a vehicle for communicating with colleagues; a scientist might see it as a way for doing statistical analysis.

Human behavior is considered goal-oriented and proactive from a symbolic interactionist perspective. People formulate plans to achieve their goals, and realization of these goals is often only possible through cooperation. Cooperation may involve the assistance of other people, a computer, or both. To establish this cooperation, meanings of things must be shared and consensual. When differences exist, an agreement must be developed through give-and-take before cooperative action is possible. Two authors working on the same manuscript, for example, need to establish an agreement regarding who will do which sections and how drafts will be exchanged (hardcopy, electronic mail, floppy disks). If the format produced by one author's favorite word processor cannot be read by the other author's editor, information can be lost or will be unusable. Resolution of this situation is possible if the authors agree to always exchange drafts using a particular size and type of disk, formatted such that both author's word processors can read the information. A symbolic interactionist would describe this as developing a *definition of the situation*.

Symbolic interactionism sees social interaction as tentative and developing. To achieve a consensus, people must continually negotiate new meanings or reaffirm old meanings. Such negotiations are evident when Human Factors personnel negotiate changes with software developers. Each person (or group) plans some actions, tries them out and then adjusts his or her plans in response to the other. Thus, social interaction inherently is somewhat unpredictable and indeterminate.

A central concept in symbolic interactionism is the process of *role taking*, in which the individual imagines how he or she looks from the other's viewpoint. If human factors people are to understand positions presented by software developers, it is important for them to view the problem with the other's eyes. The same logic applies to understanding users. As a starting point, it can be noted that users do not refer to themselves as users (Weinberg & Weinberg, 1985). People who use computers see themselves as bankers, lawyers, secretaries, scientists, or some other career label. The term *user* is a catch-all phrase applied to others by people in the computer industry.

In one of our own attempts to introduce computers into a small company, we found that the ability to put ourselves into the role of the other greatly facilitated the selection of appropriate software packages. The company provided a mail order distribution service, where incoming requests were placed in long trays and processed sequentially. Depending on what the buyer was interested in, the request was channeled to one of several points in the building. Copies of filled orders were stored in a central location in a series of metal filing cabinets. When we started to think like the workers, it was apparent that the employees symbolized these elements in their physical office in a particular way. Recognition of this metaphor provided the vehicle for translating the physical components of the environment into computer relevant terms (e.g., hard disks, floppies, and printers).

For interaction to proceed smoothly, a person must achieve consensus with respect to his or her *self* and the identity of others. Each person must answer the question "Who am I in this situation, and who are the other people?" Only when this question is answered consensually can persons understand the implications (meaning) that others have for their own plans of action. The self-concept is important to symbolic interactionism, because social order stems from self-control. Coordination between people is possible because individuals strive to control their actions from within. The goal is to maintain their own self-respect and to be respected by others.

In sum, symbolic interactionism recognizes the importance of the self in social interaction. It stresses the central role of symbolic communication and language in personality development and culture. It explicitly treats the processes in achieving concensus and cooperation. And it illuminates why people try to avoid embarrassment and maintain emotional stability. If human–human relationships and human–computer interactions stem from a similar set of processes, understanding one mode of interaction facilitates the explanation of the other.

Communication in human–computer interactions is a process of symbolic interaction (Nwankwo, 1973). People communicate with machines via symbols, but this process of symbolic communication is embedded within larger symbol systems. A person can communicate with a computer via mathematics (a symbol system), yet the process itself is contained within another symbol system: the computer as a tool or machine. Subjective interpretations of events mediate the link between social stimulus and behavioral response. To fully understand human–computer interactions, the relationship of these symbol systems must be analyzed.

If a computer is a symbol, the perception of this symbol can structure and guide a person's behavior with a computer. By manipulating symbols people can produce behavior in others (including computers) that differs from what they would normally expect. People often can't understand how a computer reacts to their use of a symbol, because the computer doesn't always behave the way they would expect it to. "When I say PRINT, I mean print on a piece of paper, not a disk storage unit." The meanings and values people extract from using symbols form the basis of knowing how to act in certain situations; they generate expectations of behavior. People expect computers to act in certain ways, because such expectations are derived from the use of symbols in other types of interaction. How people interact with one another effects how they think computers should behave and how they believe they should interact with the computer.

Emotional states arise from person–person interaction and the possibility exists that human–computer interaction can also be responsible for generating emotional states. Pecjak (1972) studied the emotional reactions expressed by two distinct cultures to a set of symbols. Results indicated that the two groups expressed different emotions to the same arrangement of symbols and that the reactions varied as a function of culture. If people hate computers, efforts should be expended to minimize adverse negative emotional effects. Such emotional states are linked to perceptions of power and status (Kemper, 1978). When people feel they are receiving less status recognition than they warrant, certain emotions are generated. Applied to human–computer interactions, interesting possibilities emerge. Interactions between computers and humans that result in the individuals feeling inferior are likely to promote negative reactions to the technology (Figure 4.7). If users feel the computer has more power (lower left quadrant), they will react with either fear or rebellion. When the users attribute the power deficit to their own abilities, the expected reaction is fear. When the deficit is attributed to the limitations of the system, the reaction is rebellion. For system designers this implies that putting the user in control minimizes adverse power differential reactions. Differential status and power perceptions of users may lie at the core of the ease-of-use concept and account for differences in subjective satisfaction. To adequately understand what happens when a person uses a computer, developers must recognize that the communication is carried out through the interchange of symbols. These symbols have a different meaning dependent on cultural background, cognitive organizing principles, language used to express symbols, and the structure of the interaction itself.

RESEARCHER'S AGENDA

Do linguistic universals exist in human–computer interactions? If yes, are the universals the same for members of different subcultures?

To what extent can linguistic universals be embedded in computer technology?

In what ways can the bandwidth of human–computer interaction be expanded to reflect human–human interaction patterns (e.g., nonverbal languages)?

Should human–computer interactions parallel human–human interactions?

What phenomena are important to people?

WHEN YOU FEEL YOU ARE THE CAUSE

	BELIEF - GUILT	BEHAVIOR - SHAME
TOO MUCH	˙ATONEMENT NEED FOR PUNISHMENT REMORSE	DEPRESSION DESIRE TO REPAY WITHDRAWAL FROM GROUP
TOO LITTLE	TRAGIC DESTINY INTENSE FEAR	LOSS OF HOPE ALIENATION

WHEN YOU FEEL SOMEONE ELSE IS THE CAUSE

	BELIEF - GUILT	BEHAVIOR - SHAME
TOO MUCH	BLAME THE VICTIM DELUSIONS OF POWER	DESIRE FOR PERFECTION HYPERCRITICISM
TOO LITTLE	REBELLION CONFUSION, DISORDER	ANGER OUTERWARD HOSTILITY

After Kemper (1978)

FIGURE 4.7
Social relational matrix of distressful emotions[1].

How do people organize these phenomena and the world around them?

What metaphors are appropriate for teaching users about a system?

What emotional tones of metaphors are conducive to user acceptance?

How do individuals cognitively chunk information about computer systems? To what extent are these chunks of information culturally variant?

To what extent do subcultures of computer users employ different mental maps of technology and the environment in which it is used?

In what ways can Bateson's ecological laws help researchers change their perspective on what to look for in human–computer interactions?

What is the pattern of communication that connects normal workflows?

How do computer users define their role within the larger organization context?

MANAGER'S AGENDA

The words people use to describe their pattern of interaction with computers provide clues for understanding underlying processes.

To understand any communication, participants must have access to the extended context of the interaction. The design of computer systems should inherently recognize the importance of this fact and build into systems a capability to facilitate people having access to the extended context of the conversations (interactions) being transmitted.

When describing a computer's metaphors to users, explicitly point out that the metaphors are not a perfect representation of the system and that the metaphors have limitations.

Given a choice between two metaphors, choose the one that is most congruent with the way the system really works. The more aspects of the system that can be "covered" by a single metaphor, the better.

When it is necessary to use more than one metaphor for a system, choose metaphors drawn from a single real-world task domain (i.e., similar enough). Do not choose objects or procedures which are exclusive alternatives from within that domain (i.e., not too similar).

Metaphors appropriate for novice users may not apply to experienced users.

Provide the user with exciting metaphors for routine work and eventually present the user with a variety of scenarios which present different views and require different actions but whose underlying structure is identical.

Understanding which chunks of information are used by groups of individuals facilitates the design of computer systems and extends their useful life as the metaphors become more differentiated.

The model of reality brought to the research/design situation can limit the identification of design alternatives. The use of ecological theory implies a search for new patterns of interaction which connect people and computers.

To understand the users of a computer system, it is necessary to view the technology from their perspective. As a starting point, it can be noted that users do not refer to themselves as users. The term user is a catch-all phrase applied to others by people in the computer industry.

APPLYING ANTHROPOLOGICAL THEORIES

Locating empirical examples of the application of theories and methods of anthropology to system design is difficult. In recent years, however, some examples have begun to appear in the technical and academic literature. We feel that, over time, anthropology will find greater relevance to system design as we learn to appreciate and account for cultural differences in the use, acceptance, and understanding of advanced technologies. Limitations to computer acceptance in today's office environment are often cultural limitations. System designers and users belong to different cultures, and difficulties in understanding arise from these differences. By employing an anthropological perspective, we can begin to realize that cultural bridges must be built between designers and users.

An Example from the Software Games Industry

The theories in anthropology can be applied to the development of any software product, but their influence is currently most pronounced in the software games industry. Because a game's outcome is often decided in a matter of seconds, the learning curve must be much shorter than other software products. To quickly and effectively communicate the objective of a game to the player, designers tend to develop a user interface rich in Western culture's symbols, rituals, and myths. Through the use of these cultural referents, computer games become more playable.

Although most designers use anthropological concepts unconsciously and haphazardly, Chris Crawford's *Trust and Betrayal: The Legacy of Siboot*, provides an exception. Trust and Betrayal makes explicit use of the theories presented here. The game's objective is to become the leader of a colony of aliens. To accomplish this task, the player must communicate with the aliens. Using a psycholinguistic consultant, Crawford developed several aliens and a language that would allow them to speak with one another as well as to the player. The language conveys the alien's culture through symbols and rituals.

The language.   Trust and Betrayal uses an artificial language called *eeyal*. Eeyal consists of a limited number of nouns, verbs, modifiers, and a simplistic syntax. Each word in eeyal is an icon representing symbols found in Western culture. A pistol pointed at a watch indicates the concept of killing time, and an icon showing one person stabbing another in the back indicates betrayal. The player constructs a sentence by picking icons off a menu. The computer lists logical choices, and the player adds icons in the appropriate places to complete the sentence.

The aliens.   The aliens in the game are also depicted with icons and come complete with a personality (likes and dislikes), and an emotional response to the player's character (some aliens like the player, others don't). To gauge the effect of a comment made to one of the aliens, the player is provided a face showing the aliens' emotional state and bar graphs which indicate fear, trust, and love. A human face rather than an alien face was provided to facilitate players' understanding of the aliens' emotions.

The culture.   A novella format is used to impart the cultural aspect of the game to the player. In the story, a mythical figure named Siboot relays the necessity of continuing the rituals of the alien society. The new leader is supposed to be the most fluent speaker of eeyal in the community and is to be chosen by a process of mental combat among the strongest eeyal speakers. The novella contains a detailed explanation of the goals and values of the society, the rituals embedded in the culture, and a history of the myths surrounding the culture. Consistent with the theories in anthropology, the culture is built upon the language. When the language changes, the culture is modified to support the linguistic change. Trust and Betrayal thus represents an interesting mix of anthropology and linguistics.

CHAPTER SUMMARY

- Anthropology is the study of the human experience. It seeks to generalize observations of behavior from overall experiences. What differentiates anthropology from other social science disciplines is the broad, holistic scope of its activities. Anthropologists are concerned with humans in all places of the world, and study all aspects of those peoples' experiences.
- Although individuals are unique in the sense that each may ascribe to a personal set of beliefs and attitudes, most individuals share a surprising number of beliefs and attitudes with other members of their society. A culture may be defined as the set of *learned* beliefs, values, and behaviors, generally *shared* by the members of a society or population. The shared customs of a subgroup within a society or population are referred to as a subculture.
- Anthropology seeks to discover the customs and ranges of acceptable behavior that comprise the culture (or subculture) of the society under investigation. It stresses the idea that any culture should be viewed in the context of that culture. To understand the needs of a subculture of computer users, the customs and ideals of that subculture must be examined directly, not interpolated from another subculture.

- Every society develops a series of cultural ideal patterns which most members of that society believe to be correct behavior. Differences between ideal and actual cultural patterns exist, but, in general, cultures are (a) adaptive to the conditions in their physical and social environment, (b) integrated to the extent that most elements in the culture are consistent with each other, and (c) culture is always changing.
- Time and space dimensions are important for understanding human–computer interactions from an anthropological perspective. The way we think and organize our world is not frozen in time or space. Perceptions of today's computer environment differ from those of the past. Anthropology provides the tools for examining the past to glean a glimpse of the future.
- Because people do not share each other's experiences directly, they must convey their ideas and feelings to each other in ways that others will understand. Symbols are signs created by humans to convey our ideas, intentions and actions to others. They are arbitrary stand-ins for what they represent. Meaning is generated from the use of symbols.
- The construction of meaning over time results in rituals for structuring meaning. Rituals represent the rules by which we combine and use symbols. Rituals are prescribed behaviors (norms) that facilitate attitude formation and provide a meaningful context. Any interaction process is bounded by normative rules.
- Myths are a narrative of events having a scared quality in which at least some of the events neither occurred nor exist in the world outside the myth. The myths associated with software development illustrate that what appears as a reasonable narrative of events can lead to misinformation and confusion. Myths associated with human–computer interaction are also evident in the narratives (stories) told by users.
- Symbols (computers) are linked to myths (stories) through rituals (behavioral prescriptions). Symbols are embedded in rituals which are in turn embedded in myths. The symbols impart meaning to behavior through the rules prescribed by rituals, but the meaning of behavior only makes sense in the context of the myths that surround that behavior.
- Theories in anthropology focus attention on societal characteristics rather than individual variations. Four major schools of thought relevant to the analysis of human–computer interaction were examined: (a) linguistics, (b) cognition, (c) ecology, and (d) symbolic interactionism.
- Linguistics is the study of how people use language. Language is composed of symbols which are linked through speech and trans-

ferred from one person to another. Language is bounded by culture and has meaning only in that context.

- Cognitive anthropology examines patterns of behavior in terms of culturally variant organizing principles. It assumes that different subcultures employ different cognitive schema. Understanding these culturally based organizing principles is important for understanding what functionality is needed for different cultures of computer users.
- Cultural ecology examines the influence of environmental factors on culture. Relative to a computer system, ecological theory is concerned with the relationships between the structure of the hardware and software, and how people perceive these relationships in a sociotechnical environment. It assumes that people interact with computing systems in symbolic and ritualistic ways. The form of this interaction is qualitatively different than the content of the interaction.
- Symbolic interactionism stresses cognitive processing, but places more emphasis on the interaction process. The theory is based on the premise that human nature and social order are products of a give-and-take process that occurs during interaction. It stresses the central role of symbolic communication in personality development and culture, and it explicitly treats the processes of achieving concensus and cooperation. Human–computer interaction is a symbolic process embedded in larger symbol systems (e.g., a computer is a tool). The theory suggests that an analysis of the relationships between these symbol systems is necessary to understand human–computer interactions.

BIBLIOGRAPHY

Agar, M. H. (1986). *Speaking of ethnography.* Beverly Hills, CA: Russell Sage.

Agar, M. H., & Hobbs, J. R. (1985). How to grow schemata out of interviews. In J. Dougherty (Ed.), *Directions in cognitive anthropology.* Urbana, IL: University of Illinois Press.

Alvarez, M. G., Gilfoil, D. M., Hakkinen, M. T., & Murray, J. T. (1984, October). *A comparison of word labels and icons in command menus.* Paper presented at the 28th Annual Human Factors Society Conference, San Antonio, TX.

Austin, J. (1962). *How to do things with words.* Cambridge, MA: Harvard University Press.

Ballinger, L. B., & Ballinger, R. A. (1972). *Sign, symbol and form.* New York: Van Nostrand Reinhold.

Bateson, G. (1970). Form, substance and difference. *General Semantics Bulletin,* No. 37.

Bateson, G. (1972). The science of mind and order. In G. Bateson (Ed.), *Steps to an ecology of mind* (pp. xv–xxvi). New York: Ballantine.

Bateson, G. (1979). *Mind and nature: A necessary unity.* New York: Dutton.

Becker, H. S. (1958). Problems of inference and proof in participant observation. *American Sociological Review, 23*(6), 652–660.

Berger, P. L., & Luckman T. (1967). *The social construction of reality.* Garden City, NY: Anchor Books.

Birdwhistell, R. L. (1970). *Kinesics in context: Essays on body motion communications.* Philadelphia, PA: University of Pennsylvania Press.

Blumer, H. (1962). Society and symbolic interaction. In A. Rose (Ed.), *Human behavior and social processes.* New York: Houghton-Mifflin.

Blumer, H. (1969). *Symbolic interactionism: Perspective and method.* Englewood Cliffs, NJ: Prentice-Hall.

Bly, S. A., & Rosenberg, J. K. (1986, April). A comparison of tiled and overlapping windows. In *Proceedings: CHI'86 Human Factors in Computing Systems* (pp. 101). New York: ACM.

Bolman, L. G., & Deal, T. E. (1984). *Modern approaches to understanding and managing organizations.* San Francisco, CA: Jossey-Bass Publishers.

Booher, H. R. (1975). Relative comprehensibility of pictorial information and printed words in procedural instructions. *Human Factors, 17,* 266–277.

Brown, R. H. (1976). Social theory as metaphor. *Theory and Society, 3,* 169–197.

Cahill, M. C. (1975). Interpretability of graphics symbols as function of context and experience factors. *Journal of Applied Psychology, 60,* 376–380.

Cairney, P., & Sless, D. (1982). Communication effectiveness of symbolic safety signs with different user groups. *Applied Ergonomics, 13,* 91–97.

Campbell, J. (1982). *Grammatical man.* New York: Simon and Schuster.

Carasik, R., & Grantham, C. (1988). A case study of computer-supported cooperative work in a dispersed organization. In *Proceedings of SIGCHI '88.* New York: ACM.

Carroll, S. M., & Thomas, J. (1982). *Metaphor and the cognitive representation of computing systems.* (IBM Research Rep. RC-8302). Yorktown Heights, NY.

Chomsky, N. (1965). *Aspects of the theory of syntax.* Cambridge, MA: Massachusetts Institute of Technology Press.

Cicourel, A. (1975). *Cognitive sociology.* New York: Penguin.

Clark, H. H., & Clark, E. V. (1977). *Psychology and language.* New York: Harcourt Brace and Jovanovich.

Cohen, P. S. (1969). Theories of myth. *Man, 4,* 337–352.

Colby, B. N. (1985). Towards an encyclopedic ethnography for use in intelligent computer programs. *Directions in Cognitive Anthropology, 4,* 269–291.

D'Andrade, R. G. (1981). The cultural part of cognition. *Cognitive Science, 5,* 179–195.

Davidson, J. W., & Zdonik, S. B. (1986). A visual interface for a database with version management. *ACM Transactions on Office Information Systems, 4,* 226–256.

Dewey, J. (1922). Communication, individual and society. In J. Dewey (Ed.), *Human nature and conduct.* New York: Henry Holt and Company.

Dolgin, J. L., Kemnitzer D., & Schneider D. (Eds.). (1977). *Symbolic anthropology*. New York: Columbia University Press.

Donahue, J., & Widom, J. (1986). Whiteboards: A graphic database tool. *ACM Transactions on Office Information Systems, 4*, 24–41.

Dougherty, J. W. D. (Ed.). (1985). *Directions in cognitive anthropology*. Urbana, IL: University of Illinois Press.

Douglas, M. (1970). *Natural symbols*. New York: Pantheon Books.

Douglas, M. (1975). *Implicit meanings*. London: Routledge and Keagan-Paul.

Dreyfus, H. (1972). *Symbol sourcebook*. New York: McGraw Hill.

Dumais, S. T., & Jones, W. P. (1985, April). A comparison of symbolic and spatial filing. In *Proceedings: CHI'85 Human Factors in Computing Systems* (pp. 127–130). New York: ACM.

Ells, J. G., & Dewar, R. E. (1979). Rapid comprehension of verbal and symbolic traffic sign messages. *Human Factors, 21*, 161–168.

Ember, C. R., & Ember M. (1977). *Anthropology* (2nd ed.). Englewood Cliffs, NJ: Prentice-Hall.

Erlandson, R. F. (1980). The participant–observer role in systems methodologies. *IEEE Transactions on Systems, Man, and Cybernetics, 10*(1), 16–19.

Firey, W. (1945). Sentiment and symbolism as ecological variables. *American Sociological Review, X*, 140–148.

Flores, F. (1982). *Management and communication in the office of the future*. Berkeley, CA: Logonet.

Flores, F., & Winograd, T. (1986). *Understanding computers and cognition*. Norwood, NJ: Ablex Publishing Corp.

Friedland, L. (1987, June). Anthropology in the boardroom. *Sky*, pp. 96–102.

Friedrich, P. (1970). Shape in grammar. *Linguistics, 75*, 5–22.

Gaylin, K. B. (1986, April). How are windows used? Some notes on creating an empirically-based windowing benchmark task. In *Proceedings: CHI'86 Human Factors in Computing Systems* (p. 96). New York: ACM.

Geertz, C. (1983). *Local knowledge: Further essays in interpretative anthropology*. New York: Basic Books.

Goffman, E. (1959). *Presentation of self in everyday life*. New York: Doubleday.

Grandjean, E., & Vigliani, E. (Eds.). (1980). *Ergonomic aspects of visual display terminals*. London: Taylor & Francis Ltd.

Grantham, C. E., & Shneiderman, B. (1984). Programmer behavior and cognitive activity: An observational study. In *Proceedings of the ACM*. New York: ACM.

Green, P., & Pew, R. W. (1978). Evaluating pictographic symbols: An automotive application. *Human Factors, 20*, 103–114.

Grudin, J., & Barnard, P. (1985, April). When does an abbreviation become a word? and other related questions. In *Proceedings: CHI'85 Human Factors in Computing Systems* (pp. 121–125). New York: ACM.

Hallowell, A. I. (1955). Cultural factors in spatial orientation. In A. I. Hallowell (Ed.), *Culture and experience* (pp. 184–202). Philadelphia, PA: University of Pennsylvania Press.

Heider, E. R., & Olivier, D. (1972). The structure of the color space in naming and memory of two languages. *Cognitive Psychology, 3*, 337–354.

Hemenway, K. (1981). Psychological issues in the use of icons in command menus. In *Proceedings: Human Factors in Computer Systems* (pp. 20–23). New York: ACM.

Hochschild, A. R. (1979). Emotion work, feeling rules, and social structure. *American Journal of Sociology, 85,* 551–575.

Homans, G. C. (1941). Anxiety and ritual: The Theories of Malinowski and Radcliffe-Brown. *American Anthropologist, 43,* 164–172.

Hudson, S. E., & King, R. (1986). A generator of direct manipulation office systems. *ACM Transactions on Office Information Systems, 4,* 132–163.

Jones, W., & Dumais, S. T. (1986). The spatial metaphor for user interfaces: Experimental tests of reference by location versus name. *ACM Transactions on Office Information Systems, 4,* 42–63.

Kamens, D. H. (1977). Legitimating myths and education organizations— relationship between organizational ideology and formal structure. *American Sociological Review, 42,* 208–219.

Keen, P., & Scott-Morton, M. (1978). *Decision support systems: An organizational perspective.* Reading, MA: Addison-Wesley.

Kemper, T. D. (1978). Toward a sociology of emotions: Some problems and some solutions. *The American Sociologist, 13,* 30–41.

Kiesler, S. (1986). The hidden messages in computer networks. *Harvard Business Review, 86,* 46–60.

King, J., & Kraemer, K. (1979). *Assessing the interaction between computing policies and problems: Toward an empirically defined stage theory of computing evolution.* Working Paper, Public Policy Research Organization, University of California–Irvine, Irvine, CA.

Kling, R. (1978). Automated welfare client-tracking and service integration: The political economy of computing. *Communications of the ACM, 21*(6), 484–493.

Kling, R. (1980). Social analysis of computing: Theoretical perspectives in recent empirical research. *Computing Surveys, 12,* 61–110.

Kling, R., & Scacchi, W. (1979). Recurrent dilemmas of routine computer use in complex organizations. In *Proceedings: AFIPS National Computer Conference* (pp. 107–115). Arlington, VA: AFIPS Press.

Levi-Strauss, C. (1963). *Structural anthropology* (Trans. by C. Jacobson & Brooke Grundfest Schoepf). New York: Basic.

Levi-Strauss, C. (1966). *The savage mind.* Chicago, IL: University of Chicago Press.

Lyytinen, K. (1987). Different perspectives on information systems: Problems and solutions. *ACM Computing Surveys, 19,* 5–46.

Mackett-Sloat, J., & Dewar, R. (1982). Evaluation of symbolic public information signs. *Human Factors, 23,* 139–151.

Maines, D. R. (1977). Social organization and social structure in symbolic interactionist thought. *American Sociological Review, 3,* 235–259.

Malone, T. W. (1983). How do people organize their desks? Implications for the design of office information systems. *ACM Transaction of Office Information Systems, 1,* 99–112.

Mandler, J. M., Seegmiller, D. & Day, J. (1977). On the coding of spatial information. *Memory and Cognition, 5,* 10–16.

Mead, G. H. (1934). *Mind, self, and society*. Chicago, IL: University of Chicago Press.

Mead, G. H. (1938). *The philosophy of the act*. Chicago, IL: University of Chicago Press.

Mick, D. G. (1986). Consumer research and semiotics: Exploring the morphology of signs, symbols, and significance. *Journal of Consumer Research, 13*, 196–213.

Miller, G. A. (1956). The magic number seven plus or minus two: Some limits on our capacity for processing information. *Psychological Review, 63*, 81–97.

Moore, G. T., & Golledge, R. G. (Eds.). (1976). *Environmental knowing: Theories, research and methods*. New York: Von Nostrand Reinhold.

Norman, D. (1983). Design Principles for Human-Computer Interfaces. In *Proceedings of 1983 SIGCHI Meetings* (pp. 1–10). Boston: Association of Computing Machinery.

Nwankwo, R. L. (1973). Communication as symbolic interaction. *The Journal of Communication, 23*, 195–215.

Oakley, K. P. (1967). *Man the tool maker*. Chicago, IL: University of Chicago Press.

Osgood, C. E. (1952). The nature and measurement of meaning. *Psychological Bulletin, 49*, 197–237.

Osgood, C. E., Suci, G. J., & Tannenbaum, P. H. (1957). *The measurement of meaning*. Urbana, IL: University of Illinois Press.

Pecjak, V. (1972). Affective symbolism of spatial forms in two cultures. *International Journal of Psychology, 7*(4), 257–266.

Pressman, R. S. (1982). *Software engineering: A practitioner's approach*. New York: McGraw-Hill.

Rae, S. G. (1986, October). Do executives really need computers? A myth of personal computing. *Business Software Review*, pp. 43–47.

Remington, R., & Williams, D. (1986). On the selection and evaluation of visual display symbology: Factors influencing search and identification times. *Human Factors, 28*(4), 407–420.

Roediger, H. L. III. (1980). Memory metaphors in cognitive psychology. *Memory and Cognition, 8*, 231–246.

Romei, L. K. (1986, July). The message is the medium. *Modern Office Technology*, pp. 47–56.

Ruesch, J., & Bateson G. (1951). *Communication: The social matrix of psychiatry*. Toronto, Canada: Norton.

Sacks, H., Schegloff, E., & Jefferson, G. (1974). A simplest systematics for the organization of turn-taking in conversation. *Language, 50*, 696–735.

Sahlins, M. (1976). Colors and cultures. *Semiotica, 16*, 1–22.

Santa, J. L., & Ranken, H. B. (1972). Effects of verbal coding on recognition memory. *Journal of Experimental Psychology, 93*, 268–278.

Sapir, E. (1921). *Language*. New York: Harcourt, Brace and Jovanovich.

Scacchi, W. (1980). *The process of innovation in computing: A study of the social dynamics of computing*. Unpublished doctoral dissertation, University of California—Irvine, Irvine, California.

Scheff, T. (1986). Micro-linguistics and social structure: A theory of social action. *Sociological Theory, 4*, 71–83.

Schein, E. H. (1986). What you need to know about organizational culture. *Training and Development Journal, 10,* 30–33.

Scherer, K. R. (1979). Non-linguistic indicators of emotion and psychopathology. In C. C. Izard (Ed.), *Emotions in personality and psychopathology.* New York: Plenum.

Schultz, A. (1964). *Collected papers.* The Hague, Netherlands: Martinus Nijhoff.

Schwartz, P., & Ogilvy, J. (1979). The emergent paradigm: Changing patterns of thought and belief. *Analytic report 7: Values and lifestyles program.* Menlo Park, CA: SRI International.

Searle, J. (1969). *Speech acts.* Cambridge, MA: Harvard University Press.

Shneiderman, B. (1980). *Software psychology.* Norwood, NJ: Ablex Publishing Corp.

Shneiderman, B. (1987). *Designing the user interface: Strategies for effective human–computer interaction.* Reading, MA: Addison-Wesley.

SRI International. (1984). *Beyond language: Visiospatial processing.* Menlo Park, CA: SRI International.

Stern, K. R. (1984). An evaluation of written, graphics, and voice messages in proceduralized instructions. In *Proceedings: 28th Annual Human Factors Society Conference* (pp. 314–318). San Antonio, TX.

Stryker, S. (1983). Social psychology from the standpoint of a structural symbolic interactionism: Toward an interdisciplinary social psychology. *Advances in Experimental Social Psychology, 16,* 181–218.

TenHouten, W. D., & Kaplan, C. (1973). *Science and its mirror image.* New York: Harper and Row.

Tyler, S. A. (1969). *Cognitive anthropology.* New York: Holt, Rinehartd and Winston.

Van Cott, H. P., & Kinkade, R. G. (1972). *Human engineering guide to equipment design.* Washington, DC: American Institutes for Research.

Weinberg, G., & Weinberg, D. (1984). The fuzzy early stages. *Journal of Information Systems Management, 1,* 71–75.

Weinberg, G., & Weinberg, D. (1985). In deepest darkest corporate America. *Journal of Information Systems Management, 2,* 63–66.

Westerlund, G., & Sjostrand, S. (1979). *Organizational myths.* New York: Harper & Row.

White, L. A. (1947). Culturological Vs. psychological interpretations of human behavior. *The American Sociological Review, 12,* 686–698.

Whiteside, J., Jones, S., Levy, P. S., & Wixon, D. (1985). User performance with command, menu, and iconic interfaces. In *Proceedings of CHI'85 Human Factors in Computing Systems* (pp. 185–191). New York: ACM.

Whorf, B. L. (1956). In J. B. Carroll (Ed.), *Language, thought and reality.* Cambridge, MA: MIT Press.

Winograd, T. (1984). Computer software for working with language. *Scientific American, 251,* 130–145.

Woodson, W. E., & Conover, D. W. (1966). *Human engineering guide for equipment designers.* Berkeley, CA: University of California Press.

Zwaga, H. J., & Boersema, T. (1983). Evaluation of a set of graphic symbols. *Applied Ergonomics, 14,* 43–54.

chapter 5
Measurement and Evaluation

Data from social science investigations often fit into one of two categories: either *obvious* because you already believe the findings, or *wrong*
because you don't believe them. Unlike computer science technical
reports where the subject of study is the performance of a system, social
research involves humans. It is therefore easier for a reader of social
science manuscripts to attribute his or her own beliefs to the subjects of
the study. For these reasons, it is incumbent upon social scientists to
translate their methods, procedures, and findings into terms that are
understandable to the users of social data. In this chapter, we attempt
such a translation.

Numerous books and articles have discussed and contrasted the
methodologies presented here. It would be pretentious for us to suggest
that our brief discussion advances existing techniques. At the same
time, it is difficult for people new to a methodology to understand the
procedures, when the examples are couched in terms of the achievement motives of Protestants and Catholics with different socioeconomic status scores, examples that are commonly used in social science
methods and statistics books. Our goal is to illustrate by way of example and simple terms how appropriate different methodological approaches are in the development and evaluation of computer applications. In doing so we hope to introduce common research terminology.
Readers interested in more in-depth discussions are referred to the
references listed at the end of the chapter.

Different approaches to software design can be found in the literature: get it right the first time, reliance on design guidelines, iterative
design. Recent articles and books emphasize the iterative nature of any
design process (Carroll & Rosson, 1985; Shneiderman, 1987). Gould
and Lewis (1985), for example, have recommended three general design principles:

1. Early focus on users and tasks
2. Empirical measurement
3. Iterative design.

The four techniques—observation of behavior, design teams, experiments, and surveys—described here are consistent with these recom-

209

mendations. The techniques can be thought of as tools that facilitate evaluation of human–computer interactions. They are similar to the extent that each is based on sound scientific reasoning and that each has advantages and disadvantages. They differ in the information they provide, the extent to which the information can be generalized, and the time and cost of collecting the information.

OVERVIEW OF THE METHODOLOGIES

Research methodologies can be compared along several dimensions (Tables 5.1 and 5.2). Observation of user behavior and design team techniques (e.g., the Delphi procedure) provide a general understanding of users' actual or reported behaviors and their beliefs and attitudes about hardware/software products (Table 5.1). They are appropriate early in the design cycle, when the developer or researcher is determining the scope of a product (Durgee, 1986). Who are the likely users of this product? What is the range of features and functionality users deem appropriate? The function of these qualitative methods is to discover, isolate, describe, and finally understand the pattern of relationships between nonmetric variables. Such methodologies are useful in unique or exploratory situations, or where little is already known. Be-

TABLE 5.1
Overall comparison of the four techniques.

| | Technique | | | |
Criteria	Observation of Behavior	Design Team	Experiments	Surveys
When to use in the design phase:	Prior to Design & After Release	Prior to Design	During Development	After Release
Number of users that can be tested	Small / Large	Small	Medium	Large
Time required to collect data	Days to Weeks	Days	Weeks	Weeks to Months
Cost of collecting data	Small	Small	Small / Medium	Small / Large

TABLE 5.2
Characteristics of the information provided by each technique.

| | Technique | | | |
| | Observation | Design | | |
Criteria	of Behavior	Team	Experiments	Surveys
Qualitative	Depends	Yes	No	No
Quantitative	Depends	No	Yes	Yes
Systematic	Depends	Depends	Yes	Yes
Reliable	Depends	Depends	Yes	Yes
Valid	Yes	Yes	Yes	Yes
Representative of Population	Depends	Depends	Yes	Yes

cause of time and cost considerations, studies with human observers are generally limited to only a few subjects. Observation research incorporating automated data collection routines are not limited by this constraint.

Experiments and surveys focus on particular aspects of a product (Table 5.1). Their application is appropriate when the software is being developed (experiments) or after the product is released (surveys). Experiments typically involve small random samples, while surveys permit larger sample sizes. The data collection period for an experiment is typically less than that required by a survey. Costs associated with both methodologies vary, depending on equipment requirements, sample size, the level of outside consulting required to complete the project, and the geographic dispersion of the surveyed audience.

Participant observation and design teams are *qualitative methods* that capture observations of events, behaviors, expressions of attitude, and environment which are difficult to measure in a numerical way (Table 5.2). Watching a user struggle with learning a new system, for example, provides a rich sense of detail that is not conveyed by the mean and standard deviation of an ease-of-use index. If such sessions are videotaped, managers and developers can be sensitized to the problems users face (Lund, 1985). These data collection procedures serve as an early warning device for larger issues, if a pattern of complaints or suggestions is noted. Qualitative methods provide a basis for detailed quantitative methods.

Quantitative indices provide a systematic basis for comparing users, computers, or applications. Any of the methodologies discussed here can be systematic in their data collection and analysis. Because computerized monitoring of users' behavior, surveys, and experiments are inherently more formal, they tend to be systematic (Table 5.2). Observation of behavior (when the observer is a human) and design team techniques can be systematic if the researcher imposes such an approach on the research.

Reliability concerns the extent to which measures are accurate and repeatable (Nunnally, 1967). If the indicators of a construct such as ease of use are internally consistent and stable, the measure is said to be reliable (Curtis, 1980). Although different methods of evaluating internal consistency exist, a common approach is to build a linear composite (e.g., an index or summated rating scale) from a set of items assumed to have some underlying structure. The reliability of the composite can be estimated using one of the internal consistency methods described by Lord and Novick (1968). When the measurement error is slight, the measure is reliable. The attitude and behavior scales presented in Chapter 2 for VOX users illustrate this approach.

Stability, the second component of reliability, refers to the extent to which scores from one investigation can be replicated in another investigation. Of the four techniques presented here, experiments and surveys readily lend themselves to reliability testing. Reliability estimation of observation techniques and design teams depends, in part, how systematically the data were collected and the extent to which the information can be quantified. Demonstrating high reliability, however, does not necessarily imply high validity.

Validity is concerned with whether a measure represents what it was intended to assess. A measure of ease of use, for example, could be constructed by asking individuals to throw their personal computers across the room. The distance people could throw the machine on one occasion is likely to be correlated with how far they could throw it on another occasion. Because the measure is repeatable, the indicator is highly reliable. Although such actions could be indicative of the frustrations users feel toward products that are not easy to use, most individuals would agree that throwing a personal computer across the room does not constitute a valid measure of the ease-of-use concept . Reliability is a *necessary* but not *sufficient* condition for validity (Nunnally, 1967). All of the techniques described here provide potentially valid indicators.

Similarly, all of the methodologies can be *representative of the pop-ulation* of interest. Because experiments randomly assign individuals to treatments and surveys allow for large sample sizes, results obtained from these procedures are more likely to be representative of the popu-lation than observation methods or design teams. At the same time, design teams and observation techniques can be representative if the team members are selected carefully and the observations involve a sufficient number of individuals.

Given the complexities inherent in each of the methodologies, the cell entries in Tables 5.1 and 5.2 should *not* be interpreted as absolutes, but rather as general similarities and differences among the ap-proaches. Readers are encouraged to briefly scan the table now. Refer-ring back to the table after finishing sections of this chapter will help to clarify the similarities/differences among the techniques.

OBSERVATION OF BEHAVIOR

Observational techniques are appropriate when the researcher's goal is to understand how users behave in various situations as they interact with computers. This section describes three techniques for the direct observation of computer users' behaviors in a work environment. We first present a research approach that is common in the social sciences (i.e., participant observation) and a currently popular method for exam-ining human–computer interaction, *Thinking Aloud*. We then discuss the potential applications of a software monitoring technique and pres-ent data from two projects to illustrate the information that can be obtained from this approach.

Participant Observation

There is little agreement in the sociological literature on the meaning of *participant observation* (McCall & Simmons, 1969; Babbie, 1979). One description identifies four roles that researchers may play: complete participant, participant-as-observer, observer-as-participant, and com-plete observer (Gold, 1958). With each approach, the researcher gathers data by placing himself or herself in the situation of interest. The tech-niques differ to the extent that those who are being observed are cog-nizant of the investigator's identity and purpose, and the extent that the researcher performs the tasks and activities of others in the situation. With complete participation, the researcher is seen by the subjects only as a participant, not as a researcher. Tasks that others perform would also be done by the investigator. At the other end of the continuum (the complete observer), the subjects recognize that the researcher is present to collect data, but the researcher does not actually participate in any of the tasks performed by the subjects.

The chief strength of participant observation lies in the depth of understanding provided (Babbie, 1979). Because the researcher is physically present in the situation (e.g., an office environment), first-hand knowledge regarding the strengths and limitations of the product/service are attainable. The method is particularly useful to designers who might normally see only a portion of the entire system. In situations where the researcher participates in the users' activities, this methodology is effective for studying the subtle nuances of attitudes and behavior. Since the researcher is also a subject, human–computer interaction processes can be observed over time; however, accurate notes must be taken if the researcher is to remember particular actions at a later date. Finally, the method is relatively inexpensive and offers considerable flexibility.

There are disadvantages associated with participant observation. The chief weaknesses are subjectivity and the lack of generalizability (Babbie, 1979; Gold, 1958; McCall & Simmons, 1969). Because the technique is time consuming and revolves around the researcher's own perceptions and behaviors, the method seldom yields precise descriptive statements about a large population. Conclusions drawn from the observations are often suggestive rather than definitive. The reliability and validity of the results depends on whether the sampled users are representative of the larger group to which the question/issue is addressed. In situations where the researcher attempts to understand the problems novice users encounter, the researcher must guard against letting familiarity with the product influence observations and conclusions. Finally, the mere presence of the observer may influence the behavior of the subject (Homans, 1965).

Thinking Aloud

The Thinking Aloud methodology has been employed to study situations that are difficult to examine experimentally (Becker & Geer, 1957; Grantham & Shneiderman, 1984). Lewis (1982) was one of the first to apply the technique to evaluations of human–computer interaction. In this context, the researcher assumes a role somewhat similar to that of a participant observer. Thinking Aloud differs from other observation techniques in that the researcher systematically questions the users as they interact with a computer. The goal of such questioning is to understand why an individual approaches a problem in a particular manner and to identify the problems encountered during the interaction. Verbal remarks from the subject provide researchers with insights into areas of a system that give the user problems (Lewis, 1982). Similar to participant observation, the method is inexpensive and is flexible.

There are, however, some disadvantages to the Thinking Aloud technique. For example, the researcher must be careful not to lead the user down a line of thinking that is different from that person's natural inclinations. In addition, some users find it difficult to talk while they are working, while others are not good at verbalizing their thoughts. These latter problems may be partially alleviated by having two individuals work on the task together (Newell & Simon, 1972). They will naturally talk while they are working, and, thus, the need for researcher induced conversation is reduced. Even with two subjects, accurate notes are still a necessity, and, similarly to participant observation, the time consuming nature of Thinking Aloud restricts the number of people that can be efficiently observed. A final disadvantage of the technique is that timing data (e.g., time to learn the system, time to complete tasks, etc.) are invalid.

Software Monitor Observation

Software monitors have been recognized as an essential tool for measuring computer system performance (Gitomer, 1984). Recently, researchers (Neal & Simons, 1984) have also demonstrated that human–computer interaction can be reliably and efficiently measured using software monitors.

A variety of monitoring/event logging packages are discussed in the literature. One type that is common to multiuser systems logs information on individuals' usage statistics for billing and accounting purposes. These standard logging packages provide a readily available source of data about actual user behavior and deserve close scrutiny when planning investigations of human–computer interaction. A second kind of software monitor can be described as a specialized software instrumentation package which utilizes data collection routines specific to the problem being investigated. Each data collection routine is activated by way of a probepoint installed in the software at a location where an event of interest occurs. The events may be interactions between a user and a particular application package; for example, output of an electronic mail facility and completed user input or keystrokes typed by the individual.

Applications of these measurement tools have observed the behaviors of subjects in laboratory settings. Neal and Simons (1984), for example, discuss a general purpose monitoring package (Playback) that has evolved over the years at IBM. Playback has been used successfully in experiments designed to improve training materials for the IBM Displaywriter (Clauer, 1982) and a database query facility (Ogden & Boyle, 1982), as well as studies of IBM Basic (Bury, 1983). Allen and Scerbo (1983) used a keystroke logging device to evaluate predictions made by the Keystroke-Level model advanced by Card, Moran, and Newell (1983). Finally, Clark (1981) used a similar technique in determining the usability of an Interactive Chart Utility prototype.

Although these laboratory investigations have resulted in ease-of-use improvements, there are benefits from studying real-world office environments (Chapanis, 1967; Nicholson, 1985). The field study reported by Nicholson (1985), for example, used system logs of mail traffic statistics along with personal interviews to evaluate the usage and acceptance of an integrated voice mail product. Hanson, Kraut, and Farber (1984) incorporated two monitoring techniques to evaluate UNIX command usage rates. The system's accounting package automatically recorded some of the commands issued by each user during each terminal session. These records were supplemented with command-line data from a smaller group of users. This latter monitor measured error messages generated by the system and commands issued by the users. Finally, Boies (1974) discusses field data from monitoring command usage on IBM's TSS/360 system.

Field studies of software users yield benefits that are not easily attainable from laboratory experiments. First, data are collected on all users of particular systems, so that differences in the behavior patterns of groups of individuals can be detected. Second, the sampling of usage via the software monitor can be distributed over a long period of time, permitting observation of trends in behavior patterns. Third, as new application programs are released, the identification of which user groups incorporate the technology into their daily work habits can be systematically and empirically determined. Fourth, the software monitor is transparent to the user, so the methodology avoids the validity problems typically associated with self-reported behaviors and eliminates the intrusions created when an observer is present. Finally, the usage is observed in a real-task situation as opposed to an artificial experimental task.

In summary, this section compared three techniques for observing the behavior of computer users. Traditional methods (participant observation) identify the behaviors and attitudes of a small group of individuals. These methods, however, do not lend themselves to large samples, because of the time required to collect the information, and, thus, the findings have limited generalizability. Similar sample size restrictions apply to the Thinking Aloud technique. The software monitor provides a more accurate and unobtrusive approach to collecting behavioral data for larger samples of individuals.

In the next section we describe the advantages and limitations of monitoring computer users in multiuser systems to observe their daily work patterns. Subsequent sections present data from two projects to illustrate the information attainable from this approach.

The Development of a Software Monitor Package

The design of a software monitor package can be described in three main steps: problem analysis, software analysis, and data processing design. *Problem analysis* involves a two-step process. The investigator first decides what aspects of system (or user) behavior are to be observed and what information is desired about that behavior. These aspects are then correlated with particular software events that occur during the normal activity of the system.

Software analysis is the process of identifying the software components that produce the events to be observed, and the data objects maintained by those components that contain information descriptive of the events. This analysis should be conducted by an experienced programmer, working with the assistance of the developers of the target software, if the application is of significant size or complexity. In many software packages equivalent events occur in more than one place, requiring multiple probes which use the same collection routine. When more than one event is observed, the data collection routines must construct output records with a unique identifier.

Data processing design is the specification of offline processing operations for summarizing the data collected by the monitor. Such operations include pattern extraction and reformatting data for input to statistical analysis packages. All manipulation of the data available at probe time should be relegated to offline processing, to keep the monitor's data collection routines short and efficient.

Special Problems of Multiuser System Monitoring

The process described in the preceding section is characteristic of software monitor application in any environment. Where the behavior to be observed occurs in a laboratory setting, this process encompasses all of the practical instrumentation problems. Subjects in such situations are usually the only users on the system, and their activities are typ-

ically constrained by an experimental script. When the software monitoring technique is transported to an operational multiuser system
being used for daily work by groups of people, additional monitor
design issues must be considered. A balance must be achieved among
three factors: (a) the level of detail in the data to be collected, (b) the
complexity needed to select only the system/user activity of interest to
the study, and (c) the processing overhead introduced by the monitoring code. One basic consideration is the need to ensure that the data
collected represents only the user activity of interest and is not con-
taminated by data reflecting people doing other things on the system.

The probe sets must also be sophisticated enough to reflect modes of
behavior employed by the most skilful users. For example, assume the
goal is observation of both user and system response times for a certain
software subsystem. Probes are placed to detect both stimuli, such as
presentation of a form on the user's screen, and user responses. Output
records contain current time of day, and are of three classes: stimulus
presentation, onset of an opportunity to respond, and response completion. To obtain this sequence of time values, the probes must be placed
at a rather low level of software organization—in various screen management components. Because these components may be employed by
other application packages besides the one being investigated, a technique is needed to switch ON collection from these probes when the
user enters the relevant package, and to switch OFF collection when he
or she leaves it. The former provision is simple, because there is usually only one way into the package. There may be, however, multiple
exits, some of which are known only to individuals who are familiar
with the package. Unless all of these exit paths trigger the cessation of
data collection, unwanted data will seriously distort postprocessing
calculations such as average response times. The solution to this problem is the use of additional probes which detect entry and exit from the
relevant package. Data collection routines for these probes must toggle
a bit in a user-local data structure, which the other data collection
routines must test.

There are also problems of output file management that must be
solved when monitoring multiuser systems over an extended time
period. The first task is to ensure that prior data are not lost in the event
of an unscheduled system restart. A second is to avoid imposing extra
duties on system operators which, if forgotten, will also result in the
loss of data. A third is to prevent the output file from growing so large
that it occupies an unduly large portion of online disk space.

To avoid unnecessary file processing overhead, the data collection
file is opened at the onset of the data collection period and remains
open until data collection is terminated. During a lengthy data collec-

tion period, system operators may have to re-initialize and restart the system occasionally. If the collection file has not been closed prior to the restart, its directory entry on disk may not reflect the data added to it since it was last opened. Even when the restart is routine, the operator may forget to terminate data collection in a natural haste to restore the system to full operation, especially if software monitoring is an unusual activity at the installation.

The solution to this class of problems is for the monitor to begin each block of output data with a unique identifier. The system's software initialization sequence can invoke a procedure which opens the data collection file, searches the existing file sequentially for the end of valid data, and then activates the software monitor. This sequence ensures that the only data lost when the system is restarted will be the relatively small amount contained in the software monitor's last, unwritten output buffer.

Preventing excessive growth of output files requires periodic transfer of its contents to another medium at appropriate intervals (e.g., once a week) depending on the amount of user data being collected. It should be done during an off hours period when no users are active to avoid loss of data.

EMPIRICAL EXAMPLES

The following examples illustrate how we have incorporated two software monitor packages (called SWM-G and SWM-S) into our research. The first demonstration focuses on general usage patterns of application programs in an integrated office automation product. The second example examines how software monitor data were used to modify the interface on a particular electronic messaging facility.

Both monitoring packages described in these examples provide useful information for system developers and marketing personnel, but the nature of the data collected makes them more or less appropriate at different stages in the evaluation process. The more general software monitor (SWM-G), if installed shortly after a product is released, provides a vehicle for recording changes in usage over time. Marketing individuals may find this information helpful in shaping realistic customer expectations regarding the short- and long-range benefits of the software. Our experiences working with electronic mail suggest that the length of this adoption period may involve several months among users who are novices with electronic communication. A second advantage of the general usage monitor is that it provides the data needed to determine systematically *when* the users have sufficient experience with the software to warrant an investigation of particular ease-of-use questions. The second example illustrates use of a monitoring package (SWM-S) for this latter purpose.

Empirical Example 1: Office Automation Usage

Data for this example were obtained from a study of all registered Office Automation (OA) users on two minicomputers (Teubner & Vaske, 1988). The OA package included nine application programs such as word processing, electronic mail, and a spreadsheet. The project had two principal objectives. One objective was to test the feasibility of using a software monitor to collect user data on a multiuser system. The second was to evaluate the popularity and utility of the nine OA applications among user groups over an extended time period.

The software monitor package (SWM-G) generated the following information: (a) number of times each application in OA was entered, (b) total time in application (in minutes), (c) average amount of time in application per session, and (d) percentage of the user's total time in OA spent in a particular application. These data can be summarized in a variety of ways. One analysis strategy is to evaluate the user-day activities for each system-week. One user-day equals the amount of activity performed by a given individual during a single day. A report of the individual's activity in OA is produced for each day during which the person uses any of the OA applications. With the user-day as the unit of analysis, an individual may appear more than once in the data, depending upon how many days the person used OA. A second strategy focuses on the user's position level in the organization. The unit of analysis for this method may represent each user's activities summed across each system/week (one record for each individual), or, alternatively, a record can be produced for each day the person uses OA. The distinguishing feature is that individuals are categorized according to organizational positions (e.g, managers/administrators, professional/technical or clericals) for analysis purposes.

The data show "Word Processing" was used more frequently and for longer periods of time than any other application in OA, irrespective of the system/week or user group (Table 5.3). The percentage of users' time in OA per user/day was statistically different for five of the nine applications. For example, communications accounted for 13.4% of individuals' time on system 83 during week 2. This percentage was significantly greater than that found on system 17 or system 83/week 1. Excluding "Word Processing," "Calendar" was the most heavily used application for managers and clericals (Table 5.4). For professional/technicals, the second most popular activity was "Electronic Mail."

TABLE 5.3
Percentage of user's total time in Office Automation spent in particular functions (per user/day).

Percentage of total time in OA in function:	Technique				
	System 17	System 83	System 17	System 83	F-value
Word Processing	92.3^a	72.1^b	89.3^a	71.7^b	12.9[**]
File Management	0.0	0.7	1.4	1.5	ns
Electronic Mail	4.3	1.9	5.7	3.1	ns
Calculator	0.3	0.2	0.0	0.1	ns
Records Processing	0.0^{ab}	6.6^a	0.0^b	4.3^b	8.1[**]
Calendar	0.0^a	5.0^{bc}	1.0^{ac}	5.9^b	6.6[**]
InfoCalc	0.7^a	6.6^b	0.5^a	0.0^a	7.6[**]
Communications	0.0^a	2.6^a	0.0^b	13.4^b	16.1[**]
System Admin	0.0	0.3	0.0	0.0	ns

Means with similar superscripts do not differ significantly at the .05 level.

[*] $p < .05$
[**] $p < .01$

These findings highlight the analyses permitted by data obtained from our general software monitor. While other comparisons are equally interesting, our goal here is to emphasize methodological considerations. Two points are pertinent. First, alternative analysis strategies result in different conclusions about the usage of OA functionality. The differences detected in Table 5.4, for example, were not apparent when the overall system/week comparisons were made (Table 5.3). The choice of one strategy over another depends on the objectives of the project. Second, computer systems need to be monitored for relatively long periods of time, if stable determination of behavior patterns are to be made.

Empirical Example 2: Electronic Mail

Data for this second software monitor example were obtained from a study (Vaske & Teubner, 1985) designed to identify aspects of the interface to an electronic messaging facility (EMail) that, if modified, would enhance the human–computer interaction process. The software monitor (SWM-S) recorded information on the interactions between the user

TABLE 5.4
Percentage of user's total time in Office Automation spent in particular functions by position level.

Percentage of total time in OA in function:	Managers/ Administrators	Professional/ Technical	Clerical	F-Value
Word Processing	87.20	80.37	89.36	3.03*
File Management	0.00	0.56	0.02	3.46*
Electronic Mail	0.71^a	7.02^b	2.32^a	5.64**
Calculator	0.01	0.02	0.18	ns
Records Processing	0.03^a	4.43^b	2.03^{ab}	3.17*
Calendar	4.48	0.84	3.79	ns
InfoCalc	0.00	0.61	1.25	ns
Communications	4.16	4.41	0.15	ns
System Admin	0.01	0.19	0.01	ns

Means with similar superscripts do not differ significantly at the .05 level.

* $p < .05$
** $p < .01$

and the EMail application.[1] The monitoring package was installed in two systems of the EMail network at each of two sites. Across all four systems, there were 152 registered EMail users, 76 in site 1 and 76 in site 2.

The software monitor data provided counts of the usage of various forms and their fields. The results suggested a number of changes to the existing interface, especially in the Read Mail and Send Mail Options forms. For example, the Read Mail Options form which allowed users to selectively scan mail items from a particular person, date or subject was almost always defaulted. Ninety-eight percent of the users at both sites never exercised the option to view their mail selectively. For most users this option simply added another layer of decision that served only to slow the interaction.

---

[1] In addition to the software monitor, questionnaires were used to describe user attitudes toward the facility.

Initial Send Mail Form

Basic Operations

    Priority: 3
    Confidential NO
    Reply NO

Acknowledgement of Action: NO
Receipt of Delivery NO

              Name   Location

TO

FROM: _____ (AUTHOR'S NAME) _____   (AUTHOR'S LOCATION)

Subject: _____

Immediate Message: _____

Next: 7   To = 1   From = 2   CC = 3   BC = 4
              Document = 5   Attachments = 6   Send = 7

Revised Send Mail Form

FROM: _____ (AUTHOR'S NAME) _____   (AUTHOR'S LOCATION)

➡ TO: Name _____   Location _____

    Subject: _____

    Document Name: _____

    Next: 7   To = 1   From = 2   CC = 3   BC = 4   Document = 5
              Attachments = 6   Send = 7   Modify Basic Operation = 8

Basic Operations

    Priority: 3
    Confidential NO
    Reply NO

Acknowledgement of Action: NO
Receipt of Delivery NO

FIGURE 5.1
Initial and revised send mail forms.

The solution was to modify the initial menu to the interface by incorporating two "read mail" options. Selection 1 (the default) took users directly to a listing of the items in their mailbox, and thus bypassed the "Read Mail Options" menu. Selection 2 on the revised initial mail menu provided those who desired to view their mail selectively with the functionality that existed in the initial version of the facility. Although the data did not suggest a need for this functionality under existing usage rates, the option may become more valuable if traffic intensity increases.

On the Send Mail Options form (Figure 5.1), data from the software monitor revealed that a number of fields were also almost always defaulted. For example, most users accepted the default values in the basic operations set of options (i.e., priority, acknowledgement of action, confidential, etc.). Similarly, the vast majority of users did not fill in more than one recipient or distribution list. The alternative send mail screen (lower half of Figure 5.1) shows the modifications suggested by the data. By moving the Basic Operations to the bottom of the screen, users were not required to sequence through fields whose default values are normally accepted. A single recipient line was deemed sufficient for this screen, since 92% of the Send mail options monitored at either site involved the use of only one name. The "To" option on the NEXT field provided users with the ability to broadcast information more widely. The arrow [–>] at the left margin of Figure 5.1 indicates the starting position of the cursor when the revised form is displayed: at the TO field of the form. This placement eliminates another instance of users' sequencing through a field for which they generally accept the default. Users modified the system-provided sender's name less than 1% of the time. Finally, the inclusion of the "Document Name" field eliminated one additional menu for the users, while maintaining the same capabilities. Follow-up interviews with some of the participants from this study suggest that the revisions enhanced the ease-of-use of the EMail product.

One could argue that, if the EMail facility had been initially designed correctly, the study described here would not have been necessary. Most software applications, however, can benefit from such studies. Design decisions that seem appropriate on paper or prototype versions may be inappropriate once the entire facility is constructed and used on a regular basis. Providing functionality for people to selectively screen their mail, for example, may be helpful for some users. As suggested by our software monitor data, however, a positive attribute can be viewed negatively when users must repeatedly exercise the option.

Summary—Software Monitor

The software monitor can be applied to any interactive application program, and the scope of system/user behavior which can be investigated is limited chiefly by the imagination of the investigator. Our examples compared usage patterns across office automation applications in a workday environment. One can also conceive of studies that relate user behavior to the overall system environment such as load imposed by other users or message delivery delays. In addition, software monitors can and have been used to investigate purely technical issues such as system performance bottlenecks (Gitomer, 1984).

The data reported here highlight some fundamental principles of scientific investigation that are too easily forgotten in one's enthusiasm for developing measurement tools. The software monitor is capable of collecting a wide range of behavioral information which can be summarized from numerous perspectives. Unless the investigators have thoroughly defined the objectives of the study, formulated hypotheses, and designed data collection and analysis procedures for testing predictions, the results are likely to raise more questions than they answer. Similar thoughts have been echoed by others. "Rather than beginning by counting or experimentally manipulating various properties of software, we should first determine what software related task we wish to understand" (Curtis, 1980, p. 1144). For these reasons, the theories presented in Chapters 2 through 4 serve as important frameworks for guiding projects.

This issue is especially crucial as one moves from a laboratory environment to the monitoring of multiuser systems. Because laboratory studies are focused on particular problems, findings from experiments tend to yield specific albeit limited conclusions about a given question. Data obtained from monitoring a multiuser production system have the advantage of reflecting broad patterns of behavior across a variety of applications and user groups; however, the results are likely to be difficult to understand unless the project has been adequately conceptualized and developed. For example, our data suggest that managers use the OA functionality differently than professional/technical types. Not indicated is why such differences exist. While one could speculate that some individuals were unaware of the system's capabilities, that some users find the existing applications more difficult to use than other alternatives, or that the tasks performed by some groups do not necessitate the use of particular functions, the software monitor by itself cannot address these issues.

The preceding reinforces the importance of incorporating attitudinal data along with the behavioral information from the monitor. Reliable estimates of behavioral patterns emerge only after the monitor has been installed for a period of time. Similarly, attitudinal data can and should be collected at a variety of times: before a user has first tried a certain application, at the time of introduction, and after an extended period of use. When merged with the behavioral data obtained from a software monitor, this sequence of attitudinal information allows the researcher to monitor shifts in perceptions about the quality of the product as a function of experience.

Ethical Issues

The unobtrusive observation of people's behavior via either a software monitor or participant observation raises certain ethical issues. Investigators must be scrupulous in selecting the data which they collect, so that they do not violate other people's reasonable expectations of privacy in the use of a computer system. The software monitors discussed here recorded users' behaviors with the sole intent of determining ways to improve the interface. The actual content of the electronic mail boxes was never examined, nor was there any attempt to interpret the findings from a productivity perspective. Computerized monitoring, however, can and has been used to assess employees' productivity. Such activities are controversial, with both pro and con arguments being advanced.

Olson and Lucas (1982), for example, suggest that computerized monitoring provides workers with more flexibility. Individuals can work at home on computers connected to the office via modems and still be credited for work. Other suggested positive outcomes include increased productivity (Bair, 1982), greater organizational control (Mintzberg, 1979) and more feedback to workers (Hackman & Oldham, 1980; Hackman, Oldham, Janson, & Purdy, 1979; Pettigrew, 1972). Finally, computerized monitoring elevates employee evaluations to a more objective level that is less susceptible to idiosyncratic tendencies of management (Schick, 1980). All of these points are consistent with structuralist approach to organizational theory (Chapter 3).

Others note negative consequences associated with computerized monitoring of user productivity. Monitoring creates a factory style atmosphere in office environments (Gregory & Nussbaum, 1982). Management efforts to gain control over employees often results in decreased worker motivation (Myers, 1967). The reliability of performance data from monitors in terms of accurately assessing production rates is questionable. Monitoring can lead to increased stress and a reduction in productivity (Walton & Vittori 1983). Finally, computerized counts of productivity may be invalid, expensive, and degrading (Johnson, Taylor, Smith, & Cline, 1983). These arguments parallel a human relations school of thinking.

To address these potential consequences, Irving, Higgins, and Safayeni (1986) compared the attitudes of workers in organizations with computerized monitoring against the perceptions of employees with similar jobs in organizations which did not have monitors installed. Results tended to confirm both the positive and negative effects. With the monitors installed, workers perceived an increase in productivity, more organizational control, and a more complete and accurate assessment of their performance. At the same time, the employees believed that managers tended to over emphasize the value of quantity and under emphasize the quality of their work. Stress increased, satisfaction declined, and the quality of the working environment decreased as a consequence of monitoring. Interestingly, the workers reacted more negatively to the way the monitors were used, than they did to computerized monitoring per se. Similar to other authors (Ackoff, 1967; Kling & Scacchi, 1980; Zuboff, 1982; Markus, 1983; Walton & Vittori, 1983), these findings again demonstrate that it is not the technology itself, but rather the way it is implemented and operated.

The guidelines used by the American Psychological Association (APA, 1981) and the American Sociological Association (ASA, 1982) provide a usable code of ethics for dealing with ethical issues:

> Research procedures likely to cause serious or lasting harm to a participant are not used.

> Except in minimal-risk research, the investigator establishes a clear and fair agreement with participants prior to their participation; for example:

> > Participants have the right to withdraw from the study at any time.

> > The researcher describes how the data will be used.

> > If the session is videotaped, a statement of how that videotape will be used.

> After the data are collected, the investigator provides the participant with information about the nature of the study and attempts to remove any misconceptions that may have arisen.

> Confidential information provided by research participants must be treated as such, even when this information enjoys no legal protection or privilege and legal force is applied.

Observance of these and other similar guidelines (e.g., Allen, 1984) will help to minimize any negative consequences for participants in human–computer interaction research and will hopefully improve the quality of software applications.

Summary—Observation of Behavior

This section has demonstrated the feasibility and potential of the software monitor technique as a tool for studying human–computer interaction in office environments. We have contrasted the technique with traditional investigative tools (participant observation and Thinking Aloud) and described the monitor's relative advantages. The technical aspects of software monitor design were discussed with special emphasis on monitoring user activities on a multiuser system. Findings from two studies were presented to illustrate the potential advantages and limitations of the technique in field research. Finally, ethical issues inherent to the observation of human behavior were presented, and guidelines for minimizing potential negative consequences discussed.

DESIGN TEAM TECHNIQUES

Design teams are common in corporations that develop products. A team of individuals representing different views (e.g., software developers, marketing, manufacturing, etc.) may be charted to assess the feasibility of a new product or service. Their objective is to provide information which will at least partially serve as a basis for planning and decision making. By including representatives from different branches of the organization, each with their own unique perspective on the product, the aim is to reach better decisions. Individuals who participate on such teams are chosen because they are judged to possess a certain expertise. Software developers, for example, might be selected because of their experiences with related applications. The marketing person has a perspective on the organization's strategic direction and the manufacturing representative is presumably familiar with the production costs associated with design decisions.

Unfortunately, many design teams are not representative of the range of individuals who are affected by the product. With many software applications, the ultimate end-users are unaware of the product until it is announced in the trade press or the application is installed on their workstations. At this stage of development little can be done to modify the existing implementation. Moreover, even if the users do identify desirable changes, there is typically no established way for them to communicate their ideas to developers.

Just as executives are reluctant to make decisions without substantial information about the technical aspects of the system, they should be equally reluctant to make decisions without information on users' behavior with and attitudes toward the computer. Data on technical differences in computer components do not make the decision for the manager, nor should input from users. Such input is merely another factor to be considered in making a decision. Consequently, one should use careful, comprehensive approaches in gathering information about users as well as the computer.

Soliciting user involvement early in the design process has advantages to both users and the organization producing the application.

First, users are experts on their own values and preferences and there is no substitute for their judgments in these matters. Applications designed to support their needs are more likely to be purchased and used. Second, by involving affected groups early, alternative designs are less likely to be questioned later. Product modifications which are costly to implement are reduced if not eliminated (Keen, 1981).

Highlighting the preferences and expectations held by constituents, however, does not make the decision easier for the executive who has ultimate responsibility for the product. If anything, a successful design team makes the decision more difficult because it identifies the range of complexities and conflicts that are easily ignored without such input (Ives & Olsen, 1984). In short, direct involvement from different groups does not make the executive's decision easier, but hopefully it makes the decision better.

Effective user involvement requires an *interactive exchange* between product designer and the ultimate end-user. The interactive nature of this process implies that user involvement is more than public relations. Good user involvement leads to good public relations, but, if it is only public relations, it is not good user involvement (Heberlein, 1976). User participation is *not* selling the user on a particular product or program. It is honestly and openly soliciting users help in the development and selection of alternatives. User involvement is not a means of achieving a consensus among different groups but procedures to determine preferences and who holds those preferences.

The first step is to realize that there is no single user.[2] Users may be separated into numerous groups or *publics*. For example, a number of individuals may use a single computer: secretaries primarily concerned with word processing applications, executives interested in using electronic mail to monitor the status of projects, analysts preparing financial reports with spreadsheets and programmers. These differences in tasks affect individuals' usage of and attitudes toward the system.

Disaggregating users into more homogeneous groups facilitates the design team process. By conducting meetings with a single public preferably in small groups and on their own turf, individuals may be more willing to discuss their feelings. By documenting the input received at these meetings, it is easier to satisfy other members of the group that their views are heard and considered in the planning process. Finally, by evaluating the input from each group separately, competing needs of users are highlighted.

Initiating contact with various groups is an important part of user

---

[2] See the Individual Differences section in Chapter 2.

involvement. Even with contacts and encouragement, however, it is necessary to establish mechanisms which facilitate rather than discourage user input. Meetings and presentations are not settings where people often communicate. Standing up in front of a group is uncomfortable for most people. Many are intimidated by their lack of expertise in such situations. The sterility of input in a formal meeting is in marked contrast to the communication which goes on in the hallways before and after the meeting and at coffee breaks. Much can be done to make meetings less formal so that individuals feel free to express their opinions. Meetings should be small, so people can talk to each other. Facilities should have a number of small rooms, so large groups can break up. Plans should be presented informally, so that individuals feel free to comment and change the plans. Flashy displays and overlays give the appearance that the plan is set even if it isn't. Line drawings on paper allow participants to draw modifications and show the audience their input is important. Seating arrangements which put the user and the developer together also help to encourage input. Each of these techniques help to facilitate user input, however, it won't happen on its own. One must make it happen.

The preceding emphasized procedures for encouraging individual participation in a group setting. Because group decision making introduces its own unique set of considerations, and groups themselves can take on a life of their own, it is equally important to consider the advantages and disadvantages of design by committee.

Advantages of Committees

Committees and groups have a number of advantages which make their use desirable under certain circumstances (Martino, 1972).

1. The amount of knowledge available in a group is at least equal to the amount of information available to any of its members. And if the group represents a diversity of interests (users, developers, marketing, planning, human factors), the total information is greater than that possessed by any single member.
2. The number of factors that have a bearing on the issue and that can be considered by the group is at least as great as for any one of the group members. For example, a software application designed to maximize consistency within its own command sequence may still be unacceptable if it deviates from other applications in the product set. By exposing the design to the scrutiny of a group, such external inconsistencies can be identified and corrected before coding begins.

3. Groups are more willing to take risks than are individuals. If a software developer believes in a design approach that is radically different from the commonly accepted methods of his or her peers, the individual may be less willing to actively pursue his or her convictions. To do so could imply a loss of professional standing among the other developers and a reduction in credibility with the person's managers. In both cases, if fellow professionals in the group agree with the individual's unpopular views, the person may be more willing to formally present the new approach inspite of the risk.

Disadvantages of Committees

Despite the above mentioned advantages, there are some disadvantages associated with design by committee (Martino, 1972).

1. There is at least as much misinformation available to the group as to any one of its members. Although the hope is that misinformation held by a committee member will be canceled out by the other participants, there is no assurance that this will take place.
2. Groups can exert strong social pressures on members to obtain agreement. If the majority view happens to be wrong, those in the minority may find it difficult to modify proposed actions, even if they are right. The probability of a group's decision being in error increases when little historical data can be brought to bear and the decision is based on only opinions. Such a situation is common in corporations which develop advanced technologies. A previous application that could serve as a role model may simply not exist.
3. Small group research (Cartwright & Zander, 1968; Michener, De-Lamater & Schwartz, 1986) has shown that the validity of an argument is sometimes less important than the number of comments for and against a proposed position. Consequently, a vocal minority who actively pursue a line of reasoning may sway a decision, even if their logic is faulty.
4. Reaching agreement in a group frequently becomes more important than a well thought out and useful decision. The result of group discussion in these cases represents the lowest common denominator, and, although a decision was reached, no one may agree with it.
5. In groups with no designated leader, a dominant individual may gain undue impact on the committee's decisions. The same scenario occurs when the appointed leader lacks the authority and power to control the group interaction.
6. Certain members of a group may have a vested interested in a given

outcome. Their objective is to win the other group members over to their viewpoint, rather than reaching a better decision. Software developers who have invested considerable effort into coding a software application, for example, may be unwilling to modify their design to conform to a set of human factors standards. The relative merits of conforming to the standard versus the cost of modifying the schedule to incorporate the changes may be discussed, but the group with the vested interest is often impervious to the facts. They may concentrate on only winning the argument.

7. If the members of a group represent a single subculture within a given area of technology, the entire group may share a common bias. If this bias deviates from the overall goals of the organization, the committee's decision may be inappropriate for the corporation.

Taken together, these observations make it apparent that although group decision making has significant limitations, it is possible to reach better decisions with a committee. The sections to follow discuss two of the more popular design team techniques—the Delphi procedure and the nominal group—that take advantage of group decision-making processes while eliminating most of the disadvantages. A case study is then presented to illustrate how design teams have been used in our research to facilitate the process.

THE DELPHI PROCEDURE

The Delphi procedure was originally developed by researchers at the Rand Corporation (Gordon & Helmer, 1964), and has proven to be a feasible and effective method of obtaining the benefits of group participation (Brown, Cochran, & Dalkey, 1969; Dalkey, 1969; Gordon, 1968; Martino, 1968). The technique is used to study highly subjective or speculative questions such as forecasting the potential sales for an as yet undeveloped product, or identifying the functionality deemed most important for a new software application. Three features differentiate the Delphi procedure from usual group interaction methods: anonymity, iteration with controlled feedback, and statistical group response.

Anonymity. All interactions in a Delphi sequence are handled anonymously through the use of questionnaires. This approach yields two advantages. First, because the originator of an idea is not identified publicly, the person can change his or her mind without losing face. Second, ideas are evaluated more on their relative merits, than on the status of the person who made the proposal.

Iteration with controlled feedback.   Two or more rounds of questioning are used. The results obtained from a given round are provided to the participants before the next round begins. The nature of the information added each time is such that respondents can place their answers clearly in the context of the range of all respondents' answers. The expectation arising from this feature is that the responses of the group tend to converge on some consensus, or at least that the degree of certainty with which respondents answer will be increased.

The person directing the Delphi sequence extracts from the questionnaire only the information that is relevant to the group. Participants in the group see only the collective opinions of others and the pro and con arguments relative to the topic. This eliminates the restatement of the same argument. Majority and minority views are heard, but not in such a way as to overwhelm opposing views simply by weight of opposition. The group is less likely to take on a separate life of its own and more likely to concentrate on the original objectives, without being distracted by self-serving goals such as winning an argument or reaching agreement for the sake of agreement.

Statistical group response.   Groups that do not employ the Delphi procedure typically produce a report that reflects decisions on which the majority of participants could agree. Unless a minority strongly disagrees with an issue, it is unlikely that there will be any indication of the degree of difference that existed among the team members. Using the Delphi procedure eliminates this problem, because the findings are presented as a statistical response which includes the opinions of the entire group. For example, the group response to a question might be presented as a median score and the two quartiles (i.e., a number such that half of the group were above it and half below, and two numbers that separate the inner half of the group from the outer quarters). Each opinion in the group is thus taken into by the median, and variances in opinion are represented by the size of the interquartile range.

Conducting a Delphi Sequence

Although variations on the Delphi procedure are discussed in the literature, this section concentrates on the basic procedures initially developed at Rand and summarized by Martino (1972). Before elaborating on the technique, the terminology must be clarified. A Delphi sequence is conducted through a series of questionnaires presented to a a panel of experts. Each successive completion of the survey is called a round. The questionnaires used in the Delphi sequence differ from those that are discussed later in this chapter. First, a Delphi questionnaire not only asks questions, but provides feedback to the respondents regarding the degree of group consensus. Second, in the initial rounds, the questionnaire is completely unstructured and open-ended. As discussed later, there are disadvantages to open-ended questions. In the Delphi procedure, however, if the survey is too structured, the panel may overlook important issues. Third, Delphi techniques are not used for surveying individuals on their past behaviors or objective characteristics of a group, although such data may be requested as an adjunct to the technique.

The groups of experts used for Delphi sequences are referred to as *panels*. In human–computer interaction research, a panel may consist of software developers, marketing personnel, planning representatives, manufacturing employees, Human Factors specialists and users. Remember, users are experts on their own values and preferences. The person responsible for collecting the panels responses is typically called the *director*. The panelists, the director, or both perform slightly different tasks during each round. Prior to round one, guidelines or background information is provided to respondents, sometimes in the form of scenarios, to ensure that all participants have minimally the same information base.

Round one.   The first unstructured questionnaire asks the panelists to make a forecast on the subject for which the panel was assembled. For example, the panel might be requested to specify the functionality that should be included in a product intended to facilitate computer supported cooperative work (CSCW). Although the open-ended items do place more of a burden on the panel members than had fixed response questions been used, it must be remembered that the panel was selected because they are experts on the topic.

The ideas suggested by each panel member are submitted to the director of the Delphi sequence who consolidates the responses into a single set. Since some panelists are likely to have described the new product in narrative form, the director must categorize these narratives into discrete events (or functionality in the above CSCW example). Similar events are consolidated and events not related to the topic are eliminated. A final list is prepared by the director in as clear terms as possible. This list of events becomes the second questionnaire.

Round two.   The panelists are presented with the consolidated list of events and asked to specify the dates by which these events will occur and/or the importance they attach to given events (e.g., functionality). They are also asked to give reasons why they believe the estimated dates are correct. In the above CSCW example, the estimated dates provided by the end-users will not be as accurate as those supplied by developers who understand the intrinsic difficulties of software development. At the same time, the end-users' response provide managers with an estimate of user expectations. After the panelists' forecasts and estimated dates are returned to the director, the director prepares a consolidated statistical summary of the panel's opinions. Included in this summary are the panelists arguments for and against an event occurring within a given time frame. The third questionnaire lists the events, the panel specified median date, the upper and lower quartile dates for each event, and the summaries of reasons for advancing or delaying the estimates.

Round three.   The panelists are presented with the events, statistical description of panel opinion, and summary arguments. Each member is asked to review the arguments and to reevaluate their estimates for each date the event is expected to occur. If their estimate falls outside the Interquartile Range of the estimates provided in Round Two (i.e., later than the upper quartile or earlier than the lower quartile), they are asked to justify their view and to comment on why their opinion deviates from the other panelists. To support their argument, the panelists are free to use whatever information they believe to be relevant. This is similar to face-to-face discussions, but here the interaction is anonymous. The director's job after the new estimates and arguments have been submitted is to recalculate the medians and quartiles and to summarize the pro and con arguments. These are compiled in a new forecast for Round Four.

Round four.   The panelists are again presented with the list of events, statistics on the estimates and pro/con arguments. They are asked to reevaluate their position and make a new forecast. Note that, if the panel reaches agreement on an event early in the sequence (e.g., Round Two), it is not necessary to carry that event through all four rounds. Also, since this is the final round, the panel may or may not be asked to present their arguments. Using this information, the director makes the same calculations as before.

The Delphi procedure has been used successfully to forecast events in the introduction of computer technology (Bernstein, 1969) and the impact of computers on worker displacement (Gordon & Helmer, 1964). More recently, Turoff, Hiltz, and Kerr (1981) used a modified version of the technique to identify desirable features of computer-mediated communication systems. In this latter investigation, software designers were presented with a list of system features and asked to rate them on two dimensions: the extent to which the feature was considered important if an ideal system were to be built, and the extent to which they were incorporated into the design of their current system. The original list of features was based on factors suggested to be important in the literature and were divided into characteristics that are common to all interactive systems and those peculiar to computer-based communication systems. Although the panel indicated more agreement for the importance and necessity of the general system characteristics as opposed to those dealing specifically with computer-mediated communication, the areas of disagreement suggested issues for further experimentation and study.[3] The Delphi procedure in this instance accelerated the synthesis of understanding each other's position and facilitated a cooperative learning environment.

THE NOMINAL GROUP

The Delphi procedure enhances group decision-making processes, but it is time consuming to conduct properly. Turoff et al. (1981), for example, suggest that the minimum time frame is probably a year when the experts are geographically dispersed and the director conducts the Delphi sequence through the mail. The nominal group technique, on the other hand, permits a faster response time while maintaining many of the advantages of the Delphi procedure.

The nominal group is a method of decision making in which individuals are gathered in a structured face-to-face encounter, resulting in a group consensus (Delbecq & Van de Ven, 1975). Seven basic steps are included:

1. define the task statement/problem
2. silent generation of ideas
3. round robin listing
4. clarification of issues
5. discussion
6. grouping of ideas
7. voting and ranking of alternatives.

The following case-study illustrates these steps with respect to a system design solution for a small distribution business. The organization had been operating successfully for over 17 years. Procedures for processing new orders, maintaining inventory, invoices, shipping, and marketing were controlled through an elaborate paperwork system. The system was efficient for small volumes of orders, but, as business increased, the management decided to automate the paper based system. Consultants were brought in to help specify requirements, assist in the procurement of hardware/software, develop applications, and, finally,

---

[3] See Turoff et al. (1981) for a description of the actual findings.

train users on the system. Design team meetings were held where the nominal group consisted of the company president, the operations manager, a senior software engineer, and the employees who would be operating the system to be installed.

Task definition (Step 1) was specified at the outset of the first meeting. The group was charged with the responsibility of developing a set of system specifications which would meet the business need to automate the paperwork. Silent generation of ideas (Step 2) began prior to the first meeting. Participants were contacted by the consultants, briefed about the task, and asked to prepare notes for a group meeting. The first meeting focused on a round robin discussion (Step 3) where participants expressed their perceptions of the problem, beliefs about the appropriate technology, and concerns about human relations issues. By the conclusion of the first session, a listing of issues, concerns, and possible courses of action had been generated. Participants were asked to evaluate the options before the second meeting.

The second meeting began by reviewing the notes from the initial session. Each participant was allowed time to question and clarify previous points and to offer additional suggestions for consideration (Steps 4 and 5). The ideas were grouped into three central issues: software/hardware requirements, cost factors, and training needs (Step 6). Alternatives under each of these major headings were discussed and an agreement was reached by all participants regarding the strategy to follow (Step 7). Interestingly, the final software/hardware configuration selected by the group differed considerably from the company president's original plan to include a large minicomputer with multitasking workstations and proprietary software. The strategy adopted by the design team called for microsystems linked together via a local area network running commercial software, a solution that was considerably less expensive than the initial configuration. The automated system has now been in operation for about a year and is meeting the needs of the company.

In summary, this section has reviewed two design team techniques— the Delphi procedure and Nominal Group. Both methods provide a structured approach to group decisionmaking. By actively seeking input from a variety of groups, a broad range of viewpoints can be aired and considered before any design decisions are finalized.

EXPERIMENTS

Experimentation is generally thought of as the most rigorous type of research, particularly in the physical sciences. In human–computer interaction research, the use of experiments has increased substantially although some of this work has been criticized for lack of experimental controls, insufficient sample sizes, and questionable generality (Brooks, 1980; Curtis, 1980; Basili, Selby, & Hutchens, 1986; Shneiderman, 1987). In this section we briefly describe controlled experimentation and identify the characteristic differences of a few basic designs. An empirical example is presented to help clarify how experimental data collected in an office environment can facilitate understanding human–computer interactions.

In a fundamental sense experiments are a point of departure from the other research methods we have been discussing. Extraneous variables in an experiment are held constant and the change in variable y (dependent variable) is observed when variable x (independent variable) is manipulated. This permits the experimenter to observe the effects of the manipulated variables upon the dependent variable in a situation where the effect of other relevant variables has been removed. With the other techniques (observation of behavior, design team techniques, and surveys), the researcher merely records the behaviors and attitudes of respondents as they are reported. Because the researcher controls what variables will be manipulated and who will receive what stimuli, the experiment is the most powerful and preferred approach for testing causal relationships. The causal ordering of variables must be inferred when using the other methodologies. Information obtained from questionnaires, for example, does not allow the researcher to identify whether the users' behavior patterns influenced their attitudes toward the product or vice versa.

Experiments differ depending on whether they are conducted in the laboratory or the field. Laboratory experiments provide more control over what is being manipulated and the influence of nonexperimental variables, but they may be artificial. Field experiments take place in the subjects' normal environment, but it is difficult to exclude extraneous stimuli which unfortunately can affect subjects much more than the stimulus under test.

Controversy over the relative merits of controlled laboratory experiments versus field studies has been debated in the computer literature for at least two decades (Chapanis, 1967; Erdmann & Neal, 1971). Chapanis (1967), for example, has questioned the relevance of laboratory work to any real-life situation, while others (Poulton, 1975) indicate the need for experimental control to eliminate observer bias. Regardless of the setting, researchers (Neal & Simons, 1984) have recognized that "it is important to provide subjects with motivation approximating that provided by a potential employer" (p. 83). The argument presented here emphasizes that both experimental and field research methods are necessary to appreciate fully the complexities of any process involving humans and computers. Our view sees the two methodologies (experimental and field research) as complementary rather than competing.

Regardless of whether or not the experiment is conducted in a laboratory or the field, the chief advantage of a controlled experiment lies in the isolation of one or more independent variables and the evaluation of their impact on one or more dependent variables. An independent variable is that which is being manipulated by the researcher. For example, assume a researcher wants to examine which of two screen layouts is easier for individuals to use. The independent variable is the two alternative screen designs. Depending on the text book, one may find a variety of names for an independent variable, such as *treatment, stimuli, predictor,* or *factor.*[4]

In the simplest experimental design, the researcher manipulates one variable and measures the effect of that manipulation on a second variable. The second variable is the dependent variable. The dependent variable in the above example is the ease of using either of the two screens. Some texts refer to the dependent variable as the criterion variable.

Since experiments are often rather limited in scope, requiring relatively little time or money, it is possible to replicate given experiments utilizing different groups of subjects. The limited scope of experiments can have some negative consequences. Unlike survey research where measures of numerous variables are taken, if a given independent variable in an experiment is empirically shown to be nonsignificant, other variables that might influence the dependent measure cannot be tested. To compensate for this limitation, experimenters often incorporate additional measures (i.e., covariates) in the study. A covariate is any variable which may interact with the independent variable to obscure the clarity of the findings. In laboratory experiments, the researcher can eliminate the confounding influence of a covariate by physically holding such variables constant. Holding the temperature at 70 degrees while examining the relationship between volume and pressure illustrates the concept. When the influence of covariates cannot be experimentally (i.e., physically) controlled, the impact of covariates can be controlled statistically by adjusting the scores on the dependent vari-

---

[4] The term *factor* in an experiment should not be confused with the concept of factors resulting from a factor analysis. In an experiment, a factor refers to a specific independent variable. In a factor analysis, a factor refers to a set of variables which share some common property.

able. Choosing the control variables so as to exclude all confounding extraneous variables, however, is difficult (Kish, 1959).

Common experimental designs

This section examines the defining features of four common experimental designs: (a) the single factor design, (b) the single factor design with blocks, (c) full factorial, and (d) Latin squares. These designs are covered in detail elsewhere.[5] For a first acquaintance with the literature on these designs it is best to consult only a few sources; otherwise, one's effort in learning experimental methodology is dissipated in learning different symbols and organization of material. The discussion below, therefore, is based on a standard text by Cochran and Cox (1957). Our goal is to highlight some of the fundamental trade-offs associated with four experimental designs.

The single factor design. The simplest and sometimes the best design pools all subjects and then randomly assigns them to categories of the independent variable. Including more subjects in a particular category cell increases the reliability of the findings without jeopardizing randomness. Because inequalities in the number of people in each category group affects statistical analysis, it is helpful to keep the number of subjects per treatment equal (Winer, 1962). This design maximizes the number of degrees of freedom ($df = t - 1$, where t is the number of treatments), since it puts the fewest constraints possible on the assignment of subjects to treatments.[6] The design is limited by the fact that subjects cannot be divided into homogeneous subgroupings. The statistical analysis of a single factor design is a t-test for two cells or an F-test for three or more cells.

The single-factor design with blocks. A block is a homogeneous group of subjects. Rather than pooling all subjects before randomization, individuals are divided into a number of smaller, homogeneous groups, and the entire experiment is repeated within each group. Examples of more homogeneous groups might include: one block for males and one for females, one block for novice users and one for experts, or

---

[5] Readers interested in a more in-depth, yet simple introduction to the field are referred to an early book (1953) by Lindquist—*Design and analysis of experiments in psychology and education.* There are also several good texts for information on specific designs; for example: Kirk (1968), *Experimental design: Procedures for the behavioral sciences.* Those interested in statistical aspects of experimental design should consult Winer (1962), *Statistical principles in experimental design.*

[6] The phrase *degrees of freedom* is used in tests of statistical inference and refers to the number of statistically independent observations.

one for secretaries and one for managers. Provided the groupings (blocks) represent meaningful clusters, this strategy helps to identify trends in the data which might not otherwise appear when all of the subjects are pooled together. If the blocks do not constitute relevant categories of individuals, this design is inferior to the single factor design because of the loss in degrees of freedom ($df = rt - 1$, where t is the number of treatments and r is the number of replications or blocks). Using blocks always sacrifices degrees of freedom, however, block designs sometimes reduce confounding differences among subjects.

Full factorial designs. Factorial experiments simultaneously manipulate two or more independent variables and evaluate their influence on a dependent variable. In contrast to a block design, where the block variable is merely a way to better observe the effects, every category in the independent variables are of substantive interest in full factorial designs. The factorial design can be thought of as a series of single factor designs. The advantage of factorial designs over single factor designs lies in their ability to determine interaction effects among the independent variables, as well as the main effects for each independent variable. Single factor experiments allow the researcher to examine only main effects. Factorial experiments are appropriate for the following situations:

1. In exploratory work where the object is to determine quickly the effects of a number of factors over a specified range.
2. In investigations of the interactions among the effects of several factors.
3. In experiments designed to lead to recommendations that must apply over a wide range of conditions. Subsidiary factors may be brought into an experiment so as to test the principle factors under a variety of conditions similar to those that will be encountered in the population to which recommendations are to apply (Cochran & Cox, 1957, p. 152).

A limitation of factorial designs lies in the number of subjects necessary to conduct the experiment. If the researcher wants to evaluate the interaction between the subjects' gender (male versus female) and their level of expertise (novice versus expert) with 10 subjects per cell, 40 individuals are needed for this 2 × 2 factorial design. If a third independent variable is added (e.g., position level in the organization— manager, scientist, and secretary), the design becomes a 2 × 2 × 3 factorial and the number of subjects increases to 120.

Latin-square designs. Latin-square designs control for the influence of confounding factors. For example, assume a researcher wants to determine which of 3 new interfaces (A, B, or C) people find easier to use. If each subject uses all three interfaces, the order in which they are evaluated might act as a confounding influence. To eliminate this influence, the Latin square design manipulates the order in which subjects view the three interfaces, for example:

A B C
B C A
C B A

In this situation, the first subject would see interface "A" first, then "B," and finally "C." The next subject would begin with interface "B," then evaluate "C," and finally "A," etc.

In summary, this section has reviewed some of the major advantages and disadvantages of alternative experimental designs. These practical considerations influence the researcher's choice of design. This is particularly true where the experimenter has less than complete control over the assignment of subjects to treatments or over the number of treatment groups. The investigator is by necessity required to combine a knowledge of experimental principles with practical experience and sound judgment.

To illustrate the application of experimental research in human–computer evaluations, the following describes a recent field experiment (Vaske & Grantham, 1985). A field experiment, as opposed to a laboratory experiment, was purposely selected for three reasons. First, field experiments are less common in human–computer interaction literature. Second, it is important for researchers to realize that experiments can be conducted in office environments as well as laboratory settings. Finally, field experiments more often than not complicate the control of extraneous variables.

EMPIRICAL EXAMPLE

The initial aim of the experiment was to compare two satellite services (satellite service X in location 1 and satellite service Y in location 2) against a terrestrial-based service that was normally used by all employees at both locations. Adopting either of the satellite services would reduce the company's per-call costs. At issue was whether or not the quality of the phone transmissions (dependent variable) would decrease with the satellite (independent variable).

Twenty-two people were randomly selected to participate at each of the two locations. All subjects were aware of the study's purpose and design. During the initial phase, individuals completed a survey designed to ascertain their attitudes and reported behaviors with respect to the existing terrestrial service. All study participants were then given access to the satellite-based service for making long distance phone calls. After one month of usage, subjects were again surveyed to identify their perceptions of satellite transmissions and to compare these beliefs against their evaluations of the land-based system.

The satellite service carrier in Location 1 unfortunately failed to route all intended phone traffic over the satellite. Some long distance calls were sent over terrestrial links, while others were routed through the satellite. Because no records were maintained by the satellite service, and because the researchers were not allowed to monitor the routing of calls, it was impossible to determine the exact routing of all calls. For these reasons, the intended comparisons for the Location 1 portion of the experiment were invalid, and only the data from Location 2 could be analyzed. Although this incident was unfortunate, it does highlight the problems encountered when attempting to conduct field experiments.

Results

Nearly two-thirds (64%) of the respondents at Location 2 rated the satellite service as "very good" or "excellent." Only 27% gave a similar response for the company's land-based system. At the other extreme, 32% felt the overall quality of the terrestrial service was "poor" or "fair," while 18% rated the satellite this low. The difference in these two distributions was significant at the .05 level, suggesting that people were generally more satisfied with the satellite than with the organization's terrestrial service.

In the first questionnaire, individuals were asked to respond to a set of 11 questions pertaining to potential problem areas on the terrestrial service. An identical set of questions was asked about the satellite in the second survey, which was distributed 1 month after the people had been given access to the satellite. Each individual's answers on the first questionnaire were compared to those in the second. Nine of the eleven tests were statistically significant, and, in each of these instances, fewer problems were recorded for the satellite (Table 5.5). No statistical differences between terrestrial and satellite were evident for clipping or transmission delays; variables that had been initially hypothesized to be especially problematic for the satellite service. The means for both of these variables indicated that the problems seldom occurred.

Taken together, these data suggest that, for this sample of users, the

TABLE 5.5
Reported frequency of specific problems with the terrestrial and satellite services.

	Frequency of problems with:[1]		
Dependent Variable[2]	Terrestrial	Satellite	t-value
Having to wait for an available line	3.9	2.7	5.92**
Getting a busy signal on the first try	3.0	2.5	2.67**
Call does not go through	3.0	2.0	5.37**
Noisy line	3.1	2.1	5.07**
Hearing voice distortion	2.6	2.1	2.30*
Having the end of words cut off (i.e., clipping)	2.2	2.0	n.s.
Experiencing too much transmission delay (time between speaking and being heard)	2.2	2.6	n.s.
Hearing an echo on the line	2.7	2.0	2.64**
Volume is too low	2.9	1.9	4.81**
Unable to hear the other party	2.8	1.3	9.24**
Getting disconnected during call	2.5	1.4	4.93**

1. Each individual evaluated the terrestrial service prior to using the satellite. Satellite evaluations were made by the same sample of people after one month of usage.

2. Variables coded on a five-point scale: (1) Never, (2) Seldom, (3) Sometimes, (4) Frequently and (5) Always.

* $p < .05$; ** $p < .01$

occurrence of problems was lower for satellite transmissions, and that the overall evaluation of the service was significantly higher than for the terrestrial service. Because such findings were contrary to our initial predictions, three covariates that may have influenced the findings were also evaluated: telephone usage patterns, expectations, and preferences.

Telephone usage patterns. One explanation for the unexpected findings is the number of long distance phone calls made by the respondents. Individuals who use the phone more frequently, for example, might experience a greater number of problems than those who make fewer calls. Results indicated that, on average, the subjects made more phone calls on the terrestrial system (M = 11) than they did during the study period (M = 6.6).

Why this difference in usage patterns exists cannot be systematically determined by the data collected here, however, plausible rationales exist. First, the respondents had not been asked to monitor their phone usage prior to completing the terrestrial survey item. Responses to the satellite usage question were completed after the individuals knew they were participants in a study concerned with evaluating the quality of different telephone services. Given that previous research has suggested that people tend to overestimate the amount they engage in certain behaviors, the increased usage for the terrestrial service may reflect a difference in the users' attention to this particular activity. Alternatively, the individuals may have simply made fewer calls during the study period than normal. Whatever the explanation, the pertinent issue is, does increased usage of the satellite increase the frequency of the problems?

The data did not support this hypothesis. Individuals who reported an average of more than five long distance calls per day on the satellite noted the same frequency of problems as those who made five or fewer calls per day (Table 5.6). Although there were three exceptions to this general pattern, the findings for one of these variables was the reverse of what would have been expected. People who logged fewer calls indicated that they were more, rather than less likely, to get a busy signal on the first try, than those who made more calls. In the other two statistically significant cases, the more frequent callers noted a higher occurrence of noisy lines and more voice distortion than those who made fewer calls. The means for the clipping and transmission delay variables were greater for the group making more calls, but the differences between groups were not significant. In summary, differences in number of phone calls made by the respondents did not account for the higher ratings for the satellite. Frequent callers reported essentially the same number of problems as infrequent callers.

Expectations. A second explanation for the differences in terrestrial and satellite evaluations concerns the respondents' expectations about the quality of the satellite. Expectations refer to specific beliefs people have about a particular service or product. For example, individuals may expect more transmission delays and clipping problems when using a satellite, as opposed to a terrestrial communication link. Such expectations stem from personal experiences or information provided by others. The surveys used in this study asked respondents to compare the expectations and quality of other phone services against

TABLE 5.6
Satellite problems reported by frequent and infrequent telephone users.

Problems with the satellite service[1]	Number of long distance calls placed on the satellite per day		t-value
	Five or fewer (n=12)	More than five (n=12)	
Having to wait for an available line	2.8	2.6	n.s.
Getting a busy signal on the first try	2.9	2.0	2.48*
Call does not go through	2.0	1.9	n.s.
Noisy line	1.7	2.7	3.11**
Hearing voice distortion	1.7	2.6	2.07*
Having the end of words cut off (i.e., clipping)	1.8	2.2	n.s.
Experiencing too much transmission delay (time between speaking and being heard)	2.3	3.0	n.s.
Hearing an echo on the line	1.8	2.2	n.s.
Volume is too low	1.9	1.9	n.s.
Unable to hear the other party	1.2	1.5	n.s.
Getting disconnected during call	1.2	1.6	n.s.

1.　Variables coded on a five-point scale: (1) Never, (2) Seldom, (3) Sometimes, (4) Frequently and (5) Always.

* $p < .05$; ** $p < .01$

the company's terrestrial system. For each of four items, individuals rated the other service as better than, about the same, or worse than the existing service.

Sixty-four percent felt that the overall quality of service they receive in their homes was better than the company's terrestrial system (Table 5.7). Since most of these individuals (73%) used AT&T at home, the comparison represented an AT&T versus terrestrial contrast. Fifteen of the individuals had used a satellite link prior to participating in this study. The reaction of most of these individuals was negative toward their earlier experiences on a satellite; 60% felt the satellite was worse than the terrestrial service. However, when asked to compare their

TABLE 5.7
Comparisons between other phone services and the terrestrial service.

Other service is:	Quality[1] of Home Service	Previous[2] Satellite Quality	Expected[3] Satellite Quality	Perceived[4] Satellite Quality
Better than the terrestrial service	64%	20%	32%	73%
About the same	36	20	50	18
Worse than the terrestrial service	0	60	18	9
Total	100% (22)	100% (15)	100% (22)	100% (22)

1. Quality of home service refers to the comparison of existing terrestrial system and the phone service used by the residents in their homes. Most of the respondents (73%) used AT&T.

2. Previous satellite quality includes the comparative evaluations of those individuals who had used satellite communications link prior to the start of this study.

3. The expected satellite quality question asked respondents to compare their expectations about satellite transmissions against the terrestrial service. This survey item was completed prior to the individual actually using the satellite.

4. The perceived satellite quality question was completed after the respondent had been using the satellite service for one month.

expectations about the satellite service they were to use in this study against the current terrestrial system, half of the respondents expected the satellite to be about the same as the terrestrial service. This difference between the users' previous experiences with satellites and their current expectations may be a reflection of the individuals' generally low evaluations of the terrestrial service. The final column of Table 5.7 examines the respondents' perceptions of the satellite used in this study against the terrestrial service. Nearly two-thirds (73%) felt the satellite was better than the terrestrial. A follow-up question comparing the satellite against their home service indicated that three-fourths felt the satellite was about the same as the service they receive at home. Taken together, these findings suggest that although the satellite performed better than expected, the service was rated only equal to the users' home service. In other words, the satellite was not perceived as inherently superior, just better than the company's terrestrial service.

TABLE 5.8
Expected versus actual problems with the satellite.

Problems with the satellite service[2]	Satellite Evaluations [1]		
	Expected Problems	Actual Problems	t-value
Having to wait for an available line	2.8	2.7	n.s.
Getting a busy signal on the first try	2.8	2.5	n.s.
Call does not go through	2.6	1.9	3.22**
Noisy line	2.7	2.1	2.43**
Hearing voice distortion	2.7	2.1	2.04*
Having the end of words cut off (i.e., clipping)	2.6	2.0	2.00*
Experiencing too much transmission delay (time between speaking and being heard)	3.3	2.6	n.s.
Hearing an echo on the line	2.9	2.0	2.71**
Volume is too low	2.7	1.9	3.50**
Unable to hear the other party	2.5	1.3	7.51**
Getting disconnected during call	2.4	1.4	4.81**

1. The expectations questions were asked prior to the individuals actual use of the satellite. Actual problems were reported after one month of using the satellite service.

2. Variables coded on a five-point scale: (1) Never, (2) Seldom, (3) Sometimes, (4) Frequently and (5) Always.

* $p < .05$; ** $p < .01$

Evaluations of the respondents' expectations were also examined by comparing the overall ratings of expected quality prior to usage against the perceptions of the service noted after one month on the satellite. Prior to using the satellite, 55% of the sample indicated that they expected the satellite would provide "very good" or "excellent" service. Given that the perceived quality of the service exceeded the users' expectations that the service would be no better than the terrestrial service, it is not surprising that the terrestrial service was by comparison rated lower.

Comparisons between the expectations for problems on the satellite against the observed frequency of these issues shows that, in all cases, the mean frequency for problems was lower after actual usage than what had been expected (Table 5.8). The difference between the two sets of observations were significant in eight of the eleven comparisons. Such findings further support the idea that the satellite service exceeded the users' expectations.

In summary, these data suggest that the respondents were not expecting the satellite to be any better than the terrestrial service. Because their perceptions of the terrestrial service were quite negative and the satellite performed better than expected, the overall evaluations of the satellite service were positive. At the same time, it is important to keep in mind that most respondents rated the satellite service as about the same as their home service. This again illustrates that the perceived superiority of the satellite is only relative to what it is compared against.

Preferences.   Preferences for a particular communication service is a third explanation for the unexpected findings. The distinction between expectations and preferences is a difference in level of specificity. Expectations represent specific beliefs about a product or service, while preferences are more general beliefs about desired or ideal conditions. Such preferences may be similar to expectations but they can differ as well. One might expect more transmission delays with a satellite but still prefer the service, because the overall quality of the service is better and the cost of making a call is cheaper.

When forced to make a choice between terrestrial and satellite, no definite preference emerged. Twelve individuals (55%) preferred terrestrial, and ten respondents (45%) preferred the satellite. Similar to the expectation variable, an individual's preferences can be influenced by other considerations. Eight issues that may have influenced the users' choice between terrestrial and satellite were included in the study. Overall transmission quality (60%), cost considerations (60%) and the number of calls that successfully go through (50%) were the three most important factors listed by those who preferred the satellite (Table 5.9). People who preferred terrestrial seemed to be motivated by the lack of transmission delays (67%) and clipping (33%) considerations, findings which can probably be attributed to the individuals' general beliefs about satellites rather than the actual occurrence of these problems.

A comparison of the percentages reported in Table 5.9 reveals rather large differences between the two groups, yet only two tests show statistical significance: cost of making a call (17% for terrestrial, versus 60% for satellite) and transmission delays (67% for terrestrial, versus 20% for satellite). In part this lack of statistical significance for six of

TABLE 5.9
Reported reasons for preferring a particular communication service.

Issues influencing the selection of a particular service [1]	Preferred Communication Service		
	Terrestrial	Satellite	Chi square
Overall quality of the transmission	33%	60%	n.s.
Cost of making a phone call	17	60	4.43*
Number of calls that successfully go through	25	50	n.s.
Static on the line	8	30	n.s.
Clipping	33	30	n.s.
Time for the call to go through	17	30	n.s.
Transmission delays	67	20	4.79*
Time it takes to dial a number	8	0	n.s.

1.   Cell entries refer to the percentage of individuals who indicated that the issues influenced their preference for a particular communication service.

the eight tests can be attributed to the sensitivity of the chi square statistic to sample size restrictions. Studies incorporating more respondents would eliminate this limitation and allow for more reliable estimates of any differences that may exist.

Although no clear preference pattern emerged, people who preferred the satellite were making their choice based on cost and overall quality of transmission considerations. Individuals who preferred the terrestrial service may have been reacting to the general beliefs that a satellite transmission will have delay and clipping problems. Interestingly, ancillary analyses that compared the frequency with which these two problems were actually noted, by people who prefer terrestrial versus those who prefer the satellite, showed no statistical difference.

Example Summary

The findings reported in this field experiment suggested that the existing terrestrial service was perceived negatively. People expected the satellite to be comparable to the land-based system prior to using the service. Because the satellite performed better than expected, the overall evaluations of the satellite were positive. The satellite was considered to be equal to the users' home service, while the company's terrestrial system rated lower in quality than the residential service. Over two-thirds of the respondents felt the company should replace the current service with the satellite service.

Although these findings supported the adoption of a satellite based transmission link for long distance telephone calls, there were at least two issues which make such a conclusion tentative. First, the relatively small sample size limited the extent to which the findings could be generalized. Second, because the respondents knew they were using a satellite link, they may have unintentionally biased their evaluations.

From the perspective of this chapter, the terrestrial versus satellite study illustrates a number of methodological issues with respect to conducting field experiments. First, the initial data from Location 1 were rendered useless because of an error on the part of the satellite company. Although this situation was unfortunate, such problems can easily occur when the researcher does not have complete control over the experimental procedures. Second, the study illustrates the importance of incorporating covariates in the design. The sponsor initially requested data only on the overall evaluations of the two services (terrestrial and satellite) and the types of problems people experienced on both systems. Given the basic findings for these variables, interpreting the results would not have been possible had the investigation not included additional measures on telephone usage patterns, expectations, and preferences.

SURVEYS

Questionnaires represent a basic tool for evaluating the attitudes and reported behavior patterns of populations. Reviews of the literature published in different disciplines have repeatedly shown surveys to be a dominant method (Rossi, Freeman, & Wright, 1979; Riddick, Deschriver, & Weissinger, 1984; Sproull, 1986). Research to improve the methodology has also generated a considerable body of literature. Dillman (1978), for example, identifies over 200 articles concerned with improving response rates and the quality of the collected data. This section compares alternative methods of questionnaire design and implementation, and provides some practical considerations for using this method.

Surveys offer five advantages to the study of human–computer interaction. First, questionnaires are particularly useful in describing the characteristics of an entire user community (Babbie, 1979). Items concerning the respondents' past history of computer usage, their attitudes, values, beliefs, and motives can all be included. Second, as the number of such variables to be analyzed simultaneously increases, a large number of cases becomes especially important (Kerlinger, 1973). Third, because large samples are feasible, surveys are more likely to be representative of the population of interest. Fourth, by presenting all respondents with the same set of questions, the reliability of the findings is enhanced. Finally, if close-ended items are used, the data are readily suitable for statistical analysis.

Despite these advantages, there are limitations to surveys. First, unlike experiments where the researcher controls what subjects receive particular treatment conditions of the independent variables, all participants in a survey complete the same questionnaire. Demonstrating cause and effect relationships through surveys is thus more susceptible to interpretation. Compared to participant observation and design team techniques, surveys are inflexible once they have been designed. Care must be taken to ensure that all questions of interest are included in the instrument before the survey is finalized. Much like the new word processing packages, what you see is what you get. Missing a key question or failing to present the questions in a clear, straightforward manner may severely limit the ability to interpret the findings.

Second, surveys have been criticized for not dealing with the context of the interaction (Babbie, 1979). Specific items can address this type of information, but, because the instrument is standardized, questions appropriate to one group may be irrelevant to another. Reducing the question set to the lowest common denominator compensates for this limitation, but the lowered social context makes the instrument less personal (Kiesler, Siegel, & McGuire, 1984). Finally, capturing the true flavor of potential emotions such as fear, anger, love, or hate that may result from human–computer interaction is difficult from a series of paper and pencil responses.

Third, a survey cannot measure the actual behavior of users, only self-reported behaviors. Although some research has shown self-report as a reasonably accurate measure of behavior (Clausen, 1968; Liska, 1974, Tittle & Hill, 1967), other evidence shows that self-report is an imperfect representation of actual behavior (Cannell & Fowler, 1967; Warshaw, Calantone, & Joyce, 1986). These distortions or response effects are influenced by both the experience level of the respondents (Root & Draper, 1983) and the medium (paper versus electronic) used to distribute the questionnaire (Kiesler & Sproull, 1986). In general, research (Sudman & Bradburn, 1974; Bradburn, 1983; Dijkstra & van der Zouwen, 1982) has shown that response effects are greater when:

1. the elapsed time between the event of interest occurs and the survey is completed increases
2. the event occurs only infrequently
3. the event is not important to the respondent
4. there are social reasons for under reporting or over reporting certain activities.

Finally, surveys are time intensive and can be expensive (Kerlinger, 1973). In a large survey, it may be months before even a single hypothesis can be tested. Sampling, developing the survey, waiting for a response, coding, and analyzing the data all take time.

The Survey Research Process

Good questionnaires are like poetry. In final form, they appear "simple, elegant and easily constructed" (Heberlein, 1980, p. 53). Unfortunately, questionnaire construction is not simple. Instructions, the arrangement of questions, and the response categories all influence the quality of the instrument. Just as poets cannot precisely describe how they write poetry, we cannot fully define how to create a questionnaire. Because survey research is a process, however, the steps necessary for developing and implementing any questionnaire can be discussed (Table 5.10).

Step 1 is to decide what information the study should seek overall. The importance of this step cannot be over emphasized. Managers and developers recognize the need for information, but do not always pose the question to the researcher clearly and specifically. If the question is unclear, the investigation will not resolve the problem, or, at least, the answer will be inadequate. Because surveys are time consuming, it is important to determine whether a survey or some other methodology provides the most appropriate data. If the researcher is interested in determining the actual usage of an application package, a software monitor is more appropriate than a survey. Alternatively, are there existing data sources (e.g., other in-house surveys or published articles) which contain answers to the questions of interest?

The solution to Step 1 is to involve the ultimate recipients of the information (e.g., management, marketing, developers, researchers, etc.) at the outset of the study. Each group is presented with a set of sample tables outlining the variables to be compared. Examination of the skeleton tables helps focus the investigation on the most important issues and eliminates variables that do not address the problem (Andreasen, 1985).

Once there is agreement on the overall purpose of the study, and a questionnaire is perceived as an appropriate component, the second

TABLE 5.10
Procedural guidelines for developing surveys.

Step 1. Decide what information the study should seek overall. For example:

    a) self-reported behavior or counts of actual behaviors (e.g., as would be obtained from a software monitor.)

    b) background information on respondents as would be available from a personnel office.

    c) historical records of an organization or a specific hardware or software product.

    d) beliefs and feelings of users and non-users of a particular system.

Step 2. Decide what the questionnaire should cover.

    a) self-reported behavior.

    b) reasons for reported behaviors and attitudes.

    c) beliefs and feelings about existing products.

    d) history of past computer usage.

    e) expectations and preferences about future or anticipated products.

    f) demographics of respondents.

Step 3. Develop a first draft of the questionnaire.

Step 4. Pre-test the questionnaire.

Step 5. Revise the questionnaire based on pre-test results.

Step 6. Develop procedures for administrating questionnaire.

Step 7. Establish procedures for:

    a) logging in completed questionnaires.

    b) follow-up reminders to nonrespondents - i.e., postcards, phone calls, etc.

    c) coding and keying the data.

    d) analyzing the data.

---

step is to decide what issues the survey should cover. If background information on the study's participants (e.g., age, sex, position in the organization, etc.) is needed to identify the individuals who are likely to buy a product, there are alternative ways to obtain the data. One source is the company's personnel office. Another technique is to incorporate a series of demographic questions in the survey. Either approach is acceptable; the choice depends on the availability of the data.

Steps 3 through 5 in Table 5.10 involve the actual process of constructing the survey, pretesting the questionnaire, and revising the instrument based on the results of the initial evaluations. The discussion to follow draws on an article by Heberlein (1980) that provides a useful set of rules to follow when formulating a questionnaire:

1. Know your population, the topic, and what the respondent thinks about the subject.
2. Use terms that make sense to the respondent.
3. Involve the respondent as a coparticipant in the research.
4. Use fixed alternatives rather than open-ended questions.
5. Make every question count.
6. Start with an interesting, easy, relevant question.
7. Break the questionnaire into sections
8. Short questionnaires are not necessarily better.
9. Avoid hypothetical questions and items of doubtful reliability.

Know your population—Involve the respondent. Although the these rules have become common maxims among human–computer interaction researchers (Ives & Olson, 1984; Gould & Lewis, 1985; Shneiderman, 1987), it is easy to revert to technical jargon when constructing a survey on attitudes toward hardware or software applications. Terms that are frequently used by systems' developers may have little or no meaning to the users of the technology. If the respondent cannot understand the question, the quality of the answers decreases and the nonresponse increases.

To protect against this pitfall, interview potential respondents to find out what they think about the topic and what terms they use in their own descriptions of the product or service. After an initial draft of the survey has been constructed, pretest the questionnaire to identify items that are unclear or ambiguous. People may not have an attitude about metafiles, but they can tell you what is liked and disliked about the application. More-specific questions, directly related to the product of interest and phrased in the respondents' own terms, yield better action items than more general items couched in technical terminology (Root & Draper, 1983). The same care and attention to detail that is used to create meaningful menus should be applied to the development of a survey.

Use fixed alternatives rather than open-ended questions. Similar to the difference between menu-driven and command-line interaction styles, it is easier for respondents to answer questions when all the alternatives are displayed. Open-ended items are difficult to answer and cumbersome to analyze. For example, asking individuals to specify what type of printer(s) they use in an open-ended question can be interpreted in several ways. Some respondents might think the researcher wants to know the brand name. Others may say laser or dot-matrix, and a few might write down the model number. If the goal is to compare different printers in terms of users' perceptions of attributes such as speed, print quality, font styles, etc., open-ended responses may not provide the information needed for grouping the answers into mutually exclusive categories. Knowing that one individual has an IBM printer and another uses a dot-matrix printer, for example, does not necessarily imply two different printers. Presenting respondents with a list of potential printers eliminates this problem, provided the response categories include the range of possible alternatives and are worded such that respondents can easily identify the type of printer they use. Because the range of possible candidates may be quite broad, the importance of rules 1 through 3 increases dramatically.

Make every question count. Surveys allow the researcher to include numerous items. Although efforts to understand human–computer interaction often necessitate information on different variables, it is equally important to determine how the answers are to be analyzed and used. If 95% of the respondents said yes to a particular item, what action would you take? If 95% said no, what would your reaction be? When the answer to both scenarios is the same, the question offers little useful information and should be eliminated from the survey.

Start with an interesting, easy, relevant question. Individuals often have strong opinions (either pro or con) toward computer products. Our experiences in doing survey research suggest that users are typically willing and sometimes anxious to let you know how they feel about software applications, especially if they believe their opinions can influence future releases. For these reasons, the survey should start with questions directly related to the product/service of interest to the study. The converse of this principle is *never* to start a survey with demographic items like age, sex, education, etc. Such questions are not interesting for the respondent to complete, can be viewed as too personal, and sometimes produce a negative reaction that results in a lower response rate. Demographic questions are better placed at the end of the survey. Respondents who have just detailed their beliefs and reactions to numerous aspects of a product/service, described their prior computing experiences and elaborated on their motivations for using the application, are more likely to see the relevance of demographic items when such questions appear at the end of the survey.

Break the questionnaire into sections. Surveys provide individuals with a chance to express their opinions toward a variety of topics. When the questionnaire is divided into discrete sections devoted to a specific issue, the individual can more easily focus on the topic and provide a more accurate reflection of his or her true beliefs and feelings. Breaking the questionnaire into sections also makes the instrument appear less monotonous, provides the respondent with a sense of psychological closure for finishing a given topic area, and allows the researcher to start numbering items in each new section. This latter point is especially pertinent for long surveys. Flipping to the end of a survey numbered consecutively, and finding out that there are 200 questions, reduces the probability that the instrument will be completed. By dividing the same questionnaire into 10 sections of 20 items each, the survey looks simpler to complete.

Short questionnaires are not necessarily better.   An analysis of the response rates reported in 214 published studies that had used mailed questionnaires indicated that response dropped approximately 5% for every 10 pages of questionnaire (Heberlein & Baumgartner, 1978). Trading off 10 pages of information for a 5% reduction in response is usually a beneficial exchange. Surveys conducted by ourselves (Grantham & Vaske, 1985; Vaske & Grantham, 1985; Vaske & Teubner, 1985) have ranged from 17 to 25 pages, with response rates in excess of 75%. Factors contributing to the success of these investigations include: the population studied (company employees), a topic of interest to the sampled individuals, and the way the instrument was put together. While researchers cannot always control the first two variables, the spacing of items and flow of questions can be manipulated. Previous experience suggests that spreading the questions out, leaving lots of white space makes the questionnaire easier to complete. A 10-page questionnaire can be easier to complete than a 2-page instrument containing the same items crammed into a smaller space. Equally important is the design of the first page. Including only a few interesting questions on the first page typically commits the respondent to completing the entire instrument. Finally, by reducing the size of the pages and putting them into a booklet makes long questionnaires appear shorter and easier to complete.

Avoid hypothetical questions and items of doubtful reliability. Individuals can describe what they like and dislike about a software application after they have had a chance to use it. As their experience increases, they can also speculate about what additional features would enhance their perceptions of the product. Difficulties arise, however, when respondents are asked to speculate on the desirable features of products for which they have no prior experience or when the information requested is too specific. For example, how many times did you login into the local area network during the last 6 months? Including such items in a questionnaire tends to frustrate the respondent and lower the response rate. Those responses that are returned are likely to be inaccurate, unreliable and invalid. If answers to hypothetical questions are desired, it is best to use one of the design team techniques discussed earlier in this chapter.

The final two steps in the survey research process (Table 5.10) are related to how the questionnaires are distributed and what you do with the information once it is collected. Before discussing the advantages and disadvantages of different kinds of questionnaires, it is important to make a few remarks regarding the analysis of survey data. Because surveys can include numerous variables, hand calculations quickly become tedious, if not impossible, for more sophisticated analyses. Fortunately, numerous statistical packages (e.g., SPSS, SPSS PC, Systat, Statgraphics, BMDP, SAS, etc.) are now available on a wide range of computers. It is strongly advised that some form of automated data reduction be available, if even modest surveys are to be conducted.

TYPES OF QUESTIONNAIRES

Three approaches to gathering survey data are traditionally discussed in the literature: mail surveys, telephone interviews and personal interviews. Computer assisted versions of these techniques (e.g., Computer Assisted Telephone Interviewing (CATI) and Respondent Completed Electronic Surveys) have also become more common as the cost of software and hardware has decreased and the popularity of electronic mail has increased. Each methodology has advantages and disadvantages. Deciding on the most appropriate type of survey depends on the problem being addressed and on time and cost considerations. The important point here is that the choice of which survey approach to use cannot be answered in the abstract. Having said this, we still need guidelines for practitioners to rely on when attempting to identify what type of questionnaire is best.[7] The following summarizes some of the observations reported by Dillman (1978) as they apply to the lessons we have learned from conducting human–computer interaction survey research.

Mail versus Telephone versus Personal Interviews

Because answers to design questions are often needed yesterday, *time* considerations play a deciding role in the choice of survey. Telephone

---

[7] Readers interested in a complete discussion of this topic are referred to Dillman (1978), *Mail and Telephone Surveys: The Total Design Method.*

interviews are generally quicker to administer than either mail questionnaires or personal interviews. Mailed questionnaires, however, allow for the inclusion of more variables in the instrument. If relatively few individuals are included in the study, personal interviews are also useful, especially if the respondents are not geographically dispersed or the researcher wishes to include open-ended items.

Another criterion when deciding on a particular type of survey is *cost*. Of the three traditional methods, personal interviews tend to be most expensive, followed by telephone interviews and mail questionnaires. If outside expertise is required to conduct the investigation, the cost per completed personal interview is roughly five times greater than the costs for a telephone interview, and 10 times more expensive than mailed surveys. Actual costs may vary considerably, depending on the length of the survey and the extent to which outside help is required to complete the investigation. What is apparent, however, is that survey research findings, even the obvious and wrong ones, do not come cheaply. For this reason, the steps outlined in Table 5.10 should not be taken lightly.

Expected *response rate* represents a third factor in the researcher's choice of survey. Most text book authors suggest that a limitation of mailed surveys is their low response rate (Babbie, 1979). Summary data reported by Dillman (1978), however, shows that the 48 mailed surveys that have followed the methods proposed in his book had an average response rate of 74%, with no survey having less than a 50% response. Similarly, our experiences with using mailed questionnaires have consistently produced response rates in excess of 75%. Thus, mailed surveys do not necessarily result in a low response; rather, mailed surveys have more variability in their response rate (Heberlein & Baumgartner, 1978). An instrument that is poorly designed, sent to a general population, and deals with a topic of no concern to the respondents will have a low response rate.

Telephone and personal interviews typically yield higher response rates (85% to 95%) than mailed surveys (Dillman, 1978). This relative advantage, however, must be evaluated against the greater costs in researcher and respondent time, and the smaller sample sizes when making a choice between survey distribution techniques (Kidder, 1981).

Time, cost, and expected response rate constraints apply to any evaluation process. When evaluating human–computer interactions, another issue influencing choice of survey method is where the product is in the *development* cycle. If a marketing department wishes to determine how a new image editor might be received by potential customers, personal interviews are more appropriate because many of the respondents in this situation will not have had any experience with this type of product. Moreover, since the researcher is present during the interview, personal interviews offer more flexibility in the flow of questions than either telephone interviews or mail surveys. Telephone interviews offer some of this flexibility, but because the investigator cannot see the facial expressions of the respondent, subtle nuances may be missed. Questionnaires distributed through the mail are more appropriate after users have had a chance to use the product and can react to structured items.

Electronic Surveys

Computers are changing the process of designing and distributing questionnaires (Freeman & Shanks, 1983). Computer Assisted Telephone Interviewing (CATI), for example, allows for more complex branch points without relying on the researchers' memory to ensure proper sequencing (Shanks, Nicholls, & Freeman, 1981). Online surveys avoid printing costs and reduce data distribution and collection efforts (Shneiderman, 1987). Finally, technologies such as the light pen are providing an easy-to-use mechanism for answering questions (Ridgeway, MacCulloch, & Mills, 1982). Given the advent and growth of these automated procedures, a number of authors have begun to examine the consequences of alternative approaches to questionnaire design and distribution (Calvert & Waterfall, 1982; Watts, Baddeley, & Williams, 1982; Root & Draper, 1983; Kiesler & Sproull, 1986).

In general, electronic surveys fall into one of two categories: those where an interviewer keys responses directly into a computer and those where the respondents themselves complete the survey online. The former represents a logical extension of telephone interviewing, while the second is analogous to mailed questionnaires.

Computer assisted telephone interviewing (CATI). In conventional paper-and-pencil interviews, follow-up questions to a given item must generally occur immediately after the lead question; otherwise, key information may be lost if branch points are missed by the interviewer. The problem is compounded in mailed surveys, where the researcher is not present to guide the respondent. Because the computer controls the sequencing of questions in CATI, the survey designer can utilize as many branch points as necessary to adequately address an issue, and the interviewer does not have to rely on memory to ensure proper sequencing (Shure & Meeker, 1978). Single complex questions are reduced to hierarchies of simpler questions.

With CATI, responses to survey questions are keyed directly to disk or other memory by an interviewer. Several benefits result from this direct entry approach (Shanks et al., 1981). First, both precoded and open-ended responses can be included in the file. Second, direct entry eliminates the need for traditional keypunching and data cleaning which may result in substantial savings for large studies. The errors associated with transferring data from the questionnaire to code sheets to a data file are also eliminated. Third, key demographic items about household members can automatically be merged with attitudinal and behavioral questions. Fourth, interrupted interviews can be restarted from a variety of points. Finally, interviewers can correct errors in previous responses and then proceed with the remaining questions.

Similar to traditional telephone interviewing, there are some costs and disadvantages associated with CATI. For example, phone lines need to be dedicated to the project and connected to the appropriate hardware and software. Answers to behavioral questions are based on respondents self-reported behaviors rather than actual behaviors. Finally, responses to attitudinal items typically refer to the person's general beliefs and feelings about a product, rather than their reactions at the time of use.

Respondent-completed electronic surveys. Researchers working in the areas of clinical psychology and psychiatry were among the first to recognize the value of respondent completed electronic questionnaires. Efforts to automate this type of psychological testing date back to at least the 1960s (Pearson, Swenson, Rome, Mataya, & Brannick, 1965; MacCulloch, 1969). The main advantages of this automation were convenience, economy, and objectivity (Gedye & Miller, 1970). The psychologist was freed from the time consuming chores of data collection, was provided with a greater standardization in the administration of the instrument, and thus could develop a closer relationship with the patients (Elithorn, Mornington, & Stavrou, 1982). The popularity of the computerized approach is evident by the number of tests which have been automated; for example: the Minnesota Multiphasic Personality Inventory (Johnson, Giannetti, & Williams, 1978), the Eysenck Personality Inventory (Ridgeway et al., 1982), the Mill Hill Vocabulary Scale (Watts et al., 1982; Wilson, Thompson, & Wylie, 1982), the Ravens Standard Progressive Matrices (Calvert & Waterfall, 1982; Watts et al., 1982), and the Personal Relations Index (Mulhall, 1977; Stevens, 1985).

Recently, studies have addressed the degree of comparability between the automated and traditional paper and pencil versions of the same test. Results generally show little or no difference between the two approaches. For example, a study by Ridgeway et al. (1982) comparing paper and machine forms of the Eysenck Personality Inventory (EPI), concluded that the construct validity of the EPI remains unchanged by the automation process. Calvert et al. (1982) examined the feasibility of automating the Ravens Standard Progressive Matrices.

Findings obtained from the automated version were comparable to the paper-and-pencil method. The machine approach had the added advantage of requiring less supervision. Similar findings were reported by Watts et al. (1982) for the same test. In this latter investigation, the time to complete the automated version was less than half that for the conventional test. There was, however, a small but consistent discrepancy in the absolute scores between the two versions, suggesting that the norms for automated versions should not be based upon the standard versions without further validation. In contrast to the study by Watts and his associates, Hansen, Doring, and Whitlock (1978) found that students took longer to answer an online exam of 100 questions than the comparable paper version of the same test. The authors, however, attribute the slower response time to design problems in the program and insufficient instructions. Finally, Stevens (1985) reports that users' reactions to the computer administered questionnaire were generally favorable, although some did feel uncomfortable with the electronic version. Given the small sample size ($n = 11$) in Stevens' study, however, it is difficult to generalize.

In summary, this section has compared and contrasted different types of surveys. The following demonstrates how we have used mailed surveys in our research. In presenting this example, our goals are to: (a) illustrate alternative ways of designing questions, (b) demonstrate the distinction between self-reported and actual behavior, and (c) show how survey data can be used in the evaluation and promotion of a computer product.

EMPIRICAL EXAMPLE

Data for this example were obtained from an evaluation of an electronic mail facility (Vaske & Teubner, 1985). Both a software monitor and a survey were employed in the data collection process. The 18-page survey included items designed to evaluate the users' beliefs about electronic forms of communication in general, as well as their specific reactions to the existing electronic mail package. For purposes of the present discussion, only variables related to the actual EMail facility are presented. Items were selected to demonstrate alternative response formats and question wording issues.

As discussed earlier, the software monitor recorded the extent to which the basic options in the EMail facility were actually used. The questionnaire also included questions to determine the users' perceptions of how frequently they used these basic features (Table 5.11). Items pertaining to the "Read Mail" and "Send Mail" options were

TABLE 5.11
Sample mail survey questions.

How frequently do you use each of the basic operations features found within EMail?	Never	Seldom	Sometimes	Frequently	Most of the time
Read Options					
Searching for mail from a particular person, subject or date	1	2	3	4	5
Send Options					
Set priority levels	1	2	3	4	5
Acknowledgement of Action	1	2	3	4	5
Receipt of Delivery	1	2	3	4	5
Confidential Mail	1	2	3	4	5
Reply Requested	1	2	3	4	5

separated to make it easier to answer the questions. A five-point scale was used to cover a range of potential behavior patterns. A seven-point, nine-point or even a two-level (no/yes) response format could also have been used. With more points on the scale, it may be more difficult for respondents to differentiate between the alternatives, and a dichotomous choice may not be sensitive enough to address the issue. Whatever scale is chosen, the findings represent the users' perceptions of their behavior and not actual behavior.

The survey was developed and pretested among representatives from marketing and software development as well as actual users of the product. The survey was distributed at the two sites where the software monitor had been installed. A total of 294 registered EMail users completed the survey, 120 in site 1 and 174 in site 2.

Selected Survey Findings

Sixty-seven percent of the respondents' indicated that they never use the Read Mail Option that allows an individual to search for mail from a particular person, subject, or date (Table 5.12). Similar percentages are shown for the basic Send Mail Options. A majority of individuals in each case indicated that they never use that particular feature. From a

TABLE 5.12
Reported usage of specific EMail options.

	Never	Seldom	Sometimes	Frequently	Most of the time
Read Options					
Searching for mail from a particular person, subject or date	67%	16%	10%	3%	4%
Send Options					
Set priority levels	77	14	5	4	1
Acknowledgement of Action	62	22	8	1	7
Receipt of Delivery	53	19	8	7	12
Confidential Mail	76	19	3	2	1
Reply Requested	66	22	9	2	1

design perspective, these findings suggest the same changes as those indicated by the software monitor observations. The percentages of people indicating "never" in the survey, however, were substantially lower than the percentage of people who were observed to accept the default (they did not use that option) in the monitor data. For example, data from the software monitor indicated that 98% of the users never exercised the option to view their mail selectively (67% of the survey respondents said they never use the "Read Mail Options" function).

Plausible explanations can be offered to account for such discrepancies. First, the monitor recorded EMail interactions for a limited period of time; 8 weeks at Site 1 and 5 weeks at Site 2. Respondents to the survey were undoubtedly reacting to their entire history of EMail usage, and, thus, some may not have utilized this functionality during the time the monitor was installed. Examination of the findings for the "seldom" and "sometimes" categories for this variable supports this observation. Twenty-six percent of the respondents checked one of these categories.

A second explanation for the difference between the survey and software monitor findings concerns the distinction between self-reported and actual behavior patterns. People do not maintain accurate records of their behaviors, especially when the behavior involves something as minor as the use of a particular screen on an electronic messaging facility. This is not to suggest that surveys should not be used in the evaluation of computer products, since questionnaires provide one of the few techniques for addressing attitudes. Rather, different data collection procedures sometimes yield different results. Researchers need to select the approach that will provide the level of information that is appropriate for answering the question and that can be realistically incorporated into the project. A software monitor provides accurate data, but the investigator must possess the programming expertise necessary to realize the benefits and have the time to collect the information.

Interestingly, the survey findings would have been useful regardless of how the numbers came out. For example, if a substantial proportion of the users indicated "yes" to the "receipt of delivery" item, the default could have been reset to the positive rather than the negative. The key word, however, is *substantial*. Based on our findings, the decision is not as straightforward. Although a majority of the respondents (53%) indicated that they never use this feature, nearly a fifth (19%) said they used the option "frequently" or "most of the time." While this breakdown probably is not sufficient to change the default from "no" to "yes," it is interesting to speculate what decision would be reached if a 60–40 or 51–49 split had occurred. The issue here is not to argue for some magical cutoff point, but rather to emphasize that empirical findings, by themselves, do not make the decision. Even with the numbers, a value judgment is required to interpret what action is necessary. Finally, it should be emphasized that, even with a software monitor, expert judgment is still required to determine what changes the developers should or should not make.

SUMMARY—SURVEYS

The use of surveys in evaluating human–computer interactions is most appropriate after initial versions of the product have been released. This section has attempted to compare and contrast alternative methods of questionnaire design and implementation, and to provide some practical considerations for individuals interested in using this approach to data collection. An empirical example was presented to demonstrate how survey results can be applied to the design process. Unlike the observation techniques presented earlier, survey methodologies provide one of the few structured vehicles for acquiring information about what people think about a potential or an existing computer product. Because large samples are feasible, survey data tend to represent the views of individuals who may normally be less vocal about their complaints. In addition, survey research often serves purposes other than information gathering. Decision makers are usually faced with unclear and changing objectives. Although collecting data on a client's attitudes and behaviors is time consuming, the process can buy developers the time needed to help clarify particular designs. From the client's perspective, knowing that someone is addressing his or her concerns, helps to alleviate the tendency to react on impulse and choose a competitors product. The empirical example discussed in this section served that function.

CHAPTER SUMMARY

This chapter has reviewed four major methodological approaches: observation of behavior, design team techniques, experiments, and surveys. Although all four tools are related, each focuses on slightly different issues and examines the human–computer interaction process with varying levels of precision and specificity. The first two techniques (observation of behavior and design teams) provide a general overview of users' actual or reported behaviors and their beliefs and feelings about hardware/software products. They are most appropriate early in the design phase or after the product has been released. The last two techniques (experiments and surveys) are more concerned with evaluating aspects of a particular product. Their application is typically most beneficial early in the design phase as the application is being developed (experiments) or after release (surveys).

Each of the methodologies has some advantages and disadvantages. For example, experiments are strong on control through randomization, but they are weak on representation. Surveys are strong on representation, but weak on control. Among the observation of behavior techniques, participant observation provides for an in-depth evaluation of a situation, but are only feasible for examining a few users. Software monitor observations can be applied to entire populations of users, but the technique is relatively expensive to put into practice. Because no single methodology is perfect, it is advisable to use several techniques when designing and evaluating products.

Selecting the right combination of methodologies is a matter of balancing:

The problem to be addressed
Amount of precision needed to answer the problem
Time availability
The number of users to be evaluated
Where the product is in the development cycle

The information presented in this chapter will not make novice researchers into experts. Rather the goal was to highlight some of the major differences among the approaches to examining human–computer interactions. Readers interested in a more complete discussion of the topics presented here are directed to the reference sources identified throughout the chapter.

BIBLIOGRAPHY

Ackoff, R.L. (1967). Management misinformation systems. *Management Science, 14,* 147–156.

Allen, R. B. (1984). Working paper on ethical issues for research on the use of computer services and interfaces. *SIGCHI Bulletin, 16,* 12–16.

Allen, R. B., & Scerbo, M. W. (1983). Details of command-language keystrokes. *ACM Transactions on Office Information Systems, 1,* 159–178.

American Psychological Association. (1981). Ethical principles of psychologists. *American Psychologist, 36,* 633–638.

American Sociological Association. (1982). *Code of Ethics.* Washington DC: ASA.

Andreasen, A. R. (1985, May–June). "Backward" market research. *Harvard Business Review,* pp. 176, 180, 182, 186.

Angle, H. V. (1981). The interviewing computer: A technology for gathering comprehensive treatment information. *Behavior Research Methods and Instrumentation, 13,* 607–612.

Babbie, E. R. (1979). *The practice of social research* (2nd ed.). Belmont, CA: Wadsworth Publishing Company, Inc.

Bair, J.H. (1982). Productivity assessment of office information systems technology. In R. Landau, J. Bair, & J. Seigman (Eds), *Emerging office systems.* Norwood, NJ: Ablex Publishing Corp.

Baroudi, J. J., Olson, M.H., & Ives, B. (1986). An empirical study of the impact of user involvement on system usage and information satisfaction. *Communications of the ACM, 29,* 232–238.

Barton, A. H., & Lazarsfeld, P. (1955). Some functions of qualitative analysis in social research. *Frankfurter Beitrage Zur Soziologie* (Band 1). Frankfurt am Main, FRG: Europaische Verlagsanstalt GmBH.

Basili, V. R., Selby, R. W., & Hutchens, D. H. (1986). Experimentation in software engineering. *IEEE Transactions on Software Engineering, 12,* 733–743.

Becker, H. S. (1958). Problems of inference and proof in participant observation. *American Sociological Review, 23,* 652–660.

Becker, H. S., & Geer, B. (1957). Participant observation and interviewing. *Human Organization, 16,* 28–32.

Bernstein, G. B. (1969). *A fifteen-year forecast of information-processing technology.* Washington, DC: Research and Development Division, Naval Supply Systems Command.

Boies, S. J. (1974). User behavior on an interactive computer system. *IBM Systems Journal, 1*, 2–18.

Bradburn, N. M. (1983). Response effects. In P. H. Rossi, J. D. Wright, & A. B. Anderson (Eds.), *Handbook of survey research* (pp. 289–328). New York: Academic Press.

Brooks, R. E. (1980). Studying programmer behavior experimentally: The problems of proper methodology. *Communications of the ACM, 23*, 591–597.

Brown, B., Cochran, S., & Dalkey, N. (1969). *The Delphi method, II: Structure of experiments* (Rand Memorandum RM-5957-PR). Santa Monica, CA: Rand Corporation.

Bury, K. F. (1983). *Prototyping in CMS: Using prototypes to conduct human factors tests of software during development.* (IBM Human Factors Center Technical Report HFC-43). San Jose, CA: IBM General Products Division.

Byers, A. P. (1981). Psychological evaluation by means of an on-line computer. *Behavior Research Methods and Instrumentation, 13*, 585–587.

Calvert, E. J., & Waterfall, R. C. (1982). A comparison of conventional and automated administration of Raven's Standard Progressive Matrices. *International Journal of Man-Machine Studies, 17*, 305–310.

Campbell, D. T., & Stanley, J. C. (1963). *Experimental and quasi-experimental designs for research.* Chicago, IL: Rand McNally College Publishing Company.

Cannell, C. F., & Fowler, F. J. (1967). Comparison of a self-report enumerative procedure and a personal interview: A validity study. *Public Opinion Quarterly, 27*, 251–264.

Card, S. K., Moran, T. P., & Newell, A. (1983). *The psychology of human–computer interaction.* Hillsdale, NJ: Lawrence Erlbaum Associates.

Carroll, J. M., & Rosson, M. B. (1985). Usability specifications as a tool in iterative development. In H. R. Hartson (Ed.), *Advances in human–computer interaction* (Vol. 1, pp. 1–28). Norwood, NJ: Ablex Publishing Corp.

Cartwright, D., & Zander A. (Eds.). (1968). *Group dynamics: Research and theory.* New York: Harper and Row.

Chapanis, A. (1967). The relevance of laboratory studies to practical situations. *Ergonomics, 10*, 557–577.

Cicourel, A. (1964). *Method and measurement in sociology.* New York: Free Press.

Clark, I. A. (1981). Software simulation as a tool for usable product design. *IBM Systems Journal, 20*, 272–293.

Clauer, C. K. (1982). Methodology for testing and improving operator publications. In *Proceedings of Office Automation Conference. American Federation of Information Processing Societies* (pp. 867–873). San Francisco.

Clausen, A. R. (1968). Response validity: Vote report. *Public Opinion Quarterly, 32*, 588–506.

Cochran, W. G., & Cox, G. M. (1957). *Experimental designs.* New York: John Wiley and Sons.

Curtis, B. (1980). Measurement and experimentation in software engineering. In *Proceedings of the IEEE, 68*, 1144–1157.

Dalkey, N. (1969). *The Delphi method, An experimental study of group reac-

tion. (Rand Memorandum RM-5888-PR). Santa Monica, CA: Rand Corporation.

Delbecq, A. L., & Van de Ven, A. H. (1975). *Group techniques for program planning*. Glenview, IL: Scott, Foresman and Company.

Denzin, N. K. (1973). *The research act: A theoretical introduction to sociological methods*. Chicago, IL: Aldine Publishing Company.

Dijkstra, W., & van der Zouwen, J. (Eds.). (1982). *Response behavior in the survey-interview*. London: Academic Press.

Dillman, D. (1978). *Mail and telephone surveys: The total design method*. New York: John Wiley and Sons.

Durgee, J. (1986, August–September). Richer findings from qualitative research. *Journal of Advertising Research*, pp. 36–44.

Elithorn, A., Mornington, S., & Stavrou, A. (1982). Automated psychological testing: Some principles and practice. *International Journal of Man-Machine Studies, 17*, 247–263.

Erdman, H., Klein, M., & Greist, J. (1983). The reliability of a computer interview for drug use/abuse information. *Behavior Research Methods and Instrumentation, 15*, 66–68.

Erdmann, R. L., & Neal, A. S. (1971). Laboratory versus field experimentation in Human Factors. *Human Factors, 13*, 521–531.

Erdos, P. L. (1970). *Professional mail surveys*. New York: McGraw-Hill.

Freeman, H. E., & Shanks, J. M. (Eds.). (1983). The emergence of computer assisted survey research. *Sociological Methods and Research, 12*(2).

Galtung, J. (1967). *Theory and methods of social research*. New York: Columbia University Press.

Gedye, J. L., & Miller, E. (1970). Developments in automated testing. In P. Mittler (Ed.), *The psychological assessment of mental and physical handicaps*. London: Methuen.

Gitomer, J. (1984). Measuring system performance with software monitors. *Journal of Information Systems Management, 1*, 50–55.

Gold, R. L. (1958). Roles in sociological field observations. *Social Forces, 36*, 217–223.

Good, M. (1985). The use of logging data in the design of a new text editor. In *Proceedings: CHI'85—Human Factors in Computing Systems* (pp. 93–97). New York: ACM.

Gordon, T. J. (1968). New approaches to Delphi. In J. R. Bright (Ed.), *Technological forecasting for industry and government*. Englewood Cliffs, NJ: Prentice-Hall.

Gordon, T. J., & Helmer, O. (1964). *Report on a long range forecasting study* (Rand Paper P-2982). Santa Monica, CA: Rand Corporation.

Gould, J. D., Conti, J., & Hovanyecz, T. (1983). Composing letters using with a simulated listening typewriter. *Communications of the ACM, 26*, 295–308.

Gould, J. D., & Lewis, C. (1985). Designing for usability: Key principles and what designers think. *Communications of the ACM, 28*, 300–311.

Grantham, C. E., & Shneiderman, B. (1984). *Programmer behavior and cognitive activity: An observational study*. Paper presented at the 23rd Annual

Technical Symposium of the Washington, DC, Chapter of the Association for Computing Machinery.

Grantham, C. E., & Vaske, J. J. (1985). Predicting the usage of an advanced communication technology. *Behavior and Information Technology*, 4, 327–335.

Gregory, J., & Nussbaum, K. (1982). Race against time: Automation in the office. *Office: Technology People*, 1, 197–236.

Hackman, J. R., & Oldham, G. R. (1980). *Work redesign*. Reading, MA: Addison-Wesley.

Hackman, J. R., Oldham, G. R., Janson, R., & Purdy, K. (1979). A new strategy for job enrichment. In *Readings in systematic management of human resources* (pp. 81–102). Reading, MA: Addison-Wesley.

Hansen, W. J., Doring, R., & Whitlock, L. R. (1978). Why an examination was slower on-line than on paper. *International Journal of Man-Machine Studies*, 10, 507–519.

Hanson, S. J., Kraut, R. E., & Farber, J. M. (1984). Interface design and multivariate analysis of UNIX command use. *ACM Transactions on Office Information Systems*, 2, 42–57.

Heberlein, T. A. (1976). Some observations on alternative mechanisms for public involvement: The hearing, public opinion poll, the workshop and the quasi-experiment. *Natural Resources Journal*, 16, 197–212.

Heberlein, T. A. (1980). Questionnaire development. In *Proceedings: Electric Rate Demonstration Conference*. Denver, CO.

Heberlein, T. A., & Baumgartner, R. (1978). Factors affecting response rates to mailed questionnaires. *American Sociological Review*, 43, 447–462.

Homans, G. C. (1965). Group factors in worker productivity. In H. Proshansky & B. Seidenberg (Eds.), *Basic studies in social psychology* (pp. 592–604). New York: Holt, Rinehart and Winston.

Irving, R. H., Higgins, C. A., & Safayeni, F. R. (1986). Computerized performance monitoring systems: Use and abuse. *Communications of the ACM*, 29, 794–801.

Ives, B., & Olson, M. H. (1984). User involvement and MIS success: A review of research. *Management Science*, 30, 586–603.

Jacob, R. J. K. (1985). An executable specification technique for describing human–computer interaction. In H. R. Hartson (Ed.), *Advances in human–computer interaction* (Vol. 1, pp. 211–242). Norwood, NJ: Ablex Publishing Corp.

Johnson, E. M., & Baker, J. D. (1974). Field testing: The delicate compromise. *Human Factors*, 16, 203–214.

Johnson, J. H., Giannetti, R. A., & Williams, T. A. (1978). A self-contained microcomputer for psychological testing. *Behavior Research Methods and Instrumentation*, 10, 579–581.

Johnson, B. M., Taylor, J. C., Smith, D. R., & Cline, T. R. (1983). *Innovation in word processing* (National Science Foundation Project ISI811079). Washington DC: National Science Foundation.

Kahn, R. L., & Cannell, C. F. (1957). *The dynamics of interviewing: Theory, techniques and cases*. New York: John Wiley and Sons.

Keen, P. G. W. (1981). Information systems and organizational change. *Communications of the ACM, 24,* 24–33.

Kerlinger, F. N. (1973). *Foundations of behavioral research.* New York: Holt, Rinehart and Winston, Inc.

Kidder, L. H. (1981). *Research methods in social relations* (4th ed.). New York: Holt, Rinehart & Winston.

Kiesler, S., & Sproull, L. S. (1986). Response effects in the electronic survey. *Public Opinion Quarterly.*

Kiesler, S., Siegel, J., & McGuire, T. (1984). Social psychological aspects of computer-mediated communication. *American Psychologist, 39,* 1123–1134.

Kirk, R. E. (1968). *Experimental design: Procedures for the behavioral sciences.* Belmont, CA: Brooks/Cole Publishing Company.

Kish, L. (1959). Some statistical problems in research design. *American Sociological Review, 24,* 328–338.

Kling, R., & Scacchi, W. (1980). Computing as social action: The social dynamics of computing in complex organizations. *Advanced Computing, 19,* 249–327.

Lewis, C. (1982). *Using the "thinking aloud" method in cognitive interface design.* (IBM Watson Research Labs. Report RC 9265). Yorktown Heights, NY.

Lindquist, E. F. (1953). *Design and analysis of experiments in psychology and education.* Boston, MA: Houghton Mifflin.

Liska, A. E. (1974). Emergent issues in the attitude–behavior consistence controversy. *American Sociological Review, 39,* 261–272.

Lord, F. N., & Novick, M. R. (1968). *Statistical theories of mental test scores.* Reading, MA: Addison-Wesley.

Loyd, B. H., & Gressard, C. (1984). Reliability and factorial validity of computer attitude scales. *Educational and Psychological Measurement, 44,* 501–505.

Lund, M. A. (1985). Evaluating the user interfaces: The candid camera approach. In *Proceedings: CHI'85—Human Factors in Computing Systems* (pp. 107–113). New York: ACM.

MacCulloch, M. J. (1969). *Aversion therapy.* Unpublished doctoral thesis, Manchester University.

Markus, M. L. (1983). Power, politics, and MIS implementation. *Communications of the ACM, 26,* 430–444.

Martino, J. P. (1968). An experiment with the Delphi procedure for long-range forecasting. *IEEE Transactions on Engineering Management, EM-15,* 138–144.

Martino, J. P. (1972). *Technological forecasting for decision making.* New York: American Elsevier Publishing.

McCall, G. J., & Simmons, J. L. (Eds.). (1969). *Issues in participant observation: A text and reader.* London: Addison-Wesley.

Michener, H. A., DeLamater, J. D., & Schwartz, S. H. (1986). *Social psychology.* San Diego, CA: Harcourt Brace Jovanovich, Publishers.

Mintzberg, H. (1979). *The structuring of organizations.* Englewood Cliffs, NJ: Prentice-Hall.

Mulhall, D. J. (1977). The representation of personal relationships: an automated system. *International Journal of Man-Machine Studies, 9,* 315–335.

Mumford, E. (1983). *Designing participatively.* Manchester, England: Manchester Business School.

Myers, C. (Ed.). (1967). *The impact of computers on management.* Cambridge, MA: MIT Press.

Nachmias, D., & Nachmias, C. (1976). *Research methods in the social sciences.* New York: St. Martin's.

Neal, A. S., & Simons, R. M. (1984). Playback: A method for evaluating the usability of software and its documentation. *IBM Systems Journal, 23,* 82–96.

Newell, A., & Simon, H. A. (1972). *Human problem solving.* Englewood Cliffs, NJ: Prentice-Hall.

Nicholson, R. T. (1985). Usage patterns in an integrated voice and data communications system. *ACM Transactions on Office Information Systems, 3,* 307–314.

Nunnally, J. C. (1967). *Psychometric theory.* New York: McGraw Hill.

O'Brien, T. C., & Shapiro, B. J. (1968). Statistical significance—What? *Mathematics Teacher, 61,* 673–676.

Ogden, E. C., & Boyle, J. M. (1982). Evaluating human–computer dialog styles: Command versus form/fill-in for report modification. In *Proceedings of The Human Factors Society 26th Annual Meeting* (pp. 542–545).

Olson, M. H., & Ives, B. (1981). User involvement in system design: An empirical test of alternative approaches. *Information and Management, 4,* 183–195.

Olson, M., & Lucas, H.C., Jr. (1982). The impact of office automation on the organization: Some implications for research and practice. *Communications of the ACM, 25,* 838–847.

Pearson, J. S., Swenson, H. P., Rome, H. P., Mataya, P., & Brannick, T. L. (1965). Development of a computer system for scoring and interpretation of Minnesota Multiphasic Personality Inventories in a medical clinic. *Annals of the New York Academy of Sciences, 126,* 682–692.

Pettigrew, A.M. (1972). Information control as a power source. *Sociology, 6,* 188–204.

Poulton, E. C. (1975). Observer bias. *Applied Ergonomics, 6,* 3–8.

Rabideau, G. F. (1971). Observational techniques in systems research and development. In W. T. Singleton, J. G. Fox, & D. Whitfield (Eds.), *Measurement of man at work: An appraisal of physiological and psychological criteria in man-machine systems* (pp. 149–158). London: Taylor & Francis Ltd.

Reece, M. J., & Gable, R. K. (1982). The development and validation of a measure of general attitudes toward computers. *Educational and Psychological Measurement, 42,* 913–917.

Richardson, S. A., Dohrenwend, B. S., & Klein, D. (1965). *Interviewing.* New York: Basic Books.

Riddick, C. C., DeSchriver, M., & Weissinger, E. (1984). A methodological review of research in *Journal of Leisure Research* from 1978 to 1982. *Journal of Leisure Research*, 16, 311–321.

Ridgeway, J., MacCulloch, M. J., & Mills, H. E. (1982). Some experiences in administering a psychometric test with a light pen and microcomputer. *International Journal of Man-Machine Studies*, 17, 265–278.

Root, R. W., & Draper, S. (1983). Questionnaires as a software evaluation tool. In *Proceedings: ACM CHI'83 Human Factors in Computing Systems* (pp. 83–87). New York: ACM.

Rosenthal, R., & Gaito, J. (1963). The interpretation of levels of significance by psychological researchers. *The Journal of Psychology*, 55, 33–38.

Ross, J., & Smith, P. (1968). Orthodox experimental designs. In H. M. Blalock, Jr. & A. B. Blalock (Eds.), *Methodology in social research*. New York: McGraw-Hill.

Rossi, P. H., Freeman, H. E., & Wright, S. R. (1979). *Evaluation of systematic approach*. Beverly Hills, CA: Sage.

Rushinek, A., Rushinek, S. F., & Stutz, J. (1984). A methodology for interactive evaluation of user reactions to software packages: An empirical analysis of system performance, interaction and run time. *Journal of Man-Machine Studies*, 20, 169–188.

Schick, M. E. (1980, January). The "refined" performance evaluation monitoring system: Best of both worlds. *Personnel Journal*, pp. 47–50.

Selltiz, C., Jahoda, M., Deutsch, M., & Cook, S. W. (1959). *Research methods in social relations*. New York: Holt.

Shanks, J. M., Nicholls, W. L., & Freeman, H. E. (1981). The California Disability Survey: Design and execution of a computer-assisted telephone study. *Sociological Methods and Research*, 10, 123–140.

Shneiderman, B. (1987). *Designing the user interface: Strategies for effective human–computer interaction*. Reading, MA: Addison-Wesley.

Shure, G., & Meeker, R. (1978). A minicomputer system for multiperson computer assisted telephone interviewing. *Behavior Research Methods and Instrumentation*, 10, 196–202.

Sieber, S. D. (1973). The integration of fieldwork and survey methods. *American Journal of Sociology*, 78, 1335–1359.

Skipper, J. K., Jr., Guenther, A. L., & Nass, G. (1967). The sacredness of .05: A note concerning the uses of statistical levels of significance in social science. *The American Sociologist*, 2, 16–18.

Smith, H. W. (1975). *Strategies of social research*. Englewood Cliffs, NJ: Prentice-Hall.

Spiliotopoulos, V., & Shackel, B. (1981). Towards a computer interview acceptable to the naive user. *International Journal of Man-Machine Studies*, 14, 77–90.

Sproull, L. S. (1986). Using electronic mail for data collection in organizational research. *Academy of Management Journal*, 29, 159–169.

Stevens, R. F. (1985). An on-line version of personal relations index psychological test. *International Journal of Man-Machine Studies*, 23, 563–585.

Steward, J. (1955). The concept and method of cultural ecology. In *Theory of cultural change* (pp. 30–42). Urbana, IL: University of Illinois Press.

Sudman, S. (1967). *Reducing the cost of surveys.* Chicago, IL: Aldine.

Sudman, S., & Bradburn, N. M. (1974). *Response effects in surveys.* Chicago, IL: Aldine.

Teubner, A. L., & Vaske, J. J. (1988). Monitoring computer users' behaviour in office environments. *Behaviour and Information Technology, 7,* 67–78.

Tittle, C. R., & Hill, R. J. (1967). The accuracy of self reported data and prediction of political activity. *Public Opinion Quarterly, 31,* 103–106

Turoff, M., Hiltz, S. R., & Kerr, E. B. (1981). Controversies in the design of computer-mediated communication systems: A Delphi study. In *Proceedings: Human Factors in Computer Systems* (pp. 89–100). Gaithersburg, MD: Association for Computing Machinery.

Vaske, J. J., & Grantham, C. E. (1985). *HVN versus satellite communications: A comparison of users' evaluations.* (Tech. Report). Billerica, MA: Honeywell Information Systems, Inc.

Vaske, J. J., & Teubner, A. L. (1985). *A comparative evaluation of Billerica and Phoenix DPS6 Email users.* (Tech. Report). Billerica, MA: Honeywell Information Systems, Inc.

Vaughan, G. M., & Corballis, M. C. (1969). Beyond tests of significance: Estimating strength of effects in selected ANOVA designs. *Psychological Bulletin, 72,* 204–213.

Walton, R. E., & Vittori, W. (1983). New information technology: Organizational problem or opportunity? *Office: Technology People, 1,* 249–273.

Warshaw, P. R., Calantone, R., & Joyce, M. (1986). A field application of the Fishbein and Ajzen intention model. *Journal of Social Psychology, 126,* 137–139.

Wasserman, A. I., & Shewmake, D. T. (1985). The role of prototypes in the User Software Engineering (USE) methodology. In H. R. Hartson (Ed.), *Advances in human–computer interaction* (Vol. 1, pp. 191–210). Norwood, NJ: Ablex Publishing Corp.

Watts, K., Baddeley, A., & Williams, M. (1982). Automated tailored testing using Raven's Matrices and the Mill Hill Vocabulary tests: a comparison with manual administration. *International Journal of Man-Machine Studies, 17,* 331–344.

Webb, E. W., Campbell, D. T., Schwartz, R. D., & Sechrest, L. (1966). *Unobtrusive measures: Nonreactive research in the social sciences.* Chicago, IL: Rand McNally.

Wilson, S. L., Thompson, J. A., & Wylie, G. (1982). Automated psychological testing for the severely physically handicapped. *International Journal of Man-Machine Studies, 17,* 291–596.

Winer, B. J. (1962). *Statistical principles in experimental design.* New York: McGraw-Hill.

Zelditch, M. (1962). Some Methodological Problems of Field Studies. *American Journal of Sociology, 62,* 566–576.

Zuboff, S. (1982). Computer mediated work—The emerging managerial challenge. *Office: Technology People, 1,* 237–243.

Author Index

A

Ackermann, D., 62, *93*
Ackoff, R.L., 227, *267*
Adamopoulos, J., 23, 60, *100*
Agar, M.H., 189, *202*
Ahl, D.H., 45, *93*
Aiken, M., 110, *156*
Ajzen, I., 37, 41, 43, 44, 45, 46, 48, *93, 96*
Akiba, E.A., 112, *156*
Al-Awar, J., 68, *93*
Albrecht, G., 110, *153*
Alderfer, C.P., 136, *153*
Allen, R.B., 216, 227, *267*
Allison, A., 125, 127, *153*
Allport, G., 1, *20*, 23, 55, *93*
Allwood, C.M., 63, *93*
Alvarez, M.G., *202*
Anderson, N.S., 6, *20*, 68, *95*
Anderson, R.E., 1, *21*
Andreason, A.R., 253, *267*
Angle, H.V., *267*
Argyris, C., 132, 133, 136, 137, 138, 140, *153, 154*
Arndt, S., 34, 38, 58, *93*
Aronson, S.A., 112, *154*
Asch, S., 27, *93*
Assunto, K., 145, 147, *154*
Atwood, M.E., 68, *100*
Auburn, P.N., 65, *99*
Austin, J., 86, *93, 202*

B

Babbie, E.R., 213, 214, 252, 259, *267*
Baddeley, A., 260, 261, 262, *274*
Bagozzi, R.P., 38, 48, *93*
Bair, J.H., 4, *20*, 226, 227
Baker, J.D., *270*
Ball, R.A., 11, *20*, 117, *154*
Ballachey, E.L., 27, *98*
Ballinger, L.B., *202*
Ballinger, R.A., *202*
Banks, O., 132, *159*
Barber, S., 112, *161*

Bariff, M.L., 63, *93*
Barnard, P.J., 68, *96*, 119, 122, *157, 204*
Baroudi, J.J., 133, *154, 157, 267*
Bartezzaghi, E., 115, *155*
Barton, A.H., *267*
Basil, V.R., 238, *267*
Bass, F.M., 147, 148, 149, *154*
Bateson, G., 165, 184, 190, *202, 203, 206*
Baumgartner, R., 257, 259, *270*
Beattie, G.W., 112, *154*
Becker, H.S., *203*, 214, *267*
Bem, D.J., 36, 51, 53, *93*
Benbasat, I., 56, *94*
Bentler, P.M., 46, 48, 49, *94*
Berger, P.L., *203*
Berkowitz, L., 81, *94*
Bernard, C., *154*
Bernstein, G.B., 235, *267*
Bevan, N., 24, 82, 85, *100*
Bikson, T.K., 10, *20*, 106, 112, *154, 156*
Birdwhistell, R.L., 185, *203*
Bjorn-Anderson, N., *20*, 109, 113, *154*
Black, J.S., 44, 51, 71, 72, 75, *94, 97*
Blake, J., 71, *94*
Blau, P., 108, 109, 118, *154*
Block, J., 30, *94*
Block, J., 30, *94*
Blumberg, P., 140, *154*
Blumer, H., 193, *203*
Bly, S.A., 63, *94, 203*
Bocker, H.D., 64, *94*
Boddy, D., 53, *94*
Boersema, T., *207*
Bogart, D.H., 112, *154*
Boles, S.J., 216, *268*
Bolman, L.G., 106, 114, 115, 117, 120, 125, 133, 140, *154, 176, 203*
Boody, D., 107, 113, *155*
Booher, H.R., 172, *203*
Booz, A., 65, *94*
Boulding, K.E., 112, 143, 144, *154, 155*
Boyes, L., 63, *97*
Boyle, J.M., 216, *272*

Bradburn, N.M., 252, *268, 274*
Brannick, T.L., 261, *272*
Braverman, H., 137, *155*
Bridwell, G.L.G., 136, *161*
Brigham, J.C., 40, *94*
Brod, C., 60, *94,* 135, *155*
Brooks, R., 1, *20,* 238, *268*
Brown, B., 232, *268*
Brown, R.H., *203*
Buchanan, D.A., 53, *94,* 107, 113, *155*
Buckley, W., 111, *155*
Brunkrant, R.E., 38, 48, *93, 94*
Bury, K.F., 216, *268*
Bush, D.M., 29, *94*
Butera, F., 115, *155*
Byers, A.P., *268*

C

Cahill, M.C., 172, *203*
Cairney, P., *203*
Calantone, R., 48, *103,* 252, *274*
Call, B., 129, *155*
Calvert, D.J., 260, 261, *268*
Campbell, A., 40, *94*
Campbell, D.T., 116, *155, 268, 274*
Campbell, J., 184, *203*
Cancian, F.M., 71, *94*
Cannell, C.F., 252, *268, 270*
Cantor, N., 37, 65, *94, 95*
Cantril, H., 1, *20*
Caporael, L.R., 1, 2, *20*
Carasik, R., 87, *95, 203*
Card, S.K., 1, *20,* 216, *268*
Carroll, J.M., 209, *268*
Carroll, S.M., 188, *203*
Carter, E.B., 108, *158*
Cartwright, D., *95,* 141, *155,* 231, *268*
Case, D., 84, *100*
Cerveny, R.P., 46, *95*
Chan, P., 66, *96*
Chantadisai, R., 135, *159*
Chapanis, A., 6, *20,* 45, 68, 84, *93, 95,*
       103, 216, 238, *268*
Chomsky, N., 182, *203*
Christensen, C.R., 136, *161*
Cicourel, A., *203, 268*
Clark, E.V., 182, *203*
Clark, H.H., 182, *203*
Clark, I.A., 68, *96,* 216, *268*
Clauer, C.K., 216, *268*
Clausen, A.R., 252, *268*
Cline, T.R., 226, *270*

Cochran, S., *268*
Cochran, W.G., 232, 240, 241, *268*
Cohen, P.S., 176, *203*
Colby, B.N., 189, *203*
Colton, K., 124, *155*
Conover, D.W., 173, *207*
Conti, J., *269*
Converse, P.E., 40, *94, 95*
Cook, S.W., *273*
Cook, T.D., 116, *155*
Coovert, M.D., 58, *95*
Corballis, M.C., *274*
Cox, G.M., 240, 241, *268*
Crane, P., 135, *155*
Crenson, M.A., 123, *156*
Crissey, B.L., 123, *156*
Crocker, J.C., 37, *102*
Cronbach, L., 76, *95*
Crowell, C.R., 23, 60, *100*
Crozier, M., 118, 143, 144, *155*
Crutchfield, R.S., 27, *98*
Cuff, R., 68, *95*
Culnan, M.J., 4, *20,* 50, *95*
Curley, P., 60, *95,* 135, *155*
Curtis, B., 212, 225, 238, *268*

D

Dainoff, M.J., 135, *155*
Dalkey, N., 232, *268*
D'Andrade, R.G., 167, 168, *203*
Danzinger, J., 109, 110, 123, *155*
Davidson, J.W., *203*
Davis, K., 71, *94*
Day, J., *205*
Deal, T.E., 106, 114, 115, 117, 120, 125,
       130, 133, 140, *154, 159,* 176, *203*
Deci, E.L., 124, 133, *155*
DeCindo, F., 86, *95*
DeLamater, J.D., 6, 7, 21, 23, 33, 36, 43,
       72, 75, 99, 231, *271*
Delbecq, A.L., 236, *269*
Delehanty, G.E., 114, *155*
DeLeeuw, L., 60, *95*
DeMichelis, G., 86, *95*
DeMichiell, R.L., 135, *158*
Denzin, N.K., *269*
DeSchriver, M., 251, *272*
Deutsch, M., *273*
Dewar, R.E., *204, 205*
Dewey, J., *203*
Dickson, G.W., 60, *103*
Dickson, W., 132, *160*

Dijk, R.B., 56, *103*
Dijkstra, W., 252, *269*
Dill, W.R., 114, *155*
Dillman, D., 251, 258, 259, *269*
DiTecco, D., 38, *101*
Dodson, V.N., 135, *160*
Dohrenwend, B.S., *272*
Dolgin, J.L., 185, *204*
Donahue, J., *204*
Donnelly, M.P., 69, *102*
Doring, R., 262, *270*
Dossett, D.L., 47, 48, *96*
Dougherty, J.W., *204*
Douglas, M., 186, *204*
Douglas, S.A., 63, *95*
Downs, A., 110, *155*
Draper, S., 252, 255, 260, *273*
Dreyfus, H., *204*
Drucker, P., 146, *155*
Dubin, R., 6, *20*
Dumais, S.T., *204*, *205*
Dunlap, R.E., *95*
Durgee, J., 210, *269*
Dutton, W.H., 85, *95*, 109, 110, 111, 123, 124, *155*, *158*
Dzida, W., 68, *95*

E
Eason, K., 143, *156*
Edinger, J.A., 85, *95*
Ehrlich, K., 38, 68, *102*, 112, 129, *156*
Eliasson, M., 63, *93*
Elithorn, A., 261, *269*
Ells, J.G., *204*
Ember, C.R., 165, 168, *204*
Ember, M., 165, 168, *204*
Erdman, H., 238, *269*
Erdos, P.L., *269*
Erikson, E., 29, *95*
Erlandson, R.F., *204*
Etzioni, A., 108, 111, 122, 132, *156*
Evans, J., 132, *156*
Eveland, J.D., 10, *20*, 112, *156*
Eyesenck, H.J., 59, *95*, *96*

F
Farber, J.M., 216, *270*
Farivar, B., 149, *161*
Faterson, H.F., 56, *103*
Fazio, R.H., 34, 43, *96*, *100*
Feltes, J., 34, 38, 58, *93*
Festinger, L., 35, 37, 53, *96*

Fink, C.F., 80, *102*
Finzer, W., 64, *96*
Firey, W., *204*
Fischer, G., 64, *94*
Fishbein, M., 35, 37, 41, 43, 44, 45, 46, 48, 73, *93*, *96*
Fitch, G., 58, *96*
Flaherty, D., 123, 132, *156*
Fleishman, J.A., 38, 68, *102*
Flores, F., 86, *96*, *204*
Floyd, C., 5, *21*
Foley, J.D., 66, *96*
Ford, W.R., 68, *93*
Forester, T., 1, *21*
Fowler, F.J., 252, *268*
Fox, M.S., 106, *156*
Fredricks, A.J., 47, 48, *96*
Freeman, H.E., 251, 260, *269*, *273*
French, J., 108, *156*
Fried, L., 107, 136, *156*
Friedland, L., 166, 168, 169, *204*
Friedrich, P., 183, *204*
Fuerst, M., 135, *161*
Furlong, M., 66, *98*

G
Gabel, D., 113, *156*
Gable, R.K., 40, *100*, *272*
Gaito, J., *273*
Gallagher, J.D., 114, *156*
Galtung, J., *269*
Gange, J.J., 60, *96*
Gardner, E., 136, *156*
Garrity, E.J., 46, *95*
Gaylin, K.B., *204*
Gedye, J.L., 261, *269*
Geen, R.G., 60, *96*
Geer, B., 214, *267*
Geertz, C., 165, *204*
Geller, V.J., 84, *96*
Georgopoulos, B.S., 111, *156*
Gerson, E.M., 135, *157*
Giannetti, R.A., 261, *270*
Gilfoil, D. M., 67, *96*, *202*
Gitomer, J., 215, 225, *269*
Gleser, G.C., 76, *95*
Goffman, E., *204*
Gold, R.L., 213, 214, *269*
Goldstein, M., 58, *95*
Golledge, R.G., 187, *206*
Good, M., *269*
Goodenough, D.R., 56, *103*

Gordon, T.J., 232, 235, *269*
Gorman, E.M., 108, *158*
Gottlieb, M.S., 135, *160*
Gough, H., 56, *96*
Gould, J.T., 209, 255, *269*
Gould, L., 64, *96*
Grandjean, E., 135, *158*, *173*, *204*
Grantham, C.E., 4, *21*, 38, 40, 48, 49, 68, 87, *95*, *96*, *102*, *106*, 112, *156*, *203*, *204*, *214*, *242*, *257*, *269*, *270*, *274*
Green, P., *204*
Gregory, J., 226, *270*
Greenburger, M., 123, *156*
Greist, J., *269*
Gressard, C., 40, *99*, *271*
Grief, I., 77, *96*
Grimes, J., 129, *156*
Grudin, J., *204*
Grucky, D., 105, *156*
Guenther, A.L., *273*
Guilford, J.P., 55, *96*
Gutek, B.A., 106, *154*

H
Hackman, J.R., 226, *270*
Hage, J., 110, *156*
Hakkinen, M.T., *202*
Hall, D.T., 53, *98*
Hall, R.H., 105, 110, 111, *156*, *157*
Hallowell, A.I., 167, 187, *204*
Hamilton, H., 65, *94*, 147, *157*
Hammond, N.V., 68, *96*, *157*
Hanak, J., 34, 38, 58, *93*
Hannemyr, G., 70, *97*
Hansen, W.J., 262, *270*
Hanson, S.J., 216, *270*
Happ, A., 135, *155*
Hebenstreit, J., 107, *157*
Heberlein, T.A., 36, 44, 51, 71, 72, 75, *94*, *97*, 229, 253, 255, 257, 259, *270*
Heider, E.R., 182, *204*
Heider, F., 37, 53, 61, *97*
Helmer, O., *157*, 232, 235, *269*
Hemenway, K., *205*
Herda, S., 68, *95*
Hewitt, C., 144, *157*
Herzberg, F., 139, *157*
Hicks, B., 66, *97*
Higgins, C.A., 226, *270*
Hill, R.J., 43, *97*, 252, *274*
Hiltz, S.R., 59, 81, 84, *97*, 235, 236, *274*
Hobbs, J.R., 189, *202*

Hochschild, A.R., *205*
Hollander, E.P., 23, *97*
Homans, G.C., 23, 71, *97*, *205*, *214*, *270*
Hopwood, A.G., 6, *21*, 111, 113, *157*
Hovanyecz, T., *269*
Hoyer, W., 66, *98*
Hudson, S.E., *205*
Hunt, R.G., 46, *95*
Hunting, W., 135, *158*
Hutchens, D.H., 238, *267*

I
Inkeles, A., 117, *157*
Inman, V., 60, *97*
Innocent, P.R., 70, *97*
Irving, R.H., 226, *270*
Iso-Ahola, S.E., 69, *97*
Ittelson, W.H., *159*
Itzfeldt, W.D., 68, *95*
Ives, B., 133, *154*, *157*, 229, 255, *267*, *270*, *272*

J
Jacklin, C.N., 56, *99*
Jackson, J., 71, 72, 73, 75, *97*
Jacob, R.J.K., *270*
Jahoda, M., *273*
Janson, R., 226, *270*
Jefferson, G., 82, *97*, 185, *206*
Jensen, S., 133, *157*
Johansen, R., 77, 85, *97*
Johnson, B.M., 226, *270*
Johnson, E.M., *270*
Johnson, J.H., 261, *270*
Johnson, M.P., 43, 44, *101*
Jones, K.C., 135, *160*
Jones, S., 172, 184, *207*
Jones, W.P., *204*, *205*
Jorgenson, A., *157*
Joyce, M., 48, *103*, 252, *274*

K
Kahn, R.L., *270*
Kamens, D.H., *205*
Kanter, J., 118, 135, *157*
Kaplan, A., 107, *157*
Kaplan, C., 164, 185, 193, *207*
Kapp, S.A., 56, *103*
Karat, J., 63, *97*
Karon, P., 77, *98*
Katz, E., 147, *157*
Katzell, R.A., 140, *157*

Kearsley, G., 66, 98
Keen, P.G.W., 123, 135, 157, 163, 205, 229, 271
Kelly, G.A., 37, 53, 98
Kelly, H.H., 53, 98
Kemnitzer, D., 185, 204
Kemper, T.D., 196, 197, 205
Kennedy, T.C.S., 60, 98
Kerber, K.W., 38, 45, 58, 98
Kerlinger, F.N., 252, 253, 271
Kerr, E.B., 235, 236, 274
Kidder, L.H., 259, 271
Kiesler, S., 4, 21, 28, 34, 76, 84, 85, 98, 107, 157, 163, 205, 252, 260, 271
King, J., 174, 205
Kinkade, R.G., 173, 207
Kirk, R.E., 240, 271
Kirs, P.J., 46, 95
Kish, L., 240, 271
Klein, D., 272
Klein, M., 269
Kling, R., 5, 21, 28, 98, 106, 109, 110, 111, 115, 123, 132, 157, 158, 163, 164, 174, 205, 227, 271
Kluckholn, C., 72, 98
Knight, G.O., 60, 65, 98, 99
Knight, G.P., 99
Kohlberg, L., 29, 98
Kornbluh, M., 66, 98
Kraemer, K.L., 65, 84, 85, 95, 98, 109, 110, 111, 124, 158, 174, 205
Kraus, W.A., 135, 158
Krauss, I., 66, 98
Kraut, R.E., 216, 270
Krech, D., 27, 98
Kremer, J.M.D., 99
Kwan, S.K., 112, 161

L
Lakshamanan, R., 135, 159
Lancaster, F.W., 84, 98
Landers, D.M., 82, 98
LaPiere, R.T., 98
Laubli, Th., 135, 158
Laudon, K., 123, 158
Lawler, E.E., 53, 98, 133, 158
Lawrence, P.R., 114, 158
Lazarsfield, P.F., 18, 21, 267
Leavitt, H.J., 99
Lee, R., 32, 39, 45, 99
Lefcourt, H.M., 58, 99
Leonard-Barton, D., 135, 158

Levi-Strauss, C., 182, 205
Levin, M.L., 147, 157
Levine, D.N., 108, 158
Levy, P.S., 172, 184, 207
Lewis, C., 209, 214, 215, 255, 269, 271
Lichtman, D., 32, 99
Licklider, J.C.R., 6, 20, 68, 95, 123, 158
Lincoln, Y.S., 106, 158
Lindquist, E.F., 240, 271
Liska, A.E., 252, 271
Long, J.B., 68, 96, 119, 157
Lord, F.N., 212, 271
Lorsch, J.W., 114, 158
Loyd, B.H., 40, 99, 271
Lucas, H., 111, 132, 158, 226, 272
Luckman, T., 203
Lund, M.A., 211, 271
Luschen, G., 82, 98
Lusk, E.J., 63, 93
Lyytinen, K., 192, 205

M
Maccoby, E.E., 56, 99
MacCulloch, M.J., 260, 261, 271, 273
Mack, D., 65, 99
Mackett-Sloat, J., 205
Mackinlay, B., 45, 46, 99
Maclean, A., 119, 157
Mahajan, V., 149, 158
Mainiero, L.A., 135, 158
Maines, D.R., 205
Malone, T.W., 105, 143, 158, 187, 205
Mandler, J.M., 205
Mann, F.C., 132, 158
March, J.G., 123, 158
Markus, M.L., 1, 21, 28, 50, 81, 99, 227, 271
Martin, J., 68, 99
Martino, J.P., 230, 231, 232, 233, 271
Maruyama, M., 111, 143, 158
Maslow, A.H., 107, 133, 134, 140, 158
Mataya, P., 261, 272
Matula, R.A., 135, 159
McCall, G.J., 213, 214, 271
McCall, R.B., 26, 99
McElhone, A., 136, 159
McGregor, D., 133, 136, 138, 140, 159
McGuire, T.W., 4, 21, 28, 34, 76, 84, 85, 98, 252, 271
Mead, G.H., 193, 206
Meade, N., 147, 159
Meeker, R., 260, 273

Merton, R., 72, 99, 107, *159*
Meyer, J.P., 61, *99*, 130, *159*
Michener, H.A., 6, 7, *21*, 23, 33, 36, 43, 72, 75, *99*, 231, *271*
Mick, D.G., *206*
Miller, E., 261, *269*
Miller, G.A., 105, *156*, 189, *206*
Miller, W.E., 40, *94*
Mills, H.E., 260, 261, *273*
Mintzberg, H., 226, *271*
Mischel, W., 37, 55, 65, *94*, *95*, *99*
Moore, G.T., 187, *206*
Moran, T.P., 1, *20*, 63, *95*, 216, *268*
Morgan, G., 5, *21*
Mornington, S., 261, *269*
Morrison, P.R., 32, 39, 45, *99*
Morton, J., 68, *96*
Mourant, R., 135, *159*
Mouzelis, N., 122, *159*
Mulhall, D.J., 261, *272*
Mumford, E., 132, 144, 145, *159*, *272*
Murray, D., 24, 82, 85, *100*
Murray, J.T., *202*
Myers, C., 226, *272*

N
Nachmias, C., *272*
Nachmias, D., *272*
Nass, G., *273*
Neal, A.S., 215, 216, 238, *269*, *272*
Newell, A., 1, *20*, 215, 216, *268*
Neuman, L.S., 44, *103*
Nicholls, W.L., 260, *273*
Nicholson, R.T., 216, *272*
Nieper, H., 64, *94*
Nixon, H.L., 81, *100*
Norman, D.A., 5, *21*, 187, *206*
Northrup, A., 111, 124, *158*
Novick, M.R., 212, *271*
Nunnally, J.C., 212, *272*
Nussbaum, K., 226, *270*
Nwankwo, R.L., 195, *206*

O
Oakley, K.P., *206*
O'Brien, T.C., *272*
Ogden, E.C., 216, *272*
Ogilvy, J., 2, *21*, 160, 165, *207*
Ogozalek, V.Z., 66, *100*
Oldham, G.R., 226, *270*
Oliver, D., 182, *204*

Olson, M.H., 133, *154*, *157*, 226, 229, 255, *267*, *270*, *272*
O'Malley, C., 107, *159*
Osgood, C.E., *206*
Otway, H.J., *159*
Ouchi, W., 5, *21*, 122, 136, 140, *159*

P
Page, T.J., 48, *94*
Pallato, J., 121, *159*
Palme, J., 81, *100*
Papert, S., 67, *100*
Parsons, T., 107, 118, *159*
Patterson, M.L., 85, *95*
Pearson, J.S., 261, *272*
Pecjak, V., 196, *206*
Pederson, P., 109, *154*
Pelto, M., *159*
Perrow, C., 108, 122, 123, *159*
Peterson, R.A., 149, *158*
Petre, P., 125, *159*
Pettigrew, A.M., 226, *272*
Pew, R.W., *204*
Phares, E.J., 58, *100*
Piaget, J., 29, *100*
Potosnak, K.M., 55, 68, *100*
Poulton, E.C., 238, *272*
Pressman, R.S., 176, *206*
Proshansky, H.M., *159*
Pryor, J.B., 23, 60, *100*
Purdy, K., 226, *270*

Q
Quintanar, L.R., 23, 60, *200*

R
Rabideau, G.F., *272*
Rachman, S., 59, *95*
Rae, S.G., *206*
Rafaeli, A., 28, 34, 53, 54, *100*
Ramsey, H.R., 68, *100*
Randles, F., 147, *159*
Ranken, H.B., 183, *206*
Rappoport, L., 26, *100*
Rasmussen, L.B., *20*
Raven, B.H., 35, *96*, 108, *156*
Reece, M.J., *100*, *272*
Regan, D.T., 34, *100*
Reitz, J.G., 18, *21*
Remington, R., *206*
Render, B., 136, *156*

Rice, R.E., 84, *100*
Rich, E., 68, *100*
Richardson, S.A., *272*
Riddick, C.C., 251, *272*
Ridgeway, J., 260, 261, *273*
Rief, W.E., 114, 115, *159*
Riegel, K.F., 26, *100*
Ringle, M., 67, *101*
Ritzer, G., 142, *159*
Rivlin, L.G., *159*
Robertson, T.S., 147, *160*
Robey, D., 113, 114, 115, 132, *160*
Roediger, H.L., *206*
Roethlisberger, F., 132, 136, *160*
Rohrer, K.M., 135, *160*
Rokeach, M., 33, 40, 41, 42, *101*
Rome, H.P., 261, *272*
Romei, L.K., *206*
Root, R.W., 252, 255, 260, *273*
Rosenberg, J.K., 63, 94, *203*
Rosenthal, R., *273*
Ross, J., 136, *156*, *273*
Rossi, P.H., 251, *273*
Rosson, M.B., 209, *268*
Rothlisberger, F.J., *161*
Rotter, J.B., 58, *101*
Ruesch, J., 184, *206*
Rule, J., 123, *160*
Rushinek, A., 133, *160*, *273*
Rushinek, S.F., 133, *160*, *273*
Ruth, S., 136, *156*

S

Sacks, H., 185, *206*
Sadler, P.F., 138, *160*
Safayeni, F.R., 226, *270*
Sahlins, M., 167, 187, *206*
Salancik, G.R., 51, *101*
Saltzstein, H.D., 72, *97*
Sanaboni, A., 86, *95*
Sanders, G.L., 46, *95*
Santa, J.L., 183, *206*
Sapir, E., 182, *206*
Sauter, S.L., 135, *160*
Scacchi, W., 174, *205*, *206*, 227, *271*
Scerbo, M.W., 216, *267*
Schafer, C., 63, *97*
Scheff, T., 87, *101*, 185, *206*
Schegloff, E., 185, *206*
Schein, E.H., 165, *207*

Scherer, K.R., 185, *207*
Shick, M.E., 226, *273*
Schlegel, R.P., 38, *101*
Schmeideck, R.A., 87, *101*
Schneider, D., 185, *204*
Schon, D.A., 140, *154*
Schultz, A., 173, *207*
Schultz, G.P., 115, *160*
Schuman, H., 43, 44, *101*
Schwartz, J., 37, *95*
Schwartz, P., 2, *21*, *160*, 165, *207*
Schwartz, R.D., *274*
Schwartz, S.H., 6, 7, *21*, 23, 33, 37, 43,
    71, 72, 73, 75, 99, *101*, 231, *271*
Scott, J.F., 38, 71, *101*
Scott, W.R., 114, 118, 130, *154*, *159*, *160*
Scott-Morton, M., 163, *205*
Sculley, J., 67, *101*
Searle, J., *207*
Sears, R.R., 65, *101*
Sechrest, L., *274*
Seegmiller, D., *205*
Selby, R.W., 238, *267*
Selltiz, C., *273*
Sewell, W.H., 29, *101*
Shackel, B., 24, 68, *101*, *102*, *273*
Shanks, J.M., 260, *269*, *273*
Shapiro, B.J., *272*
Shaw, M.E., 33, *101*
Sherif, C.W., 75, *101*
Sherif, M., 75, *101*
Shewmake, D.T., 119, *161*, *274*
Shibutani, T., 143, *160*
Shiflett, S., 78, *101*
Shneiderman, B., 1, 6, *21*, 24, 34, 58, 66,
    68, 70, 75, *101*, *102*, 119, *160*, 172,
    204, *207*, 209, 214, 238, 255, 260,
    269, *273*
Shure, G., 260, *273*
Shute, S.J., 135, *160*
Sieber, S.D., *273*
Siegel, J., 4, *21*, 28, 34, 76, 84, 85, 98,
    252, *271*
Silverman, D., 105, *160*
Sim, F., 1, *21*
Simon, H.A., 123, 124, *160*, 215, *272*
Simone, C., 86, *95*
Simmons, J.L., 213, 214, 215, 216, 238,
    271
Simmons, R.G., 29, *94*
Simone, H., *158*

Sinako, H.W., 84, *102*
Sipior, J.C., 46, *95*
Sjostrand, S., *207*
Skipper, J.K., *273*
Sless, D., *203*
Smith, D.R., 226, *270*
Smith, H.W., *273*
Smith, P., *273*
Smith, S.L., 68, *102*
Speckart, G., 46, 48, 49, *94*
Spiliotopoulos, V., 24, *102, 273*
Sproull, L.S., 251, 252, 260, *271, 273*
Stanley, J.C., *268*
Starr, S.J., 135, *160*
Stavrou, A., 261, *269*
Steiner, I.D., 78, 80, *102*
Stern, K.R., 164, *207*
Stevens, R.F., 261, 262, *273*
Steward, J., *273*
Stewart, R., 115, *160*
Stewart, T.F.M., 68, *102*
Stokes, D.E., 40, *94*
Stryker, S., 193, *207*
Stutz, J., *273*
Suchman, L., 18, 21, 82, *102*
Suci, G.J., *206*
Sudman, S., 252, *274*
Sutton, R.I., 53, *100*
Swanson, B., 132, *160*
Swenson, H.P., 261, *272*

T
Tannebaum, A.S., 111, *156*
Tannenbaum, P.H., *206*
Tapscott, D., 84, *102*
Tarde, G., 147, *160*
Tuasky, C., 122, *160*
Taylor, F., 118, 122, *160*
Taylor, J.C., 226, *270*
Taylor, R.N., 56, *94*
Taylor, S.E., 37, *102*
TenHouten, W.D., 164, 185, 193, *207*
Teubner, A.L., 4, 6, 21, 40, *103, 161,* 220, 221, 257, 262, *274*
Thomas, E.J., 80, *102*
Thomas, J., 188, *203*
Thomas, R.J., 149, *160*
Thompson, C.R., 135, *160*
Thompson, D.A., 68, *102*
Thompson, J.A., 261, *274*
Thompson, J.D., 114, *160*
Thorngate, W., 1, 2, *20*

Tigert, D., 149, *161*
Tittle, C.R., 252, *274*
Trauth, E.M., 112, *161*
Trigg, R., 82, *102*
Trist, E., 132, 145, *161*
Turke, S., 30, 31, *102*
Turoff, M., 84, 97, 235, 236, *274*
Tweed, D.L., 69, *102*
Tyler, S.A., 186, *207*

U
Ullrich, R.A., 139, *161*

V
Vancott, H.P., 173, *207*
Van de Ven, A.H., 236, *269*
Van Der Veer, G., 55, 59, 62, 64, *102*
Van der Zouwen, J., 252, *269*
Van Liere, K.D., *95*
Van Muylwijk, B., 55, 59, 62, 64, *102*
Van Praag, J., 66, *100*
Vaske, J.J., 4, 6, 21, 38, 40, 48, 49, 68, 69, *96, 102, 103, 106, 129, 156, 161,* 220, 221, 242, 257, 262, 270, 274
Vassallo, R., 86, *95*
Vaughan, G.M., *274*
Vezza, A., 123, *158*
Vigliani, E., 173, *204*
Vittori, W., 226, 227, *274*
Vroom, V.H., 133, 139, *161*

W
Waern, Y., 55, 59, 62, 64, *102*
Wagner, L.G., 115, *161*
Wahba, M.A., 136, *161*
Wallace, V.L., 66, *96*
Walton, R.E., 226, 227, *274*
Warshaw, P.R., 48, *103*, 252, *274*
Wasserman, A.E., 119, *161, 274*
Waterfall, R.C., 260, 261, *268*
Watts, K., 260, 261, *274*
Webb, E.W., *274*
Weber, M., 118, *161*
Weeks, G.D., 84, *103*
Weick, K.E., *161*
Weigel, R.H., 44, *103*
Weinberg, D., 166, 167, 194, *207*
Weinberg, G.M., 57, 64, 66, *103,* 166, 167, 194, *207*
Weinburg, S., 135, *161*
Weiner, N., 111, *161*
Weisgerber, S., 63, *97*

Weissbach, T.A., 40, *94*
Weissinger, E., 251, *272*
Weizenbaum, J., 23, *103*
Welmers, H., 60, *95*
Westerlund, G., *207*
Westrum, R., 118, *161*
Whisler, T.L., 114, 115, *160, 161*
White, L.A., *207*
Whiteside, J., 172, 184, *207*
Whitlock, L.R., 262, *270*
Whorf, B.L., 182, *207*
Whyte, W.F., 132, *161*
Wicker, A.W., 43, *103*
Widom, J., *204*
Wiggins, J.S., 55, *103*
Williams, D., *206*
Williams, E., *103*
Williams, J.G., 65, 84, *99*
Williams, L.K., 132, *158*
Williams, M., 261, 262, *274*
Williams, T.A., 260, 261, *270*
Wilson, S.L., 261, *274*
Winer, B.J., 240, *274*
Winograd, T.A., 86, *103*, 185, *204, 207*

Witkin, H.A., 56, *103*
Wixon, D., 172, 184, *207*
Woodson, W.E., 173, *207*
Wright, J.M., 33, 40, *101, 103*
Wright, S.R., 251, *273*
Wylie, G., 261, *274*
Wynne, B.E., 60, 103, 113, *161*

Y
Yankelovich, D., 140, *157*

Z
Zajonc, R.B., 38, *103*
Zaleznick, A., 136, *161*
Zander, A., 95, 141, 155, 231, *268*
Zanna, M.P., 34, 43, *96*
Zdonik, S.B., *203*
Zelditch, M., *274*
Zeller, A., 61, *103*
Zmud, R.W., 55, 56, 58, 62, 68, *103*
Zoltan, E., 35, 45, 69, *103*
Zuboff, S., 227, *274*
Zwaga, H.J., *207*

Subject Index

A

Achievement need, 59–60
Additive tasks, 80–81
Affiliation need, 135
Age(ing), 65–66
Affect, *see* Attitudes
Altair, 39
Anonymity, 232
Anthropology, 14–16, 163–207
  concerns of, 14, 163
  scope of, 166–167
Anthropology theories
  cognitive, 180, 186–187, 189, 192, 201
  ecology, 180, 189–192, 201–202
  linguistics, 180–182, 186, 200–201; *see also* Language
  symbolic interaction, 180, 193–195, 201–202
Anxiety
  reasons for, 53, 60–61, 123, 135–136
  reducing, 61
Apple computer, 67, 119, 125, 172, 187
Applied versus basic research, 18–19
AT&T, 127, 168
Attitudes, 9, 32–42, 132, 165, 167
  definition of, 9, 32–33
  structure of, 36, 45–46
  components of, 33–42
  formation of, 34, 38, 53
  behavior and, 43–51, 165
  prediction of behavior, 9, 43–51
  measurement of, 35, 37–38, 46
  scales, 40, 49
  situation context, 45–46
  specificity, 43–45, 51
  organization and change of, 9, 35–41
    balance theory, 37, 53
    cognitive dissonance theory, 37, 53–54
    cognitive structure, 36–37, 50–51
    self-perception theory, 53
Attribution theory, 53, 60–61

Authority, 107–108, 110, 115, 117, 119, 125–126, 128, 142, 152

B

Balance theory, 37, 53
Bass model
  parameter estimation, 148–149
  empirical example, 149–151
Behavior, 165, 168, 174, 193, 195
  attitude and, 51–54
  norms of, 175
  rites of initiation, 178
Behavioral intentions, 41, 43–44, 46–49
Beliefs, 170, 178, 179, 200; *see also* Attitudes
  definition of, 35
  evaluative, 35
  horizontal structure, 36
  measurement of, 35
  organization of, 35–40, 165, 167, 169
  vertical structure, 36
Bureaucracy, 12, 118–122
  characteristics of, 118–119
  changes in, 118
  computers influence, 120
Burroughs, 126

C

Calculative rationality, 118–119
CHAOS, 86
Chunking, 188–189
Cognitive, 166, 180, 186–187, 189, 192, 201; *see also* Anthropology theories
  chunking, 187–189
  environmental knowing, 187
  mental maps, 187, 189
  mental schemata, 187, 189
  organizing principles, 186
  phenomenon, 186, 190, 192; *see also* Symbolic interaction
  relativism, 165

Cognitive anthropology, 16, 186–189
Cognitive consistency, 53–54, 170
Cognitive development stage theory, 29
Cognitive differentiation, 38–39
Cognitive dissonance theory, 37, 53–54
Cognitive integration, 38–39
Cognitive style, 10, 55–56, 62–64
  application of, 62–63
  definition of, 62
  field (in)dependent, 56, 62–63
  flexibility versus rigidity, 64
  sex differences, 56
  systematic/heuristic, 63
  verbalizers/visualizers, 63–64
Committees
  advantages of, 230–231
  disadvantages of, 231–232
Communication, see also Patterns
  computer mediated, 165, 185–186
  voice mail, 150
Communication networks
  definition of, 82
  patterns of, 82–83
Community, 166
Computers
  diffusion of, 1–2, 123, 135
  forums, 178
  trends, 3, 109, 113, 193
  paradigm shifts, 2, 5, 165
  resistance toward, 135, 169
Computer-assisted telephone interviewing
  advantages of, 260
  disadvantages of, 261
Computer supported cooperative work, 4, 59, 77–89
  definition of, 77
  current research, 85–86
  empirical example, 86–87
Conversational templates, 86
Computer mediated communication, see also Electronic mail
  social psychological aspects of, 82–85
Conjunctive tasks, 80–81
Context, 174–175, 179, 185–186, 201
Cooperative management, 122
Cooperative work, 10, 193; see also Computer supported cooperative work
Coordinator, 86–89
Covariate
  definition of, 239

Culture, 14, 179, 182, 183, 186, 187, 195, 199
  adaptation, 169–170, 201
  change, 165, 169, 201
  characteristics of, 168–170
  concept of, 167–170
  definition of, 167–168
  corporate, 105, 141, 147, 153
  evolution, 175
  goals, 166
  integration, 169–170, 201
  norms, 172
  relativity, 168
  subcultures, 164, 167, 186, 189, 200
Cultural anthropology, 180
Cultural ecology, 16
Customs, 168
Cyberphobia, 60, 135

D
Defense mechanisms, 61–62
Degrees of freedom
  definition of, 240
Delphi
  overview of, 210
  characteristics of, 232–233
  conducting, 233–235
  examples, 235–236
Dependent variable
  definition of, 239
  example, 242
Design teams
  objectives of, 228
  advantages of, 228–229
  limitations of, 229
Desktop metaphor, 187
Demographic variables, 56, 64–67
Digital Equipment Corporation, 125, 129
Digital Research, 183, 187
Disjunctive tasks, 80–81
Divisible tasks, 79

E
Education, 66–67
Ecological theory, 180, 189–193, 201–202; see also Anthropology theories
  concerns of, 190
  laws, 190–191
Electronic mail, 3, 34, 40, 59, 73, 77, 81, 84–85, 107, 169, 185, 112, 220–224, 262–265

Electronic surveys, 260–262
Emotions, 196
Environment, 108, 111, 114–115, 120–121, 124–126, 129, 137, 141, 144, 153
Environmental knowing, 187
Epistemology, 192
ESPIRIT, 127
Ethical issues, 226–227
    guidelines for, 227
ETHICS, 145–146
Ethnography, 189
Eureka, 127
Expectations, 23, 54, 107, 133–134, 175, 245–249; see also Norms
Experiments
    overview of, 211
    advantages of, 239
    disadvantages of, 239
    controversies, 238–239
    common designs, 240–242
    empirical example, 242–251
Extraversion–introversion, 59
Eysenck personality inventory, 261

F
Field (in)dependent, 56, 62–63
Fixed alternative responses, 255–256
Flexibility versus rigidity, 64
Full factorial experimental designs, 241

G
GEM, 183–184, 187
General Electric, 126–127, 129
General psychology, 26–28, 189
Generative rationality, 119
Goals, 106, 111, 114, 120, 121, 124, 126, 136, 138, 140
Groups
    cohesiveness, 81–82
    goals of, 77
    size, 80–81
    decision making, 228–232
    tasks, 78–79
Group productivity, 4, 59
    definition of, 77–78
    factors affecting, 78–82
Growth (of organizations), 125–126, 144
Guttman scaling, 193

H
Hawthorne effect, 132
Help facilities, 59–60

Honeywell, 45, 49, 126–127, 129–130, 150
Human factors, 109, 111, 127, 129, 132, 194
Human relations theory; see also Organization theories
    assumptions of, 133
    critique of, 141–142

I
IBM, 34, 106, 119, 122, 129, 187
Icon(s), 173, 183–184, 199, 200
Independent variable
    definition of, 239
    example, 242
Information theory, 108–109, 111, 115, 120, 148
    feedback, 112
    input/output, 112
    signal/noise, 112
Individual differences, 9–10, 16
    indicators of, 55–69
Innovation, 118, 124, 127, 131, 145, 147
Iterative design, 209, 228–229

J
Job enrichment, 139–140
Job involvement, 53

K
Knowledge workers, 65

L
Language, 166, 191, 195, 199, 201
    definition of, 181
    body language, 185
    nonverbal, 185–186, 193
    paralanguage, 185
Leadership, 125, 127
Latin square experimental designs, 241–242
Linguistics, 16, 180–182, 186, 200–201; see also Language
    definition of, 181
    characteristics of, 181
    hypotheses, 182–183
    pragmatism, 181, 184–185
    relativity, 182
    structuralist approach, 181–183
        morphology, 181
        semantics, 181, 189
        syntax, 181, 199
    universals, 182
Locus of control, 58

M

Macintosh, 35, 67, 119, 172, 174–175, 187
Mail surveys, 258–260
Management by objective, 122
Meaning Structures, 163, 164, 172, 184–185, 187–188, 193–194, 201–202
negotiation of, 194
Mental maps, 189
Metaphor, 163, 187–189, 195
Microelectronics Computer Corporation, 126
Microsoft, 187
Mill Hill vocabulary scale, 261
Minnesota multiphasic personality inventory, 261
Motivation, 53, 133, 139
Myths, 141, 144, 153, 164, 171, 180, 199, 201
definition of, 15, 176
characteristics of, 176
examples of, 176–178
reality and, 176–177

N

Needs hierarchy theory, 107, 134–136
Needs human, 107, 133, 136, 138–139
Nominal group
conducting, 236
example, 236–237
Nonverbal
cues, 83–84, 185–186
interaction, 185
Norm(s)(-ative), 10–11, 40, 70–76
definition of, 71
cultural, 185
structural characteristics, 75–76
social, 72, 88, 174–175
personal, 72–73
response time standards, 70–71, 73–77
models, 73–77

O

Observation of behavior
overview of, 210, 213
summary of, 227–228
Open-ended questions, 255–256
Open systems theory; see also Organization theories
overview of, 143–145
sociotechnical design, 145–147

models of innovation, 147–149
empirical example, 149–151
Organizational commitment, 53–54
Organization theories, 12–14
relation to human–computer interaction, 12–13
scientific management, 12, 118, 122–125, 130, 132
structural, 12, 117, 120, 124, 130, 143, 152
human relations, 117, 130, 132, 140–143, 152
system theories, 117, 143–149, 152
Theory X, 136–137, 140
Theory Y, 136–137, 140
Theory Z, 140–141
Organizations
conflict, 110, 139–140
complexity, 106, 110–111, 152
effectiveness, 105, 111, 117, 120, 152
efficiency, 105, 111, 117–119, 122–123, 152
function of, 106–107
human–computer interaction and, 105–106
personality and, 138–140
problems in, 127–130
nature of, 106–107
size, 106, 110, 115, 126, 152
structure of, 82, 106, 117

P

Pacific Bell, 86
Participative management, 140
Participant observation, 213–214
advantages of, 214
disadvantages of, 214
Patterns of,
behavior, 168, 176, 202
communication, 143, 145, 147, 149, 152–153, 164
connection, 193
culture, 168–169, 202
ideal, 169
interaction, 180, 190–192
sound, 181
work, 176
Pattern recognition, 166, 192
People and Organizations, 133, 138–139, 144–145, 153; see also Organizational theories

Personal interviews, 258–260
Personal relations index, 261
Personality, 9, 55–65
    definition of, 55
    development of, 65
Personality traits, 9–10, 56–64
    definition of, 57
    measurement of, 57
Power, 107–108, 110, 120, 141, 142, 152, 196
Preferences, 175, 249–250
Prior experience, 38, 46–49, 53–54, 67–68, 70–71
Productivity, 107, 113, 122, 132, 141
Psychoanalytic theory, 61–62
Public relations, 116, 229

Q
Qualitative methods
    function of, 210–212
Quality circles, 140
Quantitative methods, 212

R
RAND Corporation, 112–113
Rapid prototyping, 46, 119
Ravens standard progressive matrices, 261
Reliability, 212, 257
Representativeness, 213, 228
Repression, 61–62
Return potential model, 73–77
Rituals, 141, 144, 153, 164, 171, 178, 180, 199, 201
    changes in, 175
    definition of, 15, 174
    function of, 175

S
Scientific management, 12, 118, 122–125, 130, 132; see also Organization theories
    assumptions of, 123–124
Self actualization, 134, 136, 139
Self concept, 195
Self esteem, 134–136, 139
Self-perception theory, 53
Semiconductor Research Corporation, 126
Single factor experimental designs, 240–241

Sex differences, 56
Sex typing, 65
Signs, 173, 201
Social change, 26, 31, 33–34
Social facilitation theory, 60–61
Social groups, 72
Social influence, 9, 24–25, 117
    examples of, 9, 28, 33–34
Social networks, 107, 153, 164
    analysis, 112
    formal versus informal, 132
Social psychology, 106, 116, 141, 153, 165, 170, 180, 193
    definition of, 23–25
    scope of, 25–28
    major concerns, 7–11, 26
Socialization, 10–11
    definition of, 29
    in adolescence and adulthood, 30–31
    agents of, 30
    examples of, 30
Sociotechnical analysis, 132, 145–147, 152, 164
Software games, 199–200
Software monitors, 215–227
    types of, 215–216, 219
    advantages of, 219, 225
    limitations of, 225
    development of, 217
    laboratory studies, 216, 225
    field studies, 216, 219–225
    empirical examples, 219–224
    summary, 224–225
    ethical issues, 226
    reliability of, 226
Speech acts, 86
Sperry, 126
Stability, 212
Stage theories
    definition of, 29
    hypotheses, 29
Standards, see Norms
Statistical packages, 258
Status, 196
Stress, see Anxiety
Structural theories, see also Organization theories
    bureaucracy, 118–122
    scientific management, 118, 122–124
    applying, 124–130
    summary of, 130

Structure (of Organizations), 105–107, 110, 114–115, 117, 119, 120–122, 124–127, 130, 132, 150
  bureaucracy, 118, 120, 124, 130, 142–143
  function and, 106, 117, 122, 124
  centralization/decentralization, 114–115, 122
  hierarchy, 117, 134
Subculture, see Culture
Suppression, 61–62
Surveys
  advantages of, 251–252
  limitations of, 252–253
  construction of, 253–258
  length of, 257
  types of, 258–262
  response rates, 257, 259
  empirical example, 262–265
  response formats, 263
  summary of, 265–266
Symbol(s), 15–16, 141, 144, 153, 164, 178, 185, 189, 193, 195, 199, 201
  definition of, 171
  examples of, 172–173
  interpretation of, 172
  types of, 172–173
  systems of, 181–182, 193
  symbolic, 163, 173
Symbolic Interaction, 180, 193–195, 201–202; see also Anthropology theories
  definition of situation, 194
  meaning, 163, 202
  role taking, 194, 237
System theories, see also Organizational theories
  general, 143–144
  open, 12, 143–145
  closed, 143–144
Systematic/heuristic, 63

T
Technological fix, 2
Technological impacts, 1–2, 13–14, 17, 108, 115, 120, 125–126, 129, 135–136
  descriptive component, 13
  evaluative component, 13–14
  impact interrelationships, 17
  examples of, 49–51, 53–54, 70–71, 75–76, 107, 109, 111, 123, 129

Technology
  computer as, 113, 114
  diffusion, 145, 147–149, 153
  transfer, 170
Technostress, 60, 135
Telephone interviews, 258–260
Telephone usage patterns, 242–245
Theories
  definition of, 6
  development of, 6–7
  integration of, 17, 165
  differences between, 11–12, 14, 17, 26, 40, 56–57, 116–117, 167, 180
  similarities between, 26–27, 107, 139–140, 169
  overview of
    social psychology, 7–11, 23–27
    social organization, 11–14, 106–107, 116–117
    anthropology, 14–16, 163–166
Theoretical perspectives, see Theories
Theory X, 136–137, 140; see also Organization theories
Theory Y, 136–137, 140; see also Organization theories
  assumptions of, 137
Theory Z, 140–141; see also Organization theories
Thinking aloud, 214–215
Transaction cost approach, 122
Two-factor theory, 139–140

U
Unisys, 126
Unitary tasks, 78–81
Unix, 178
User involvement, 229
User profiles, 68–69

V
Validity, 212
Values, 168–170, 173
Verbalizers/visualizers, 63–64
Visual display terminals, 135
Voice store-and-forward, 40, 49–51
VOX, 49, 150

W
Wang, 125, 129
Workflow, 146
Workgroups, 124, 193